The Devils' Alliance

Hitler's Pact with Stalin,
1939–41

Microcosm:
Portrait of a Central European City
(with Norman Davies)

Killing Hitler:
The Third Reich and the
Plots against the Führer

Berlin at War:
Life and Death in Hitler's Capital,
1939–45

The Devils' Alliance

Hitler's Pact with Stalin, 1939–41

ROGER MOORHOUSE

THE BODLEY HEAD
LONDON

Published by The Bodley Head 2014

2 4 6 8 10 9 7 5 3 1

First published in Great Britain in 2014 by
The Bodley Head
20 Vauxhall Bridge Road,
London SW1V 2SA

www.bodleyhead.co.uk
www.vintage-books.co.uk

Addresses for companies within The Random House Group Limited can be found at:
www.randomhouse.co.uk/offices.htm

The Random House Group Limited Reg. No. 954009

A CIP catalogue record for this book
is available from the British Library

ISBN 9781847922052

The Random House Group Limited supports the Forest Stewardship
Council® (FSC®), the leading international forest-certification organisation. Our books
carrying the FSC label are printed on FSC®-certified paper. FSC is the only forest-certification
scheme supported by the leading environmental organisations, including Greenpeace. Our paper
procurement policy can be found at www.randomhouse.co.uk/environment

Typeset in Dante MT Std by Palimpsest Book Production Limited,
Falkirk, Stirlingshire

Printed and bound in Great Britain by
Clays Ltd, St Ives plc

To my mother
and the fond memory of my father

Contents

Author's Note

It is always a challenging task to try to make sense of the shifting sands of Eastern Europe's place names. For this book, in which frontiers move and rival languages intrude, I have employed a policy of using names appropriate to the period under scrutiny.

So, to take the example of what is now the Ukrainian city of L'viv: in September 1939, it was the Polish city of Lwów, but when it passed to Soviet control, the name was Russified to Лbвов (transliterated as L'vov). Incidentally, the modern Ukrainian version, L'viv, only came into official use with the dissolution of the USSR in 1991.

In addition, where there is an accepted Anglicised form – such as Warsaw, Brest or Moscow – then I have naturally used it throughout.

POLAND DIVIDED

Poland under German and
Soviet occupation.
September 1939 – June 1941

LITHUANIA

R. Neman

Königsberg

Danzig

Wilno

EAST PRUSSIA

Grodno

Białystok

Poznań

R. Vistula

Warsaw

Pińsk

R. Warta

Łódź

R. Bug

N

Łuck

R. San

Rowno

GERMANY

Kraków

Przemyśl

Lwów

U.S.S.R.

Tarnopol

SLOVAKIA

0   100 miles

0   200 km

HUNGARY

ROMANIA

Annexed to the Reich	Occupied by Nazi Germany
General Government	
Administerd by Lithuania	
Annexed by the U.S.S.R.	
Poland's pre-war frontier	

THE POLISH EASTERN PROVINCES
UNDER SOVIET OCCUPATION:
October 1939

The former Polish eastern frontier ......
The 'Boundary of Peace': the line of partition
between Nazi Germany and the USSR ———
International frontiers as at October 1939 ----

LATVIA

LITHUANIA

BALTIC
SEA

R. Neman

Braslav
(Bracław)

Vilnius
(Wilno)

N

Königsberg

EAST PRUSSIA

Grodno

Minsk

Augustów

Jedwabne

Novogrudok
(Nowogródek)

Belostok
(Białystok)

BYELORUSSIAN SOVIET

SOCIALIST REPUBLIC

R. Vistula

Warsaw

Brest
(Brześć)

Pinsk
(Pińsk)

R. Pripyat

Kovel (Kowel)

GERMAN OCCUPIED

Lutsk
(Łuck)

Rovno
(Rowno)

POLAND

Rava-Russkaya
(Rawa-Russka)

Dubno

R. San

Kraków

L'vov
(Lwów)

UKRAINIAN SOVIET

Sambor

SOCIALIST REPUBLIC

Tarnopol

Boryslav
(Borysław)

Czortkov (Czortków)

SLOVAKIA

Kamieniec Podolski

Stanislav
(Stanisławów)

HUNGARY

0   100 miles

0   200 km

ROMANIA

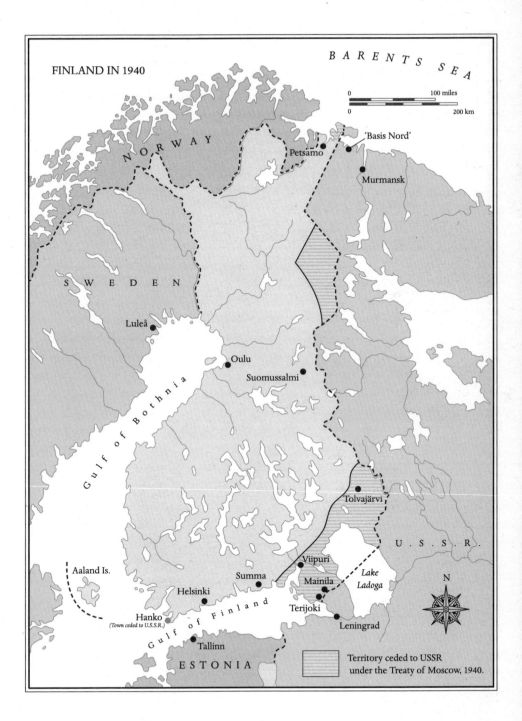

FINLAND IN 1940

B A R E N T S   S E A

0   100 miles
0   200 km

N O R W A Y

'Basis Nord'

Petsamo

Murmansk

S W E D E N

Luleå

Oulu

Suomussalmi

Gulf of Bothnia

Tolvajärvi

U . S . S . R .

Aaland Is.

Viipuri

Summa

Mainila

Lake
Ladoga

Helsinki

Terijoki

N

Hanko
(Town ceded to U.S.S.R.)

Leningrad

Gulf of Finland

Tallinn

E S T O N I A

Territory ceded to USSR
under the Treaty of Moscow, 1940.

SWEDEN

Stockholm

FINLAND

Helsinki

Leningrad

Narva

TALLINN

ESTONIA

BALTIC SEA

Hiiumaa

Pärnu

Tartu

Saaremaa

Gulf
of Riga

GOTLAND
(Sweden)

Pitrags

Litene

Ventspils

RIGA

Maslenki

LATVIA

Liepaja

R. Daugava

Daugavpils

N

Telšiai

Šiauliai

Memel

Kunigiškiai

LITHUANIA

U. S. S. R.

R. Neman

Kaunas

Königsberg

VILNIUS

Minsk

GREATER
GERMANY

THE BALTIC STATES 1939–1941
Soviet Socialist Republics from
August 1940

0   100 miles

0   200 km

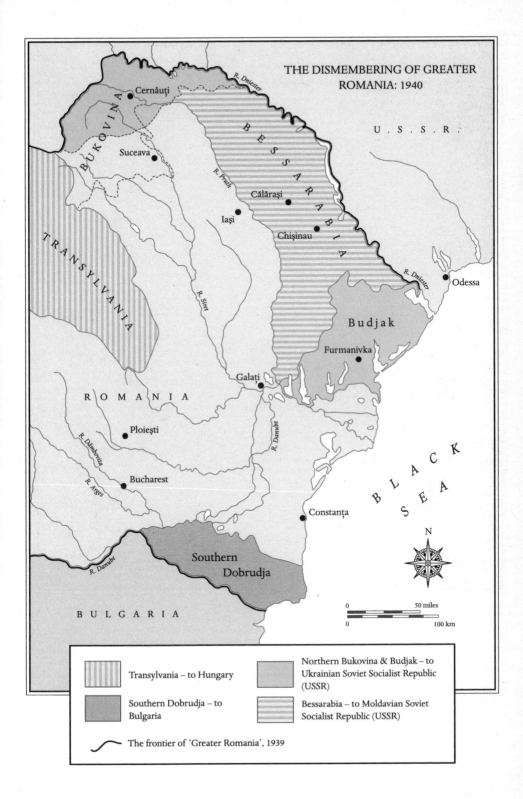

THE DISMEMBERING OF GREATER
ROMANIA: 1940

U. S. S. R.

R. Dniester

Cernăuți

BUKOVINA

Suceava

BESSARABIA

R. Pruth

Călărași

Iași

Chișinau

R. Dniester

Odessa

Budjak

Furmanivka

TRANSYLVANIA

R. Siret

Galați

ROMANIA

R. Danube

Ploiești

R. Dâmbovița

R. Argeș

Bucharest

Constanța

BLACK

SEA

N

Southern
Dobrudja

R. Danube

BULGARIA

0   50 miles

0   100 km

Transylvania – to Hungary

Northern Bukovina & Budjak – to
Ukrainian Soviet Socialist Republic
(USSR)

Southern Dobrudja – to
Bulgaria

Bessarabia – to Moldavian Soviet
Socialist Republic (USSR)

The frontier of 'Greater Romania', 1939

'LET'S DIVIDE THE WHOLE WORLD':
Europe on the Eve of Barbarossa, June 1941.

ICELAND

N

FINLAND

NORWAY

SWEDEN

ESTONIA

LATVIA

LITHUANIA

DENMARK

HOLLAND

BYELORUSSIA

IRELAND

U.K.

BELGIUM

GREATER
GERMANY

UKRAINE

MOLDAVIA

OCCUPIED
FRANCE

SWITZ.

SLOVAKIA

HUNGARY

VICHY
FRANCE

CROATIA

SERBIA

ROMANIA

ITALY

BULGARIA

ALBANIA

TURKEY

PORTUGAL

SPAIN

GREECE

CYPRUS

CRETE

MALTA

U · S · S · R

0   300 miles

0   600 km

	Neutral States		The Soviet Union
	Allied Powers and their areas of occupation		Axis-aligned
			Axis Powers, their allies and their areas of occupation

Chronology

1939

March

 10 Stalin's speech to the 18th Communist Party Congress

 15 German forces occupy Bohemia and Moravia

 31 Britain extends a guarantee to both Poland and Romania

May

 3 Stalin replaces Foreign Minister Maxim Litvinov with Vyacheslav Molotov

August

 12 Anglo-French-Soviet talks begin in Moscow

 19 German–Soviet Credit Agreement signed in Berlin

 21 Soviet talks with the British and French are suspended

 23 German–Soviet Treaty of Non-Aggression or 'Nazi–Soviet Pact' signed in Moscow

 25 Anglo-Polish Military Alliance signed in London

 31 Soviet forces defeat the Japanese at Khalkhin Gol

September

 1 German forces invade Poland

 3 Britain and France declare war on Germany

 15 Soviet forces agree a ceasefire with the Japanese in Manchuria

 17 Soviet forces invade Poland

 22 German and Soviet forces stage a joint parade at Brest-Litovsk

28   German–Soviet Boundary and Friendship Treaty
      signed in Moscow

28   Soviet–Estonian Mutual Assistance Treaty signed in
      Moscow

October

5   Soviet–Latvian Mutual Assistance Treaty signed
6   Last pockets of Polish resistance are defeated
10   Soviet–Lithuanian Mutual Assistance Treaty signed

November

26   Mainila Incident provides Moscow with a *casus belli*
      against Finland
30   Soviet forces invade Finland

1940

February

10   First Soviet Mass Deportation from Poland begins
11   German–Soviet Commercial Agreement signed

March

12   Treaty of Moscow signed between Finland and Soviet
      Union bringing the Winter War to an end

April

3   Katyn Massacres begin
9   German forces invade Norway and Denmark
13   Second Soviet Mass Deportation from Poland begins

May

10   German forces invade France and the Low Countries
31   The heavy cruiser *Lützow* arrives in Leningrad

June

15   Soviet forces invade Lithuania
17   Soviet forces invade Estonia and Latvia
22   Armistice signed between Germany and France
28   Romania heeds a Soviet ultimatum and withdraws from
      the provinces of Bessarabia and Northern Bukovina
30   Third Soviet Mass Deportation from Poland begins
30   Soviet occupation of Bessarabia and Northern
      Bukovina is complete

July

    14/15 Rigged elections are held in Latvia, Lithuania and Estonia

August

    2 Moldavia (Bessarabia) becomes a republic of the Soviet Union

    3 Lithuania becomes a republic of the Soviet Union

    5 Latvia becomes a republic of the Soviet Union

    6 Estonia becomes a republic of the Soviet Union

September

    27 Tripartite Pact signed between Germany, Italy and Japan – establishing the Axis powers.

November

    12 Molotov arrives in Berlin for talks with Hitler

    20 Hungary joins the Axis

    23 Romania joins the Axis

December

    1 German–Soviet Tariff and Toll Treaty signed

    17 Danubian Conference breaks up in acrimony

    18 Hitler gives the order for Operation Barbarossa, the attack on the Soviet Union

    23 Opening of the Red Army High Command Conference in Moscow

1941

January

    10 German–Soviet Border and Commercial Agreement signed in Moscow

March

    1 Bulgaria joins the Axis

    25 Yugoslavia joins the Axis

    27 Coup d'etat in Yugoslavia

April

    6 Soviet–Yugoslav Treaty of Friendship and Non-Aggression signed

    6 German forces invade Yugoslavia

    13 Soviet–Japanese Neutrality Pact signed in Moscow

May

June

July

List of Illustrations

Guderian and Krivoshein at Brest-Litovsk *(Bundesarchiv, Berlin)*.

German and Soviet troops fraternise in September 1939 *(© IWM)*.

The signature of the Nazi–Soviet Pact *(akg-images/Universal Images Group/Sovfoto)*.

Stalin and Heinrich Hoffmann drink a toast *(bpk/Bayerisches Staatsarchiv/ Archiv Heinrich Hoffmann)*.

Harry Pollitt's pamphlet 'How to Win the War' *(author's collection)*.

David Low cartoon, *Evening Standard*, 20 September 1939 *(courtesy of British Cartoon Archive, University of Kent, www.cartoons.ac.uk; Solo Syndication)*.

Hitler announces declaration of war on Poland *(Bundesarchiv, Berlin)*.

German troops in Poland *(R. Schäfer, private collection)*.

Molotov announces the Soviet invasion of Poland *(Fundacja Ośrodka KARTA)*.

The Red Army enters Poland *(akg-images/Universal Images Group/ Sovfoto)*.

Hitler reviews the victory parade in Warsaw, October 1939 *(Bundesarchiv, Berlin)*.

Execution of Poles *(akg-images/East News)*.

Red Army parade in L'vov, 1939 *(Fundacja Ośrodka KARTA)*.

A few of the exhumed corpses at Katyn *(Bundesarchiv, Berlin)*.

Jews being deported from Łódź *(Bundesarchiv, Berlin)*.

Volksdeutsche from Bessarabia coming 'Home to the Reich' *(Bundesarchiv, Berlin)*.

Soviet deportation from Riga, Latvia, 1941 *(Collection of the Occupation Museum of Latvia)*.

A deported Polish family outside their new 'home' in Soviet Kazakhstan *(Fundacja Ośrodka KARTA)*.

The *Lützow* being towed into Leningrad, 1940 (*Russian Naval Archive/ public domain*).

A German engineer checks a delivery of Soviet oil (*akg-images/picture-alliance*).

Molotov arrives in Berlin, November 1940 (*bpk/Bayerisches Staatsarchiv/ Archiv Heinrich Hoffmann*).

Molotov in talks with Hitler (*bpk/Bayerisches Staatsarchiv/Archiv Heinrich Hoffmann*).

Goebbels announces the attack on the Soviet Union, June 1941 (*akg-images*).

Muscovites hear a radio announcement of the German invasion (*akg-images/RIA Nowosti*).

German troops welcomed in former Bessarabia (*bpk/Hanns Hubmann*).

Red Army prisoners with their Wehrmacht captors (*Klaas Meijer, private collection*).

T-34 tank knocked out, July 1941 (*akg-images/interfoto*).

A statue of Stalin is taken away for disposal, Białystok (*Bundesarchiv, Berlin*).

The signature of the Sikorski–Maisky Agreement (*Fundacja Ośrodka KARTA*).

Lietukis Garage Massacre, June 1941 (*DÖW*).

Victims of the NKVD in L'vov (*Fundacja Ośrodka KARTA*).

Baltic Way, Estonia, August 1989 (*Museum of Occupations, Tallinn, Estonia*).

Šiauliai Protest (*Rimantas Lazdynas*).

Acknowledgements

Any book of breadth and ambition involves a degree of collaboration, and this one is no exception. For every word that makes it on to the page, dozens have been unearthed from archives, retrieved from libraries, translated or transcribed. Hence, a number of debts must humbly be acknowledged.

Firstly, this project required a considerable degree of foreign-language research assistance, sometimes in parts to which the shrinking author's advance will scarcely stretch. Consequently, help was ably tendered by Evgeny Panin in Russia, Oleg Medvedevsky in Belarus, Neringa Pangonyte in Lithuania, Dr Jakub Tyszkiewicz in Poland, Axel von Wittenberg and Philipp Rauh in Germany, and Andreea Minca and Andreea-Lavinia Mocanu in Romania. In addition, James Simpson, Saskia Smellie, Sebastian Palfi, Vicky Davis and Owen Emmerson did sterling work in the UK.

Secondly, thanks must also be extended to colleagues and friends who gave advice, answered questions, read chapters, or otherwise gave their time and knowledge, including: Jaroslaw Garlinski, Mel Huang, Dr Alex Drecoll, Professor Edward Ericson, Klaas Meijer, Robin Schäfer, Bill Russ, Nigel Jones, Dr Martin Folly, Professor Richard Overy, Dr David Kirby and – as ever – Professor Norman Davies.

Having worked in many archives, libraries and academic institutions, I would like to single out two – where much of this book was researched and written – for special praise: the German Historical Institute in London and the library of the UCL School of Slavonic and East European Studies. Where other institutions put up obstacles and present an uncaring face to their readers, they make the sometimes onerous task of researching and writing a genuine pleasure.

I would also like to thank those of the surviving community of

Kresowcy and *Sybiriacy* – the Poles deported to Siberia and elsewhere by the Soviet Union in 1940–1 – that I met in researching this book. It was a truly humbling experience to hear their stories of unimaginable hardship, stories which – sadly – rarely receive an airing in 'the West'. While this book is not strictly about their enforced exile, I hope that I have nonetheless done them justice in, at least in part, bringing their plight to a wider audience. Thanks are also due to the Polish Social & Cultural Centre 'POSK' in West London, for arranging the meetings.

All of this would be for nought, of course, were it not for the commitment, passion and persuasion of my agents, Peter Robinson in the UK and Jill Grinberg in the US, and the vision of my respective commissioning editors, Stuart Williams at the Bodley Head in London and the brilliant Lara Heimert at Basic Books in New York. An honourable mention must also be made for my inestimable editor in London, Jörg Hensgen, who has had the dubious honour of working on all of my previous books and brought his valuable insights and expertise to this one as well.

Lastly, convention dictates that an author should close with a saccharine paean to his or her family. Mine is as simple as it is heartfelt. To my wife, Melissa, and to our children, Oscar and Amelia, I offer my profound thanks: thank you for your perennial enthusiasm for the book that has taken shape in your midst and thank you for the patience, the love and the understanding that you have shown to its occasionally ill-tempered author. 'This time next year . . . !'

Introduction

On 23 August 1939, Stalin drank to Hitler's health. Though the two dictators would never meet, the agreement they forged that day would change
the world. As the 'Nazi–Soviet Pact', the 'Hitler–Stalin Pact' or the
'Molotov–Ribbentrop Pact', it was in force for less than two years – ending
with Hitler's attack on Stalin's Soviet Union on 22 June 1941 – but it was
nonetheless one of the salient events of the Second World War.

When I started researching this book, I was occasionally asked what
I was working on by friends and acquaintances beyond history circles,
and I would reply 'the Nazi–Soviet Pact'. The blank looks and furrowed
brows that I saw in response spoke volumes. Except in Poland and the
Baltic states, the pact is simply not part of our collective narrative of
the Second World War. It is my firm conviction that it really should be.

Our ignorance of the subject is surprising. While every other curiosity,
campaign and catastrophe from the Second World War has been interpreted and reinterpreted, assessed and reassessed, the pact remains largely
unknown – passed over often in a single paragraph, dismissed as a dubious
anomaly, a footnote to the wider history. It is instructive, for example,
that almost all of the recent popular histories of the Second World War
published in Britain give it scant attention. It is never considered to warrant
a chapter, and usually attracts little more than a paragraph or two and a
handful of index references.

When one considers the pact's obvious significance and magnitude,
this is quite astonishing. Under its auspices, Hitler and Stalin – the two
most infamous dictators of twentieth-century Europe – found common
cause. Their two regimes, whose later confrontation would be the
defining clash of the Second World War in Europe, stood side by side
for twenty-two months, almost a third of the conflict's entire time span.

We forget the link, perhaps, but the pact led directly to the outbreak of war; isolating Poland between its two malevolent neighbours and scuppering the rather desultory efforts of the Western Powers to thwart Hitler. The war that followed, therefore, carried the pact's odious stamp. While the Western Powers endured the so-called 'Phoney War', Poland was invaded and divided between Moscow and Berlin. With Hitler's connivance, the independent Baltic states were occupied and then annexed by Stalin, as was the Romanian province of Bessarabia. Finland, too, was invaded and conquered by the Red Army. When Hitler turned west, invading first Scandinavia, then the Low Countries and France, Stalin sent his congratulations. Behind the scenes, meanwhile, the Nazis and the Soviets traded secrets, blueprints, technology and raw materials, oiling the wheels of each other's war machines. For a time it seemed that the two dictatorships – or 'Teutoslavia' as one British politician called them – were ranged together against the democratic world. The British and French even considered a pre-emptive attack on the Soviet Union in 1940.

This aspect of Soviet belligerence is more than just a curiosity. Post-war writing on the Nazi–Soviet Pact – such that there is – has tended to parrot the Kremlin's post-war exculpatory line that Stalin was merely buying time by signing the pact, fending Hitler off while he could prepare Soviet defences to meet an expected attack. This interpretation, still hawked by apologists, does not tally with the evidence, however. As this book shows, Stalin was much more proactive and anti-western in signing the pact than has conventionally been appreciated. On one level at least, he was seeking to exploit Nazi aggression to his own ends, to speed the fall of the West and the long-awaited collapse of the capitalist world. An unwilling or passive 'neutral', he was not.

Viewed in this way, as it was by many contemporaries, it is not surprising that the Nazi–Soviet Pact turned the political world upside down, making – as one commentator memorably put it – 'all our -isms into -wasms'. It was a close-run thing, but it was the Soviets and world communism that were most profoundly damaged by the connection. Whereas Nazism had precious little moral capital left by 1939, and would soon disgrace itself entirely by launching the Holocaust, communism still liked to pride itself on its moral aspect. The acrobatics that loyal members were obliged to make, therefore, to accommodate Hitler and the Nazis as their fraternal allies were all the more humiliating, and as a result party memberships fell and the little political integrity that communists were perceived as having beyond their own milieu vanished in a puff of contorted dialectic. The pact with Hitler left an indelible stain on world communism, like the Soviet invasion of Hungary would do in 1956, or the suppression of the Prague Spring in 1968. It was only Stalin's hard-fought victory against Nazism after 1941 that would temporarily rescue its blackened reputation.

The Nazi–Soviet Pact was hugely influential, therefore. But away from the high politics and ideology, its baleful consequences were most keenly felt in central and eastern Europe, where – at a rough estimate – 50 million people were directly affected. By facilitating Hitler's war, the pact ushered in the brutal occupation of western Poland, with all its attendant cruelties and injustices. Though the Holocaust itself was yet to get properly under way in this period – beginning in earnest in the autumn of 1941 – Poles and Jews in Nazi-occupied Poland were subjected to a horrific regime of exploitation and persecution, with hundreds of thousands expropriated, deported or killed.

The pact also affected those Poles, Jews, Latvians, Estonians, Lithuanians, Byelorussians, Ukrainians and Romanians who became Soviet citizens under its aegis, their homelands annexed by the USSR. A few of them, certainly, welcomed the change. The vast majority did not. Huge numbers suffered persecution, torture and death at Soviet hands, the most notable examples being the 22,000 Polish army officers and officials murdered in the Katyn massacres of 1940.

Many more suffered deportation and exile to the Soviet interior. From eastern Poland alone, as many as 1.5 million people were deported in 1940–1. Tens of thousands were also deported from the Baltic states and Bessarabia. All were destined for the wild depths of the USSR – Kazakhstan, Siberia, the Polar north – and a life of hard labour and misery in the many Gulag camps, which only the strongest would survive. For those in any doubt about the grim reality of Stalin's Gulag, it is worth remembering that the Soviet camps had a higher death rate than Hitler's concentration camps. Some of those survivors and their descendants are still there today.

It is frankly scandalous that this grim chapter does not find a place in the western narrative of the Second World War. Six decades after Stalin's death, and over twenty years since the demise of the Soviet Union, it is high time that this changed. For, just as Hitler 'ethnically cleansed' the lands under his control, so Stalin 'politically cleansed' those under his. Yet though Hitler's crimes are well known and well documented – discussed in the media and the subject of school and university syllabuses the world over – Stalin's crimes scarcely penetrate the public consciousness. In fact, Hitler and Stalin were birds of the same totalitarian feather and far from being anomalous, the Nazi–Soviet Pact might be seen as symptomatic of their shared misanthropy.

It is worth clarifying that the Nazi–Soviet Pact was not an alliance as such, it was a treaty of non-aggression. Consequently, aside from the metaphorical title used here – *The Devils' Alliance* – I generally refrain from referring to Hitler and Stalin as 'allies' or their collaboration as an 'alliance'. However, that clarification should not blind us to the fact that the Nazi–Soviet relationship between 1939 and 1941 was a profoundly important one, which consisted of four further agreements after the pact of August 1939 and was, therefore, close to an alliance in many respects. Certainly it was far more vital and far more crucial to both sides than, for instance, Hitler's alliance with Mussolini's Italy. Hitler and Stalin were allies in all but name.

Though it ended in 1941, the pact would have a curious afterlife. Torn up by the Nazis and excused by the Soviets as a strategic necessity, its effects have persisted long after its death. Indeed, the map of eastern and central Europe that we see today is largely its product: the boundaries hastily drawn by Ribbentrop and Molotov have proved to be astonishingly durable. More immediately, two generations of Lithuanians, Latvians and Estonians would endure life within the hated USSR, where bitter memories of the Soviet annexation and occupation of 1940–1 would fuel post-war resistance movements. Poetically, it would be the protests in the Baltic states on the fifteenth anniversary of the pact's signature in 1989 that would begin the process of the USSR's dissolution.

For all its brevity then – it lasted only twenty-two months and its seven short paragraphs contain barely 280 words – the Nazi–Soviet Pact was profoundly important. Far from a sideshow or a curiosity, it is of vital importance to our understanding not only of the Second World War, but also of the broader story of twentieth-century European history. It fully deserves to be rescued from the footnotes and restored to its rightful place in our collective narrative of the Second World War in Europe. I can only hope that this book might make some small contribution to that process.

A Meeting on the Boundary of Peace

It was probably not the rattle of tanks that surprised the citizens of Brest that chill September morning in 1939. Their city in eastern Poland had already been occupied by German forces for the best part of a week, so they would have become grimly accustomed to the din of barked orders and military traffic. Rather, it was the accompanying voices that would have shocked them. Not the harsh, guttural intonations of German, this time, but the slurred sing-song of a language that was much closer to their own, and was instantly recognisable: Russian.

For some in Brest, the arrival of the Red Army was seen as a liberation. Many among the city's Byelorussian and Jewish communities viewed the Soviet Union as their protector against what they saw as the intolerant nationalism of the Polish state. In some eastern suburbs, therefore, there was a celebratory atmosphere, with the traditional Slavic greeting of bread and salt being extended to the arriving soldiers, while a band played the Soviet anthem, the 'Internationale'.[1] Others were rather more wary. The city's Polish population had endured a torrid few weeks, fretting over the military situation, fearing the arrival of German troops or the use of poison gas, and worrying that their Byelorussian neighbours might turn against them. Those with longer memories would have recalled the bitter Polish–Soviet War of 1920–1, or the long decades of Russian occupation that had preceded 1914, only a generation or so earlier. For them, the arrival of Soviet troops was an echo of dark times and an ominous portent of bad days to come.

The Soviet troops themselves did little to ease tensions. Generally shabby and unkempt in appearance, they were evidently under orders not to interact with the locals, although it seems that some had little choice but to ask the peasantry for food or to change their exhausted horses.[2] Nonetheless, they were sometimes approached by the brave or curious. One of the latter was fifteen-year-old Svetozar Sinkevich, a Byelorussian, who was initially excited by the arrival of what he called 'his' people. He was quickly disillusioned: 'Their faces were grey, unshaven', he recalled,

> greatcoats and short quilted jackets looked baggy, the tops of their boots were made of a canvas-like material. I went up to one of the trucks and tried to talk to the soldiers, yet all of them kept silent, averting their gaze from me. Finally one of them in a uniform cap with a star on his sleeve said that the Party had sent the Red Army to liberate us from the Polish landlords and capitalists. I was perplexed.[3]

Many in Brest would have shared his confusion. Historically, at least, the city was used to the violent intrusion of the outside world. In the 900 years since its foundation, it had been repeatedly fought over by Poles, Mongols, Russians, Swedes and Teutonic Knights. Within living memory, too, it had seen considerable upheaval. In 1915, the Russians had abandoned the city to a German occupation that had lasted until the end of the First World War. Then, with the collapse of the Russian Empire in 1917, the city had made headlines worldwide for the first time. As 'Brest-Litovsk', it had played host to the German–Soviet negotiations and the peace treaty between the two of March 1918 that would bear its name.

In 1939, however, events had moved with a rapidity that had been unimaginable a generation before. Far from the plodding, stalemated immobility of the First World War, the Polish campaign of 1939 had witnessed something of the revolution in military tactics. Though it was to develop organically and was yet to earn the status of an official military doctrine, the blitzkrieg, with fast-moving armoured spear-heads penetrating far into the enemy's rear to disrupt defences, heralded a new era in tactical thinking. So, though located deep in eastern Poland, Brest had quickly found itself a focus of the German advance, primarily because of the formidable nineteenth-century fortress on its western fringe that might serve as a defensive strong-point for hard-pressed Polish forces.[4] Such had been the speed of the German advance, indeed, that when their armies first appeared before

Brest on 13 September, less than two weeks after the opening of the invasion, some within the city believed that the soldiers had to be paratroopers, dropped behind Polish lines.[5]

Confusion was still the order of the day when the Red Army arrived in the city five days later. Aside from those citizens that hurried to greet the Soviets as liberators, others fervently hoped that the Red Army was coming to their aid against the invading Germans, a fiction that had evidently been propagated by elements of the Polish military.[6] Yet, official declarations of the Soviet authorities – which had been issued in Polish translation by the local Wehrmacht command, in a cosy example of collaboration between the two – would dash all such hopes by stating categorically that the Red Army's invasion was merely the result of Poland's supposed military and political collapse, and was intended solely to protect the Ukrainian and Byelorussian peoples living there.[7] Far from rushing to engage the invading Wehrmacht, then, those Soviet soldiers – riding on the open backs of trucks or clinging to the sides of their tanks – were heading west through the city to greet their German counterparts.

Late on the morning of 18 September, the first contacts were made. Across the city, German and Soviet troops began fraternising: olive green met 'field-grey', the vanguard of Stalin's communist revolution came face to face with Hitler's Wehrmacht. Warily at first, mindful of their previously strained relations, the two sides shared rations and communicated as best they could, using sign language and goodwill. An easy entrée was the sharing of cigarettes: *papirosi*, crude, hand-rolled examples from the Soviet side, would be exchanged for German manufactured articles, which would be much prized by the Red Army men. Tanks and armoured cars were clambered upon and inspected, with the ever-present rejoinder from both sides that 'ours are better'. For all their ideological differences, the smiles that day seem to have been genuine. An eyewitness recalled seeing Wehrmacht soldiers on one side of the street greeting their Soviet counterparts on the other with the words: 'Communists! Good!'[8]

Contact was also made at more senior levels. At around 10.30 a young Soviet officer arrived in an armoured car at the German headquarters in the city. According to contemporary German records, the discussions that followed were 'friendly', and mostly concerned with delineating a demarcation line between the Soviet and German forces.[9]

The local German commander, General Heinz Guderian, was rather less enthusiastic. He had endured a difficult few days, losing his adjutant Lieutenant Colonel Robert Braubach to a Polish sniper – a 'painful loss' – and then being obliged to assist the bishop of Danzig, Edward O'Rourke, who had found himself in the war zone and had been eager not to fall into Soviet hands. Consequently, he was frustrated that the deadline agreed for a German withdrawal from Brest, only two days later, gave his men too little time to evacuate their own wounded or recover their damaged vehicles.[10] Nonetheless, the Soviet officer was given lunch, and an agreement was made that a formal cession of the city to Soviet control would follow on the afternoon of 22 September.

On the morning of the handover, preparations went smoothly. According to the agreement, Soviet forces took sole control of the city, and its fortress, from 8.00 a.m. Two hours later a joint commission met to clarify any remaining points of confusion or friction. Soon after that Guderian met with his opposite number, Brigadier General Semyon Krivoshein, commander of the Soviet 29th Light Tank Brigade. An impassioned communist and a Jew, Krivoshein was a short, wiry man, who sported a Hitleresque toothbrush moustache. Like Guderian, he was a pioneer in the use of tanks; indeed the two may have known each other from their time at the Kama tank school at Kazan in the 1920s, during an earlier blossoming of German–Soviet collaboration. Speaking together in French, he and Guderian discussed staging a joint military parade to mark the formal handover of the city. Though Krivoshein was less than entirely keen, stating that his men were weary after their long march west,[11] he nonetheless agreed to release a couple of units to take part in a march past of Wehrmacht and Red Army forces for that afternoon.

At 4.00 p.m., the two generals reconvened on a small wooden platform, which had been hastily constructed in front of the main entrance to the former German command, the regional administration building on Union of Lublin Street. Standing before a flagpole bearing the swastika'd German *Kriegsflagge*, Guderian grinned broadly, looking resplendent in his red-lined greatcoat and black leather jackboots. At his side, Krivoshein was similarly attired, in a belted leather coat and leather boots to keep out the autumn chill.

Surrounding the two, beyond a knot of senior German military personnel, a mixed crowd of Wehrmacht and Red Army soldiers thronged the route of the parade, pockets of German field-grey mingling with the black leather coats of Soviet officers, the olive drab of the infantry and the dark overalls of the tank crews. Beyond them, civilians lined the street. Among them was twenty-year-old Raisa Shirnyuk, who remembered how word of the parade had spread: 'There was no official announcement,' she recalled, 'but the rumour mill had worked well; already that morning everyone in the town knew that the troops would be marching there.'[12] According to one German account, the crowd was enthusiastic, being made up primarily of Brest's non-Polish communities – Byelorussians and Jews – who welcomed the Red Army with flowers and cheering.[13]

To the blare of a military band, the parade began. German infantry led the way, their smart uniforms and precision goosestep drawing admiring comments from the assembled crowds. Raisa Shirnyuk was one of those impressed by their military bearing, noting that their commanding officer kept the men in line, shouting *Langsam, langsam, aber deutlich!* ('Slowly, slowly, but clearly!').[14] Motorised units followed: motorcycles with sidecars, trucks and half-tracks laden with soldiers and towing artillery pieces. Tanks, too, clattered along the cobbled street. As each group filed past the reviewing stand, they drew a crisp salute from both Guderian and Krivoshein, who spent the moments between in amiable conversation.

Inevitably, some of those watching drew comparisons between the two forces on display. The somewhat primitive Soviet T-26 tanks, for instance, contrasted rather obviously with more modern Wehrmacht vehicles, especially when one of the former slithered off the road not far from the reviewing platform.[15] Stanislav Miretski noticed other differences: the Soviets' belts were canvas rather than the German leather, and while the Germans employed trucks to haul their artillery, the Red Army used 'stunted and unsightly' horses with inferior harnesses.[16] Raisa Shirnyuk concurred, noting that the Red Army men, with their 'dirty boots, dusty greatcoats and stubble on their faces', compared rather unfavourably with their German fellows.[17] Another eyewitness drew a chilling conclusion from the poor appearance of the Soviet infantry. Boris Akimov was accustomed to seeing elegantly dressed Polish officers, so the 'poverty and slovenliness' of the Red Army struck him. But their smell and dirtiness prompted a much more profound question: 'What sort of a life', he wondered, 'will they bring to us?'[18] An answer of sorts was provided when an elderly lady pushed her way through the crowd to approach the Soviet soldiers with tears in her eyes, muttering 'My kin, my boys.' To the astonishment of those watching, she was roughly pushed away by a soldier, shouting 'Get back, woman!'[19]

While the military hardware trundled past and the future was being pondered, the attention of the crowd turned skyward as two dozen or so Luftwaffe fighters made a low pass over the tribune. Guderian, struggling to make himself heard over the roar of their engines, shouted 'German aces! Fabulous!' 'We have better!' Krivoshein replied, determined not to be impressed by the display of German air power.[20]

After some forty-five minutes, with the parade drawing to a close, Guderian, Krivoshein and the senior officers around them all turned to face the flagpole. As the military band struck up the German national anthem, 'Deutschland, Deutschland über alles', and the assembled officers solemnly saluted, the blood-red *Kriegsflagge* was lowered, to be replaced by the deeper red of the Soviet hammer and sickle. With that, the band played the 'Internationale' – out of tune, as one eyewitness recalled[21] – before Guderian and Krivoshein shook hands for the last time. Then the German general joined his men as they departed to the west, across the river Bug, the new German–Soviet frontier. As Krivoshein recalled: 'At last, the parade was over.'[22]

In his post-war memoir, doubtless mindful of the rather compromising nature of events at Brest, Krivoshein made much of his unwillingness in his dealings with Guderian and the Germans, giving the impression that he was 'holding his nose' throughout. He claimed to have set his men various maintenance tasks, thereby leaving only one battalion to take part in the parade, and mischievously suggested that Guderian's men and machines were looping around the block to make them appear more numerous than they were.[23] Despite his later protestations of reluctance, however, Krivoshein's true sentiments are perhaps indicated by the account of a couple of German war reporters who caught up with him, the following day, at his nearby field headquarters. They noted that the Soviet brigadier general was in high spirits, treating the two to a lavish lunch and raising a toast to both Hitler and Stalin as 'men of the people'. As the reporters left, he even gave them his Moscow address and invited them to visit him 'after the victory over capitalist Albion'.[24] Politics, it seems, can do strange things to people's memories.

Though the Soviet media appear not to have mentioned the parade at Brest, the German propaganda machine made much of it, describing it as a 'meeting on the boundary of peace'.[25] Grainy footage of the tanks and vehicles rumbling past the reviewing stand was duly included in the weekly newsreels that were shown in cinemas across Hitler's Reich that autumn. The propaganda value of the images was immense, providing as they did a startling visual confirmation of the Nazi–Soviet agreement that had been forged the previous month. As if to hammer the point home, the newsreel commentary taunted Germany's enemies by stating that the meeting with the Soviets at Brest had 'scuppered the pious plans of the Western Democracies'.[26]

One German news reporter went further. Writing in the Nazi Party newspaper – the *Völkischer Beobachter* – Kurt Frowein described the scene in lyrical terms: the 'keen autumn day', the 'rising crescendo of tank tracks', the homage to a city 'captured with German arms . . . now being returned to its rightful owners'. For him, the handshake between Guderian and Krivoshein was 'a symbol of the friendly coming together of two nations' which announced 'that Germany and Russia are uniting in order to jointly decide on the fate of Eastern Europe'.[27] Frowein was right to employ hyperbole. The events of that day signified such a seismic political shift that his words would have been unthinkable barely a month before.

For those who had taken to heart all the fulminations and insults that the Soviet Union and Nazi Germany had hurled at one another over the previous six years, these were strange days indeed. The parade at Brest vividly demonstrated the reality and currency of the pact agreed a month earlier in Moscow, tanks and soldiers now replacing the images of smiling men in smoky Kremlin offices. As events at Brest demonstrated, Europe's two mightiest dictatorships – whose bitter enmity had largely defined the 1930s – were now standing side by side as allies, collaborating in a joint conquest of their mutual neighbour.

Contemporary observers were bewildered. Communists around the world baulked at the ideological gymnastics that they were suddenly obliged to perform, while many Nazis harboured deep-seated misgivings about their country's new collaborator and bedfellow. In the West, meanwhile, there was profound disquiet, as though the world had shifted slightly on its axis and the old political certainties had proved themselves to be merely transient. Many would have wondered just how this peculiar turn of events could have come to pass.

I

The Devil's Potion

A month earlier, soon after midday on 23 August 1939, two Focke-Wulf Condors emerged from the clouds and began their descent towards Moscow's Khodynka airfield. The planes – sleek, modern, four-engined examples – had begun their journey the previous afternoon, stopping overnight at the eastern German city of Königsberg, before continuing their route to the Soviet capital. Each one contained around twenty officials: advisors, translators, diplomats and photographers. The party was led by the German foreign minister, Joachim von Ribbentrop.

As they circled, preparing to land, those on board whiled away the time as best they could. It had been a five-hour flight from Königsberg, and many of them were restless. The vain, pompous Ribbentrop had endured a rather stressful night, fretting about his task, poring over official documents and making copious notes.[1] Others were more relaxed. Hitler's photographer, Heinrich Hoffmann, for instance, was sleeping off the excesses of the previous night. Renowned as something of a drinker and bon viveur, he had earned the nickname of 'Reichssäufer', or 'Reich drunkard', and, true to form, he had taken the opportunity of the hotel stay in Königsberg to spend a 'cheery night' in a nearby bar. Woken just prior to landing, he was delighted that he had 'slept like a babe' for the entire flight.[2]

Most of those on board peered down at the airfield and the city below. For all of them, flying was still a rather novel experience, and the bird's-eye view was something that could be both thrilling and terrifying. Moreover, Moscow itself had more than a whiff of the exotic about it. Not only was the Soviet capital geographically far removed from all that most of them knew, it was also laden with sinister political connotations as the home of proletarian revolution: the fountainhead of world communism. 'There was a feeling of ambivalence', one of the party later wrote, 'that fate should lead us to Moscow, which we had previously fought bitterly as the enemy of European culture.'[3]

Once the two aircraft landed, it became clear that a substantial welcome had been arranged, as both the airfield and its two-storey terminal building were bedecked with German and Soviet flags, the swastika juxtaposed with the hammer and sickle, a sight that Heinrich Hoffmann – like many others – had considered inconceivable only days before.[4] Evidently, the Soviet authorities had considered it similarly implausible, and had encountered considerable difficulty in finding sufficient swastika banners for the purpose, finally requisitioning them from local film studios, where they had recently been used for anti-Nazi propaganda films.[5]

As Ribbentrop descended the steps from the plane, a military band struck up first 'Deutschland, Deutschland über alles' and then the 'Internationale'. Introductions followed, with smart handshakes and smiles all round for the Soviet welcoming delegation and their German guests. A few of the German participants remembered the welcome with more than a dash of cynicism. Johnnie von Herwarth, a junior diplomat at the German embassy in Moscow, stood with a colleague watching a group of Gestapo officers shaking hands with their counterparts from the Soviet secret police, the NKVD. 'They're obviously delighted finally to be able to collaborate', his colleague said, adding 'but watch out! This will be disastrous, especially when they start exchanging files.'[6] Hitler's senior interpreter, Paul Schmidt, meanwhile, was amused to see that they were being met by the Soviet deputy foreign minister, Vladimir Potemkin. As an educated man, he knew that an eighteenth-century namesake of Potemkin, one of Catherine the Great's regional governors, had constructed fake settlements in the Crimea to impress the visiting empress, which became known as 'Potemkin villages'. So, for Schmidt, Potemkin was a name that was neatly symbolic of the unreality of the scene.[7] Pilot Hans Baur was rather less cynical. Watching Ribbentrop inspect a guard of honour taken from elite Soviet air force squadrons, he was simply struck by the surreal sight of watching the German foreign minister marching briskly along the line with his arm outstretched in the Hitler salute. 'My God', he said to himself. 'Wonders will never cease!'[8]

That sense of amazement would have been widespread on both

sides. After all, the Nazis and the Soviets had spent most of the previous decade insulting one another. As an opposition politician in the later 1920s, Hitler had made political capital by portraying both communism and the Soviet Union as malevolent, alien forces, threatening the German people and their way of life. He had persistently railed against Moscow, habitually referring to the 'Jewish tyrants' and 'bloodsuckers' in the Kremlin, and labelling Bolshevism as 'an infamous crime against humanity' and an 'infernal abortion'.[9]

Once established in power from 1933, Hitler had scarcely softened his anti-Soviet rhetoric. In time, a tone of unremitting hostility had developed, with few opportunities being missed to deliver violent condemnations of Moscow and its agents, and laud Nazi Germany's role in the front line of the fight against communism. Hitler's keynote speech to the Nazi Party Congress at Nuremberg in September 1937 was perhaps typical. In it, he was keen to stress the community of civilised nations: the 'great European family of peoples' that had 'given each other models, examples and lessons . . . pleasure and many things of beauty' and in whose company 'we have every reason to harbour mutual admiration instead of hate'. Against this, he countered with the image of a 'Bolshevist plague', a 'totally alien element which has not the slightest contribution to make to our economy or our culture, but instead wreaks only havoc'.[10] Hitler was an opportunist politician, certainly, but anti-communism was one of his guiding principles.

The Soviets had reciprocated. As relations soured between Berlin and Moscow from the mid-1930s, an increasingly Germanophobic tone emerged, in which Stalin and his paladins competed to criticise Hitler and Nazi Germany in the press and in public speeches. Hitler was often portrayed as insane, an 'idiot' or a man 'possessed by a demon'.[11] The Nazi regime, too, was pilloried as 'modern-day cannibals . . . the descendants of Herostratus' who would 'drown in their own blood'.[12] Blood, indeed, was a common leitmotiv, and rarely was fascism or Nazism mentioned in the Soviet press in the 1930s without the adjective 'bloody' being appended to it.

The enmity was not merely cosmetic or tactical: it was underpinned by ideology. As the world's first communist state, and one that openly espoused the spreading of revolution, the Soviet Union had originally seen territorial expansion against a hostile outside world not only as desirable, but as crucial to its survival. And though it had, in time, evolved less overtly bellicose ideas, Moscow still held a special place for Germany in its geopolitical ambitions. According to the precepts of Marxist–Leninist doctrine, the establishment of communism in pre-industrial Russia had been anomalous, the accidental product of the chaos of the Bolshevik Revolution. In order to secure a future for itself, therefore, communism had to be exported to Europe's industrial heartland – Germany – where it was expected that an advanced, ideologically sound proletariat was itching to throw off the shackles of bourgeois democracy and embrace the heirs of Marx and Lenin.[13]

German thinking, meanwhile, was also couched in geopolitics, but drawing on dubious theories of race, rather than the dry precepts of socioeconomics. Long before the Third Reich, German statesmen and generals had liked to envision the vast expanses of Russia and Ukraine as an area ripe for German expansion and colonisation; a modern re-imagining of the medieval *Drang nach Osten* or 'drive towards the East'. It was an attitude that had been amply expressed by the punitive Treaty of Brest-Litovsk of March 1918, which had ended Russian involvement in the First World War, and had forced Bolshevik Russia to cede vast swathes of territory – including Ukraine and the Baltic states – along with a quarter of its population, to the victorious Germans. Though the cessions proved to be short-lived, being superseded by Germany's defeat on the western front later that year, the idea of German expansion at Russia's expense refused to die.

Indeed, as Germany endured post-war tribulations of her own, the concept of territorial expansion was increasingly seen by those on the right as a panacea for the combined ills of poverty, hunger and over-population. In time, Hitler was to add a new ideological gloss to such sentiments, railing against the perversities and excesses of the Bolsheviks and advocating German expansion at their expense. In *Mein Kampf*, written in 1925, he had clarified his own, rather half-baked, ideas on the subject. Russia, he wrote, had been deprived of its 'Germanic ruling class' by the revolution, and had been taken over by the Jews, so now was in a 'ferment of decomposition' and was 'ripe for dissolution'. Consequently, he suggested, it was time for the German people to 'turn [their] eyes towards the lands of the East', for it was there that their shortage of living space – *Lebensraum* – would be rectified.[14]

Of course, the partnership that was on offer in 1939 was a long way from the merciless conquest that Hitler had envisaged or the westward expansion foreseen by Stalin, but it could nonetheless be regarded by both as a first step. Stalin would have been well aware of Lenin's dictum that history proceeds, not by straight lines, but by 'zig-zags and roundabout ways', and Hitler had done much to advance the Nazis' goals through opportunism and realpolitik, so it was not illogical for either to conclude that a pact with his enemy might advance his cause. Both, therefore, could have been forgiven for believing that they were fulfilling their ideological destiny.

The German foreign minister would certainly not have been immune to such grandiose thoughts. Conceited and arrogant, Ribbentrop was deeply unpopular, even among his fellow Nazis. A former champagne salesman, he had married into money, added a spurious aristocratic 'von' to his name and bluffed his way into the upper echelons of the Third Reich, where his international contacts had earned him a role as Hitler's favourite foreign policy advisor. From there, his oleaginous and ingratiating manner had secured an appointment as ambassador to London in 1936, before he finally landed the position of foreign minister early in 1938. Bellicose and incompetent in equal measure, Ribbentrop had contributed greatly to the poisoning of international relations over the previous months. Faithfully and belligerently echoing his master's voice, he had been instrumental in the slide towards what he viewed as an inevitable, even desirable, conflict to establish German hegemony in Europe. In this respect, Ribbentrop had also been a key player in the developing relationship with the Soviet Union, which – ideological differences aside – offered Germany not only a secure eastern flank, but also the prospect of an economic collaboration that would be essential for the coming conflict. The pact that he was coming to negotiate would be a volte-face that would shock the world, but it would give Hitler his war on hugely favourable terms. Ribbentrop knew that this would be his finest hour.

After the welcome at Khodynka, the members of the German delegation were taken to the former Austrian legation building, which had been allocated to them as a residence. Many then took the opportunity to experience something of the city, and the regime, of which they were guests. Heinrich Hoffmann visited the Novodevichy cemetery to see the grave of Stalin's second wife, Nadezhda Alliluyeva, which he described as one of the 'most beautiful' he had ever seen.[15]

Paul Schmidt, meanwhile, opted for a short tour of the capital, accompanied by a translator. 'At first sight', he recalled,

> there was an almost disappointing similarity to the other European cities. But, upon closer inspection, the key differences occurred to me. The happiness that one was used to seeing upon the faces of people on the street in Berlin, Paris or London appeared to be absent in Moscow. The people looked serious and stared straight ahead with a haunted air. Only very occasionally did I see a smiling face.[16]

If Schmidt was perhaps guilty of allowing his prejudices to colour his experience, pilot Hans Baur was left in little doubt about the realities of life in the Soviet Union. Leaving the German military attaché's residence by car, Baur's guide pointed out the secret policeman, whose task it was to inform the authorities of their departure and where they were going. Soon, the guide explained, 'another car would tack itself on to us and follow fifty yards or so in the rear, and wherever we went and whatever we did, the [secret police] would be on our heels'.[17] Politically rather naïve, Baur had to be repeatedly warned not to take photographs, and caused a scene when he tried to tip the Russian driver for his efforts. 'The man was furious', he recalled. 'He wanted to know whether this was the thanks he got for having done his best for us – to get him into prison. We knew perfectly well that it was forbidden to take tips.'[18]

At the embassy, meanwhile, a lavish buffet had been laid on for the new arrivals. Heinrich Hoffmann was astonished, as he had not expected to find such opulence in the Soviet capital. He was soon disabused of the assumption that the food on display had been supplied locally, however: 'everything had come from abroad – the bread, even, from Sweden, the butter from Denmark and the rest from various sources'.[19] The complexities of the food situation in Moscow had already been made plain to Hans Baur earlier at the airfield. Seeking to dispose of food left over from the inbound flight, Baur had offered rolls, biscuits and chocolate to the team of Soviet mechanics and cleaners busying themselves with his planes. But, to his surprise, his offer had been declined, with the foreman telling him that it was forbidden and that the Russian people had enough to eat. Bemused, but determined not to let the food go to waste, Baur resolved to leave the items out on a bench in the hangar; very soon, they all duly disappeared.[20]

While his entourage thus acquainted themselves with the Soviet capital, Ribbentrop was eager to open talks with his Soviet counterparts. Against the advice of his embassy colleagues – who had suggested a more measured approach, so as not to appear too keen – Ribbentrop hurried, upon arrival, straight into his first session of discussions with the Soviets.[21] There were other concerns. Embassy advisor and translator, Gustav Hilger, recalled being pulled aside by Ribbentrop as they left for the Kremlin, in an unexpected show of paternal concern. 'You look so worried', Ribbentrop said. 'Is there any reason?' Hilger, who had been born in Moscow and had lived in Russia for most of his life, voiced his misgivings about their mission, stating 'I believe that what you are about to do in the Kremlin will go well only as long as Germany remains strong.' Ribbentrop was unmoved, replying: 'If that is all, then I can only tell you that Germany will be able to deal with any situation that comes up.'[22]

With that, Ribbentrop and Hilger, accompanied by the German ambassador to Moscow, Friedrich-Werner von der Schulenburg, and the chief of Stalin's bodyguard, Nikolai Vlasik, boarded a limousine of the Soviet NKVD to be whisked through Red Square. Entering the Kremlin beneath the impressive Spassky Gate, the party were driven to the Senate, an elegant, three-storey building on the Kremlin's north-eastern side, just across the wall from Lenin's mausoleum. Throughout, an unseen bell tolled ominously to mark their arrival.

Descending from the car, the party were met by the bald, fleshy Alexander Poskrebyshev, chief of Stalin's personal chancellery, and led up a short flight of stairs to the prime minister's office, located on the first floor. There, amidst the spartan, functional furnishings, stood Stalin himself, simply attired in a plain tunic jacket over baggy woollen trousers and calf-length leather boots, his narrow, yellowing eyes and pockmarked skin making him instantly recognisable. Alongside him stood Vyacheslav Molotov, his foreign minister, a diminutive, rather nondescript figure in a plain grey suit, his signature pince-nez perched on his nose above a neatly trimmed greying moustache. It was rare for a foreigner to encounter such a concentration of Soviet power, and Schulenburg reportedly gave a squeak of surprise when he saw Stalin; despite serving in Moscow for five years as ambassador, he had never met the Soviet leader. Ribbentrop, too, was impressed, and would later wax lyrical about Stalin as 'a man of extraordinary calibre', who justified his reputation.[23] For his part, Stalin usually avoided foreign visitors on principle, so his presence there was most probably a calculated strategy, intended to intimidate his guests and throw them off guard.[24] Whatever the motivation, it was certainly proof of how seriously the negotiations were being taken.

After an initial exchange of introductions and pleasantries, in which Stalin was 'simple and unpretentious', behaving with 'jovial friendli-ness'[25] towards his guests, the four principal players – Stalin and Molotov, Ribbentrop and Schulenburg – seated themselves around a table and proceeded to the business at hand. To Stalin's rear sat his translator, the youthful Vladimir Pavlov, while Hilger, acting as Ribbentrop's interpreter, positioned himself between his foreign minister and Ambassador Schulenburg. The negotiations they began that afternoon would cause a political earthquake.

In truth, it was a process that had started in earnest a few months earlier. Despite the opprobrium that both sides had heaped upon one another during the mid-1930s, contacts between the Nazis and the Soviets had never been entirely broken off, and talks – first on economic ties, then political matters – had tentatively begun in May 1939. Hitler's position had been fairly clear. Irritated by what he saw as western meddling in frustrating his ambitions at Munich the previous autumn, he had resolved to accelerate Germany's expansion – by force if neces-sary – while his perceived advantage in armaments and trained personnel still held good. And if that meant thinking outside of the ideological box, then so be it.

To this end, Ribbentrop had initially courted the Poles with a view to enticing them away from the Anglo-French camp. The flirtation had begun in October 1938, when Ribbentrop had requested the disputed Free City of Danzig, offering Warsaw a twenty-five-year guarantee of the German–Polish border in return. The following January, the Polish foreign minister, Józef Beck, had been invited for talks with Hitler at the Berghof, where German support for Polish ambitions in Ukraine had been dangled by way of an incentive to broker a deal. The flirtation was no ruse. Hitler initially directed little of the hatred towards the Poles that he reserved for the Czechs, and had lauded Poland's role as a bulwark against communism. Indeed, true to his anti-Soviet instincts, he had even floated the idea of a joint anti-Soviet alliance, with Poland – naturally – as Germany's subordinate, junior partner. 'Great possibilities' existed in Polish-German co-operation, Ribbentrop minuted optimistically to the German ambassador in Warsaw, above all in the pursuit of 'a common Eastern policy' against the USSR.[26]

Yet the Poles would not be swayed, either by German offers or by veiled threats. Poland's territorial integrity and independence, newly restored only a generation before, after 123 years of foreign occupation, were far too precious to her politicians to be bartered away in return for dubious promises and vassal status, so a strict policy of even-handedness – the so-called 'Doctrine of Two Enemies' – governed her relations with her two largest neighbours. Thus, while Warsaw was willing to negotiate on minor details, the seizure of Danzig and the surrender of the Polish Corridor were not open to discussion and any attempt to take them by force would be interpreted in the Polish capital as an act of war.

This brief, aborted dalliance with Poland would not be without consequence. That same spring, as Ribbentrop was flirting with Warsaw, Hitler had designs on another European capital. On the morning of 15 March, German troops had marched – at Czech 'invitation' and unopposed except for a snowstorm – into the Czechoslovak capital, Prague. Hitler, following in their wake, had proclaimed the final dissolution of the Czechoslovak state – Slovakia had been persuaded to declare its independence the previous day – and announced that the remaining Czech lands, Bohemia and Moravia, would henceforth become a 'protectorate' of the Greater German Reich.

Hitler's motives for invading the rump of Czechoslovakia in the spring of 1939 are not entirely clear. He certainly seems to have wanted to thumb his nose at the Western Powers, whose interference had so irritated him the previous autumn. As he commented to an aide at the time of Munich, 'that fellow Chamberlain has spoiled my entry into Prague'.[27] Hitler was not a man to be denied his wishes for long. There were other, more cogent, justifications, however. Bohemia and Moravia were rich in raw materials and industry, and the two territories represented a vast salient protruding into Greater Germany's south-eastern flank. But the move was also calculated to intimidate Poland. At a time when Poland's intransigence in negotiations was stymying Hitler's strategic ambitions, the taking of the Czech lands was a demonstration both of German power and – Hitler hoped – of western impotence. Hitler gambled that the British and French would do nothing to aid the state that they had 'defended' barely six months before at Munich, and the clear implication was that the Poles should accede to German demands.

Yet the West would not be nearly as supine as Hitler had hoped. Indeed, the annexation of Bohemia and Moravia served belatedly to galvanise western opinion, representing as it did Hitler's first acquisition of a substantial non-German population, and thereby giving the lie to his earlier protestations that he was merely righting the historic wrongs of Versailles, and returning ethnic German populations 'home' to the Reich. Those in London, Paris and elsewhere who had been sceptical of the appeasement of Hitler's Germany were now clamouring for a much more robust response.

Consequently, on 31 March 1939, the British government extended a guarantee to Poland, which it considered to be the next target of Hitler's aggressive intentions, stating that 'if any action clearly threatened Polish independence, and if the Poles felt it vital to resist such action by force, Britain would come to their aid'.[28] Of course, there was very little that Britain could practically do to aid Poland in the event of a German invasion: her resources of men and material simply did not make active intervention in central Europe a realistic proposition. But the guarantee was nonetheless an expression of solidarity and support, which was intended not only to bolster Polish resolve, but also to reassure the French that Britain remained committed to continental European affairs. Most importantly, it was intended to mark a line in the sand to Hitler, a signal that further German aggression would not be tolerated. It was, as one historian has described, the diplomatic equivalent of a game of 'chicken'.[29]

Hitler was predictably furious at this British checkmate. When he received word of the guarantee, he was in the Reich Chancellery in Berlin, and – as Admiral Wilhelm Canaris reported – he could barely contain his annoyance. 'Hitler flew into a passion', Canaris recalled:

With features distorted by fury, he had stormed up and down his room, pounded his fists on the marble table-top, and spewed forth a series of savage imprecations. Then, with his eyes flashing with an uncanny light, he had growled the threat: 'I'll brew them a devil's potion.'[30]

The following day, before a mass rally at Wilhelmshaven, he gave his response. 'No power on earth', he warned, would be able to break German might, and if the Western Allies expected Germany to stand by while they marshalled their 'satellite states' to act in their interests, then they would be sorely mistaken. Hitler concluded ominously that 'whoever declares himself willing to pull the chestnuts out of the fire for the great powers should expect to burn his fingers'.[31]

It was at this point that the idea of a new rapprochement with Moscow seems to have occurred to the leadership in Berlin. Initially intended as a *'petit jeu'* to intimidate the Poles, it was first aired in mid-April, with Göring rather than Ribbentrop playing a key role.[32] In his diary, the Nazi ideologue Alfred Rosenberg would recall that he had spoken with Göring about the possibility of an alignment such as this. 'When Germany's life is at stake', he wrote, 'even a temporary association with Moscow must be contemplated.'[33] Hitler was also lukewarm on the idea, reminding Ribbentrop that he had 'fought communism' all his life, but according to the latter he changed his mind in early May, when he was shown footage at the Berghof of Stalin reviewing a military parade. Thereafter, Ribbentrop alleged, Hitler was intrigued, taking 'a fancy' to Stalin's face and saying that the Soviet leader looked 'like a man one could do business with'. With that, Ribbentrop got permission to pursue his negotiations.[34] It remained to be seen whether the idea would gain any traction with the Soviets.

In fact, the Soviet Union was ripe for a change of tack in foreign policy. A late convert to the principle of 'collective security' to deter fascist aggression, it had hoped that concerted action – whether via the Comintern's 'Popular Front' policy or via the high ideals of the League of Nations, which it finally joined in 1934 – might contain and defeat Hitler. By the spring of 1939, however, it had begun to shift its position. With 'collective security' already discredited by the international failure to confront German revisionism and Italian aggression against Abyssinia, the Soviets had been terminally disillusioned by the West's lack of vigour at Munich, and became increasingly convinced

that the British and the French would be happy to cut a deal with
Hitler at their expense.[35] At around the same time as Göring was
hatching his '*petit jeu*', therefore, Stalin was open to new suggestions
in foreign policy, even erring towards a policy of unilateralism, in
which practical bilateral arrangements would replace the previous
multilateral commitments.

Indeed, in a speech to the 18th Communist Party Congress on 10
March 1939, only days before Hitler sent his troops into Prague, Stalin
had struck a novel note in vociferously attacking the West. A 'new
redivision of the world' was under way, he said, in which the 'aggressor
states' were gaining spheres of influence and colonies at the expense
of the 'non-aggressor states'.[36] Yet, instead of standing up to aggression, he explained, as the principles of collective security had
prescribed, the British and the French were colluding with the
aggressor states, drawing back and retreating, 'making concession
after concession . . . eager not to hinder [them] in their nefarious
work'. Far from being motivated by mere cowardice, Stalin went on,
the Western Powers wanted to encourage the aggressors to become
mired in a war with the Soviet Union, whereby both sides would
'weaken and exhaust one another', until the 'enfeebled belligerents'
would be ready to have conditions dictated to them once again by
the capitalist world. This, he said, was the 'true face' of 'the policy
of non-intervention'.[37]

Though there undoubtedly were a few of the more hawkish anti-
Bolsheviks in the West who might have subscribed to this view, it was
certainly not a fair reflection of mainstream western opinion or policy.
Rather, it was very much the result of Stalin trying to make sense of
the outside world through the blinkers of communist ideology and
the fog of his own paranoia. The primary ideological problem that
Stalin had was his inability – following the precepts of Marxism–
Leninism – to differentiate clearly between Nazism and 'ordinary'
western capitalism. Both were, according to communist doctrine,
merely two sides of the same malevolent coin, albeit with Nazism
considered to be further down the road to its 'inevitable' demise.
Consequently, from the Soviet perspective, relations with the outside
world – democratic and totalitarian alike – could never be normal.
Every relationship was viewed in Moscow as a zero-sum game, with
the only governing ideal being the benefit and security of the USSR.

The Soviet Union, therefore, had little interest in assisting its ideological enemies in maintaining the status quo, and was unafraid of fomenting conflict between its rivals, so as to then be able to exploit the unrest and upheaval that might follow, to its own benefit. In this regard, Soviet thinking was actually much closer to that of the Nazis. As Stalin later explained – somewhat clumsily – to the British ambassador Stafford Cripps:

> the USSR had wanted to change the old equilibrium . . . England and France had wanted to preserve it. Germany had also wanted to make a change in the equilibrium, and this common desire to get rid of the old equilibrium created the basis for the rapprochement with Germany.[38]

In private, Stalin was more honest about his motivations. It is suggested that he made his thoughts plain in a secret Politburo meeting on 19 August 1939, in which he advocated accepting Hitler's proposal of a non-aggression pact in the expectation that conflict between Germany and the West would be inevitable and that the USSR could 'remain on the sidelines' and 'hope for an advantageous entry into the war'. Stalin, it is said, went further, giving a number of resulting scenarios in which the prospects for 'world revolution' would be enhanced. He closed by stating that the USSR 'must do everything to ensure that the war lasts as long as possible in order to exhaust both sides'.[39]

This text, which Stalin himself dismissed as 'nonsense', is now generally considered to have been a wartime forgery, intended to discredit the Soviet Union.[40] However, despite this, much of its content rings broadly true and indeed chimes with comments made by Stalin and others at the time. A few days after the pact with Germany was signed, for example, Stalin explained to his acolytes that the agreement and the war that followed it presented an opportunity to undermine capitalism itself:

> A war is on between two groups of capitalist countries for the redivision of the world, for the domination of the world! We see nothing wrong in their having a good hard fight and weakening each other. It would be fine if, at the hands of Germany, the position of the richest capitalist countries (especially England) were shaken. Hitler, without

understanding it or desiring it, is shaking and undermining the capitalist system . . . We can manoeuvre, pit one side against the other to set them fighting with each other as fiercely as possible.[41]

Molotov expanded on those ideas in a meeting the following summer with the Lithuanian communist Vincas Krėvė-Mickevičius, where he mused on what the war might mean for the Soviet Union: 'We are more firmly convinced now than ever that our brilliant comrade, Lenin, was not mistaken when he assured us that the Second World War will help us to gain power throughout all Europe as the First helped us to gain power in Russia.' Molotov then elaborated, explaining how the pact with Nazi Germany dovetailed with this overarching ideal. 'Today we support Germany', he said,

> but just enough to keep her from being smothered before the miserable and starving masses of the warring nations become disillusioned and rise against their leaders. Then the German bourgeoisie will come to an agreement with its enemy, the allied bourgeoisie, in order to crush with their combined forces the aroused proletariat. But at that moment we will come to its aid, we will come with fresh forces, well prepared, and in the territory of Western Europe, I believe, somewhere near the Rhine, the final battle between the proletariat and the degenerate bourgeoisie will take place which will decide the fate of Europe for all time. We are convinced that we, not the bourgeoisie, will win that battle.[42]

This last part was, almost certainly, a flight of Stalinist fancy; a calculated exaggeration to enthuse and inspire a provincial communist functionary, but it is nonetheless telling that such grand ambitions were being floated in Moscow at all, as it shows that they were undoubtedly part of the narrative.

Soviet policy in 1939 is still routinely described – particularly by those who cleave to a rosy view of the Soviet Union – as being essentially 'defensive' in nature; motivated by a desire to hold Hitler off, and buy time to prepare for an inevitable attack. This has, at the very least, a modicum of retrospective logic to it, but it finds no contemporary echo whatsoever.[43] When Molotov confessed, much later in life, that his task as minister for foreign affairs was 'to expand the borders'[44] of the USSR, he was not simply exaggerating or playing to the gallery; he was expressing a fundamental truth. The Soviet Union saw territorial expansion and the spreading of communism as part of its *raison d'être*: it had sought to expand west in 1920, and did so with spectacular results in 1944–5. There is no reason to suppose that westward expansion was *not* part of the plan in 1939. Far from being defensive, therefore, Stalin's motives in 1939 are at the very least 'passive-aggressive', exhibiting a profound underlying hostility to the outside world in general, yet portraying it as 'non-aggression' and 'neutrality'. The Nazi–Soviet Pact presented Stalin with a golden opportunity to 'shake the tree': to set the world-historical forces into motion, while remaining outwardly neutral, preserving the Red Army for future battles – whether they were to be on the Rhine, or elsewhere.

In seeking to take advantage of the opportunity that a rapprochement with Germany might represent, Stalin needed first to remove his long-time foreign minister Maxim Litvinov. Litvinov – who was already in his sixties by 1939 – was very much a Bolshevik of the old school; a man who had spent a good deal of his career prior to 1917 in exile, aiding the communist cause as a gun-runner, a propagandist and only later as a diplomat. From 1930, he had served as Stalin's foreign minister and in this capacity had become synonymous with the policy of collective security, using his urbane charm to bring the Soviet Union back in from the cold and into a modicum of diplomatic respectability.

Yet, by the early summer of 1939, Litvinov was on thin ice. In fact, given that the policy of collective security had so demonstrably failed by that point, it is remarkable that he had not been removed beforehand. By May, his close connections to the discarded policy made him surplus to Stalin's requirements. Moreover, as a Jew and someone with a track record as a persistent critic of the Nazis – who loved in return to refer to him mockingly as 'Litvinov-Finkelstein'[45] – Litvinov clearly lacked the flexibility that might be required in a new and challenging international situation. Citing his former foreign minister's 'disloyalty' and his failure to 'ensure the pursuance of the party line',[46] Stalin had Litvinov removed from office. Far from receiving a gold watch and being shuffled into retirement, however, Litvinov was arrested by the NKVD, his office surrounded, his telephone cut off and his aides interrogated, evidently in an attempt to elicit some compromising information.[47] He would be fortunate to survive the experience.

Litvinov's successor as foreign minister was Stalin's most faithful acolyte, Vyacheslav Molotov, a man whose loyalty to the 'party line' – and to Stalin personally – was unswerving. Born Vyacheslav Skryabin in 1890, he had enjoyed a rather stereotypical apprenticeship as a revolutionary: the conspiratorial existence, the spells of Siberian exile, even – like Lenin and Stalin – the adoption of a *nom-de-guerre*, his deriving from the Russian word for 'hammer', '*molot*'. With the revolution of 1917, Molotov had found himself in Petrograd, editing the communist party newspaper, *Pravda*, and soon emerged as a leading member of the Petrograd Soviet and, in time, a protégé of Stalin. Never a military man or an inspiring orator, the slight, bespectacled Molotov considered himself primarily a journalist. According to his contemporaries, he was somewhat colourless: a plodding bureaucrat, a stickler for Bolshevik doctrine, who was dubbed 'Comrade Stonearse' for his ability to sit through interminable Kremlin meetings. As pedantic as he was loyal, he was even known to correct those who dared to use the moniker, claiming that Lenin himself had christened him 'Ironarse'. He did not do so with a smile. Petty and vindictive, he did not hesitate to recommend the death penalty for those who crossed him.[48]

These qualities enabled Molotov to climb the greasy pole of Soviet politics, becoming first head of the Moscow Party organisation and then chairman of the Council of People's Commissars in 1930, in which capacity he oversaw the brutal collectivisation campaign in Ukraine in 1932–3. Absolutely and unquestioningly loyal to Stalin, Molotov survived the purges of the late 1930s, even personally authorising thousands of executions. As he later admitted with brutal flippancy: 'I signed most – in fact almost all – the arrest lists. We debated and made a decision. Haste ruled the day. Could one go into all the details?'[49] So, by the time he was appointed as Stalin's foreign minister, Molotov was not so much the 'colourless bureaucrat': he was thoroughly steeped in blood. Yet he had no experience of foreign affairs, knew little about the outside world, spoke no foreign languages and had only once briefly been abroad. Indeed, he has been described by one prominent historian as 'one of the most inexorably stupid men to hold the foreign ministership of any major power in this century'.[50] Molotov's only qualification was that he was Stalin's man.

Stalin's appointment of Molotov was a bold move, then, and an indication that foreign policy was now very much in the leader's own hands. It did not necessarily signify that collective security was dead, but it did send a strong signal to the outside world – and to Nazi Germany in particular – that *all* foreign-policy options were now up for consideration in Moscow. In case the message of Litvinov's demise was missed in Berlin, Stalin also instructed that the foreign ministry was to be purged of Jews, for good measure. 'Thank God', Molotov faithfully remembered later in life. 'Jews formed an absolute majority in the leadership and among the ambassadors. It wasn't good.'[51]

Curiously, just as Stalin's appointment of Molotov had concentrated the levers of foreign policy in the Soviet dictator's hands, a similar process had taken place the previous year in Berlin, with Ribbentrop's appointment as Hitler's foreign minister. Though Ribbentrop had refrained from ushering in any wholesale clear-out of foreign-office mandarins, he nonetheless was not above promoting his own, often ill-qualified favourites into important positions. The rise of Martin Luther is instructive in this regard. Brought into the German foreign office on Wilhelmstrasse on Ribbentrop's coat-tails in February 1939, Luther headed the new 'Party Liaison Office', which essentially concerned itself with protecting Ribbentrop's interests in the endemic infighting of the Third Reich. In due course, he would end up as one of Wilhelmstrasse's most influential players, even representing the foreign office at the infamous Wannsee Conference in 1942. Yet his pedigree for such exalted office was dubious to say the least: Luther's main qualification was that he had been Ribbentrop's interior decorator, furniture remover and 'fixer' during the latter's spell as ambassador in London.[52]

Aside from his questionable choice of acolytes, however, it was primarily Ribbentrop's fawning sycophancy towards Hitler that had been instrumental in his advancement. This made his career a curious parallel to that of Molotov. The appointment of both, 'yes men' and nonentities, marked the concentration of decision-making, effectively, in the hands of Hitler and Stalin themselves. With no moderating voices to restrain them or advise them otherwise, the two dictators were free to negotiate with one another.

Despite this, however, German policy had actually been rather slow to wake up to the possibilities that an arrangement with Stalin might present. Of course, there were some in the German foreign office – sometimes referred to as 'Easterners', such as Moscow ambassador, Schulenburg – who had long advocated some sort of reimagining of the Rapallo Treaty of 1922, whereby Germany and Soviet Russia had enjoyed a season of economic and military co-operation, while jointly thumbing their noses at the Western Powers. But, for all the appeal that such an arrangement might have had, its advocates had generally been drowned out in the 1930s by those who were more in tune with the anti-Bolshevik zeitgeist. Göring's *'petit jeu'*, however – cynical manoeuvre though it was – had momentarily given the Easterners their head, and for a brief period at least, their ideas were taken seriously. They had much to argue in their favour: not only might a pact with Moscow free Hitler to deal with Poland and the Western Powers, it could also ensure that Germany would be immune to the worst effects of any British blockade, by sourcing its food and raw materials from the USSR.

In order to square the ideological circle, some in Berlin managed to convince themselves that the Soviet Union was 'normalising', with Stalin's policy of 'Socialism in One Country' supposedly marking a departure from the expansionist communism of old into a new, more nationally minded direction. Ribbentrop said as much when explaining the pact to his foreign missions in August 1939. 'Russian Bolshevism has undergone a decisive structural change under Stalin', he wrote. 'In place of the idea of world revolution there has emerged an attachment to the idea of Russian nationalism and the concept of consolidating the Soviet state on its present national, territorial and social bases.'[53] In other words, Moscow's dark days of fomenting class war and spreading worldwide revolution were now to be considered a thing of the past.

This was largely post facto wishful thinking, of course, but there were other, wiser heads than Ribbentrop's that also claimed to see similarities. A month earlier in late July, for instance, German negotiator Karl Schnurre had drawn the attention of his Soviet counterpart to the question of ideology. 'Despite all the differences in their respective world view', he said, there is one common element in the ideologies of Germany, Italy and the Soviet Union: opposition to the capitalist democracies. Neither we nor Italy have anything in common with the capitalist West. Therefore it seems to us rather unnatural that a socialist state would stand on the side of the western democracies.[54]

Ribbentrop struck a similar note in the opening salvoes of his flirtation with Moscow in August 1939, stating that 'differing philosophies do not prohibit a reasonable relationship' and suggesting that 'past experience' should dictate that it was 'the capitalistic Western democracies' that were 'the implacable enemies of both National Socialist Germany and Soviet Russia'.[55] If nothing else, the Nazis imagined that they and the Soviets could at least find common ground in their shared antipathy towards Britain and France. Stalin and Hitler, it seemed, were edging ever closer.

For his part, Hitler was largely immune to such ideological flourishes. For him, the logic behind the move was brutally simple. According to Goebbels, he had arrived at the idea of the pact with Stalin partly from the dawning realisation that he had backed himself into a corner. 'The Führer believes he's in the position of scrounging for favours and beggars can't be choosers . . . In times of famine', he noted darkly, 'the devil feeds on flies.'[56] The gloss that Hitler put on the decision was a little more positive. On the Obersalzberg, on 22 August, he addressed his paladins and senior generals on the challenges that lay ahead of them. In justifying the pact with the Soviets, he explained, 'there are only three great statesmen in the world, Stalin, I and Mussolini. Mussolini is the weakest.' What was more, he added, Stalin was 'a very sick man'. The pact was only temporary, he explained, serving to isolate Poland and defeat the British blockade by providing access to Russian raw materials. Then, 'after Stalin's death . . . we will break the Soviet Union. Then there will begin the dawn of the German rule of the earth.'[57]

Meanwhile, the British and French had not been idle, and had made a tentative effort to bring Stalin onside, sending a joint delegation consisting of a British admiral and a French general, which arrived in the USSR in mid-August. Everything about that mission, however, appeared to be almost comically counterproductive. Firstly, finding a secure route to Moscow had proved difficult, and the delegation had

THE DEVILS' ALLIANCE

opted to travel aboard an ageing merchantman, *The City of Exeter*, whose leisurely six-day voyage up the Baltic did little to convince the Soviets of Allied seriousness. Secondly, the head of the mission – Admiral Sir Reginald Ranfurly Plunkett-Ernle-Erle-Drax – was unlikely to curry much favour with the prophets of proletarian revolution with his quadruple-barrelled name.

But there were also more practical concerns. For all their evident status, Admiral Drax and his French counterpart General Joseph Doumenc were no foreign ministers, and they lacked the authority to undertake serious material negotiations with the Soviets. Moreover, it is highly doubtful that any deal was ever really intended to be struck. Many in the West were just as wary of Moscow as Moscow was of them. In March 1939, British prime minister Neville Chamberlain confessed to a friend 'the most profound distrust of Russia'. 'I distrust her motives,' he explained, 'which seem to me to have little connection with our ideas of liberty, and to be concerned only with getting everyone else by the ears.'[58] It is easy to understand, therefore, why the Allied delegation to Moscow was sent with the instruction to 'go very slowly', dragging out any resulting negotiations so as to effectively 'talk out' the summer campaigning season and thereby rob Hitler of his opportunity to invade Poland.[59] Motivated by their governments' instinctive anti-Bolshevism, its members were going through the motions – holding their noses while talking to the Soviets – apparently in the hope that their mere presence in Moscow, raising the spectre of an Anglo-French-Soviet alliance, would be enough to deter Hitler. Never, one historian has written, was an alliance pursued less enthusiastically.[60]

The shortcomings of that approach were exposed almost immediately. Poland was naturally key to the negotiations. As Hitler's next target, and the country geographically doomed to be squeezed between the rock of Berlin and the hard place of Moscow, Poland was bound to loom large in the diplomatic horse-trading of that summer. Yet Drax quickly found that he could offer the Soviets little beyond participation in a principled preservation of the status quo. Hemmed in by the Anglo-French guarantee to Poland, earlier that year, he and his party could give nothing of substance, and even failed to secure agreement from the Poles for a suggested passage of Soviet troops through the east of the country to meet any German threat. Polish intransigence was not mere obstinacy. Poles were acutely mindful of the Soviet invasion of their homeland during the Polish–Soviet War of 1919–21, an earlier attempt by Moscow to spread communism westwards, which was only narrowly defeated at the gates of Warsaw.[61] In addition, given that Poland's eastern regions contained fractious minorities of Byelorussians and Ukrainians, Warsaw rightly had its doubts that the Red Army, once allowed in, would ever leave.

As Drax and Doumenc sat down with Soviet Defence Commissar Marshal Kliment Voroshilov on 14 August to discuss the possibilities for common action, this flaw in the Anglo-French plan was swiftly made clear. When Voroshilov pointedly asked whether Soviet forces would be allowed passage across Polish territory, the general and the admiral could only squirm and prevaricate, answering with platitudes and evasions, promising vaguely that such matters would be cleared up in due course. Voroshilov was unimpressed, and brought the meeting to a close by expressing his 'regret' that this 'cardinal question' had not been considered. It was no great surprise, perhaps, that negotiations stalled.[62]

The Germans, however, had no such inhibitions, and were happy to offer genuine territorial and strategic gains to the Soviets – at other people's expense – to secure agreement. As Johnnie von Herwarth would confess after the war: 'We were able to make a deal with the Soviets because we were able without any problems with German opinion to deliver the Baltic states and eastern Poland to Russia. This the British and the French, with their public opinions, were unable to do.'[63] Thus, in stark contrast to the hesitancy and impotence exhibited by Admiral Drax, Ribbentrop's telegram to his Moscow ambassador of 14 August exuded confidence and optimism. 'There exist no real conflicts of interests between Germany and Russia', he wrote. 'There is no question between the Baltic and the Black Sea which cannot be settled to the complete satisfaction of both parties.'[64]

What was more, Ribbentrop was willing to fly to Moscow to negotiate in person. Berlin had considered sending Hitler's legal expert and later Governor General of Poland, Hans Frank, to carry on the negotiations, but Ribbentrop was selected in his stead.[65] It is not clear from the archival record whether this change was the result of a fit of ego on Ribbentrop's part or the hard-headed calculation that a senior minister would have more of an impact in the Soviet capital.

Ribbentrop's own account of the episode claims that he was selected by Hitler because he 'understood things better'.[66] Whatever the truth, it is certain that Molotov was most impressed by the prospect of the German foreign minister coming to negotiate in person; as Schulenburg noted to Berlin on 16 August, Molotov found it 'very flattering person-ally' and 'proof of our good intentions', contrasting favourably with the status of previous foreign visitors.[67]

Impressed by this ecumenical and businesslike approach, the Soviets continued their clandestine negotiations with Berlin, while maintaining their public, and increasingly desultory, talks with the British and the French. For all the Machiavellianism on show in the Soviet capital, there seemed to be a genuine sentiment at its core. As Johnnie von Herwarth recalled, there was 'near unanimity among the Western embassies in Moscow that summer that Stalin had a higher regard for the Germans than for the other Western Powers, and that he certainly trusted them more'.[68] Consequently, through most of August, sound-ings with Berlin were taken, meetings conducted and respective posi-tions clarified, such that by the penultimate week of the month, draft treaties had already been drawn up, exchanged and provisionally agreed.[69] The process had been driven on by Hitler's overriding desire to wrap up the pact in time for his invasion of Poland, initially planned for 26 August, and so present the West with a fait accompli. Drawing upon these discussions, a German–Soviet economic agreement was signed in Berlin, in the early hours of 20 August, allowing for an exchange of Soviet raw materials for German finished goods and a credit facility of 200 million Reichsmarks. Goebbels was unusually laconic in his diary comment of 'Times change',[70] but he knew very well that the agreement's primary significance was that it was seen by both sides as the necessary precursor to the all-important political treaty.

That same day, events far to the east further contributed to Soviet decision-making. In its flirtation with Berlin, Moscow had been consist-ently worried about bringing an end to German support for the Japanese campaign against the Red Army in the Far East, raising the issue several times in negotiations. On 20 August, however, the problem appeared to have finally solved itself. After a summer of inconclusive skirmishing on the border between Mongolia and Manchuria, Soviet forces attacked the Japanese Imperial Army that day, close to the Khalkhin Gol river, seeking the decisive result that would drive the Japanese back. While the ensuing battle raged – and it would last for eleven days before the Japanese forces were finally routed – Stalin would be unsure whether further military commitments would be necessary on his eastern border, and consequently would have been wary of entering new commitments in the west – particularly those of the sort suggested, however half-heartedly, by the British and the French. If Hitler's offer of territorial gain for non-belligerence was not already attractive enough, the battle at Khalkhin Gol must have conspired to make his mind up for him.[71]

From there, events moved with astonishing rapidity. On the morning of 21 August, a final meeting was held between Drax's delegation and their Soviet partners, but neither side, it appeared, had anything further to report, so the meeting was adjourned *sine die*. The western policy of procrastination had run out of tomorrows. In contrast, discussions with the Germans on the draft text of the pact were progressing apace, and though Stalin would have welcomed a delay, pending some clarity on the situation on his south-eastern frontier, Hitler was determined to force matters along. The previous evening, the Führer had sent a personal telegram to Stalin, in which he had asked that Ribbentrop be received in Moscow to tie up the final details without delay.[72] This highly unorthodox move would have made a distinct impression on the Soviet leader. Accustomed to being treated as a toxic and malevolent outsider in world politics, Stalin craved the recognition and respect that a direct approach such as Hitler's implied. That afternoon, his reply – agreeing to Ribbentrop's arrival for talks on 23 August, and expressing the hope that the proposed pact would be a 'turn for the better' in Soviet–German relations[73] – was telegraphed to Hitler on the Obersalzberg. According to Albert Speer, who witnessed the scene at the Berghof, Hitler 'stared into space for a moment, flushed deeply, then banged on the table so hard that the glasses rattled, and exclaimed in a voice breaking with excitement, "I have them! I have them!"'[74]

Stalin might have countered with a querying '*Kto kogo poimal?*' ('Who has whom?'). Certainly when the negotiations began in the Kremlin on the afternoon of 23 August, he performed like a man convinced that he held all the cards. After the opening pleasantries had been concluded, the four – Ribbentrop, Stalin, Molotov and Ambassador Schulenburg – got down to business. Draft treaties had already been agreed in the preceding days, so all that needed to be done was to finalise terms and draw up the necessary paperwork. Nonetheless, Ribbentrop began with a bold suggestion, most likely calculated to steal the initiative, proposing on Hitler's behalf that the Nazi–Soviet non-aggression pact should have a hundred-year term. Unfazed, Stalin's response was cool. 'If we agree to a hundred years', he said, 'people will laugh at us for not being serious. I propose the agreement should last ten years.'[75] Deflated, Ribbentrop meekly concurred.

Discussion swiftly moved to the essence of the Nazi–Soviet arrangement, the so-called 'secret protocol' by which both parties were to divide the spoils of their collaboration. The initiative came from the Soviet side.[76] Realising that Hitler was impatient to proceed with his invasion plans for Poland, Stalin sought to extract the maximum possible territorial concession. 'Alongside this agreement', he announced, 'there will be an additional agreement that we will not publish anywhere else', adding that he wanted a clear delineation of 'spheres of interest' in central and eastern Europe.[77] Taking his cue, Ribbentrop made his opening offer. 'The Führer accepts', he said, 'that the eastern part of Poland and Bessarabia as well as Finland, Estonia and Latvia, up to the river Dvina, will all fall within the Soviet sphere of influence.' This was exceedingly generous, but Stalin was not satisfied and demanded *all* of Latvia. Ribbentrop stalled. Though he had been given the authority to agree terms as was necessary, he utilised the negotiating trick of breaking off talks to refer a question to a higher authority. Replying that he could not accede to the Soviet demand for Latvia without consulting Hitler, he asked that the meeting be adjourned while a call was made to Germany.[78]

Hitler was still at the Berghof on the Obersalzberg, anxiously awaiting news of the negotiations. It was a hot summer's evening, and he spent his time on the terrace, enjoying the spectacular view north across the valley to the Untersberg where, according to legend, King Frederick Barbarossa lay sleeping, waiting to re-emerge at Germany's hour of need. As Hitler's Luftwaffe adjutant, Nicolaus von Below, recalled, the highly charged mood of anticipation seemed to be mirrored by the weather. 'As we strolled up and down', he wrote in his memoir, the eerie turquoise-coloured sky to the north turned first violet and then blood red. At first we thought there must be a serious fire behind the Untersberg mountain, but then the glow covered the whole northern sky in the manner of the Northern Lights . . . I was very moved and told Hitler that it augured a bloody war. He responded that if it must be so, then the sooner the better; the more time went by, the bloodier it would be.[79]

Shortly afterwards, the mood had scarcely lightened when word came through from Moscow. 'Groups of ADCs, civilian staff, ministers and secretaries were standing around the switchboard and on the terrace', recalled SS-Adjutant Herbert Döhring, 'everybody was tense, they waited and waited.'[80] When the telephone finally rang, Hitler was initially silent as he listened to Ribbentrop's brief summary of progress and Stalin's demand for all of Latvia. Within half an hour, after consulting a map, Hitler returned the call, consenting to the alteration with the words 'Yes, agreed.' According to Johnnie von Herwarth, who received the call in Moscow, the speed of Hitler's reply was testament to his eagerness to conclude the pact.[81] For Stalin, it marked an astonishing success: with a single evening's negotiation and a single phone call, he had regained almost all of the lands lost by the Russian Empire in the maelstrom of the First World War.

Once the 'spheres of interest' had been cleared up, the essential business of the pact was concluded and discussion in Moscow turned to current events and the wider ramifications that a Nazi–Soviet agreement and non-aggression pact might have. Japan was top of the agenda, and Stalin was keen to know the status of Germany's links with Tokyo. Ribbentrop reassured him that German–Japanese friendship was in no way directed against the Soviet Union, and even offered to intercede in settling disagreements between Moscow and Tokyo. Stalin again was rather cool in response, stating that he would be happy for an improvement of relations, and for German assistance in that regard, but he did not want it known that the initiative had his sanction.

Talks then ranged over Italy, Turkey, France and Britain, the last of which, it seems, excited both Ribbentrop and Stalin greatly, and provided an arena for common ground and some competitive damnation of 'perfidious Albion'. England was weak, Ribbentrop opined, echoing the tone of Stalin's speech of March that year, and was keen to use others to further its 'arrogant claims to world domination'. Stalin concurred, stating that the British army was feeble and that the Royal Navy was no longer worthy of its reputation. 'If England has dominated the world it is only because of the stupidity of other countries', he said. 'It's astonishing that only a few hundred British ruled India.'[82]

But, Stalin warned, the British could fight stubbornly and skilfully. Ribbentrop replied that – unlike the British and French – he had not come to ask assistance: Germany was perfectly capable of dealing with both Poland and her Western Allies on her own. According to Ribbentrop, Stalin thought for a moment before responding:

> The viewpoint of Germany . . . deserves attention. However, the Soviet Union is interested in preserving a strong Germany, and in the event of military conflict between Germany and the western democracies, the interests of the Soviet Union and Germany coincide completely. The Soviet Union shall never tolerate letting Germany fall into difficult straits.[83]

By the end of their discussions, there was evidently even room for some wit. When Ribbentrop began a rather unconvincing explanation of how the Anti-Comintern Pact – the anti-communist alliance agreed between Germany and Japan three years earlier – had not really been directed against the Soviet Union, but against the western democracies, Stalin replied that it had been the City of London and 'English shopkeepers' that had been most frightened by the move. Ribbentrop concurred, adding that German opinion on the matter was clear from a recent Berlin joke which quipped that Stalin himself was now considering joining the Anti-Comintern Pact.[84] For the otherwise humourless Ribbentrop, it was almost funny.

After this *tour d'horizon*, a draft communiqué, hastily drawn up in two languages in an anteroom, was finally presented to the negotiators for their consideration. Ribbentrop had scripted an elaborate, gushing preamble to the original Soviet draft of the treaty, full of references to the 'natural friendship' between the Soviet Union and

Germany. Stalin, however, who was rather more sober in his senses, was unmoved. 'Don't you think', he asked,

> that we have to pay a little more attention to public opinion in our two countries? For many years now, we have been pouring buckets of shit on each other's heads, and our propaganda boys could not do enough in that direction. And now, all of a sudden, are we to make our peoples believe that all is forgotten and forgiven? Things don't work so fast. Public opinion in our country, and probably in Germany too, will have to be prepared slowly for the change in our relations that this treaty is to bring about.[85]

Outplayed again, Ribbentrop could only humbly agree, and the preamble reverted to that of the original Soviet draft. With a few minor alterations, the text of the treaty – a short document of only seven brief paragraphs – was then checked and accepted by the parties. Both agreed to desist from any aggressive action against each other and to maintain constant contact for the purposes of consultation on their common interests. Disputes were to be settled by the friendly exchange of opinion, or, if necessary, through arbitration. Unusually, the treaty would come into force immediately upon signature, rather than upon ratification.

The secret protocol accompanying the treaty was similarly terse, with only four articles delineating the Nazi and Soviet 'spheres of influence' that were to apply 'in the event of a territorial and political rearrangement'. Accordingly, the Soviet Union laid claim to Finland, Estonia and Latvia, up to the border of Lithuania, with the latter earmarked for Germany. In Poland, the boundary between the two signatories would be the line of the San, Narew and Vistula rivers, thereby neatly dissecting the country. To the south, Moscow expressed its 'interest' in the Romanian province of Bessarabia, while Germany registered its 'complete political disinterest'. Finally, both sides agreed that the protocol was to be treated as 'strictly secret'.[86] With its pious, high-flown rhetoric about the pernicious 'Imperialists' and their cynical 'spheres of interest', the Soviet Union could scarcely admit to having similar arrangements of its own. Such was the sensitivity of the secret protocol, indeed, that it has been speculated that, on the Soviet side, only Stalin and Molotov knew of its existence.[87]

The hard work done, the signatories and their respective entourages were treated to a small, impromptu reception. At around midnight, samovars of black tea appeared, followed by caviar, sandwiches, vodka and finally Crimean champagne: 'our treat', as Molotov would later recall.[88] Glasses were filled and cigarettes were lit, and the atmosphere became – according to one of those present – 'warmly convivial'.[89] As is the Russian way, an interminable round of toasts followed. Stalin began proceedings, exclaiming to a hushed room: 'I know how much the German nation loves its Führer. I should therefore like to drink to his health.'[90] Once the glasses had been refilled, Molotov proposed a toast to Ribbentrop, and Ribbentrop in turn toasted the Soviet government. All of them then drank to the non-aggression pact as a symbol of the new era in Russo-German relations.

In the early hours, when the draft treaty had been retyped, the photographers were ushered in to record its ceremonial signature. Entering the 'smoke-laden room', Hitler's photographer, Heinrich Hoffmann, introduced himself to Molotov and received a 'hearty handshake' from Stalin. Then he set to work. Flanked by a Soviet photographer with 'a prehistoric camera and an antediluvian tripod' as well as his own colleague Helmut Laux, he began recording the scene for posterity.[91] Stalin insisted on only one condition: that the empty glasses were cleared before the photographers began; he clearly did not want anyone to think that he had signed the pact while drunk.[92] At one point, soon after, Laux took a photograph of him and Ribbentrop together, with glasses of champagne raised in a toast. Spotting him, Stalin remarked that it would probably not be a good idea to publish the picture, in case it gave a false impression to the German and Soviet peoples. With that, Laux immediately began to take the film out of his camera, ready to hand it over to Stalin, but the latter stopped him by waving his hand, assuring him that he 'trusted the word of a German'.[93]

After that brief halt, Hoffmann and Laux resumed their work. Between them they would produce the iconic images of the pact's signing: Molotov and Ribbentrop, seated at the desk, pen in hand; to their rear, the Chief of the General Staff, Boris Shaposhnikov, looking like a silent-film star with his slicked-back, parted hair; the interpreters Hilger and Pavlov seemingly startled to be sharing the limelight; and finally Stalin, beaming broadly in his smart light-coloured tunic. Behind them all, glaring down from a large framed photograph, was Lenin.

Taking their turn, Molotov and Ribbentrop then appended their signatures to the treaty and smiled for Hoffmann's camera. With that, the lives of millions of Europeans would be changed for ever.

2

Bonded in Blood

Eight days, almost to the hour, after the Nazi–Soviet Pact was ceremonially signed in the Kremlin, war returned to Europe. Before sunrise on the morning of 1 September 1939, the elderly German cruiser *Schleswig-Holstein* – a veteran of the battle of Jutland, making a 'friendship visit' to the Free City of Danzig – slipped her moorings and opened fire at close range on the Polish garrison of the nearby Westerplatte. The signal was thereby given, in brutal and dramatic fashion, for the German invasion of Poland.

The week that had preceded those opening salvoes had had a heavy, oppressive flavour to it. Though the precise details of the pact remained opaque, most contemporary commentators were agreed that it marked an unprecedented shift. 'It is a stunning blow,' Romanian diarist Mihail Sebastian wrote, 'the whole course of world politics has suddenly changed.'[1] Moreover, there was a grim consensus that the pact was rather more than just another chapter in Europe's ongoing crisis, and that it would, most likely, herald war. Thus, the world's statesmen urged circumspection. Roosevelt sent Hitler a personal appeal, suggesting 'alternative methods' in solving the crisis; French premier Edouard Daladier followed suit, urging the German dictator to step back from the brink, otherwise 'Destruction and Barbarism will be the real victors'. British prime minister Neville Chamberlain, meanwhile, was disconsolate, confiding to the US ambassador that 'the futility of it all is the thing that is frightful'.[2] Others began preparing for the worst. London's museums started evacuating their treasures to the countryside; hospitals were cleared of non-essential cases, and railway stations installed blue lights to comply with the expected blackout. Everywhere sandbags were filled and stacked, and windows were taped. While Chamberlain prepared to move into the Central

War Room, newly completed beneath Whitehall, orders were prepared for the evacuation of children from Britain's towns and cities, to begin on the morning of 1 September. The public mood was dark. 'Poor weary world,' one diarist wrote, 'what a mess we people have made of it.'[3]

While the rest of the world digested the news of the Nazi–Soviet Pact and considered the prospect of war, Ribbentrop had travelled back to Germany with his entourage to a rapturous reception from Hitler, who hailed his returning foreign minister as 'a second Bismarck'.[4] As Ribbentrop was being feted, Hoffmann was busy developing his photographs of the signing ceremony in Moscow. When he met with Hitler, he was dismayed to find that the Führer was more interested in his opinion of Stalin than his pictures. 'Does he actually issue orders,' Hitler asked eagerly, 'or does he cloak them in the guise of wishes?' 'What about his health?' he wondered, adding 'Does he really smoke so much?' and 'How did he shake hands with you?' Bizarrely, he also asked about Stalin's earlobes, whether they were 'ingrown and Jewish, or separate and Aryan'. Hoffmann replied that the Soviet leader's earlobes were separate, to Hitler's evident satisfaction. Clearly, the Führer was most impatient to learn as much as he could about his new ally.[5]

When they finally came to look at Hoffmann's pictures, Hitler was disappointed. 'What a pity', he said. 'There is not a single one that we can use.' To Hoffmann's protests he replied that in every photograph Stalin was smoking: it was, Hitler said, 'out of the question . . . The German people would take offence.' He explained: 'The signing of a Pact is a solemn act, which one does not approach with a cigarette dangling from one's lips. Such a photograph smacks of levity! See if you can paint out the cigarettes.' So it was that the photographs that were released to the German press were all doctored by Hoffmann, with no cigarettes visible.[6]

Other frustrations were to follow. Hitler had originally foreseen a swift campaign against Poland, having ordered an attack on 26 August, but had been forced to postpone it because of last-minute diplomatic manoeuvres and fruitless negotiations with the British. He was also obliged to cancel the annual showpiece Nazi Party rally at Nuremberg, which had been due to start on 2 September. Ironically, this year's event had been given the theme of 'Peace'. Then, on 31 August, Hitler issued his first 'war directive', ordering an attack on Poland to commence the following morning and stipulating that 'a solution by force' had been decided upon but that it was vital to leave 'responsibility for the opening of hostilities unmistakeably to England and France'.[7]

Stalin, meanwhile, had wasted little time reflecting on the niceties of the pact's signature. Meeting his entourage the following day for a supper of freshly shot duck, and 'seeming very pleased with himself',[8] he had mused on the new relationship with Hitler: 'Of course, it's all a game to see who can fool whom. I know what Hitler's up to. He thinks he's outsmarted me but actually it's I who has tricked him.'[9] When presented to the Supreme Soviet on the last day of August, the pact was duly applauded, with Molotov echoing Hitler's line criticising the 'ruling classes of Britain and France', who, he claimed, had been so keen to involve Nazi Germany and the USSR in conflict. In the coming war, he stated, the Soviet Union would maintain 'absolute neutrality'.[10]

By the following morning, 1 September, that conflict was already raging. In the grey light of a late summer dawn, German troops moved off from their forward positions across the 2,000 km Polish– German border. Sixty divisions, incorporating over 2,500 tanks and over a million troops, advanced into Polish territory from Silesia in the south-west, Pomerania in the north-west and East Prussia to the north. German armour and weaponry were comfortably superior to those of the Poles, and swift gains were registered on all fronts. In the air, the sleek Messerschmitts and screaming Stukas of the Luftwaffe were little threatened by the obsolete – if bravely flown – fighters of the Polish air force.

Outnumbered and outgunned, Polish resistance was nonetheless spirited. On the opening day, for instance, at the battle of Mokra in southern Poland, the German advance was temporarily halted at considerable cost to the 4th Panzer Division; while in the north at Krojanty, a brief engagement between Polish cavalry and German tanks would spawn a durable myth about the romantic futility of Poland's defence. Despite such actions, Polish forces were inexorably driven back by the German advance, and by the time of the campaign's largest battle – on the river Bzura, ten days later – Warsaw itself was already being threatened. When the old tsarist forts defending the Polish capital were finally overwhelmed later that month, it was only a matter of time before the city fell.

Long before the campaign had been decided, however, the Wehrmacht's conduct demonstrated that the world had entered a new era of warfare. Prior to the invasion, Hitler had told his military commanders to 'Close your hearts to pity. Act brutally.'[11] They complied. Right from the outset, Nazi forces were pitiless in their treatment of Polish subject populations. Units of special forces – *Einsatzgruppen* – were instructed to follow the front-line troops to ruthlessly suppress any resistance in the rear areas. And, as the Poles quickly discovered, 'resistance' could have an extremely broad definition and was invariably punished by summary execution. In the first five weeks of military action, German forces would burn 531 Polish towns and villages and carry out over 700 mass executions,[12] the worst examples being at Częstochowa, where 227 civilians were murdered on 4 September, and at Bydgoszcz, where as many as 400 were executed in reprisal for the alleged Polish killing of ethnic Germans.[13] As one eyewitness recalled, the brutality could be baffling:

> The first victims of the campaign were a number of Boy Scouts, from twelve to sixteen years of age, who were set up in the marketplace against a wall and shot. No reason was given. A devoted priest who rushed to administer the Last Sacrament was shot too . . . Among the [other] victims was a man whom I knew was too ill to take any part in politics or public affairs. When the execution took place he was too weak to stand, and fell down; they beat him and dragged him again to his feet. Another of the victims was a boy of seventeen, the only son of a surgeon who had died the year before . . . We never heard of what the poor lad was accused.[14]

In truth, there was often little logic to the killing and some atrocities were sparked by the slightest pretext. At Kajetanowice, for instance, seventy-two Polish civilians were massacred in response to the death of two German horses in a 'friendly fire' incident.[15] According to the most comprehensive study, the German military executed over 12,000 Polish citizens in September 1939 alone.[16]

The speed and ferocity of the German advance were a surprise not only for the Poles. Stalin, too, was caught off-guard by the Wehrmacht's swift progress. Having anticipated an active Anglo-French intervention, as well as a more protracted campaign in Poland itself – similar to the style of attritional warfare that had been seen in the First World

War – he was quickly forced to revise his plans. Stalin's hand had hitherto been stayed by concern about the West's reaction to Soviet participation in the attack and by the ongoing operations against the Japanese on the Mongolian frontier. However, when German troops appeared on the territory earmarked for the Soviet Union already on 12 September, and Ribbentrop himself was urging a Soviet advance, Stalin was obliged to act to secure those areas promised to him by the pact.[17] After mobilising on 11 September, the Red Army was assembled beyond the Polish border in two 'fronts' – the 'Byelorussian' and the 'Ukrainian' – to the north and south of the Pripyat river. These two army groups comprised twenty-five rifle divisions, sixteen cavalry divisions and twelve tank brigades with a total of nearly 500,000 men.[18] Molotov then asked Berlin to send word when Warsaw was due to fall, so that the Soviet intervention could be timed accordingly.[19]

By 17 September, with the situation on the Mongolian frontier stabilised by the signature of a peace treaty with the Japanese, and with the absence of any Anglo-French offensive against Germany in the west, Stalin resolved to act. At 3.00 that morning, the Polish ambassador in Moscow, Wacław Grzybowski, was summoned to the Kremlin, where he was presented with a note from the Soviet government outlining the grounds for its intervention. As if to emphasise the impossibility of Poland's predicament, the note itself had been drawn up jointly by the Soviets and the German ambassador in Moscow, Schulenburg.[20] It claimed that 'The Polish government has disintegrated', and that 'the Polish state no longer exists'. Given this apparent collapse, it went on, 'the Soviet government cannot remain indifferent at a time when brothers of the same blood, the Ukrainians and the Byelorussians, residing on the Polish territory have been abandoned to their fate'. Consequently, the Red Army had been ordered to 'cross the border and take under their protection the lives and property of the inhabitants of Western Ukraine and Western Byelorussia'.[21] By 'Western Ukraine' and 'Western Byelorussia', the note meant eastern Poland.

Faced with this apparent fait accompli, Grzybowski gamely refused to accept the note, protesting about Soviet dishonesty and the blatant violation of international law.[22] He also argued, quite correctly, that Poland's dire straits had no bearing on her sovereignty. Did anyone question Russia's existence, he asked, when Napoleon occupied Moscow?[23] His efforts were in vain, however. Within an hour, Red Army troops would cross the border on to Polish territory, and the note would simply be delivered to his office with the morning post. Now redundant in a hostile capital, Grzybowski was not accorded the usual diplomatic immunity and found himself arrested by the NKVD. By a quirk of fate, he was rescued by Schulenburg, who used his good odour with the Soviets to secure Grzybowski's release and subsequent escape from the USSR. The Polish consul at Kiev, Janusz Matuszyński, was not so fortunate; arrested by the NKVD, he was never seen again.[24]

The Soviet advance that followed was rather chaotic. Having been eviscerated by the purges, and given only days rather than weeks to mobilise, the Red Army was in no state to engage in serious offensive operations, lacking vehicles, spare parts and effective leadership. Fortunately for Moscow, however, Poland's defence was by this point similarly disorganised, with the few units stationed in the east of the country devoid of heavy weapons, unsure as to how to react to the Soviet advance, and lacking clear instructions from the increasingly desperate high command. Polish indecision was not aided by deliberate Soviet deceptions and the resulting rumour that the Red Army was advancing in defence of Poland to meet the German invasion.[25]

For civilians caught up in the Soviet advance, it could be a profoundly confusing time, with fear of the unknown tempered only by the hope that the Red Army might be coming to their aid. Most, only vaguely aware of the wider political constellation, were unsure of how to react. Janusz Bardach was fleeing the Nazis, heading east, towards Rowno, when he was stopped at night by an army patrol:

> Two men shined flashlights in our eyes, while others surrounded us . . . I was astonished to see Soviet military uniforms and hear the Russian language – we were still a long way from the border. I couldn't imagine what Soviet soldiers were doing on Polish territory and could only hope that the mighty Red Army had come to fight the Nazis and expel them from Poland. I wanted to express my joy at seeing them, but someone ordered us to put up our hands.[26]

In the months and years that followed, Bardach's youthful enthusiasm for the Soviet Union and for communism would be tested to destruction.

A minority – of communists as well as some Jews, Ukrainians and Byelorussians – had fewer doubts, however, and rushed to welcome the Red Army as their liberators. One such scene was recorded in the north-eastern town of Jedwabne, where a few locals not only greeted Soviet soldiers with the traditional Slavic offerings, but also erected a large banner reading 'We Welcome You'.[27] Though comparatively rare, events such as this served, in the public mind, to confirm the long-standing association between Jewishness and communism. Early twentieth-century Jewish intellectuals had often gravitated towards the left of politics, partly as a result of their rejection by the nationalist mainstream. Interwar communist parties had consequently had large Jewish representation in both membership and leadership, with Rosa Luxemburg in Germany, Bela Kun in Hungary and Leon Trotsky in the USSR being the salient examples. This link was seized upon by right-wing parties as a means to smear both enemies, falsely arguing that since many communists were Jews, so many Jews had to be communists. The resulting concept of 'Judaeo-Bolshevism' – that communism itself was little more than a Jewish conspiracy to take over the world – quickly became a mantra across the extreme right wing of politics, not least in Hitler's Nazi Party, which was the most efficient and determined propagator of the fiction. It was a link that was explicitly made in *Mein Kampf*: 'We ought to recognise in Russian Bolshevism', Hitler wrote, 'the kind of attempt being made by the Jew . . . to secure dominion over the world.'[28]

Those Jews and others who welcomed the Red Army in 1939 were certainly not agents of any grand conspiracy. They had a variety of motivators; some were expressing a firmly held conviction, others were giving voice to their frustrations over the perceived iniquities of the Polish state; some, perhaps, were just tacking with the political wind. However, theirs was an act that would not be forgotten easily by their neighbours. By siding with the new oppressor, and by giving apparent confirmation to the grotesque Nazi caricature of 'Judaeo-Bolshevism', they would unwittingly provoke profound and bloody consequences.

The Polish defence against the Soviet invasion was largely ad hoc, with most of the lightly armed border guards preferring to lay down their weapons, or simply evade both the Soviets and the Germans, and head south-west towards the Romanian border. In all, there are thought to have been about forty clashes between the Poles and the Soviets.[29] One of these was the battle of Szack on 28 September, in which the eponymous small town, south of Brest, was briefly liberated from Soviet control by Polish forces, which routed a Red Army infantry division in the process.[30] Another was the battle of Grodno, where a brilliantly improvised defence was organised by Polish general Józef Olszyna-Wilczyński, holding up the Soviet advance for two days and inflicting heavy losses on the invaders. Both the general and his adjutant were among some 300 of the town's defenders who would pay for their temerity with their lives, being executed by the Red Army upon capture.[31] Such actions were sadly not unique. The Red Army's instinctive hatred for the Polish officer class, as Catholics, aristocrats and Poles, would lead to other atrocities, and the execution of captured officers quickly became the norm. At Pińsk, for instance, thirty officers of the river flotilla were separated from the other ranks after their surrender and led away for execution.[32]

A few Polish commanders had the dubious honour of facing both sets of invaders that autumn. Perhaps the best example is that of General Franciszek Kleeberg, whose 'Polesie Independent Operational Group' first confronted Guderian's forces near Brest in the early phase of the war before pressing westwards with the Soviet invasion on 17 September, ostensibly to aid the besieged Warsaw. Overrun by events, however, Kleeberg's force was attacked by Red Army units at Milanów at the very end of September, before once again fighting the Germans in early October at the battle of Kock, the last engagement of the Polish campaign. Having run out of ammunition, the remains of the Polesie Independent Operational Group surrendered to the Germans on the morning of 6 October after a four-day battle. Kleeberg was the last to leave his post; he would not survive German captivity.[33]

In most cases, Soviet and German forces kept clear of each other, adhering to demarcation lines and avoiding contact. Indeed, they were supposed to maintain a 25 km distance from one another.[34] Yet despite this there were examples of co-operation and concerted action. From the outset, for instance, the Soviet authorities agreed to allow signals to be broadcast from Minsk to aid Luftwaffe navigation.[35] In addition, the two sides shared intelligence on the size and disposition of Polish units on the ground, and collaborated in their neutralisation.[36] One example of this is the battle of Lwów, the south-eastern regional capital, which was already under siege by the Germans when the Soviet 6th Army arrived on the outskirts on 19 September. Despite having taken numerous casualties in the battle, the German forces were instructed to withdraw, leaving the city's Polish commander, General Władysław Langner, to surrender to the Soviets, under the assurance that his men would be correctly treated. Langner was misled, however, as an eyewitness recalled: 'Hardly had they laid down their arms when they were surrounded by Russian troops and marched off.'[37] Throughout, the Soviets were all smiles towards their new German allies, with one Red Army lieutenant greeting his counterpart enthusiastically with cigarettes and the hastily learned slogan *'Germanski und Bolsheviki zusammen stark'* ('Together Germans and Bolsheviks are strong').[38]

In the sphere of public relations there was also widespread co-operation, with both sides reporting each other's successes and issuing joint communiqués. On 20 September, for example, *Izvestia* (the mouthpiece of the Soviet Communist Party) carried a front-page directive – evidently passed by Berlin and Moscow – giving a cynical and disingenuous explanation of the actions of German and Soviet troops in Poland. 'In order to prevent any kind of groundless rumours concerning the task of Soviet and German troops currently in the field in Poland', it ran,

> the governments of the Soviet Union and Germany announce that the function of these troops is not to pursue any particular aims . . . conflicting with the spirit of the non-aggression pact agreed between Germany and the Soviet Union. On the contrary, the task of these troops is to maintain peace and order in Poland, which have both been compromised by the collapse of the Polish state, and to help the population rebuild the conditions necessary for the existence of the state.[39]

This collaborative attitude was perhaps best and most wickedly demonstrated at a meeting in Warsaw in late October 1939 of the joint German–Soviet Border Commission. After a celebratory lunch, hosted by Hitler's representative in Poland, Hans Frank, he and the Soviet senior delegate, Alexander Alexandrov, smoked together. Frank remarked: 'You and I are smoking Polish cigarettes to symbolise the fact that we have thrown Poland to the wind.'[40]

★   ★   ★

Once installed on Polish territory, the two regimes wasted little time in formalising arrangements between themselves. On 27 September, Ribbentrop returned to Moscow to sign a supplementary agreement, the 'Boundary and Friendship Treaty', which tied up some of the loose ends left by the signature of the pact a month previously. In those discussions, the new-found friendship between the Nazis and the Soviets was given full expression. As Ribbentrop himself reported, it was like being in a 'circle of old comrades'.[41] Stalin stated that Nazi Germany and the Soviet Union together represented such a force that no combination of powers would be able to resist them. Moreover, he promised that 'should Germany unexpectedly get into difficulties, it could be sure that the Soviet people would come to Germany's aid and would not allow it to be strangled'.[42]

The practical business of the meeting was to regulate Nazi–Soviet relations in the wake of Poland's looming defeat. To this end, both parties agreed not to resurrect any Polish state and to collaborate in combating all agitation to that end. They also agreed a framework within which an exchange of populations could take place, enabling ethnic Germans to travel west, and Byelorussians and Ukrainians in German-occupied areas to move east. Most importantly, perhaps, the demarcation line previously agreed between the two regimes in eastern Europe had to be revised, with the Soviet frontier in occupied Poland being moved eastwards to the line of the river Bug, and Lithuania being awarded to Moscow as compensation. In this way, Poland was neatly divided almost in half, with Germany taking 72,800 square miles of territory and 20 million citizens, and the USSR receiving 77,720 square miles and 12 million inhabitants.[43] While Stalin publicly claimed that the shift was intended to remove any potential source of friction with his new ally, he clearly had one eye on London and Paris, as the revised frontier was much more readily defensible to western opinion, coinciding as it did, very broadly, with the ethnographic limit of Polish habitation. For the sake of clarity a map was produced from the German embassy, and a black line was added to mark the new German–Soviet border. Next to it were appended the signatures of Ribbentrop and – in a flourish of thick blue crayon – Stalin. The Soviet leader quipped to his German guest: 'Is my signature clear enough for you?'[44]

Once the formalities were agreed, the two regimes set about remaking their respective parts of the conquered territory in their own image. On the German side of the line, the former Polish lands were divided into two parts: the northern and western districts being annexed directly to the Reich – and most of it rechristened the Warthegau – and the southern and central areas being established as a separate entity – the *Generalgouvernement* or General Government – including both Warsaw and Kraków, which though nominally autonomous was nonetheless entirely dependent on the whim of Berlin. In both areas, the native Polish population enjoyed scant civil rights, being deliberately reduced to the status of an underclass whose sole purpose was to dutifully serve their new German overlords.

The first priority for the German authorities in Poland was to ensure that the Polish elite – religious leaders, teachers, military officers, intellectuals, even Boy Scouts – was effectively neutralised. To this end, the rather random killings of the early phase of occupation became more targeted and more overtly political in motivation. In the so-called 'Valley of Death' near Bydgoszcz, for instance, in October 1939 over 1,200 priests, doctors and others were killed by firing squads of the *Einsatzgruppen* and local ethnic German militias.[45] In total, actions such as these, 'pacifications' in Nazi parlance, would account for as many as 50,000 Polish deaths in that first autumn and winter of the German occupation.[46]

November 1939 saw *Sonderaktion Krakau* ('Special Action Kraków'), when Nazi cynicism matched Nazi barbarism. At midday on the 6th of that month, the entire staff of the prestigious Jagiellonian University – one of the oldest universities in the world – were summoned to a meeting with the new Gestapo chief for the city, Bruno Müller, to learn about the Nazis' plans for education. Rather than hear a lecture, however, the assembled 184 professors were summarily arrested and taken for interrogation, after which they were sent, en masse, to Sachsenhausen concentration camp outside Berlin. Though they would be released the following spring after international protests – not least from Benito Mussolini and the Vatican – some sixteen of the Jagiellonian professors would not survive their ordeal. The university itself was closed, meanwhile, along with all of Poland's secondary and higher-educational establishments, for the duration of the Nazi occupation. Poles would require no more than the most rudimentary learning.

In the spring and summer of 1940, the Germans began another wave of repression in their zone of occupied Poland, to remove so-called 'leadership elements' from what remained of Polish society. The resulting *AB Aktion*, or 'Extraordinary Pacification Action', followed what would become a familiar pattern. Prisoners were removed from their cells in local jails; a charge, verdict and sentence would be read out; and they would be taken by truck to nearby woods, where they would be executed with a shot to the head, or machine-gunned, into waiting pits. In this way, 358 prisoners from Pawiak prison in Warsaw were killed in Palmiry Forest in June 1940; 400 were killed near Częstochowa in July; and 450 people were murdered near Lublin on the night of 15 August 1940. In total, it is thought that the *AB Aktion* cost around 6,000 lives.[47]

In administrative terms, too, the Nazis and the Soviets recast their respective zones of occupation according to their own norms. So, while the Germans employed brute force and the dictatorial hierarchy prescribed by the *Führerprinzip* or 'leader principle', in the Soviet zone the new administration adorned itself with the illusion of democratic legitimacy. A month after the Red Army's arrival, the Soviets staged rigged elections (with a closed list of candidates) for new assemblies in the two annexed territories of 'Western Byelorussia' and 'Western Ukraine'. A week or so later, those new assemblies petitioned the Supreme Soviet in Moscow with a request that they be permitted to join the Soviet Union, which was duly granted in mid-November 1939. 'Western Ukraine' and 'Western Byelorussia' were then annexed to the existing Soviet Republics of Ukraine and Byelorussia respectively, and the newly elected 'national assemblies' were dissolved. Within two months, the Polish eastern borderlands or *Kresy* had been seam-lessly absorbed into the USSR.

From that point on, Soviet norms applied throughout. Private prop-erty was abolished, businesses were nationalised and all former citizens of Poland had to register as Soviet citizens. The Polish zloty was with-drawn from circulation in mid-November. With no conversion permitted to Soviet roubles, this measure left many among the old middle and upper class impoverished overnight – divested of their property, their savings worthless. Sovietisation naturally had profound effects; not only was economic and social life for the majority turned on its head, but many now found themselves liable to retroactive arrest for anti-Soviet activities, such as having fought in the 1920 Polish–Soviet War. Membership of the former bourgeoisie or the intelligentsia suddenly became a potentially life-threatening condition.

In fact, a remarkable symmetry emerged between the occupation policies adopted by the Nazis and the Soviets, with both sides using very similar methods for dealing with their respective conquered populations. Just as the Germans were effectively 'decapitating' Polish society in the west, so the Soviets were doing the same in their area of occupation: measures adopted against the racial enemy in one half of Poland were virtually indistinguishable from those applied to the class enemy in the other. In the Soviet zone, numerous prominent personalities – military and political – were arrested in a conscious effort to remove opinion formers and commentators who might adversely affect the smooth transition to Soviet rule. Others were detained more speculatively, considered suspect after a chance conversation perhaps, or picked up off the street. A favourite NKVD tactic was to arrest two people talking together in public and then interrogate them separately, asking specifically what they had been talking about prior to their arrest. If there were discrepancies in the two accounts, then they were clearly hiding something and the interrogation would continue. Most would be arrested for some minor transgression – real or imagined – which could be construed as oppositional; service to the pre-war Polish regime, for instance, was enough for an individual to be branded a supporter of 'fascism'.[48] Of course, the irony that Stalin himself was supporting fascism via his pact with Hitler was not allowed to intrude.

Some of those arrested had actually committed an offence. Czesław Wojciechowski was nineteen years old when he was detained for distributing anti-Soviet leaflets in the northern town of Augustów. Sentenced to eight years in the Gulag labour camps of the Soviet interior, he was taken away in the clothes in which he had been captured and never saw his family again.[49] He was one of an estimated 100,000 Poles seized by the NKVD in occupied Poland for criminal offences, half of whom were sent to the Gulag.[50] For those sent to local jails, conditions were little better. Aleksander Wat was sent to the overcrowded main prison in Lwów in January 1940. None of the prisoners there had been incarcerated for more than three months, yet the poor conditions were such that all of them looked like old men. 'I couldn't tell the difference between 40-year-old and 70-year-old men', Wat recalled.[51] Little wonder that the grim joke soon began to circulate in Poland that the initials NKVD (or NKWD in Polish) stood for *Nie wiadomo Kiedy Wrócę do Domu* ('Impossible to tell when I will return home').[52]

Perhaps the most infamous example of this process of 'decapitation' takes the name of one of the sites where the unfortunate prisoners were murdered – Katyn. After the Soviet invasion of eastern Poland, around 400,000 Polish prisoners of war, policemen, prison officers and others were arrested by the NKVD. Through a process of interrogations and political screening, this number was then whittled down, with many enlisted men being released and others being assigned to labour battalions. This left around 15,000 men by the end of 1939 – predominantly army officers – interned in the Soviet prison camps at Starobelsk, Kozelsk and Ostashkov, where they were subjected to lengthy nocturnal interrogations in order to ascertain their attitude towards the Soviet Union and to communism. The prisoners considered that they were merely being screened prior to their release, but it was much more serious than that: their very lives were at stake. As Poles, officers, aristocrats and Catholics, most of them were damned many times over in Soviet eyes, and accordingly fewer than 400 of them were deemed to be 'of use' and were saved from execution; one of them was Zygmunt Berling, later commander of the 1st Polish Army, which would fight alongside the Red Army all the way to Berlin. For good measure, around 7,000 other Poles – priests, policemen, landowners and intellectuals – from other camps were added to the execution list. Then, on 5 March 1940 – the very same week that the *AB Aktion* was ordered in Berlin – the instruction was given in Moscow to apply 'the supreme punishment: shooting'.[53]

The following month, the 15,000 or so officers were shipped out of their camps in batches of a few hundred at a time. They all enjoyed a hearty send-off, in the belief that they were being released, with their fellow officers sometimes forming an honour guard through which they would pass to board the buses that would take them away. 'There was not the slightest suspicion', one eyewitness recalled, that they were 'in the shadow of Lady Death'.[54] Their journey was a comparatively short one, however. Taken to NKVD prisons and safe houses, they were held for a time longer, while their identities were again checked. One diarist, Major Adam Solski, maintained his journal right up to that moment. 'We have been brought somewhere to a forest; it looks like a summer resort', he recorded. 'Here a thorough personal search. Roubles, belt and pocketknife are taken.'[55] It was to be his last entry.

Though it seems that other methods were tried, the NKVD quickly worked out the most effective technique for dealing with the prisoners. One by one they were led, arms bound behind their backs, to a cellar room with makeshift soundproofing provided by sandbags. Before the prisoner could make sense of his surroundings, he was grasped from both sides by two NKVD men, while a third approached him from behind and fired a single shot into the base of his skull with a German-made pistol, the bullet generally exiting through the victim's forehead. A skilled executioner, such as Stalin's 'favourite', Vasily Blokhin, could carry out as many as 250 such executions in a single night. Working at the NKVD jail at Kalinin that spring, Blokhin wore a leather apron and gauntlets to prevent being sullied by his victims' blood.[56]

Immediately afterwards, the bodies of the victims would be loaded on to trucks and driven into the nearby forests for disposal in mass graves, where they would be stacked perhaps twelve deep and limed to speed decomposition.[57] The 7,000 or so other victims on the list were executed in NKVD prisons in Ukraine and Byelorussia. In total, at least 21,768 Polish prisoners met their end in this way, including one prince, one admiral, twelve generals, eighty-one colonels, 198 lieutenant colonels, twenty-one professors, twenty-two priests, 189 prison guards, 5,940 policemen and one woman, Janina Lewandowska.[58]

By such measures, and by the analogous massacres and executions carried out by the Nazis, Poland's ruling and administrative class was effectively destroyed. It is perhaps not surprising that a few unfortunate families would find siblings divided by the war yet meeting identical fates at Soviet and Nazi hands. One such was the Wnuk family from Warsaw. Army officer Jakub Wnuk was in his mid-thirties when he was taken by the Soviets to the camp at Kozelsk and thence to Katyn, where he was murdered in April 1940. His older brother Bolesław – a former Polish MP – was arrested by the Germans in October 1939, before being executed near Lublin on 29 June. The latter left a farewell note: 'I die for the fatherland with a smile on my lips.'[59]

With the 'leadership elements' thus removed, and the immediate sources of possible resistance neutralised, both the Soviet and Nazi occupiers embarked upon a simultaneous cleansing of Polish society – the Nazis motivated primarily by concerns of race and the Soviets mainly by class-political criteria. The German-occupied areas of Poland, therefore, became a vast laboratory for an extended experiment in racial reorganisation. All citizens were required to register with the Nazi authorities and would be allocated to one of four categories: *Reichsdeutsch* (German nationals), *Volksdeutsch* (ethnic Germans), *Nichtdeutsch* (non-Germans) and *Juden* (Jews). One's category would dictate one's ration allocation and where one was permitted to reside. Entire populations were sifted and sorted, expropriated and expelled. Jews were confined to the newly established ghettos at Warsaw, Łódź and elsewhere, and Poles were often shunted out of the annexed Warthegau – making way for the arrival of ethnic Germans, *Volksdeutsche*, arriving from the east – to be concentrated in the General Government. By the spring of 1941, around 400,000 Poles had already been deported in this way.[60]

The procedure was that lists of deportees would be prepared by the Nazi authorities with the aid of local *Volksdeutsche*, which were then presented to the affected households by officers of the SS or Wehrmacht. Deportees were generally given an hour to pack and were permitted to take a single suitcase each, containing warm clothing, food, identity documents and up to 200 zloty in cash. Everything else was to be left behind. As one of those affected recalled, the instructions that were given were very particular: 'the flat must be swept, the plates and dishes washed and the keys left in the cupboards so that the Germans who were to live in my house should have no trouble'.[61] Once the deportees were ready, they were loaded on to trucks to be taken to the local railway station, for their onward journey. The deportation process that followed could be brutal, with little thought given to the provision of even the most basic amenities for those arriving at their destinations. The first large-scale deportation, for instance, was carried out in December 1939, when some 87,000 Poles were taken by train from the Warthegau to the neighbouring General Government. With many of the deportees spending hours waiting in the snow, or arriving at unfinished internment camps, the number that perished in the process was substantial; as the laconic report of the Nazi administration admitted, 'not all the deported persons, especially the infants, arrived at the destination alive'.[62]

Those Poles that survived were reduced to the status of second-class citizens: forbidden to use public parks and swimming pools; banned from all cultural, political and educational activity; and required to step aside to allow a German to pass. Any show of the slightest dissent – a glance or an ironic smile – could mean a death sentence. As the head of the General Government, Hans Frank, boasted to a journalist early in 1940, if he had to hang out a placard for every seven Poles shot, as was done in the German Protectorate of Bohemia, 'then the forests of Poland would not suffice to produce the paper'.[63] It was little wonder, perhaps, that the Poles would establish the largest and most effective underground resistance organisation in Europe.

Paradoxically, at the same time as Poles were being actively 'cleansed' from the Warthegau, the need for labour on the Nazi home front meant that many thousands of Poles would also be taken west, into the very heart of the Reich. Some volunteered, keen to improve their lot, but most were coerced, rounded up on the streets, or press-ganged from church congregations. In one instance, a village was required to provide twenty-five labourers, but none volunteered, so German gendarmes set a few houses on fire and would not permit the inhabitants to tackle the blaze until the requisite numbers of workers had 'volunteered'.[64] The able-bodied, therefore, were just as likely to end up being deported to Berlin as to Warsaw; and already by the middle of 1940, some 1.2 million Polish POWs and labourers were working in Germany.[65] Once there, they would be subject to harsh conditions: underfed, underpaid and, as one of their number recalled, 'treated worse than dogs'.[66]

Jews occupied the very bottom rung of the Nazis' racial hierarchy and were treated accordingly. In the opening days of the Polish campaign they had been subject to the same murderous caprice as their Polish neighbours, with many falling victim to arbitrary killings. At Błonie, west of Warsaw, for instance, fifty Jews were shot on 18 September; four days later another eighty were massacred at Pułtusk, to the north of the capital.

In time, other policies developed, including the expedient of simply pushing Jews eastwards, into the Soviet sector. On 11 September, for instance, Himmler's deputy, Reinhard Heydrich, was already ordering his *Einsatzgruppen* to 'induce' Jews to flee eastwards, despite the fact that the Soviet zone had not yet even been established.[67] German forces complied. Later that month, over 3,000 Jews were transported over the river San in southern Poland (which had been intended to mark the Nazi–Soviet demarcation line) and told to 'go to Russia'.[68] In another example, a transport of 1,000 Czech Jews was unloaded in the town of Nisko, not far from the new frontier, which had briefly been intended to serve as a Jewish 'reservation'. After the fittest among them had been removed for a labour detail, the remainder were simply ordered to march east and not to return.[69] On a single day, 13 November 1939, over 16,000 Jews were thus forced across the border at various locations. In some cases, groups of deportees were fired upon by German troops to encourage them on their way.[70]

Most needed no such encouragement. Many thousands would voluntarily follow suit across occupied Poland, finding few obstacles to their departure. As one Jewish diarist in Warsaw recalled, enthusiasm for the Soviet Union was – initially at least – widespread among the Jews. 'Thousands of young people went to Bolshevik Russia on foot,' he wrote, 'that is to say, to the areas conquered by Russia. They looked upon the Bolsheviks as redeeming Messiahs. Even the wealthy, who would become poor under Bolshevism, preferred the Russians to the Germans.'[71] That enthusiasm could be short-lived, however. Some of the 300,000 Polish Jews who are thought to have fled to the Soviet zone would attempt to return after a few weeks or months, either through homesickness or disillusioned by the poor conditions that they found there.

Those Jews that remained in the German-occupied regions would soon find themselves confined to ghettos. Starting in Łódź, then spreading to Warsaw, Kraków and elsewhere, ghettos were seen by the Nazis as a useful way to concentrate and isolate Jewish populations, while their ultimate fate was still undecided. In the Nazi mind, 'ghettoisation' had the added appeal that unsanitary conditions and disease would serve to reduce the Jewish population through 'natural wastage'. That euphemism would conceal countless horrors. Starvation spread, with the very young and the old most immediately affected. 'Bread is becoming a dream', one ghetto inhabitant wrote, 'and a hot lunch belongs to the world of fantasy.'[72] Typhus, too, was soon commonplace, spurred by poor hygiene. In the Łódź ghetto, for instance – which contained 163,000 people in the spring of 1940 – only 294 apartments were registered as having a toilet, and fewer than 400 had running water.[73] Those that endured the ghettos could scarcely have imagined that their stay there was only a prelude to an even worse fate.

In the Soviet area of occupation, meanwhile, the NKVD was rolling out a 'cleansing' procedure of its own which – in addition to the 'decapitation' process already under way – sought to screen Polish society for all those that it perceived might be antagonistic towards Soviet rule. Again, it was a category that could be extremely elastic in interpretation. As well as teachers, businessmen and priests, the Soviets chose to arrest many who were simply damned by their knowledge of the outside world, including philatelists, postmasters and even Esperantists.[74] Others qualified for arrest by being what the Soviets called *beloruchki*, literally 'those with white hands', meaning those who did not do manual labour. By a particularly vicious twist of fate, the families of those killed in the Katyn massacres were also rounded up, their names and addresses having been gleaned by the NKVD through intercepting correspondence with their doomed loved ones.[75]

For all of those affected, the procedure was generally the same. Households would be woken in the early hours by an urgent hammering on the door and bellowed instructions in Russian from small groups of men, usually consisting of one or two NKVD NCOs along with a couple of Red Army privates and a local militiaman. While the property was searched for any incriminating evidence, and the family held at gunpoint, the NKVD officer would read a prepared decree outlining the offence and the punishment – deportation. No details were generally given of the destination; some officers were deliberately vague or misleading, while others might show a flicker of sympathy. One NKVD man tried to soothe a crying child by handing her a toy doll. When she refused it, he gave it to her older sister saying: 'Take it with you, there will not be dolls like that where you're going.'[76]

In most cases, instructions would then be given on the procedure to follow: time allowed for packing, for instance, or suggestions for what should be taken on the journey, although some NKVD men were more interested in looting valuables and persecuting their victims. In one case, a family woke to the sight of a group of soldiers already inside the bedroom:

> No one dared move because he would be killed on the spot. They tied Daddy up with a chain, and the others searched for weapons and at the same time stole whatever was valuable. The oldest militiaman shouts that in half an hour we have to be ready to leave . . . They caught Mummy, tied her up and threw her on the sleigh.[77]

Even when instructions were given, for many of those affected the details were lost in a haze of fear and panic. As one peasant woman recalled:

> He tells us to listen [to] what he will read and he read a decree that in half an hour we must be ready to leave, wagon will come . . . I immediately went blind and got to laugh terribly, NKVD man screams get dressed, I run around the room and laugh . . . son keeps packing what he can . . . children are begging me to pack or there will be trouble, and I have lost my mind.[78]

One mother was so traumatised that her young son had to pack for her. When she arrived in rural Kazakhstan, she found that he had included his French dictionary, a recipe book and some Christmas decorations.[79]

Soviet practice was generally to deport households together, according to the names on the list that accompanied the NKVD officers. Thus, extended non-resident family members were usually excluded and allowed to leave, as were occasional guests, but absent family members would be actively sought. Teenager Mieczysław Wartalski was on the list, and though he had already made good his escape when the NKVD arrived, he returned to his family because he feared that his mother would not cope without his help and he remembered his father's parting instruction to take care of his brothers and sisters. All five of them would be deported together to Kazakhstan.[80]

The NKVD was similarly conscientious, and permitted few exceptions. In one example, a man pleaded in vain that his paralysed father and infant son might be excused deportation; neither would survive the journey.[81] One of the only digressions allowed, it seems, was when would-be deportees were absent and NKVD officers decided to find replacements to fulfil the quota. In one such instance, a young woman was snatched off the street to 'replace' a teenage daughter who had run away when the NKVD arrived. The woman's screams and protests were countered with the ominous reply that 'Moscow will put it right.'[82]

After collection, the deportees were taken to their local railway stations and packed into goods carriages. Conditions were atrocious as the primitive wagons were scarcely equipped for transporting human cargo: a few were fitted with wooden bunks and stoves, but most were simply bare carriages, with barred windows, and no sanitary facilities beyond a hole in the floor. Confined sixty or so to a carriage, 2,500 per train, the deportees had little room to sit.

Once under way, supplies of water and food for the deportees were intermittent at best, particularly as the carriages would often only be opened days into the journey. Water supply was consistently short, with those on the winter transport forced to scavenge for snow from the roof of the carriage, which was often blackened with soot from the locomotive. Those deported in summer did not even have that option. Food was similarly meagre, being supplied on average every two to three days and consisting perhaps of a thin, indistinct soup, sour bread or sometimes simply hot water, all of which had to be collected by child volunteers from each carriage. Occasionally, a train was rather better supplied. One deportee recalled that Soviet soldiers would walk along the train during a stop, attempting to sell ham, fruit and the other supplies, which, it was suspected, had been provided free of charge for the passengers' benefit.[83]

In such difficult conditions, exhaustion and disease took a hideous toll and the primary task whenever the train stopped was often to remove the dead bodies – mainly those of the elderly and the young. One deportee remembered seeing a Red Army officer moved to tears by the sight that greeted him when the doors of the train were opened.[84] Another, from a winter transport, recalled the grisly sight of Soviet soldiers moving from one wagon to the next, with tiny corpses under their arms, asking 'Are there any frozen children?'[85] In summer, meanwhile, the deportees would try to push the dead out of the carriage windows themselves, for fear of spreading disease. Summer or winter, requests that a formal burial be permitted were routinely refused, and the bodies would be left where they fell, or simply stacked, anonymously, by the side of the tracks.

For many, the agony of deportation would last for up to four weeks, until they reached their destinations, where the new agonies of a life of hard labour and exile awaited them. Many found themselves in the Soviet far north, in the district of Arkhangelsk Oblast, or in Siberia, where they were mainly put to work logging. Most of the remainder ended their journey in Kazakhstan, working on collective farms or labouring to construct railways. For all of them, the Soviet maxim ran: 'Who doesn't work, doesn't eat.' Death tolls were substantial, with an estimated annual death rate of around 30 per cent.[86] Deportation to the wide expanses of the Russian interior was a policy whose roots went back to the time of the tsars, but the criteria applied by the Soviets were based on raw class politics. As those left behind in Poland were told:

> This is how we annihilate the enemies of Soviet power. We will use the sieve until we retrieve all bourgeois and kulaks, not only here, but in the entire world. You will never see again those that we have taken away from you. *Tam propadut kak rudaia mish* [They will disappear over there, like a field mouse].[87]

The four main deportations from eastern Poland – in February, April and June 1940, and again in June 1941 – were all carried out in the same way. The precise numbers involved are not known for certain, and have long been assumed to have totalled over a million.[88] Though recent scholarship, drawing on research from the NKVD's own archive in Moscow, has revised this figure downward,[89] it is suspected that the Russian archival record tells only one aspect of the story, and does not include those condemned by summary courts, or otherwise unregistered. For every convict or official deportee, it seems, there may have been three or four who went unrecorded, making the figure of 1 million – according to Poland's foremost western historian – a 'very conservative estimate'.[90] Whatever the true totals, few would ever return.

Even those newly arrived in the Soviet zone from the west could find themselves en route to the Gulag. The Soviet authorities could be royally inhospitable, with many officials viewing refugees simply as spies or provocateurs. In one instance, a group of around 1,000 Jews were expelled across the border by the Germans, only for a nearby Soviet commander to attempt to force them back into the German zone some fifteen kilometres away, thereby causing a tense stand-off with the local Wehrmacht units.[91] Most refugees that were caught close to the frontier by the Soviet authorities were liable to arrest and a sentence in the Gulag. This would be the fate of the Dreksler family in the autumn of 1939. Having entered the Soviet zone without being apprehended, they were stopped in Lutsk, where they were asked to fill out various forms by the communist authorities. However, their answer to the question of where they ultimately intended to settle – 'Palestine' – so irritated their interrogating officer that he sent them instead to a work camp at Archangel.[92]

Viennese Jew Wilhelm Korn was one of the few who sought to escape his fate. Expelled across the river Bug by the SS, with the instruction to 'go over to your Bolshevik brothers', he did not believe Soviet promises of work, accommodation and good treatment, and so decided to abscond. Recaptured and interrogated by the NKVD, Korn was accused of being a German spy and was sent back across the border and to Vienna. Remarkably, he would survive the war.[93]

Unsurprisingly, perhaps, the Soviet authorities grew so frustrated by the volume of refugees entering their zone – willingly or unwillingly – that they complained to the Germans that future collaboration between the two on the sensitive issue of population exchanges was being jeopardised. With that, 'wild' deportations were brought to an end, and border controls were tightened. The ethnic and political reorganisation of the Polish lands required a degree of Nazi–Soviet co-operation.

Beginning in December 1939, therefore, both the Nazis and the Soviets began the process of registering those desiring to leave their respective zones of occupation. On the German side of the frontier, some 35,000 Ukrainians and Byelorussians were found – mainly former Polish POWs – applying to be evacuated east into the Soviet zone, but the larger number of ethnic Germans wanting to go in the opposite direction was more of a challenge. In the Soviet zone, then, joint

Nazi–Soviet 'resettlement commissions' – consisting of four SS officials from the ethnic German office, the *Volksdeutsche Mittelstelle*, accompanied by four members of the NKVD – began touring the towns and cities in December 1939 to oversee the registration of all those claiming to be ethnic Germans and enable them to travel west into Germany. Over the next six months, 128,000 *Volksdeutsche* would successfully apply to be 'repatriated' to the Reich, with the first group of settlers being welcomed at Przemyśl on the Soviet–German border by Heinrich Himmler himself.[94]

Naturally, this process was not without complications. For one thing, the Soviets seemed to be committed to frustrating the operation, often vetoing applications in what appeared to their German counterparts to be an arbitrary fashion.[95] The primary problem was that – embarrassingly for the Soviets – many more people beyond the ethnic German community evidently wanted to leave the Soviet zone, including many of the Jews who had only recently arrived. Some years later, the then Communist Party head in Ukraine, Nikita Khrushchev, would recall in his memoirs with incredulity, the 'long lines of Jews . . . waiting to register to leave for the west'.[96] Another account tells of a similarly incredulous German officer, watching the queues and saying 'Jews, where are you going? Don't you know that we will kill you?'[97]

One of those who chose to return was the Jewish writer Mieczysław Braun, who had fled to Lwów with the outbreak of war, but soon regretted his actions when he found himself forced to conform to the expected Soviet norms. 'I have never been in such a humiliating and absurd situation', he wrote to a friend:

> Every day we have a meeting. I sit in the first row and they look at me,
> I hear propaganda, nonsense and lies. Whenever they mention Stalin my
> supervisor starts clapping and everyone present follows suit. I also clap,
> and I feel like a court jester . . . I don't want to clap, but I am forced to.
> I don't want Lwów to be a Soviet city, but a hundred times a day I say
> the opposite. All my life I have been myself and an honest person, and
> now I am playing the fool. I have become a scoundrel.[98]

Racked by the contortions that he was obliged to make, Braun opted to return to Warsaw and take his chances with the German occupation. He died in the Warsaw ghetto in 1941.

In fact, very few of those who applied to emigrate from the Soviet zone were granted permission, with only around 5 per cent of applicants being successful.[99] Those who were rejected would not be spared the self-righteous wrath of the Soviet state. Given that they had, implicitly, expressed their rejection of communism, and had been obliged to register their details to do so, they were now doubly exposed to the attentions of the NKVD. The Soviet authorities did not hesitate in exacting their revenge. In June 1940, once the Resettlement Commission had completed its work and departed, the recalcitrants were collected for transport to the Soviet interior. Some were even told to present themselves at their local railway station for emigration to the *west* – thereby saving the authorities the trouble of physically rounding them up – only to then be loaded on to trains and deported in the opposite direction.[100] Of those involved in this third large Soviet deportation from eastern Poland, in June 1940, nearly 60 per cent are thought to have been Jews, and the vast majority were those who had unsuccessfully applied to leave the Soviet zone.[101]

It is, of course, invidious to attempt any comparison of the Nazi and Soviet occupation regimes in this period, yet as these accounts demonstrate, it was a comparison that many Poles and Polish Jews were forced to make.[102] In truth, Poles of all faiths and all classes faced an impossible choice: either to remain where they were and accept the inevitable hardships that their occupiers would impose, or to attempt to better their situation by moving to the other zone. In weighing this decision, they had little information beyond rumour and hearsay. Few of them made their decision on political or ideological grounds; rather, they were motivated primarily by essential self-preservation, seeking a modicum of security for themselves and their families. It was a dilemma that was neatly summed up in one story from the period, which told of two trainloads of Polish refugees encountering each other crossing the Nazi–Soviet frontier – one going east, the other going west – with each group astonished that the other was fleeing into the zone from which they were trying to escape.[103] It is a scene that eloquently sums up the Polish predicament in 1939.

Even Polish communists, it seems, could be less than totally enamoured of life in the Soviet zone. Some were disappointed by the apolitical avarice of the Red Army. 'We waited for them to ask how was life under capitalism', one complained, 'and to tell us what it was like in Russia. But all they wanted was to buy a watch. I noticed that they were preoccupied with worldly goods, and we were waiting for ideals.'[104] Marian Spychalski's complaints were more immediate. He had fled to Lwów in the Soviet zone in November 1939, but was so shocked by Soviet treatment of the Poles there that he lasted barely two weeks before escaping back into the German zone and heading for Warsaw.[105] Organising resistance in the former capital, Spychalski was joined by another prominent Polish communist, Władysław Gomułka, who had also fled from Lwów to take his chances with the Germans in the General Government.[106] Despite their sobering experiences of life under the Soviets, both Spychalski and Gomułka would later become senior politicians of the post-war Polish communist state: Spychalski as minister of defence, Gomułka as First Secretary of the Communist Party.

For all the hardships that they endured, Spychalski and Gomułka would have counted themselves fortunate. Some 5,000 of their fellow Polish communists – practically the entire active membership of the party – had already fallen victim to Stalin's purges. The only members spared had been those who had found themselves in Polish jails at the time.[107] Other communists would soon be targeted by Berlin. Already in November 1939, Ribbentrop had stated to Molotov that the continued imprisonment of German citizens in the Soviet Union was incompatible with good political relations between Moscow and Berlin.[108] He was referring to the 500 or so political emigrants from Germany – mainly communists – who were thought to have found refuge in the Soviet Union after the Nazi seizure of power. Ironically, by 1939 many of them had also fallen foul of the NKVD's terror machinery, and those who had escaped execution in the purges often found themselves in the myriad labour camps of the Gulag. Now, after enduring the NKVD's attentions, they were to be returned to the clutches of their original tormentors, the Gestapo.

German officials would provide lists to their Soviet counterparts with the details of those German, Austrian and Czech citizens that they believed had escaped to the Soviet Union. The NKVD would check its own records to determine the precise fate of the individuals in question and any survivors would be rearrested and deported.

Peculiarly, for some of the prisoners, a period in Moscow was allowed in which they could be 'fattened up' after the rigours of the Gulag. Otto Raabe recalled a sojourn in Moscow with feather pillows, bedsheets and good food as well as an in-house tailor and a cobbler to prepare him for his return to Germany. Unsurprisingly perhaps, many of the prisoners did not want to go, but they were told that they had no choice. At German insistence, they would be taken by train direct to crossing points on the new German–Soviet border in occupied Poland, thereby avoiding possible escape attempts. In total, around 350 individuals were delivered back to Germany in this way.[109]

One of those affected was Margarete Buber-Neumann, the wife of a prominent German communist, Heinz Neumann, who had fled to the Soviet Union in 1935. After her husband had been arrested and shot by the NKVD in 1937, Buber-Neumann had been sentenced to five years' labour in the Gulag, before she was arrested once again in January 1940 and brought for questioning to the infamous Butyrka prison in Moscow. The following month, she was deported with a group of twenty-nine others back to Germany, being taken by train to Brest-Litovsk. 'We got out on the Russian side of the Brest-Litovsk bridge', she recalled. After a while, a group of NKVD men crossed the bridge, returning with some SS officers: 'The SS commandant and the NKVD chief saluted each other. The Russian . . . took some papers from a bright leather case and began to read out a list of names. The only one I heard was "Margarete Genrichovna Buber-Neumann".' With that, she was handed back to the SS. As she was crossing the bridge, she could not resist a glance back to the communist refuge that had betrayed her: 'The NKVD officials still stood there in a group watching us go. Behind them was Soviet Russia. Bitterly I recalled the Communist litany: Fatherland of the Toilers; Bulwark of Socialism; Haven of the Persecuted.'[110] Already a veteran of the infamous Soviet camp at Karaganda, she would spend the next five years in Ravensbrück concentration camp.

One group crossing the German–Soviet frontier that is not often considered is Allied POWs. In the opening phase of the war many, mainly British, prisoners found themselves in German POW camps, some of which were located in the eastern provinces and the Polish lands annexed directly to the Reich. For them, Soviet-occupied Poland represented the closest 'neutral' territory, and therefore potential refuge, available. The prisoners of Stalag XXA at Thorn (Toruń) north-west of Warsaw, were a good case in point. Fifteen of their number made successful escapes to Soviet territory, only 150 miles to the east, in 1940. One of those who attempted the feat was Airey Neave, who 'dreamed of [his] triumphant arrival in Russia' and believed that, should he reach the demarcation line at Brest-Litovsk, he would be 'ushered into the presence of the British ambassador, Sir Stafford Cripps'.[111] Neave was to be disappointed, however. Posing as an ethnic German, he was captured en route to Brest at Iłow, near Warsaw, in April 1941. He might have considered himself lucky. The reception that escapers received from the Soviets, according to the official MI9 report, was 'always cold', and many of the prisoners were even maltreated. Most of them, indeed, were subsequently sent to Siberia.[112] Neave would later succeed in scoring a 'home run' from the high-security POW camp at Colditz.

Though they were obliged to intern escapees, the Soviets' treatment of escaped POWs could be positively hostile. One escapee who swam the river San to present himself to Soviet authorities in March 1941 was promptly arrested and spent the next year in a succession of NKVD jails, usually in solitary confinement.[113] In some cases, escapees were even handed back to the Germans. Polish underground couriers, for instance, were bemused to discover that sixteen Allied airmen whom they had spirited out via Kiev in the winter of 1940 had returned to Warsaw as prisoners of the Gestapo.[114] 'Internment', it seems, could have various definitions.

The question of co-ordination between the Nazis and the Soviets is one that still exercises many today, with fevered speculation in some quarters about high-level meetings between the NKVD and the Gestapo, supposedly with the likes of Adolf Eichmann in attendance. Tantalisingly, Khrushchev states in his memoir that Ivan Serov, the head of the NKVD for Ukraine, had 'contacts with the Gestapo'.[115] Of course, given that both sides were united in their common efforts to exchange refugees as well as destroy Poland's elite, a degree of co-operation is to be expected, and to this end it should not be surprising that a number of planning meetings would have been held. And it is certainly notable in this regard that both the NKVD's Katyn massacres and the Gestapo's *AB Aktion* were ordered within a few days of each other, thereby suggesting at least an element of imitation, if not concerted action. As yet, however, broader high-level collaboration between the Gestapo and the NKVD finds no echo in the documentary record.

Yet Nazi–Soviet collaboration found expression in other spheres. In the first week of the war the luxury ocean liner SS *Bremen* found an emergency berth at Murmansk after escaping internment in New York and playing hide-and-seek with the Royal Navy in the Atlantic. With Soviet assistance, most of the ship's complement were evacuated by train back to Germany, while the captain later sneaked the *Bremen* back to German territorial waters under cover of the polar night, narrowly avoiding a British submarine on the way.[116]

The *Bremen* was not an isolated case. Indeed, in the opening three weeks of the war alone, eighteen German ships had sought refuge from the attentions of the Royal Navy in Murmansk.[117] Mindful, therefore, that a friendly port in the Soviet Arctic might be beneficial, in October 1939 the German admiralty submitted a request to the Soviets for a naval base in the Arctic north, for the service and supply of U-boats. After some wrangling and a few shifts of location, the request was granted and *Basis Nord*, or 'Base North', was established that December on a sheltered inlet, away from all prying eyes and all semblance of civilisation. Though the base never became fully operational, rendered superfluous by the Nazi conquest of Norway the following summer, its brief existence was fraught with difficulties.[118] Not only was the terrain utterly inhospitable that winter, but the reflexive paranoia and secrecy of the Soviets served to exacerbate the already trying conditions for the German sailors stationed there. According to a ship's doctor on a German supply vessel, the provision of food was 'terrible', causing cases of scurvy, while the sense of isolation and futility fostered a pervasive atmosphere of depression. Matters were not helped by the hostile attitude exhibited by their Soviet liaison officers, one of whom the doctor described as 'mentally malnourished, disingenuous' and 'an unusually evil subject [who] mistrusts and harasses us whenever possible'.[119]

That Soviet mistrust was not merely force of habit. As Allied seamen aboard the Arctic convoys would discover later in the war, the Soviet authorities could be astonishingly inhospitable when it came to foreign servicemen trespassing on their soil. Another factor fed the psychosis.

Stalin was very eager to maintain the outward fiction of Soviet 'neutrality' in the war, and any military action which openly assisted his German ally risked jeopardising that cover. Fear of discovery, then, seems to have spurred the already unhelpful Soviet authorities to new heights of obstructionism.

Other joint ventures proved rather more fruitful, not least in exploiting Soviet 'neutrality' to German advantage. In December 1939, for instance, the German auxiliary cruiser *Kormoran* evaded the British blockade by disguising herself as a Soviet merchantman; appropriately enough, the name chosen was the *Vyacheslav Molotov*.[120] In the following spring, Soviet assistance was more active, providing Germany with access to the Pacific via the Northern Passage, over the Arctic north of the USSR. An ex-merchantman was duly refitted as a surface raider, complete with torpedo tubes, an array of weaponry and a crew of 270. The *Komet*, as she was named, sailed from Gdynia in July 1940, skirting Scandinavia en route for the Soviet Arctic, where she was met by the icebreaker *Stalin* of the Red Fleet. By September, with Soviet assistance to clear a path through the ice floes, the *Komet* crossed the Bering Strait into the Pacific Ocean, where she attacked Allied shipping disguised as a Japanese merchant vessel, the *Manyo Maru*. In this guise, she would sink eight ships, including the RMS *Rangitane*, totalling over 42,000 tons, before being torpedoed in 1942.[121]

This story would be remarkable by any measure, not least for the sheer chutzpah and the feats of seamanship involved. Yet the 'war diary' of the *Komet*'s captain reveals an amicable collaboration with the Soviets that stands in stark contrast to the grim experience of those at *Basis Nord*. 'The relationship was good,' he noted at the outset, 'we liked them. We saw they were good people.' In due course, the connection would strengthen further still. Indeed, when an attack on the British was celebrated by the German crew, their Soviet counterparts joined in. 'You can't fake that,' the captain recorded in his diary, 'that was real . . . The Russians were on our side.'[122] Indeed, when the *Komet*'s Arctic adventure was at an end, Admiral Erich Raeder wrote in person to thank his Soviet opposite number, Admiral Nikolai Kuznetzov: 'It falls to me to have the honour of expressing the German Navy's sincerest thanks to you, esteemed Commissar, for your invaluable support.'[123]

★   ★   ★

In mid-December 1939, Adolf Hitler sent birthday greetings to his new ally, Joseph Stalin, expressing his 'most sincere congratulations [and] very best wishes for your personal good health and for a happy future with the peoples of a friendly Soviet Union'. Ribbentrop's note, predictably, was more effusive and rather more laboured, recalling the 'historic hours at the Kremlin which marked the beginning of a decisive change in the relations of our two countries' and ending with his 'most cordial congratulations'.[124]

Apart from the hyperbole, Hitler had every reason to be pleased with the political and strategic developments of the previous few months. In collaboration with the Soviet Union, his forces had crushed and dismembered Poland, leaving his eastern frontier secure and allowing him to devote his energies to confronting the British and the French in the west. In concert with the Soviets, his forces had begun the racial reorganisation of the Polish lands, and set in motion exchanges of political prisoners and ethnic Germans. Economic agreements forged with Moscow would also prove beneficial, it was hoped, not least in enabling Germany to avoid the worst effects of the British blockade of the European continent.

Stalin, too, would have been satisfied. Collaboration with the Germans was proceeding well. Poland – one of Moscow's historic enemies – had been wiped off the map, and territory had been gained at her expense which made good many of the losses sustained by the Soviet Union during the chaos of the revolution and its aftermath. Beyond that, Stalin could be well pleased with the Soviet Union's strategic situation. From a position of almost perpetual insecurity only a few months before, he was now allied to the pre-eminent military and economic power on the continent, with a freshly minted economic arrangement promising vital German military hardware in return for Soviet raw materials. What was more, the Soviet Union was at peace, having declared itself neutral in the war that had broken out between his German partner and the Western Powers. In his more hawkish moments, Stalin could doubt-less envisage the Germans and the West becoming embroiled in a costly, murderous rerun of the First World War, after which he would be the one to pick up the pieces, remaking all of Europe in the Soviet image in the process.

Little wonder, then, that Stalin's reply was similarly effusive, proclaiming that 'the friendship between the peoples of the Soviet Union and Germany, cemented in blood, has every reason to be solid and lasting'.[125] He might have added that it was a friendship that had been cemented largely in Polish blood.

3

Sharing the Spoils

Ribbentrop was thoroughly feted in Moscow on his second visit to the Soviet capital in late September 1939. Though he was there for the serious business of agreeing and signing the German–Soviet Boundary and Friendship Treaty, the prevailing mood of success infecting both parties after their joint destruction of Poland was so pervasive that he was treated with all the pomp and ceremony that the Soviet state could muster, including a performance of *Swan Lake* and a twenty-four-course gala banquet.

As Ribbentrop was returning to Molotov's office for the evening session of negotiations, however, he had the opportunity to see the other side of Soviet 'hospitality'. Waiting in an anteroom with his entourage, he encountered the Estonian foreign minister, Karl Selter, as he was leaving a meeting with Molotov.[1] The two certainly knew one another; Selter had been in Berlin only four months earlier to sign a non-aggression pact with Ribbentrop. Yet their chance meeting in Moscow would certainly have been rather more strained. History does not record whether anything other than the usual diplomatic platitudes were exchanged between the two, but Selter would have had every reason to have betrayed a rather hunted look.

It was Selter's second visit to Moscow that week. A tall, seasoned diplomat, considered one of the ablest politicians in the Estonian government, he had trained as a lawyer before entering politics, and had served in a number of ministerial and diplomatic posts before being appointed foreign minister the previous year. This would be his sternest test. On 24 September, he had attended a meeting with Molotov, where he had expected that a new trade treaty would be signed, but instead the Soviet foreign commissar had wanted to discuss political matters.

Soviet–Estonian relations were in something of a crisis, with the Estonians still unsettled by what the Nazi–Soviet Pact might mean for them, and the Soviets rather exercised by the ongoing war. To add to the tensions, the previous week, the Polish submarine *Orzeł* had escaped from Tallinn harbour and Moscow was aggrieved, arguing that the Estonian authorities should have done more to detain the vessel. In response to this perceived 'provocation', Red Army troops had been massed on Estonia's eastern border and the Red Air Force was overflying Estonian airspace, apparently carrying out reconnaissance.

When Molotov met Selter for talks that evening in the Kremlin, therefore, the mood was commensurately strained. Molotov began by airing his concerns about the implications of the recent *Orzeł* crisis for Soviet security, claiming that the Estonian government was either unwilling or unable to 'keep order in its country' and demanding guarantees to the contrary, embodied in the proposal of a mutual assistance pact. Undaunted, Selter replied that there were no shortcomings in Estonia's ability to keep order, and that the suggested pact was unnecessary, was unwanted by the Estonian people and would impair Estonian sovereignty. Molotov was unmoved, however, giving Selter the assurance that the pact with the Soviet Union would bring no perils with it. 'We are not going to force Communism on Estonia', he said, adding: 'Estonia will retain her independence, her government, parliament, foreign and domestic policy, army and economic system. We are not going to touch all this.'[2] When Selter protested further, Molotov cut to the chase, saying 'The Soviet Union is now a great power whose interests need to be taken into consideration . . . If you do not want to conclude a mutual assistance pact with us, then we will have to guarantee our security in other ways, perhaps more drastic, perhaps more complicated. I ask you: do not compel us to use force against Estonia.'[3]

If Selter had the impression of being a mouse caught in the claws of a playfully malevolent cat, he would not have been far wrong. Requesting leave to discuss the Soviet 'proposal' with his government, he was told that the matter 'cannot be delayed', and a direct telephone line to Tallinn was produced. Selter protested that such delicate discussions could not be carried out in that way, and asked that he be permitted to return to the Estonian capital the following day. As he left, Molotov told him: 'I advise you to yield to the wishes of the Soviet Union in order to avoid something worse.'[4]

An hour after leaving the Kremlin, Molotov's office then telephoned him again to request another meeting at midnight the same evening. This time, Selter was presented with a unilateral Soviet draft of the disputed 'mutual assistance pact' and forced into a discussion of the locations – including the capital, Tallinn – that might be 'of interest to the Soviet Union' as possible military bases. Once again, Molotov hectored him on the urgency of the matter and the inadvisability of any delay, adding that the agreement was 'ready for signature'.

Returning to Tallinn the next day, Selter discussed the Soviet proposal with his cabinet colleagues. German diplomatic circles were also sounded out, but their response – that Estonia was essentially on its own – caused consternation. Given the non-aggression pact that they had agreed with Germany in June 1939, the Estonian cabinet was justified in expecting some assistance from the Germans when faced with Soviet intimidation. German inaction, therefore, tended to confirm what some of them had already feared; that the political constellation had shifted with the signature of the pact between Moscow and Berlin, and Estonia was being cut adrift. Despite some defiant rhetoric, sober realism was the order of the day and Selter was dispatched again to Moscow with instructions to conclude the best terms possible with the Soviet Union. The alternative was unthinkable: 'To refuse the Soviet proposal', President Konstantin Päts intoned, 'would mean to knowingly send the entire Estonian people to their death.'[5]

Yet when Selter returned to Moscow on 27 September – accompanied, rather superfluously, by two Estonian experts on international law – he found that the goalposts had already shifted. Just as he had used the case of the *Orzeł* to undermine the Estonian position three days earlier, Molotov now used the alleged sinking of the Soviet merchantman *Metallist* in the Baltic, the previous day, to undermine Selter once again. On the unsubstantiated assumption that the *Metallist* had been sunk by the *Orzeł*, Molotov asserted that the previous proposals were no longer sufficient: Soviet security now required additional Estonian concessions.

In response to Selter's protestations of his country's innocence,

Molotov called upon Stalin himself to join the discussion. The Soviet leader showed his avuncular side upon entering the room soon after, joking with the Estonians, but quickly got down to business. Once apprised of the essentials he stated ominously: 'What is there to argue about? Our proposal stands and that must be understood.'[6] What passed for negotiations continued for the next couple of hours, the Soviets insisting on the placing of 35,000 Red Army troops in Estonia to 'protect order' and demanding a base in Tallinn itself, and the Estonians desperately trying to resist, yet sticking to the diplomatic niceties that their opponents had long since abandoned. Browbeaten, berated and bullied, the Estonian delegation returned the following day having decided that they could do nothing except yield. Yet, with Ribbentrop waiting in the wings, they were again met with additional demands and the threat that 'other possibilities' existed for ensuring Soviet security. Agreement on the mutual assistance pact was finally signed at midnight on 28 September and ratified by the Estonian president a week later. Nominally, the treaty obliged both parties to respect each other's independence, yet by allowing for the establishment of Soviet military bases on Estonian soil, it fatally undermined Estonian sovereignty. Estonia was effectively at Stalin's mercy.

If the Estonians had thought that they were alone in their torturous negotiations with the Soviets, they were mistaken. They were just the first on the list. Once the treaty with Estonia had been agreed, Moscow's focus turned to the other countries promised to it by the secret protocol to the Nazi–Soviet Pact and the follow-up agreement signed by Ribbentrop. Stalin was putting down a marker, as much for Berlin's attention as for the rest of the world, that the Baltic states were now under his 'protection'.

A week after the Estonian treaty, therefore, a similar pact was forced on Latvia, requiring the cession of bases at Liepāja, Pitrags and Ventspils on the Baltic coast and the stationing of Red Army garrisons totalling 30,000 troops. Again, Latvian sovereignty was not supposed to have been affected by the agreement and the government in Riga was left untouched for the time being. Yet, like their Estonian neighbours, the Latvians were under few illusions about their predicament, and knew that little help would be forthcoming from Germany. Molotov would later boast that he 'pursued a very hard line' with the Latvians, telling their minister for foreign affairs, Vilhelms Munters, that he 'would not go home' until he had signed an agreement.[7] Stalin was even blunter, informing the hapless minister 'frankly' in early October 1939 that 'a division of spheres of interest has already taken place. As far as Germany is concerned, we could occupy you.'[8]

In Lithuania, Soviet advances received a slightly more positive response, if only because the mutual assistance pact of 10 October 1939 had been sweetened by Moscow's agreement to hand the disputed city of Vilnius (the former Polish Wilno) over to Lithuanian control. Nonetheless, the terms on offer were identical in their essentials to those agreed with Estonia and Latvia: mutual aid in event of attack and the stationing of large numbers of Red Army troops. Moreover, Soviet methods, it seemed, were unchanged; as one of the Lithuanian delegation noted, arguing with Molotov was akin to 'throwing peas against a wall'.[9] The threat of violence – implicit or explicit – combined with the new strategic realities of war, had left Latvia, Lithuania and Estonia helplessly exposed to Moscow's designs. Unable to sensibly resist, they had been forced to accommodate Soviet demands and now existed very much under the Soviet shadow. By mid-October 1939, barely six weeks after the signature of the pact, Stalin had moved to exercise control of most of the territory that he had been promised by Hitler, extending his reach to the Baltic coast and securing the stationing of around 70,000 Red Army troops in the three Baltic states, a larger force than the combined standing armies of the three countries.[10]

While the Baltic politicians had wrestled, the Germans had merely squirmed. Right from the opening of the Soviet invasion of Poland, the Baltic governments had telegraphed Berlin repeatedly requesting that Germany explain its position, not least given the non-aggression pacts that she had signed with Latvia and Estonia only four months before. Berlin was well aware of the Baltic predicament; indeed, Stalin had informed Hitler of his intentions in late September, at which point the negotiations on a 'defence treaty' with the Lithuanian government had been halted, effectively abandoning that country to the Soviet 'sphere of influence'.[11] Nazi ideologue Alfred Rosenberg, himself born in Tallinn, was clear on the potential consequences, confiding to his diary that: 'If the Russians now march into the Baltic states, then the Baltic Sea will be strategically lost to us. Moscow will be more powerful than ever.'[12] Yet, in response to repeated requests for clarity, if not assistance, Ribbentrop was unyielding, finally replying in a circular to all three German legations in the region with an explanation of the new frontier arrangements agreed with Moscow, and stating tersely that 'Lithuania, Latvia, Estonia and Finland do not belong to the German sphere of interest.' He added that his representatives in the affected countries were to 'refrain from any explanations on this subject'.[13] The Baltic states were being abandoned to their fate.

As if to reinforce the sense of foreboding and isolation that was spreading in the region, Hitler chose that autumn to call all ethnic Germans *'Heim ins Reich'* – 'Home to the Reich' – thereby further signalling his abandonment of the region to Stalin. While Ribbentrop had been in Moscow in late September, the possible 'repatriation' of the *Volksdeutsche* in those areas was raised for discussion, ostensibly in response to Stalin's intention to assert his influence in the Baltic. With agreement secretly reached with the Soviets, the Germans approached the still-independent Estonians and Latvians to agree on procedures and compensation. In wooing the *Volksdeutsche* themselves, they primarily stressed the supposed benefits of joining the German 'national community', but the secondary message was an implicit warning of the difficult times that were to come.[14]

Many Baltic Germans took a good deal of persuading, not least because some of them were leaving lands that they had lived in for generations. Aside from their personal tribulations, some saw it as a betrayal, not only of their own history and culture, but of a civilisation. 'I found it very difficult', one evacuee recalled after the war, 'that an old culturally European land, a land in which the Germans had, for centuries, been the leading stratum and that in many respects bore a German face, was simply relinquished with a few words and the stroke of a pen.'[15] Even some staunch National Socialists were appalled. One noted in his diary the 'terrible shock' that news of the resettlement brought. 'Everything for which we had lived,' he wrote, 'everything our ethnic group had established in the course of 700 years . . . was to disappear, just like a melting snowman.'[16]

Nonetheless, despite the profound upheaval involved in relocating to a country of which many of them had little knowledge, the Baltic Germans responded to Hitler's call in large numbers. Already in mid-October 1939, the first ship carrying ethnic Germans left Riga en route for Germany. Over the two months that followed a further eighty-six vessels would depart from the region's ports, carrying over 60,000 people 'home' to the German Reich, or at least to the annexed region of the Warthegau. In fact, such was the growing anxiety about the future in the Baltic states that the operation even attracted some Jewish applicants.[17] For the Baltic populations that remained, the departure of the *Volksdeutsche* was an ominous sign: an augury of an uncertain future. As one Estonian-German remembered:

> They [the Estonians] saw the danger from the east . . . they under-stood how difficult it was for us to leave Estonia. And, as we boarded ship in Tallinn to leave our homeland and 'Deutschland über Alles' was played, followed by the Estonian national anthem, many broke into tears.[18]

Events in Finland that winter would spur the exodus. Like their Baltic neighbours, the Finns were invited to Moscow to discuss 'political questions' in early October 1939. Like their neighbours, they attended, sending a delegation led by the veteran diplomat Juho Paasikivi to receive the Soviet proposals, which included a northward extension of the border in the Karelian Isthmus, close to Leningrad, and a thirty-year lease on the port of Hanko, at the mouth of the Gulf of Finland. For their part, the Soviets seem to have assumed that the Finns would be as cowed and helpless as the Baltic governments before them; as Khrushchev recalled in his memoirs: 'All we had to do was raise our voice a little bit and the Finns would obey.'[19] Certainly there would be no intervention from Berlin. As with the Baltic states, Ribbentrop refrained from any comment beyond a pious wish that Finland might 'settle matters with Russia in a peaceful manner', and reacted with horror at the prospect of the former Finnish president coming to Berlin for talks. The German ambassador in Finland, meanwhile, was privately instructed to 'avoid any commitments . . . which would disturb German–Soviet relations'.[20]

Yet, despite their isolation, the Finns saw fit to resist Soviet threats. They tabled two counterproposals and sought to draw out negotiations for much of the following month, convinced that Moscow was bluffing and that 'right' was on their side. Molotov, it seemed, had met his match in the wily Paasikivi and snapped ominously at the final meeting between the two men that 'since we civilians don't seem to be making any progress, perhaps it's the soldiers' turn to speak'.[21]

In due course, the soldiers would indeed find their voice. On 26 November 1939, a Soviet border post near the village of Mainila in Karelia came under artillery fire, killing four Red Army men and wounding nine. Molotov hurried to blame the Finns for the 'deplorable act of aggression',[22] despite the fact that the post was beyond the range of Finnish gunners, who had been withdrawn from the frontier as a precaution. Summoning Helsinki's representatives to Moscow once again, he declared that his government was henceforth freed from the obligations of the existing Soviet–Finnish non-aggression pact and that normal relations could no longer be maintained. Just as Hitler had manufactured the 'Gleiwitz Incident' three months earlier to provide him with a *casus belli* against Poland, so Stalin had done the same at Mainila, giving communists worldwide the spurious argument they needed to justify Soviet aggression. Within four days the Red Army was on the march.

At first sight, it is difficult to imagine more of a military mismatch. The twenty-six divisions and 500,000 soldiers deployed by the Soviets should have been sufficient easily to sweep aside the 130,000 soldiers fielded by the Finns. In every sphere, the Red Army had an overwhelming advantage, with three times as many soldiers and thirty times as many aircraft. On the Karelian Isthmus, for example, where the main Soviet attack was expected, the Finns could field only 21,000 men with seventy-one artillery pieces and twenty-nine anti-tank guns against a Red Army force comprising 120,000 men, 1,400 tanks and over 900 field guns.[23] In addition to its numerical advantage, Moscow was convinced that the Finnish working class would rise up in support of their communist 'liberators' and serve as a 'fifth column' behind enemy lines, disrupting logistics and undermining morale. Soviet confidence was naturally high, therefore, with senior military personnel allocating only twelve days to the operation and anticipating such a swift advance that Red Army commanders were even warned not to cross the border into neutral Sweden – 300 km distant – by mistake.[24]

The reality was to be rather different. Materiel and numerical advantages would count for little in the extreme conditions of a Finnish winter, where temperatures would plummet as low as $-40°C$. In addition, much of the terrain through which Soviet soldiers would have to trudge was a trackless, snowbound wasteland of deep pine forests, punctuated by frozen rivers, lakes and swamps – all but impassable to a modern mechanised army. As if to make the situation harder still, the Karelian Isthmus, north of Leningrad, had been fortified in the interwar period and now boasted an extensive (though incomplete) network of bunkers, trenches, natural obstacles and earthworks, known as the Mannerheim Line, after Finland's military commander-in-chief. The Red Army would clearly not be having things all its own way.

The Soviets' numerical superiority was also lessened by the differing quality of the opposing troops. For its part, the Red Army was mired in something of a crisis. Still reeling from the purges that had cut a murderous swathe through its ranks in the mid-1930s and had accounted for over 85 per cent of senior officers,[25] it was hamstrung by poor leadership, defective training regimes and low morale. And though well armed in comparison with the Finns, its ranks lacked winter clothing, skis and camouflage, with both the infantry and their tanks going into battle that November sporting their traditional olive-green colour scheme, making them an easy target for their opponents. Tactically, too, the Red Army was lacking, with invention and initiative among the officer class proving to be a secondary casualty of the purges. What passed for military doctrine, then, was often simply a massed, frontal assault, with shortcomings exacerbated by insufficient co-ordination between the various branches of the armed forces.

The Finns, meanwhile, were highly motivated. And, far from welcoming the Soviets as Moscow had predicted, they were imbued with a staunch patriotism, which ensured that what their soldiers might have lacked in materiel, they made up for in morale. They were also able to draw on a large pool of trained reservists to bolster their standing forces and many of them brought vital local knowledge with them, as well as excellent fieldcraft and survival skills. One quip that did the rounds that winter summed up their optimism despite facing such an apparently powerful foe: 'They are so many and our country is so small', they would say. 'Where will we find room to bury them all?'[26]

Typically, the Soviet assault on Finland was both political and military. So, as Soviet bombers hit Helsinki and Viipuri, and tanks and infantry made their first sallies against the Mannerheim Line, a pro-communist puppet government was established at Terijoki, the first small town across the old Soviet–Finnish border. The 'Finnish Democratic Republic' was led by veteran communist Otto Kuusinen, whose main claim to fame was that he had survived the Soviet purges. Yet despite assiduously courting the trade unions and the moderate left, Kuusinen found himself ignored, recognised solely by his Moscow masters, with his writ running only in those areas 'liberated' by the Red Army.

Such political misjudgements were allied to serious strategic failings. For all its materiel superiority, the Red Army could be remarkably inflexible: the archetypal 'colossus with feet of clay'. Its tactical naïvety, it seems, was often matched by a very cautious approach, in which an advance could be held up for hours by the slightest Finnish resistance. In the conditions – with only a few roads and tracks providing a passage through largely impenetrable forests – this naturally played into the defenders' hands and Soviet assaults quickly deteriorated into enormous armoured traffic jams.

As the Red Army advance stalled, the Finns moved to counter-attack, showing all the guile and ingenuity that their opponents lacked. Small units of mobile ski-troops would outflank the invaders and separate them from their supply columns, utilising the long nights of the Scandinavian winter to harry and ambush their foes under cover of darkness. Infantry, meanwhile, employed improvised explosives, such as satchel charges, or the famed 'Molotov cocktail' – a petrol bomb containing kerosene and tar, which could be remarkably effective when aimed at the air intakes of Soviet tanks. The weapon got its nickname after Molotov had claimed in public that Soviet bombing missions were in fact dropping food packages over Finland. Soviet cluster bombs were then ironically dubbed by the Finns as 'Molotov breadbaskets', and the humble petrol bomb was named as 'a drink to go with the food'.[27] For all the mocking humour, the Molotov cocktail – mass-produced in a Finnish distillery – would prove to be a formidable weapon.

In time, Finnish tactics, which had hitherto been largely ad hoc, evolved into a recognised method. After isolating and containing each Soviet advance, the Finns would systematically reduce the enemy columns, with relentless probing attacks and the harsh winter weather combining to sap Soviet resistance. This tactic became known as the *motti*, from the Finnish term for timber stacked prior to being chopped. The sinister implication was that Soviet forces, thus encircled, were merely waiting to be dealt with, either by Finnish soldiers or by the elements.

The harsh Nordic winter could be a fearsome foe. While the Finns were used to the freezing conditions and tended to dress appropriately, the Red Army soldiers had little protection against the cold. All too often, then, the weather wrought as great a death toll as military action, and Finnish troops grew grimly accustomed to finding their enemies frozen solid where they crouched or lay, supposedly poised for action. In some cases, the survivors made for an even more gruesome spectacle. On one occasion, a Finnish officer took delivery of two Red Army prisoners who had been brought in with snow-blindness and severe frostbite to their hands and feet. 'After a while', an eyewitness reported, 'the Russians became aware of the heat from the stove and stumbled towards it. Then they both put their hands on the red-hot iron. They kept them there. They couldn't feel a thing. And there they stayed with their hands sizzling like rashers of bacon.'[28]

Aided by the weather and their own ingenuity, the Finns scored some remarkable successes. By Christmas Eve 1939, both the Soviet 139th and 75th Rifle Divisions had been effectively wiped out at the battle of Tolvajärvi, north of Lake Ladoga, while the 44th and 163rd Divisions were annihilated further to the north at Suomussalmi in early January. The latter battle was perhaps the most exemplary of Finnish methods. After the Red Army's 163rd Division had encountered stiff resistance, the 44th Division was sent in support, but both suffered a similar fate. Strung out along the narrow roads, hemmed in by lakes and forests with their forward progress prevented by a fortified Finnish roadblock, the two divisions were harassed by fast-moving ski-troops and ambushes, and gradually broken up into smaller and smaller sections, exposing the enemy soldiers to the ravages of the cold and hunger as well as combat. Each dwindling pocket was then wiped out, one by one. When the two divisions were finally eliminated, the Finns discovered over 27,000 frozen corpses littered along the forest road, amidst the scattered remains of their equipment.[29] It was a horrific scene. As a reporter discovered, the dead were everywhere:

> On the sides of the road; under the trees; in the temporary shelters and dugouts where they had tried to escape the relentless fury of the Finnish ski-patrols. And all along both sides of the road, for all these four miles, are lorries, field-kitchens, staff-cars, ammunition carts, limbers and every other kind of vehicle you can imagine.[30]

In the face of such morale-sapping setbacks, Red Army justice was swift and harsh. The commander of the 44th Division, General Aleksei Vinogradov, who had escaped the slaughter and returned to Soviet lines, was court-martialled a few days later and executed in front of his few surviving soldiers. NKVD reports suggested that the rank and file approved of the punishment.[31]

In the *motti* battles, snipers were used to devastating effect by the Finns. Their deployment had an important psychological aspect, as they were well able not only to spread fear but also to maximise the mental anguish suffered by their opponents, by targeting commanding officers, for instance, or concentrating their fire on field kitchens, or on those huddled around a campfire. A few snipers even targeted soldiers while they were relieving themselves, reinforcing the impression among the survivors that nowhere was safe. Utilising their exceptional camouflage and fieldcraft skills, the Finnish marksmen were expert at concealing their positions and took a heavy toll among the Soviet troops. As one Red Army colonel later complained: 'We couldn't see [the Finns] anywhere, yet they were all over the place . . . invisible death was lurking from every direction.'[32]

Most famous among the snipers was Simo Häyhä, a slight, unassuming 34-year-old corporal serving with the 34th Jäger Regiment in the snowy wastes north of Lake Ladoga. Though working only with an aged variant of the Russian Moisin–Nagant bolt-action rifle, equipped with standard iron sights, he was able to 'score' over 500 confirmed kills in barely a hundred days on the front line: the highest figure of any sniper in the Second World War. Targeted with artillery strikes and counter-sniping, Häyhä survived the war, despite being shot through the face. He was known to the Soviets as *Belaya Smert*, 'The White Death'.[33]

As the Red Army's forces ground to a halt in early January 1940, stalemate ensued. Bolstered by their successes, the Finns were also buoyed by expressions of international support. Right from the outset, Helsinki had benefited from an outpouring of sympathy, most tellingly perhaps when the Soviet Union was expelled from the League of Nations for its attack and the League Council called for its members to assist the Finns. For many in the West, Finland became a cause célèbre, a moral test case and a fillip for those still dismayed by their impotence over Poland. It was in this spirit, perhaps, mindful of Poland's fate, that Neville Chamberlain declared in January 1940 that: 'Finland must not be allowed to disappear from the map.'[34] Churchill echoed that sentiment in his own inimitable style: 'Only Finland,' he said in a radio address, 'superb, nay sublime, in the jaws of peril, shows what free men can do.'[35]

The case of Finland, it seemed, suggested a juxtaposition of Stalin's aggression with that of his ally Hitler, as the *Daily Sketch* argued in an editorial: 'Our task in this war is to defeat Hitlerism, but it is still Hitlerism if the aggressor is called Stalin.'[36] As a result of such sentiments, a huge relief effort was launched, with Sweden, Britain and France in the vanguard, collecting military hardware to be sent to Helsinki, including half a million hand grenades, 500 anti-aircraft guns and nearly 200,000 rifles.[37] Meanwhile, some 11,000 volunteers – mainly Swedes, Danes and Norwegians – registered their willingness to fight for Finland's cause, with the American president's cousin Kermit Roosevelt among them. Many of Finland's Baltic neighbours joined up, in some cases eager for the fight that their own governments had not dared to invoke. In the former Lithuanian capital of Kaunas, for instance, over 200 volunteers crowded into the Finnish consulate.[38]

Altruism, of course, is a rare quality in politics, and it should be noted that there was precious little of it in Allied planning to aid the Finns. Though individuals may well have been motivated by high principles and ideals, the politicians had other concerns, not least using any putative campaign to help Finland as an opportunity to hinder Hitler. Consequently, when tentative Allied plans

were drawn up to assist the Finns, it was rather ambitiously foreseen that any landing force would travel via Narvik in northern
Norway and Luleå in northern Sweden, both of which lay on the
route used by the Germans for the extraction of the Swedish iron
ore that was so vital to the German war effort. In this way, Finland's
cause was neatly subsumed by the Western Allies into the wider
one of fighting Hitler. Unsurprisingly perhaps, the plan came to
nought.

Stalin, meanwhile, was furious: a campaign that should have lasted
only two weeks had lasted three times that and with no success in
sight. The Red Army was being humiliated before the eyes of an
outside world that was growing restive, and – as Khrushchev believed
– events would be watched by the Germans with 'undisguised glee'.[39]
Certainly, the Red Army's difficulties in the Winter War had been
noted with interest in Nazi military and political circles, with many
doubtless seeing the apparent weaknesses of the Soviets as an important revelation. Goebbels, for instance, clearly noted the Red Army's
failings: 'Russia, as expected, is not making especially swift progress',
he wrote in his diary on 4 December, adding: 'Her army is not much
good.'[40] Elsewhere, the appropriate conclusions were being drawn. As
the German ambassador in Finland wrote to Berlin in January 1940:
'In view of this experience the ideas on Bolshevist Russia must be
thoroughly revised.' The Red Army's inability to 'dispose' of such a
small country as Finland, he argued, suggested that a change of
approach towards Moscow might be advisable. 'In these circumstances', he wrote, 'it might now be possible to adopt an entirely
different tone toward the gentlemen in the Kremlin from that of
August and September.'[41]

Yet for all that, Nazi Germany's attitude towards the conflict was
rather more nuanced than Khrushchev would have imagined. Public
opinion, for instance, broadly sympathised with the Finns and was
perturbed to see a Nordic nation and a traditional ally of Germany
being apparently sacrificed to communist expansion. But, at the same
time, concerns were expressed about the wisdom of Helsinki's decision to stand firm against the might of Moscow.[42] Some were rather
more forthright in their opinions. The conservative diplomat Ulrich
von Hassell, for instance, decried Germany's collusion with the Soviet
Union, stating that 'In such company, in the eyes of the world, we

now appear to be a big gang of robbers.'[43] The Italian foreign minister, Count Galeazzo Ciano, would have concurred. He noted in early December 1939 a growing anti-German sentiment in Italy and claimed that the fate of the Finns would be of much less concern to the Italian people were it not for the fact that the Soviets were the allies of Germany: 'In all Italian cities', he wrote, 'there are sporadic demonstrations by students in favour of Finland and against Russia. But we must not forget that the people say "Death to Russia" and really mean "Death to Germany".'[44]

The official line from Berlin, meanwhile, was one of resolute non-intervention and disinterest. Indeed, the message circulated to all foreign-office personnel from Wilhelmstrasse was that 'Germany has no part in these events [and that] sympathy is to be expressed for the Russian standpoint.' For good measure, it was added: 'I request that you refrain from any expression of sympathy for the Finnish position.'[45] True to the letter of the Nazi–Soviet Pact, the German government refused to allow any support to be given to its partner's opponent, even halting Italian deliveries of weapons, destined for Finland, that were in transit through Germany. Any remaining debate on the issue within Germany was settled that same month by the *Völkischer Beobachter*, in which an article – thought to have been penned by Hitler himself – stated that, though 'the German *Volk* has nothing against the Finnish people', it was 'both naïve and sentimental' to expect Germany to support Finland, when Finland had treated Germany with such 'haughty disapproval'.[46] It was a line that was echoed, more bluntly, in Goebbels' diary. 'The Finns are whining that we offer them no help', he wrote, when they 'never helped us'.[47]

In fact, if there was any help being offered by Berlin, it was being offered to the Soviets. Talks began on the provisioning of Soviet submarines operating in the Gulf of Bothnia immediately upon the outbreak of the Finnish War, with the Germans keen to co-operate in anticipation of a quid pro quo elsewhere. A merchantman was found and converted, and a crew was raised, compete with three undercover Soviet officers. But then the Soviets seemingly got cold feet and called the operation off, perhaps wary about being too heavily indebted to their new ally.[48] Berlin's alacrity in the matter had been noticed, however, and the Finns consequently tended to view Germany more as an 'accomplice of the Soviet Union' than anything else.[49]

Despite such expressions of support, Stalin's annoyance at the humiliation of his Red Army at this most sensitive juncture was barely assuaged. At a meeting at his dacha outside Moscow in January 1940, he raged at the commander of the Finnish campaign, Marshal Kliment Voroshilov, who replied in the same tone, claiming that Stalin was to blame for the fiasco as he had had all the best generals killed during the purges. Voroshilov then smashed a plate of food in fury.[50] With that, a wholesale reorganisation of the Finnish operation became inevitable, and Marshal Semyon Timoshenko – one of the Red Army's ablest commanders and the mastermind of the Polish invasion four months earlier – was brought in to replace Voroshilov.

Timoshenko quickly set to work. Abandoning the costly eastern front, where the *motti* battles had so decimated Soviet forces, he concentrated his efforts on the Karelian Isthmus, packing the Soviet side of the front with 600,000 troops, backed by massed artillery and the newest tanks. In addition, he tightened the control and co-operation between the different branches of service in the Red Army, and issued a revised tactical doctrine. The Finns were to be forced to fight a conventional war for the narrow strip of the Mannerheim Line, against crushingly superior enemy forces. Finland would have its Thermopylae.

Timoshenko's assault began at dawn on 1 February 1940, with a rolling barrage of 300,000 shells pulverising defences and reviving memories of the First World War; in the town of Summa, for instance, 400 Soviet shells per minute rained in on Finnish positions.[51] Over the days and nights that followed, repeated artillery barrages combined with probing attacks by armoured columns, with massed infantry support, served to systematically degrade the defensive strongpoints, blockhouses and bunkers of the Mannerheim Line. After ten days of intense combat, the Finnish defenders were forced to withdraw to a secondary line of fortifications, but even that could not be held. Soviet spearheads were once again breaching the Finnish lines, with some Red Army infantry even circumventing the defences by a perilous detour across the ice of Lake Ladoga.[52] By the end of the month, Finland's forces were no longer able to resist.

Facing the inevitable, a Finnish delegation travelled to Moscow for negotiations on 7 March. In truth, there was little to negotiate, but keen to end the war and forestall the looming foreign intervention, Stalin offered remarkably moderate terms. Karelia, including the city of Viipuri as well as all of the Mannerheim fortifications, was to be ceded to Moscow, with further territorial losses mainly in the Arctic north and east. In addition, the Hanko peninsula at the western end of the Gulf of Finland would be leased to the USSR as a naval base for a period of thirty years.[53] Beyond that, there was to be no Soviet occupation, no puppet government, and no infringement of Finnish sovereignty. Kuusinen was pensioned off to run the rump Karelo-Finnish Soviet Republic, which incorporated the ceded lands and stood in wait to incorporate more Finnish territory – or indeed all of Finland – should the necessity arise. The resulting Treaty of Moscow was signed on 12 March, and the guns fell silent the following day. Some 25,000 Finns had been killed over barely a hundred days of fighting. The Soviet death toll – still disputed – is estimated at over 200,000,[54] but as Khrushchev candidly admitted, 'our people . . . were never told the truth'.[55]

Considering such losses, and the horrors of the Winter War itself, the people of the Baltic states might have been forgiven for thinking that they had got off lightly by acceding to Moscow's demands and submitting merely to the establishment of Soviet bases on their territory. Certainly, Molotov was keen to emphasise the benign nature of the new arrangements. As he stressed to the Supreme Soviet in October 1939: 'These pacts are inspired by mutual respect for the governmental, social and economic system of each of the contracting parties', adding that 'foolish talk of Sovietisation of the Baltic states is useful only to our common enemies'.[56] His Baltic counterparts, meanwhile, did their best to put a positive spin on events, but they were soon to be disabused of any such optimism.

The emptiness of Soviet promises of 'non-intervention' in the internal affairs of the Baltic states was exposed almost from the very outset. Though relations were outwardly correct, behind the scenes there was considerable friction. Arriving teams of Soviet military personnel, charged with setting up the bases agreed with Moscow, routinely demanded more than had been stipulated in the treaties. In Latvia, for instance, an additional coastal strip – fifty kilometres wide – was requested as a Soviet 'military zone',[57] while in Lithuania the Red Army demanded the right to establish a garrison in Vilnius.[58] In Estonia, meanwhile, two additional airfields and further bases were ceded to the Soviets. Across the region, the numbers of incoming troops quickly exceeded those initially agreed, and rental and compensation packages – stipulated by the treaties – were ignored. The attitude of one Soviet major was perhaps emblematic of Moscow's high-handed attitude towards its new 'allies': 'The Red Army knows only one government', he said, 'and that is the government of the Soviet Union.'[59]

Despite such distinctly unneighbourly attitudes, the degree of premeditation and conspiracy involved in the Soviet subversion of the Baltic states is traditionally exaggerated. Most writers on the subject cite an NKVD document from October 1939, known as 'Order 001223', which is presented as proof of Moscow's intention to 'cleanse' the Baltic states of all 'anti-Soviet elements', in effect anticipating the deportations of 1941 already in 1939, at a time when the Baltic states had not yet been annexed. However, this is incorrect. 'Order 001223', which has never been published in the West, is thought to relate to affairs in newly annexed eastern Poland, but has habitually been confused with the instruction with regard to the Baltic states which was issued by Ivan Serov in the spring of 1941 and is quoted below (p. 251).[60] In fact, it seems sensible to suggest that Soviet plans regarding the Baltic states were much more gradualist in nature, evidently based on the belief that the close relationship fomented by the 'bases agreements' would inevitably lead to a groundswell of popular enthusiasm in favour of union with the USSR. When Comintern chief Georgi Dimitrov wrote about the Baltic mutual assistance pacts in his diary in the autumn of 1939, he betrayed Moscow's rather optimistic thinking on the issue. 'We have found the right form to allow us to bring a number of countries into the Soviet Union's sphere of influence', he wrote. 'We are not going to seek their Sovietisation. The time will come when they will do that for themselves!'[61]

The reality would be rather more prosaic. It is likely that the decision to occupy and Sovietise the Baltic states crystallised gradually through the early spring and summer of 1940. In the first instance, underground communist activity in the Baltic region spiked in March of that year, provoking an inevitable deterioration in relations between the Baltic governments and Moscow. In due course, incidents involving the Soviet 'guests' began to multiply: in Estonia, Soviet warships fired on an Estonian aircraft over Tallinn,[62] and in Latvia a local man was shot dead by two drunk Soviet officers.[63] Increasingly, local populations who were already predominantly anti-communist began to view the Soviets with open contempt and tensions rose further. While politicians tried to play such incidents down and maintain a positive commentary on relations with Moscow, in private some were beginning to feel the chill. At the end of April 1940, for instance, the Lithuanian ambassador in Moscow reported home that 'a black cat [had] crossed the road of Soviet–Lithuanian relations'.[64]

The 'black cat' did not go unnoticed. Already in May 1940, contingency plans were being prepared by the Latvian and Lithuanian governments, arranging for powers to pass to selected diplomatic representatives in the event that contact with the home country was broken. The Estonians, meanwhile, arranged for some of their gold reserve, along with a part of the state archives, to be shipped abroad. In desperation, the Lithuanian president, Antanas Smetona, even offered his country as a protectorate to the Germans.[65]

For their part, the Soviets presented a litany of complaints. They protested that the Baltic elites had hampered the deployment of the Red Army the previous autumn, delaying negotiations and dragging their feet on construction. They also claimed to have been troubled by the inevitable climate of hostility. In Latvia, for instance, it was suggested that civilians who so much as spoke to Soviet personnel were liable to arrest, and a 'malevolent atmosphere' encouraged espionage against Soviet installations.[66] Moscow was also doubtless frustrated because it had been obliged to revise its earlier idea that the ordinary working people of the Baltic states would welcome its soldiers' presence, and that they would prove amenable to a Soviet-style revolution. Unsurprisingly, then, relations had become strained by the early summer of 1940. In time, events far to the west would provide the catalyst for a further, terminal, deterioration.

Hitler's share of the spoils from the Nazi–Soviet Pact had not been insubstantial. Not only did he get his desired campaign against the Poles, dividing Poland with Stalin in the process, but he also had the prospect of Soviet economic aid helping him to sidestep the worst effects of the expected British blockade of Germany. Yet most important perhaps for Hitler was the question of *Rückendeckung*: the fact that the pact with Stalin had covered his rear, allowing him to turn west with impunity, thereby avoiding the spectre of a two-front war. So it was that Hitler sent his troops into Scandinavia in April 1940, essentially to forestall a planned British operation to occupy Narvik in northern Norway, and to secure the strategically vital Norwegian western coast. The occupation went relatively smoothly; in Denmark only a few dozen casualties were incurred in an operation that lasted barely six hours. Norway was rather more complex, seeing stiff resistance from the Norwegian army as well as an attempted Allied intervention at Narvik, which was finally defeated in mid-June.

By that time, after six months of the so-called 'Phoney War', the campaign in the west of Europe was already under way. When Hitler's tanks finally rolled into France and the Low Countries on 10 May 1940, it appeared to the rest of Europe and the world that battle had finally been joined – that the crucial contest to decide who would control the continent of Europe was now afoot. As the British general Alan Brooke noted in his diary on the first day of the campaign: 'one of the greatest battles in history' had begun.[67]

It was certainly substantial. Between them, the opposing forces on the western front amounted to 285 divisions and over 7 million men. They were evenly matched in manpower and materiel – with French tanks even considered superior – but a German advantage in morale and strategy was decisive. Bypassing the Maginot Line and driving through the Ardennes forests, German armoured spearheads out-thought and outpaced the British and French, forcing them inexorably backwards and into one of the most catastrophic defeats of modern military history. Far from the static, plodding rerun of the First World War that Stalin and others had envisaged, it would be a campaign that was characterised by rapid movement – the very epitome of what came to be known as the blitzkrieg.[68]

With the world's attention thus focused on events on the Maginot Line, Sedan and the forests of the Ardennes, Moscow appears to have sensed an opportunity to consolidate its grip on the Baltic. On 16 May, an article in *Izvestia* used the recent experience of Belgium,

Luxembourg and the Netherlands to claim that 'the neutrality of small states . . . is a mere fantasy' and warned that such states should be reminded that 'the policy of neutrality could not be called anything but suicide'.[69] The warning was to be instantly and grimly prophetic.

Two days before the *Izvestia* article, Molotov had been informed by his Lithuanian counterparts about the case of a junior Red Army officer by the name of Butaev, who had apparently been kidnapped in Lithuania and had since died in mysterious circumstances. Ordinarily, perhaps, such an event – though troubling – would not cause an international incident, but May 1940 was no ordinary time. The Soviet response was not slow to materialise. On 25 May, just as British and French forces were reeling under the German onslaught in the west, Molotov requested the presence of the Lithuanian ambassador in the Kremlin. He informed his guest that, in addition to Butaev, two further Red Army soldiers had gone missing in Lithuania, alleging that they had been plied with drink, involved in criminal activities and induced to desert. Responsibility for such events, Molotov asserted, lay with the Lithuanian authorities, who clearly desired to provoke the Soviet Union, and he closed by demanding that the Lithuanian government should 'take the necessary steps . . . to halt such provocative action', lest he be forced to 'take other measures'.[70]

Soviet ire was evidently not restricted to the Lithuanians. On 28 May, an article in *Pravda* criticised the 'loyal attitude' that it perceived among the Estonian intelligentsia towards Great Britain, complaining that the University of Tartu, for instance, was a veritable hotbed of 'pro-British propaganda'.[71] An Estonian delegation at a book exhibition in Moscow personally experienced the abrupt change of climate. Arriving on 26 May, they had been warmly welcomed and feted, but two days later the atmosphere became so hostile that they were obliged to return home ahead of schedule.[72]

As the British and French faltered before German aggression in the west, so the Baltic states were exposed to the full fury of Molotov's diplomatic offensive. On 30 May – while the Dunkirk evacuation was at its height – formal accusations were levelled at the Lithuanian government, alleging official collusion in the recent 'outrages' against Red Army soldiers. Hurrying to Moscow,

Lithuanian prime minister Antanas Merkys found Molotov in
unyielding mood. On 7 June, the Soviet foreign minister demanded
that two prominent members of the Lithuanian cabinet should be
removed; two days later he accused Lithuania of conspiring with
Estonia and Latvia to establish an anti-Soviet military alliance. On
the third meeting, on 11 June, with Merkys and the Lithuanian
cabinet offering everything possible to placate him, Molotov was
determined not to be mollified and poured scorn on Lithuanian
protestations of innocence. After only an hour, the meeting broke
up and Merkys returned to Vilnius, unaware that his efforts had had
little purpose because the Red Army was already preparing its
invasion.[73]

On the night of 14 June 1940, while the world was transfixed by
the entry of German troops into Paris, Molotov delivered the *coup
de grâce*. Submitting an ultimatum to the Lithuanians, he demanded
the arrest and trial of the two cabinet members of whom he disap-
proved, and the formation of a new government that would be
capable of repairing relations with Moscow. Finally, an unspecified
number of additional Soviet troops were to be allowed to enter
Lithuanian territory to help preserve order. An answer was required
by 10 o'clock the following morning.

Lithuania's agony was soon shared by her neighbours. On 15 June,
as the government in Vilnius collapsed and the Red Army began its
unopposed invasion, Estonia was already blockaded. Now the same
ultimatum that had been handed to the Lithuanians was issued to
Latvia and Estonia. As if to heighten tensions still further, Soviet
forces staged provocations against Baltic targets. At Masļenki on
15 June, five Latvian border guards and civilians were ambushed and
killed by NKVD troops; the day before, a Finnish civilian aircraft –
the Kaleva – had been shot down by Soviet bombers en route to
Helsinki from Tallinn, with the loss of all nine passengers and crew
on board, as well as a bag of French diplomatic mail, which was
picked up by a Soviet submarine.[74] The furore that followed both
incidents was quickly silenced by the Soviet invasion.

There would be a chilling symmetry between events at either end
of the European continent that June. On 17 June, only days after
Wehrmacht troops paraded down the Champs-Elysées in Paris, the
Red Army trundled on to the streets of the Latvian capital, Riga.

The watching civilian populations of both cities were similarly dismayed and fearful. While the world had been distracted by Hitler's spectacular victory over the French and British in the west, Lithuania, Latvia and Estonia had quietly surrendered their independence. The followng day, Molotov extended his 'warmest congratulations' to Schulenburg on the 'splendid success of the German armed forces' in France.[75] He might have expected the compliment to be returned.

As the respective national leaders of the Baltic states shuffled their governments, trying desperately to find communists and fellow travellers who might be deemed acceptable to Moscow, a few of the senior national politicians stayed in place, hoping perhaps that something of value might be salvaged from the crisis. It was an attitude that was typified by the response of the Latvian president, Kārlis Ulmanis, who stressed continuity to his people in a radio address: 'I will stay in my place, you stay in yours.'[76] He would indeed remain in office until he was arrested by the NKVD.

Others would not be so accommodating. General Ludvigs Bolšteins, commander of the Latvian Border Guards, committed suicide, leaving a scathing note to his superiors: 'We, the Latvians, built ourselves a brand new house – our country. Now an alien power wants to force us to tear it down ourselves. In this I cannot take part.'[77] The Lithuanian president, Antanas Smetona – who had been an advocate of armed resistance against the Soviets – fled to the safety of German East Prussia by wading across a brook; the Soviet press reported mockingly that he turned his trousers up to do so.[78] Smetona's foreign minister, Juozas Urbšys, who was already in Moscow on diplomatic business, was simply arrested. Such people were soon replaced. On the same day that Smetona fled, Stalin's representative Vladimir Dekanozov arrived in Vilnius, followed by Andrei Zhdanov in Estonia and Andrei Vyshinsky in Latvia. These three senior Moscow officials would oversee the rapid incorporation of the Baltic states into the USSR. As Molotov made clear to the new Lithuanian foreign minister, Vincas Krėvė-Mickevičius, there was to be no alternative:

> You must take a good look at reality and understand that in future small nations will have to disappear. Your Lithuania, along with the other Baltic nations . . . will have to join the glorious family of

the Soviet Union. Therefore you should begin to initiate your people into the Soviet system, which in future shall reign everywhere, throughout all Europe.[79]

To his credit, Krėvė-Mickevičius would resign in protest, once he had returned home, exclaiming that he did not want to participate in the burial of Lithuanian independence.[80]

Events moved with dizzying speed that summer. After their experience in eastern Poland the previous autumn, the Soviets were already well practised in the art of 'democratic demolition'. Within a month, across all three Baltic states, elections were called by the newly formed, Moscow-friendly governments. This in itself would have been quite a novelty, as all three states had spawned authoritarian – albeit largely benign – governments in the 1930s, but the Soviet variant of democracy was even less worthy of the name. Only approved candidates were permitted to stand, all others were removed from the ballot and arrested. Voting was compulsory, with those spoiling their ballot or refusing to vote risking arrest: 'Only enemies of the people stay at home on election day', warned one Estonian newspaper.[81] To reassure the people, Soviet representatives were at pains to stress that the independence of the Baltic nations would be respected, vehemently denying that incorporation into the USSR was in the offing. The results were preordained, to the point that they were even accidentally announced in Moscow before the polls had closed: 97.2 per cent of Latvian voters were said to have voted for the approved list, 99.2 per cent in Lithuania and 92.8 per cent in Estonia.[82] Voter turnout was also unfeasibly high, ranging between 84 and 95 per cent; one electoral precinct in Lithuania even achieved the remarkable feat of voter turnout reaching 122 per cent. The true figure across all Lithuania has been estimated at barely 16 per cent.[83]

Once compliant 'people's parliaments' were installed, all that was left for them was to vote themselves out of existence. The first act of each, therefore, upon meeting in late July, was to petition Moscow for accession to the USSR as a constituent republic. After a period of 'consultation' the Supreme Soviet in Moscow duly granted the requests: Lithuania became a Soviet republic on 3 August 1940, Latvia followed two days later and Estonia on 6 August. In Vilnius, Riga and Tallinn, there were confusion and humiliation as people sought to take in what had happened to them, and to the independent states that they had once inhabited. In desperation, a few took to the forests to fight the Soviet occupiers; others chose more passive forms of protest such as placing flowers at national memorials, or singing patriotic songs. Khrushchev would later write in his memoirs, without a hint of irony, that the annexation of the Baltic states was a 'great triumph' for the Baltic peoples, as it gave them 'the chance to live in conditions equal to those of the working class, peasantry, and labouring intelligentsia of Russia'.[84]

Germany's leadership was swift to recognise the new reality – all of which, of course, was in accordance with the agreed terms of the secret protocol to the Nazi–Soviet Pact and its successor agreement – but it was a little more difficult to carry domestic opinion, which still tended to be distrustful of the Soviet Union. As if to sweeten the pill, Hitler ordered another round of evacuations of ethnic Germans from the Baltic region, which proved a godsend for those *Volksdeutsche* who had previously opted to remain behind and had now seen their worst fears realised. Accordingly, once procedures were formalised in January 1941, there was a second wave of evacuations from the former Baltic states, including many with only the most tenuous claims to German nationality. In Lithuania, over 50,000 volunteered to leave for Germany, despite the country's remaining German population being estimated at barely 35,000. In Estonia, meanwhile, it was observed by one official that, if the Soviets had allowed it, the vast majority of the Estonian population would have asked to be resettled.[85]

German largesse was very much restricted to the *Volksdeutsche*, however. If the Baltic states had imagined that they would receive a sympathetic hearing in Berlin, they were sorely mistaken; the procedures ordered by the German foreign ministry were scrupulously correct, but perceptibly cool. A circular from 17 June reminded all staff that Soviet actions in the region 'are the concern of Russia and the Baltic states' and warned them to 'refrain . . . from making any statement which could be interpreted as partisan'.[86] A week later, after Latvian and Lithuanian diplomats in Berlin had both lodged notes of protest with their German counterparts over the formal incorporation of their countries into the Soviet Union, those notes were duly returned – 'in a friendly manner' – with the reminder that such protests could only be accepted if they were presented in the name of their governments.[87] As the diplomats no longer spoke in this capacity, they were effectively redundant. For one of them, it was all too much. Lithuanian chargé Kazys Škirpa had questioned German press reporting on the crisis complaining that only the Soviet version of events had been aired and that no sign of sympathy for Lithuania was in evidence. When he was told that German officials were refraining from any comment on the issue, according to the foreign-office record, he 'burst into tears and could not recover for some time'.[88] While German officials obfuscated, Goebbels – in his diary at least – was brutally honest. 'Lithuania, Latvia and Estonia transferred . . . to the Soviet Union', he wrote. 'This is the price we pay for Russian neutrality.'[89]

The West withheld its blessing. The British, painfully aware of their own impotence, refused to recognise the Soviet annexations, but refrained from making any specific comment on events and continued to deal as before with the – now exiled – representatives of the Baltic governments. Nonetheless, in British government circles the idea of a de facto recognition of the annexations was soon floated as a possible sop to bring Stalin onside. The American reaction was rather more principled. Undersecretary of State Sumner Welles issued a formal statement – the Welles Declaration – condemning Soviet aggression and refusing to recognise the legitimacy of Soviet control in the region, citing 'the rule of reason, of justice and of law', without which, he said, 'civilization itself cannot be preserved'.[90] In private he was more forthright, and when the Soviet ambassador, Konstantin Oumansky, opined that the United States should applaud Soviet action in the Baltic, as it meant that the Baltic peoples could enjoy 'the blessings of liberal and social government', his response was withering. 'The US government', Welles explained, 'sees no difference in principle between the Russian domination of the Baltic peoples and the occupation by Germany of other small European nations.'[91] Strong words, perhaps, but the point that they expressed was moot; barely six weeks after the Red Army invasion, the Baltic states had effectively ceased to exist.

At the same time that the Baltic littoral was being drawn inexorably into Moscow's orbit, Stalin turned his gaze south-west towards

Romania and the province of Bessarabia, which had been lost by Moscow in the aftermath of the First World War. As in the Baltic example, Molotov's sense of urgency was spurred by the awareness that the fall of France offered a unique opportunity for him to act while the world was looking the other way. France and Britain had offered a guarantee to Romania in March 1939, so with the defeat of the Western Allies on the continent, Bucharest was effectively at the mercy of Moscow. As Deputy Defence Commissar Lev Mekhlis wrote the day before France fell: 'Bessarabia must be snatched from the thieving hands of the Romanian aristocrats.'[92]

Officially at least, Germany's position on Bessarabia mirrored that which she had adopted towards the Baltic states. When the German ambassador in Moscow, Schulenburg, was sounded out to ascertain Berlin's intentions with regard to the region, he gave Molotov the green light – reiterating the 'political disinterest'[93] that had been expressed when the secret protocol had been drawn up nearly a year before. Yet beyond that, there was a concern in Berlin that the Soviets were edging ever closer to Germany's vital interests – the Romanian oilfields at Ploiești – and to this end Ribbentrop had privately sought to defuse the crisis, fearing that the region could become a battle-ground. However, flushed with his recent successes, Molotov would not be deterred and on 26 June 1940 issued an ultimatum to the Romanian government in Bucharest, demanding the evacuation of all civil and military representatives from Bessarabia, and requesting a reply within twenty-four hours. Bessarabia, it read, had been taken by Romania while the Soviet Union was weak, and was now to be returned. In addition, by way of 'compensation . . . for the tremendous loss' which the Soviet Union had suffered, the neighbouring region of Northern Bukovina was to be transferred to Soviet control as well.[94]

Like their unfortunate Baltic counterparts, the Romanian government toyed with the idea of resistance – the firebrand former prime minister Nicolae Iorga exclaimed: 'Curse us all if we don't fight!'[95] – but cooler heads within the cabinet prevailed, particularly when they were urged to comply by their German allies. On the morning of 28 June, they agreed to submit to Soviet demands with the words: 'In order to avoid the serious consequences which might follow the use of force and the opening of hostilities in this part of Europe, the Romanian government finds itself obliged to accept the . . . evacuation.'[96] The Romanian withdrawal from the region began that same day, and within two days the Red Army had taken their place.

It was an arrival that often came as a shock to the inhabitants. At Cernăuți (Czernowitz), on the morning of 28 June, an eyewitness recalled that: 'You had the feeling that hell was upon the earth.'[97] Another described the reaction: 'churches rang their bells, as if tolling a death-knell. People were running. Some knelt down to pray. Many were in a state of shock. A low wail was resounding down the streets'. He went on to describe the desperate civilian evacuation:

> The atmosphere of desolation was intensifying hour by hour. Hundreds upon hundreds of people were heading for the railway station carrying what they had collected in just a few hours. All goods, vans and cattle wagons were lined up in a hurry. People were asked to pack in so that the space should hold as many as possible.[98]

As the last train left Cernăuți, at 2 o'clock that afternoon, the first Soviet spearheads were already entering the city. Communists, naturally, were much more positive. Jacob Pesate had journeyed from Budapest to Cernăuți the day before the Red Army's arrival – just as many Bessarabians were fleeing in the opposite direction – as he wanted to greet the soldiers personally 'with flowers'.[99] Meanwhile, Red Army Marshal Timoshenko took the time to pay a propaganda visit to his native village of Furmanivka in southern Bessarabia, where he was supposedly greeted as a returning hero.[100]

Bessarabia and Northern Bukovina were swiftly incorporated. In early August 1940, the two provinces were divided between neighbouring Soviet Ukraine and the new Moldavian Soviet Socialist Republic, adding 3.5 million citizens and 50,000 square kilometres of territory to the Soviet Union. In total, as Molotov would gleefully inform the seventh session of the Supreme Soviet, the annexations of that summer had brought an additional 10 million souls under Moscow's control, in addition to the 13 million added with the expansion into eastern Poland the year before.[101] Though the two provinces would be erased from the map, they would not disappear from popular memory. As diplomat Alexander Cretzianu recalled, their loss and the brutal circumstances of their annexation caused a 'deep-seated resentment' in Romania and 'a desire for revenge'.[102]

Life in the new Soviet Socialist Republics of Estonia, Latvia, Lithuania and Moldavia was quickly co-ordinated to conform to that in the remainder of the Soviet Union. Over the weeks and months that followed the annexations, the Soviet constitution and law code were adopted and all political parties that were deemed 'unfriendly' to the Soviet Union were banned. The old regional administrations were ruthlessly purged: in Lithuania, for instance, eleven out of twelve mayors of principal cities were removed, as well as nineteen out of twenty-three town mayors and 175 out of 261 regional gover-nors.[103] Police forces were disbanded and replaced by communist militias, often comprised of former political prisoners. Planned economies were introduced, with private property outlawed and businesses and industries nationalised and placed under central administrative control. A partial collectivisation of the land was carried out affecting the largest estates, with a number of collective farms being established and land redistributed. All youth and student organisations were banned or else forcibly incorporated into the youth organisations of the Soviet Union, with cultural and peda-gogical output being thoroughly Sovietised, and Marxist–Leninist principles adopted across academic and intellectual life. A list of banned books – those with nationalist or 'reactionary' content – was produced and all offending titles were removed from bookshops and libraries to be pulped, or in some cases burnt. Schoolbooks were also 'edited', with offending pages being simply torn out and discarded. The churches, although nominally spared closure, were nonetheless harassed and persecuted, with clergy and congregations placed under surveillance or subjected to arbitrary arrest and services disrupted by 'atheist brigades'.[104]

Some, certainly, did not experience the change as dramatically as others. One Latvian, for instance, remembered the early period after the annexation as surreal rather than immediately threatening, with everyday life continuing on its course, despite the ubiquitous pres-ence of Soviet troops and the jaunty marches incessantly played by Red Army bands.[105] Yet for all the apparent normality, the Soviet regime was already showing its teeth, with those who displeased the NKVD facing arrest, interrogation and torture. The first to feel

Soviet wrath were the old political elites. Now surplus to requirements, the former president of Latvia, Kārlis Ulmanis, and the acting
president of Lithuania, Antanas Merkys, were arrested by the NKVD
and deported. They had stayed on in the hope of salvaging something from the catastrophe, but would now form the vanguard of
their countrymen shipped to an uncertain fate in the Soviet interior.
They would be followed by the majority of their fellow politicians:
fifty-one of the fifty-three former ministers of the Estonian government, for instance, were arrested in 1940–1,[106] as were all but one of
the thirteen serving ministers of the Latvian government, the sole
exception being the minister for social affairs, Alfrēds Bērziņš, who
escaped to Finland in 1940.[107] In Lithuania the situation was no
different. Already on the eve of the elections of that summer, the
NKVD had rounded up 2,000 or so of the political class, who were
deemed to be a potential threat.[108] One of them was the former
minister of justice, Antanas Tamošaitis, a professor of law and a
socialist, who had chaired a commission to investigate the earlier
Soviet claims about Red Army soldiers being 'encouraged' to desert.
He was tortured to death in Kaunas prison.[109]

One story testifies to the collective horror. Konstantin Päts was
already sixty-six when he was arrested by the NKVD in the summer
of 1940. A veteran politician, who was in many ways the godfather
of independent Estonia, he had served in most senior positions in
government, and finally as president from 1938. In 1940, when the
Soviets arrived, Päts had hoped that by remaining at his post, he
could ameliorate the worst effects of Soviet rule, but he was
mistaken. Arrested with his family on 29 June, he was deported a
month later and spent a year in provincial obscurity at Ufa in the
Urals, under house arrest. In July 1941, he was picked up by the
NKVD once again, separated from his family and sent to prison,
convicted of counter-revolutionary sabotage. Päts would end his
days consigned to a psychiatric hospital, declared insane by the Soviet
authorities because he persistently claimed that he was president of
Estonia – which, morally perhaps, he still was.[110]

As well as the political class, the military forces of the Baltic states
also faced violent upheaval and 'co-ordination'. Though the vast
majority of ordinary soldiers were simply incorporated wholesale
into the Red Army in the autumn of 1940 – from which many would

subsequently desert – their officers would face a much more sinister fate. NKVD methods were simple: suspect elements would be ordered to attend special 'training courses' at remote army camps, where they would then be selected for deportation to the Soviet interior or simply shot. As one Lithuanian eyewitness recalled:

> Commanders of battalions, companies and some platoons were called to the headquarters of the regiment, told that they were going on reconnaissance training, put into trucks, and taken into the forest. There they were brutally disarmed, robbed, squeezed into cattle cars at the Varėna railroad station and deported.[111]

As many as 6,500 officers and men of the Lithuanian army are thought to have been deported in this way or shot. A similar fate awaited members of the Latvian armed forces. At Litene, for example, around 200 officers were executed and over 500 were deported to the camp complex at Norilsk in the Soviet far north – dubbed the 'Baltic Katyn' – where they would perform hard labour in horrific conditions in nickel and copper mines. As one of the deportees noted years later: 'A quick death . . . would have been a far kinder fate than all of those terrible years spent in the hell camps of the north.'[112] Fewer than one in five of his fellows would survive the experience.[113]

Once the political and military elites had been dealt with, the Soviets moved on to ordinary citizens picked up for minor transgressions or considered guilty by association. Those arrested would generally be charged under the catch-all of 'anti-Soviet activities', whether carried out privately or in their public life. In this first phase, it is estimated that over 7,000 people were arrested or deported in Estonia, 7,000 in Latvia and 12,000 in Lithuania.[114] In Bessarabia and Northern Bukovina, meanwhile, some 48,000 are thought to have been arrested, with 12,000 deported and as many as over 8,000 executed or dying during NKVD interrogation.[115]

Many of those who survived the NKVD's jails testified to the bestial nature of the tortures that they endured, with sleep deprivation, threats and casual violence as the basis for most interrogations. Other methods included electrocution, choking or drowning, and the infamous 'manicure', where needles were inserted beneath the victim's nails. After enduring such techniques, many exhausted prisoners were willing to sign their 'confessions', especially if it meant that the threat of further questioning was removed. As one prisoner recalled: 'NKVD official Sokolov began talking to me in a calm voice, saying "You see what we have made of you . . . We know how to turn a man into nothing, to push him into the dark. But we also know how to wash dirt from a man. If you admit your guilt, we will call off the interrogation."'[116] It took a brave man to resist.

Some of the 'crimes' recorded were extremely petty. Andres Raska, for instance, was a 24-year-old student imprisoned in 1940 for distributing lapel ribbons in the Estonian national colours.[117] Deported to the Soviet Union, he died in a camp in Kirov in the summer of 1942. Ironically, at the time of Raska's arrest, the pre-war Estonian flag still had official status, but in the Kafkaesque world of the Soviet occupation, its distribution was enough to earn him deportation to the Gulag.

Other cases reflected the prevailing Soviet paranoia or the mania for revenge against former anti-Bolsheviks. Ex-'Whites' from the Civil War were often among the first to be targeted. One of them was Oleg Vasilkovski, who was over sixty when he was arrested in the summer of 1940. A general in the Tsarist Army in the First World War, he had drifted into Yudenich's 'White' Army in 1919, before settling in Tallinn, where he had eschewed politics and worked as a chandler. Deported to Leningrad in 1941, he was sentenced to death. His precise fate is unknown.[118]

Priests, too, were singled out for especially harsh treatment. In Bessarabia, in late August 1940, NKVD troops interrupted Mass at an orthodox church in Călăraşi and attempted to arrest the priest, Alexandru Baltagă. Baltagă bravely refused to leave his flock until Mass was finished, so the officers returned the following night and took him for interrogation to nearby Cernăuţi, where he was accused of having supported the union of Bessarabia with Romania back in 1918, and challenged to 'show your God'. Predictably, after a lengthy interrogation, he was sentenced to a spell of re-education in the Gulag. Already frail, Baltagă would not survive the experience: he died, aged eighty, in 1941.[119]

A final chilling example was recorded by Menachem Begin, the later prime minister of Israel. Born in Brest, Begin had fled to Vilnius on the outbreak of war in 1939, but was arrested by the NKVD in September 1940, accused of being a British agent. Under interrogation, he was alarmed to discover that Soviet 'justice' was an extremely elastic concept, which was not restricted by time or national borders. When asked by his interrogator if he knew the section of the Soviet law code under which he was being charged, Begin confessed that he did not. 'You are charged under Section 58 of the Criminal Law of the Soviet Socialist Russian Republic', he was told, with the added detail that the section had been 'written by Vladimir Ilyich Lenin himself'. Begin was confused. 'But how can it apply to what I did in Poland?' he asked. 'Ach! You are a strange fellow, Menachem Wolfovitch', the NKVD officer replied. 'Section 58 applies to everyone in the world. Do you hear? *In the whole world*. It is only a question of when he will get to us, or we to him.'[120]

And so Stalin and Hitler divided much of Europe between them in 1940. Hitler occupied Norway, Denmark, Belgium, Holland, Luxembourg and northern France – a total of over 800,000 square kilometres. Although Great Britain remained technically undefeated, she was confined to her island; and the USA, while increasingly antagonistic towards Germany, was still neutral. Nazi Germany, therefore, became the pre-eminent power on the continent of Europe. Stalin did less well territorially, with only around half of Hitler's haul at 422,000 square kilometres, but was arguably better placed to actually absorb his gains, given that all of them were long-standing Russian irredenta, with some tradition of rule from Moscow, and all were neatly contiguous to the western frontier of the USSR.

In occupying those lands, of course, Stalin was just taking that which had been promised to him by Hitler in August 1939. Only the tiny territory of Northern Bukovina – barely 5,000 square kilometres – lay beyond the list of lands ascribed to him under the Nazi–Soviet Pact. Hitler could have few complaints, therefore. This was the price that he had agreed to pay to secure his rear while he turned west to fight the British and the French; it was the price of his dramatic solution to the 'Polish Question', and of the economic relationship that was supposed to render the British blockade ineffective.

Neither can Hitler have seriously cried foul about Soviet tactics in securing and 'pacifying' its new territories. Certainly the NKVD operated with exemplary rigour and brutality in annexing the Baltic states, Bessarabia and Northern Bukovina and 'co-ordinating' their respective societies to Soviet norms. Yet Hitler's Gestapo and SS were no less rigorous or brutal in enforcing their 'New Order' in Poland and the west: the two sides even employed similar tactics – deportation, hard labour and execution.

And yet Hitler was clearly disquieted by Soviet actions in the summer of 1940. He first learned of the Soviet intention to occupy Bessarabia while he was visiting Paris in late June, with his architect Albert Speer and sculptor Arno Breker in tow. He was said to have flown into a rage, demanding that Ribbentrop show him a copy of the secret protocol as he could not believe that he would have agreed to such a move. When he was presented with the proof, he could do nothing but seethe and have Ribbentrop register a protest.[121] His irritation was such that his Moscow ambassador, Schulenburg, sought desperately to conceal Stalin's strategic motives from Hitler, instead attributing the move to the influence of a mythical Ukrainian clique in the Kremlin. Acknowledging the truth, Schulenburg knew, would be to imply a looming clash of interests.[122]

Hitler had no particular love for Romania, of course, seeing that country as a corrupt Francophile kingdom that had been a recipient of the Anglo-French guarantee eighteen months earlier. But Romania's loss of Bessarabia nonetheless worried him, not only because of the proximity of Soviet forces to the vital Romanian oilfields, but also because he interpreted it as a dangerous westward move and a symbol of Stalin's undiminished territorial ambition. Though he said nothing in public, Hitler complained to his adjutants that the Soviet annexation of Bessarabia signified 'the first Russian attack on Western Europe'.[123]

Goebbels concurred, at least in his diary. On 28 June, when the Romanian government submitted to a Soviet ultimatum, he was damning. 'King Carol is a coward', he said, 'but Stalin is seizing the moment. Grave-robber! All down to our success. We make victory easy for others.' Already the following week, he was speculating whether 'maybe we will have to move against the Soviets after all'.[124] A month later, doubtless echoing his master's voice, he had clearly begun thinking seriously of some sort of reckoning with Stalin's

USSR. Writing in his diary in August 1940, he pondered whether: 'Perhaps we will be forced to take steps against all this, despite everything. And drive this Asiatic spirit back out of Europe and into Asia, where it belongs.'[125]

4

Contortions

In the first week of September 1939, Harry Pollitt sat down in his office, in London's bustling Covent Garden, to write a pamphlet. Round-faced with a receding hairline and prominent dark eyebrows, the 48-year-old Pollitt was general secretary of the Communist Party of Great Britain, and it was part of his role as leader to provide a commentary on current events that not only delineated the position of the Communist International, but also explained matters in terms that could be readily digested by the thousands of ordinary workers who made up the party's membership. To this end, he had penned numerous titles in previous years, including *Towards Soviet Power, Save Spain from Fascism* and *Czechoslovakia Betrayed*. This, however, would be his most controversial piece of work.

Pollitt was certainly well regarded within the communist movement. Growing up in Manchester, he had imbibed his socialist radicalism with his mother's milk, trained as a boilermaker, and graduated as an industrial militant working in the Southampton docks during the First World War. Joining the nascent Communist Party upon its foundation in 1920, he was a talented and impassioned public speaker, so much so that he was even kidnapped briefly by his fascist opponents in 1925 to prevent him from attending a party meeting in Liverpool. Rising through the ranks, propelled by the power of his oratory, as well as by his unswerving loyalty to the communist cause and the Soviet state, Pollitt was appointed general secretary in 1929.

Through the 1930s, then, it was Pollitt who had charted the course of British communism. Aided by the rather more arid, theoretical abilities of Rajani Palme Dutt, the party's senior ideologist, he spearheaded an impressive rise in communist fortunes in Britain, skilfully exploiting the economic and social woes of the age, and showing a natural capacity for leadership. Pollitt was especially passionate about events in Spain, where he would be a regular visitor in the late 1930s to galvanise British volunteer battalions. As one of his later biographers would suggest, his anti-fascism was not mere communist orthodoxy, it stemmed from a deep emotional commitment, derived largely from the Spanish Civil War.[1] Yet, by the summer of 1939, the ideological clarity of that bipolar world of communist versus fascist seemed to be fading. Pollitt did not yet realise it, but he was approaching something of a personal and political watershed.

Initially, the events of that first week of September 1939 had appeared to conform to the old, comfortable idea of a left–right conflict. Pollitt had not been unduly perturbed by the signature of the Nazi–Soviet Pact a week previously, contriving to see that agreement as 'a victory for peace and socialism',[2] and as damning proof of the unwillingness of Britain's ruling class to deal fairly with the USSR. The German invasion of Poland on 1 September and the British declaration of war two days later had then surprised many on the left, who had expected to see some sort of accommodation reached between the 'semi-fascist' government of Chamberlain, as they saw it, and the über-fascist government of Hitler. Nonetheless, a new 'party line' had quickly crystallised, sanctioned by the Comintern[3] and penned by Pollitt himself, calling for a 'two-front war' against Hitler abroad and Chamberlain at home.[4]

It was by way of clarification of this rather complex position that Pollitt resolved to write his pamphlet, entitled *How to Win the War*. In thirty-two closely typed pages, he laid out the British Communist Party's position on the war then beginning. In one memorable passage, he proclaimed that:

> to stand aside from this conflict, to contribute only revolutionary-sounding phrases, while the fascist beasts ride roughshod over Europe, would be a betrayal of everything our forebears have fought to achieve in the course of long years of struggle against capitalism.

Just as the Abyssinians had been right to fight the Italians, he wrote, and just as the Spanish had been right to take up arms against Italian and German invaders, so 'the Polish people are right to fight against the Nazi invasion that is now taking place'. Although Pollitt reiterated the policy of a 'two-front' conflict, to combat Chamberlain politically and Hitler militarily, he was nonetheless absolutely unequivocal: 'The Communist Party supports the war,' he wrote, 'believing it to be a just war which should be supported by the whole working class and all friends of democracy in Britain.'[5] Priced at one penny, with a rather unappealing portrait of its author on the cover, *How to Win the War* was published on 14 September, with a print run of 50,000 copies.

The reception among the party's rank and file was mixed. As good Marxists, they had interpreted the travails of the 1930s as the death-throes of capitalism, with fascism seen as the purest expression of that demise. So the sight of Stalin cosying up to Hitler would have been rather disquieting: an apparent refutation of the entire political constellation as they had previously understood it. Of course, to the hardened communists among them, this was not a problem. True to their convictions, they were unperturbed, safe in the knowledge that the Soviet Union knew best how to protect the communist experiment. As the party member Douglas Hyde explained: 'The Soviet leaders had a responsibility to the working class of the world to defend the USSR and could, if necessary, for this reason make an alliance with the devil himself.'[6]

Others, however, were rather more perplexed, and for them Pollitt's pamphlet restored a modicum of clarity, providing a line that they could defend both to the wider world and to themselves. As the later Labour minister Kenneth Robinson recalled, the pact was 'a bombshell: We just did not know what to do. But I remember that we all welcomed a statement by Harry Pollitt . . . that we must now fight a war on two fronts – one against Nazi Germany, and one against the Establishment.'[7] Even Pollitt's comrade Dutt was enthused, describing the pamphlet as 'one of the finest things' that the leader had ever produced, 'so clearly and simply presented'.[8]

Yet Pollitt's problems began almost as soon as the pamphlet was published. That same day, a telegram arrived from Moscow explaining the new line on the war that was to be adopted by all fraternal communist parties and made known to every member. 'The present war', it proclaimed, 'is an imperialist and unjust war for which the bourgeoisie of all belligerent states bear equal responsibility. In no country can the working class or the Communist Parties support the war.' 'Tactics must be changed,' it went on, 'under no conditions may the international working class defend fascist Poland', adding that in the light of the conclusion of the Nazi–Soviet Pact, 'the division . . . into fascist and democratic states has now lost its former sense'. The message ended with an ominous warning: 'Communist Parties which acted contrary to these tactics must now correct their policy.'[9]

Pollitt must have been dismayed, and his first instinct was to suppress the telegram in the hope, perhaps, that he could ride out the crisis. But he couldn't. Dutt had also got wind of the new line from Moscow and he was too much of an opportunist and a loyal Stalinist to allow the matter to go unchallenged. He asked that the party's Political Bureau reconvene to reconsider its position. Pollitt tried to resist, holding out for his line, but when Dave Springhall – the party's representative at the Communist International in Moscow – returned in late September with specific instructions, he was doomed. Consequently, the Central Committee was convened to resolve the issue on 2 October.

At the meeting, called at the party's Covent Garden headquarters that morning, Dutt was ruthless in espousing the revised line from Moscow and advocating its acceptance. The party had 'failed to understand' the 'new period' that the Nazi–Soviet Pact and the outbreak of war had signified, and in that 'new situation' it was necessary to 'adjust our perspective' and 'face, frankly and openly, that our line was a wrong line'.[10] Citing Lenin and numerous theoretical concepts and '-isms' that must have impressed his listeners, he went on to explain in less than perfect clarity why the new Muscovite line was correct. In closing, he warned that:

> the Party is now on trial as it has never been since the beginning of its history . . . We are going to need all forces in the conditions that we have to face, and in the fight that we have before us we want no half-hearted supporters, no vacillators, no faint-hearts. Every responsible position in the Party must be occupied by a determined fighter for the line.

For those still in doubt as to their fraternal responsibility, he added that 'the duty of the communist is not to disagree but to accept', and warned that 'any member who . . . deserts from active work for the Party will be branded for his political life'.[11] It was not difficult to determine at whom that closing threat was aimed.

Pollitt was not the first to respond; that task fell to Willie Gallacher, a firebrand Scot and the party's only Member of Parliament. He was scathing towards Dutt, retorting that he had never listened to a 'more unscrupulous and opportunist speech', and had never known 'anything so rotten, so mean, so despicable, so dirty'.[12] But, for all his righteous indignation, Gallacher was very much in a minority. Member after member of the Central Committee stood up to voice their undimmed 'faith in the Soviet Union' and their agreement with 'Comrade Dutt's position'. Then Pollitt finally had the floor.

Though he must have harboured the distinct impression that the party he had led for a decade was measuring him for a coffin, Harry Pollitt was initially conciliatory, stating that it would be easy for him 'to say I accept and let us kiss and be friends and everything in the garden would be lovely'. But, he said, that would be dishonest to his convictions. Reiterating his visceral anti-fascism – his desire, as he put it, to 'smash the fascist bastards' – he expressed his dismay at the fact that the 'fight against fascism' had disappeared, and that, due to its pact with the Soviet Union, fascism now seemed to have taken on a 'progressive role' and was no longer to be considered as the main enemy of the communist movement. 'May I say without offence', he went on, doubtless offending many in the room, 'that I don't envy the comrades who can so lightly in the space of a week, and sometimes in the space of a day, go from one political conviction to another.'

Pollitt also had a personal response for Rajani Palme Dutt, whose oblique threats must have raised his ire. 'Please remember, Comrade Dutt,' he said, 'you won't intimidate me. I was in this movement practically before you were born and will be in the revolutionary movement a long time after some of you are forgotten.' If he could not trump Dutt on his loyalty to Moscow, Pollitt could at least pull rank. He ended on a note of sadness rather than anger, explaining how he felt 'ashamed at the lack of feeling . . . that the struggle of the Polish people has aroused in our leadership'. His comrades were deceiving themselves if they thought that the pact with a country that they hated did not 'leave a nasty taste in the mouth'. As far as Pollitt was concerned, the party's honour was now at stake and it was impossible for him to continue as leader in the circumstances. His eloquent response failed to move his comrades, however, so he declared his resignation.[13] The committee voted by 21 to 3 to accept the new line outlined by Dutt, with the only dissenters being Pollitt, Gallacher and the *Daily Worker* editor, Johnny Campbell.

Ten days later, it was reported in *The Times* that Pollitt had been 'relieved of his office' as 'the policy of the British Communist Party was found to be altogether out of step with Moscow's'. A revised manifesto, composed on 7 October, was declared to correct the previous policy espoused by Pollitt on the outbreak of war.[14] At the end of the month, a new pamphlet would appear, penned by Rajani Palme Dutt and entitled *Why This War?*, giving the communist argument for neutrality. Pollitt's pamphlet was quietly withdrawn.

In line with its universalist pretensions, Soviet communism boasted an international organisation, known as the 'Communist International' or 'Comintern'. Founded in 1919 and based in Moscow, the Comintern spearheaded the international class struggle against the bourgeoisie and promoted communism and the Soviet system to the world, acting in effect as the Soviet Union's unofficial foreign-policy agent, the handmaiden of global revolution. It was through the Comintern that all affiliated communist and revolutionary socialist parties would be guided in their political mission, advised of how they should interpret events, informed of the line that they were required to take. To the loyal communist, the Comintern's word was law.

So it was in 1939, when the international communist movement was faced with the profound challenge of the Nazi–Soviet Pact. Stalin's deal with Hitler had reverberations across the world, blindsiding the Comintern itself and requiring every affiliated party to toe the new Muscovite line. And, as Harry Pollitt found to his cost, local perspectives – however honourable, logical or well intentioned – counted for little against the brute political force of Moscow. The result could be an uncomfortable stand-off, and the apparent conflict between ideology and realpolitik caused many to call their communist faith into question. For some, the malaise had a troubling moral aspect. Communism, for many of its followers, boasted a self-proclaimed moral superiority, espousing 'progressive values', concern for one's fellow man, and defiance of fascist aggression. The sight of Molotov and Ribbentrop smiling together in the Kremlin undermined that, sullying the image that world communism had of itself.

George Orwell, ever the perspicacious critic, diagnosed the problem accurately. 'The Russo-German Pact', he wrote in early 1941, 'brought the Stalinists and the near-Stalinists into the pro-Hitler position', thereby at a stroke undermining not only communism's primary 'anti-fascist' appeal, but also its primary complaint against the status quo. Where communists had once damned their bourgeois governments for appeasing Hitler with their shabby deal-making, they were now obliged to defend Moscow for doing the very same. The result, Orwell wrote, was the 'complete destruction . . . of left-wing orthodoxy'.[15]

The fascists faced similar difficulties. Hitler, who had made a career from combating communism, and had once claimed that alliance with Russia 'would be the end of Germany',[16] now had to explain an embarrassing volte-face, which potentially undermined much of what Nazism as well as the wider fascist movement had stood for. To complicate matters, both sides – communists and Nazis – saw themselves tainted by their association with one another. Their respective regimes, therefore, which had revolutionised the use of propaganda, news manipulation and what Hitler had once cynically called the 'big lie', would be faced with a public-relations challenge of the first order: that of selling the agreement between the two to their sceptical followers. As well as unleashing war in the autumn of 1939, the Nazi–Soviet Pact plunged both the communist and fascist movements into an existential crisis.

On the British left, at least, at one remove from continental troubles, the reaction to that crisis would span the spectrum. For some, their faith in communism was undimmed. Eric Hobsbawm, for instance, a young graduate just down from Cambridge, found the ideological somersaults easier to perform than most. He was unfazed by the speed of developments as war erupted in the late summer of 1939, despite the fact that the war was 'not the war we had expected', nor was it the war 'for which the Party had prepared us'. What he laconically called the 'line change' also bothered him little, in spite of the fact that, as he later confessed, the idea 'that Britain and France were as bad as Nazi Germany made little emotional or intellectual sense'. Nonetheless, as an obedient communist, he accepted the line with 'no reservations'. After all, he added airily, 'Was it not the essence of "democratic centralism" to stop arguing once a decision had been reached, whether or not you were personally in agreement?'[17]

Others were rather more conflicted. The veteran socialist Beatrice

Webb was horrified by the announcement of the Nazi–Soviet Pact. As someone who had spent her life promoting socialism and who had famously lauded the USSR as 'a new civilization', she found Stalin's accord with Hitler to be a 'holy horror' and a 'great disaster' for everything that she had stood for. 'Knocked senseless' by the pact, she described it in her diary in the most damning terms, as 'dishonourable', 'disgraceful' and a 'terrible collapse of good faith and integrity'. Within a few days, however – her equilibrium at least partially restored – she was again looking for the positives, seeking as ever to provide an optimistic explanation of Soviet actions. 'No wonder Stalin prefers to keep his 170 million out of the battlefield', she wrote, 'while the anti-Comintern Axis and the Western capitalist democracies . . . destroy each other.' Though 'disreputable', she commented, Stalin's policy was nonetheless 'a miracle of successful statesmanship'.[18]

However, if she thought that she had made sense of Stalin's actions, the Soviet invasion of Poland in mid-September would throw her once again into turmoil. 'Satan has won hands down', she wrote the day after the Red Army's invasion. 'Stalin and Molotov have become the villains of the piece', and their entry into Poland was 'a monument of international immorality'. It was, she said, 'the blackest tragedy in human history', not because of the grim fate of the Poles, but because her beloved USSR had squandered its 'moral prestige'.[19] The socialist writer Naomi Mitchison, meanwhile, saw the invasion as a personal blow: 'I feel like hell deep down because of the Russian news', she wrote in mid-September, adding that Soviet actions were 'knocking the bottom out of what one has been working for all these years'.[20] Others had rather more mundane concerns. One communist shop steward was devastated: 'Bugger Uncle Joe, bugger Molotov, bugger the whole bloody lot of them! How the hell am I to explain this to the factory tomorrow?'[21]

Yet darker days were to follow for Britain's communists and their fellow travellers. After swallowing the line-change in early October, they were shaken once again when the Red Army invaded Finland on the last day of November. So, as Comrade Dutt chimed in to publicly accuse hapless Finland of being a 'semi-fascist state', Beatrice Webb appeared to have given in to disillusionment, writing that it was the manner of the invasion, 'hard hatred and parrot-like repetition of false

– glaringly false – accusations' that were 'so depressing'. The leaders of the USSR had not yet 'learnt good manners', she chided, and 'they will have to suffer for it'.[22]

For those more in touch with the righteous wrath of the British people, it was about much more than 'good manners' or diplomatic niceties. According to Douglas Hyde, sellers of the *Daily Worker* were obliged to run the gauntlet from an angry public, being 'spat upon and assaulted in the streets . . . doors slammed in their faces, even chamber-pots emptied on their heads from upstairs windows'.[23] Moscow's Winter War against Finland was one of a series of events that autumn that tested communist credibility in Britain, with some of the newer recruits and the less ideologically convinced becoming disillusioned and leaving the party.[24]

There were some high-profile names among the defectors. John Strachey was one. A former acolyte of Oswald Mosley and a prominent Marxist theorist, Strachey had been taken aback by the signature of the Nazi–Soviet Pact, but only abandoned the party following the Nazi invasion of Norway in 1940, claiming that the 'inter-Imperialist aspect of the struggle was subsidiary to the necessity to prevent a Nazi world-conquest'.[25] Left-wing publisher Victor Gollancz did not wait so long. Appalled by the pact, he broke his long-standing connection with the Communist Party in protest and published an open letter to its members entitled *Where are You Going?*. It was a typically woolly, verbose attack, but nonetheless one that landed a few punches, not least in asking its readers to try to recall the days before the pact:

> You regarded Hitler-fascist aggression, did you not, as a deadly menace, as *the* deadly menace, to everything in which we believe, and to every hope of further progress and advance . . . You were horrified at the tortures in the concentration camps; you loathed Hitler's ideological repudiation of liberty, objectivity, mercy, pity and kindness, and his glorification of force and submission to force.[26]

Yet, he went on, the Nazi–Soviet Pact had now created a new line, of 'revolutionary defeatism', which had brought communist propaganda to the uncomfortable position of aligning itself with Hitler's once-despised Nazi Germany, and so was 'running the terrible risk . . . of bringing about the very catastrophe' which it had struggled to prevent.[27] He urged party members to take a moment to reconsider the position that the Communist Party was asking them to adopt.

In the United States reactions were similarly mixed. Although as many as 2,000 American volunteers had fought against fascism in the ranks of the Abraham Lincoln Brigade in the Spanish Civil War, a sizeable contingent of them were able to jettison their anti-fascism and march in Moscow-sponsored opposition to American entry into the war in the autumn of 1939.[28] Popular ire against the stance of the US Communist Party (CPUSA) did prompt the winding up of the Comintern-funded 'American League for Peace and Democracy', but under the leadership of the Soviet spy Helen Silvermaster, it promptly morphed into the 'American Peace Mobilization' and continued campaigning against American aid to Britain and against the 'warmonger' President Roosevelt.

Alongside its stooges, the CPUSA was also extremely active in campaigning for 'peace' and against any American intervention in what it called the 'European Imperialist War'. All its anti-fascist propaganda was duly halted, and the line that was touted in the pamphlets of the CPUSA's leader Earl Browder, such as *Whose War Is It?*, parroted Comintern slogans by stressing the culpability of the British, the French, and the Poles, while minimising any criticism of Hitler's Germany. According to Browder, Stalin's actions in signing the Nazi–Soviet Pact had been proved correct 'a hundred times over'. The Soviet Union, he claimed, was a force for peace, which had even halted the Nazi advance by 'redeeming more than half of Poland' and was 'utilizing the contradictions among the imperialists to prevent them from carrying through their . . . schemes of oppression and war'.[29]

Such sophistry did little to endear the political far left to the American public, and the CPUSA suffered accordingly, with membership falling by around 15 per cent in the opening six months of the war, and seeing a virtual collapse in new membership in 1940.[30] The American political establishment was similarly unimpressed, and in October 1939 a federal grand jury indicted Earl Browder on charges of passport fraud, following the latter's public admission that he had travelled abroad on falsified papers. Despite it being an overtly politically motivated case, Browder was found guilty, sentenced to four years' imprisonment and temporarily disappeared from the political stage.[31] The party's subsequent 'Free Earl Browder' campaign foundered on public distrust and continuing resentment of Stalin's flirtation with Hitler. The pact had dealt American communism a blow from which it would never recover.

While Gollancz wrestled with his conscience, and American communists battled public suspicion, a few on the left contrived to see the Nazi–Soviet alignment simply as a genuinely new political constellation. Indeed the idea that the two regimes had more similarities than differences was one that had gained ground prior to 1939 and one which, with the signature of the pact, appeared to have been very publicly confirmed. It was not as outlandish an idea as modern minds might imagine. After all, the origins of Hitler's Nazi Party had been in an amalgam of socialist and nationalist principles. 'National Socialism' had been sincerely meant, and though its socialist element had been corrupted and diluted in the interim, it had never been removed entirely and it is clear that Hitler and many of his acolytes still saw themselves broadly as socialists.[32]

Consequently, the idea that Hitler and Stalin were converging, or even that they shared some political DNA, enjoyed a season of currency. An editorial in London's left-wing *New Statesman*, for instance, accused Stalin of 'adopting the familiar technique of the Führer'. The piece pulled few punches: 'Like Hitler', editor Kingsley Martin wrote, Stalin

> has a contempt for all arguments except that of superior force. Like Hitler, he would argue that in the world today only force counts . . . By the inexorable laws of its dialectic, Bolshevism brought into being its antithesis, National Socialism. Today the question being asked is whether the ugly thing that now reigns from Vladivostok to Cologne is turning into the inevitable synthesis, National-Bolshevism.[33]

Journalist Henry Brailsford was also plainly baffled by the pact – referring to it as the 'central enigma' of the war – but he nonetheless concurred that some sort of convergence between the two regimes might be afoot. Both were revolutionary regimes, he noted in the *New Republic* that autumn, and both despised the West. Was it not possible that the two were pursuing the same aims: waging a crusade against the 'effete liberalism of the pluto-democracies'?[34]

This apparent convergence of Nazi and Soviet aims was not merely theoretical. In the United States in October 1940, a British merchant seaman was arrested in Boston after offering to supply the local German spy network with information on the Atlantic convoys. George Armstrong was a 39-year-old communist from Newcastle who had been motivated by a speech made by Molotov in which he had encouraged all Allied merchant seamen to desert as soon as they reached a neutral port. Deported to Britain, Armstrong was tried for aiding the enemy – the first Briton of the war to be tried for spying – and was sentenced to death. He would have been bemused to learn that, by the time of his execution in July 1941, the Nazi–Soviet 'friendship' in whose name he had committed treason was already a thing of the past.[35]

Yet, while communists in Britain and the United States enjoyed the comparative luxury of indulging in the theoretical, the abstract and the downright contrary, for some of their comrades elsewhere the events of that autumn and winter had a more perilous immediacy. The French Communist Party, for instance, was thrown into chaos by the pact. At the outset, it attempted to convince its followers that Stalin's alignment with Hitler changed nothing, indeed that it marked a 'new success of the Soviet Union' and 'an incomparable service to the cause of peace', which 'will not deprive any people of its freedom' or 'hand over a single acre of any nation's land'.[36] Yet few were convinced. As the journalist Adam Rajsky recalled, news of the pact's signing 'resounded like a thunderclap', leaving communist intellectuals such as himself to attempt to 'explain the inexplicable'.[37] In due course, despite stressing its *patriotisme*, the party found itself under investigation by the French government, on the charge that Stalin's pact with Hitler had rendered the communist movement a passive ally of the Nazis and thereby, potentially, a fifth column. Even before August 1939 was out, the party's newspaper, *L'Humanité*, was closed down.

If that were not difficult enough, the Muscovite change of line subsequently threw many into despair. According to one former party member, the reaction of French communists to Stalin's directive was one of 'extraordinary discipline, unique in the history of humanity'. Once the new line was given, he claimed, there was a 'sudden reorientation . . . towards a policy diametrically opposed to the policy of the day before'.[38] But such obedience was far from universal. Some members tore up their party cards in disgust, and there were a number of high-level defections, including twenty-one of the Communist

Party's seventy-three parliamentary deputies. A group of dissidents even made a public appeal in which they condemned the Nazi–Soviet Pact and pledged to continue resisting the Nazi aggressor and supporting the democracies.[39] The main French trade union, the CGT, was also resolute, deciding to expel all those of its members who refused to repudiate the pact. Finally the French government banned the Communist Party, and the dissemination of its propaganda was declared an offence, with a maximum penalty of five years' imprisonment. With some of his members now facing arrest, party leader Maurice Thorez fled to Moscow. Tried in absentia for desertion from the army, he was sentenced to death.

The party that Thorez left behind was in crisis. By the spring of 1940, the government clampdown had resulted in over 3,000 arrests, with a further 2,500 party members being dismissed from their posts in municipal administrations. Forced underground, the party was obliged to propagate the new Muscovite line through clandestine means such as fly-posting and pamphleteering. Communist propaganda was no less effective for being underground, with industrial go-slows and even incidents of sabotage resulting, but its defeatist tone went dangerously close to implying collaboration with Hitler's Germany. Even on 15 May 1940, as Hitler's panzers were already on French soil, the underground communist press was still attacking the 'imperialists of London and Paris'.[40] By performing such contortions, the French Communist Party, the largest sister party outside the Soviet Union, had thoroughly disgraced itself.

If it were possible, the German Communist Party (KPD) was in an even more parlous state. Outlawed since the Nazi seizure of power in 1933, it had been forced underground, its members subject to arrest and persecution, and given only limited succour via often tortuous lines of communication with their superiors in Moscow. The fate of its leader, Ernst Thälmann, was indicative of how far the party had fallen. Once a giant of the political scene who had contested the presidency in 1925 and 1932, Thälmann was arrested by the Gestapo barely a month after Hitler came to power. Kept in solitary confinement, he was repeatedly questioned, abused and beaten – losing four teeth in one interrogation – but was never granted the dignity of a trial. He simply disappeared, shunted between a succession of prisons and concentration camps, from which he would never re-emerge.

By 1939, the German communists had been reduced to an underground fringe movement, isolated and largely swimming against the tide of public opinion, with its lines of command fractured, compromised and unreliable. Little wonder that the Nazi–Soviet Pact was initially viewed with utter bewilderment in German communist circles. Officially, at least, it was greeted as a potential lifeline, with the party announcing its approval of the pact as a 'blow for peace' and expressing the hope that further, similar pacts would follow.[41] Some German communists went further, speculating that the pact would signal an end to the persecution, with the expectation that they would soon be able to hold their meetings without hindrance and that Thälmann and other prisoners would be released. There was even a wild rumour that the Nazi Party itself was to be wound up and that *Mein Kampf* would be withdrawn from publication.[42]

Aside from such daydreams, news of the pact's signature caused a serious split in communist ranks, between those loyal to Moscow, who welcomed it as the precursor to the desired war between the Nazis and the 'Imperialists' of Britain and France, and communist idealists, who were dismayed by what they saw as Stalin's betrayal of the international working class. The later East German leader Erich Honecker was one of those who were firmly in the former camp, receiving the news with equanimity in his prison cell outside Berlin, and declaring the pact to be a 'diplomatic success' for the Soviet Union in its struggle against the West.[43] Others reacted with outrage and incredulity, however. Exiled novelist Gustav Regler, for instance, was in despair, asking 'How could Stalin do that to us?' Thorwald Siegel, a German communist émigré in Paris, was so distressed by the Soviet invasion of Poland that he committed suicide.[44]

Undoubtedly, a good many communists and their sympathisers were simply confused. The playwright Bertolt Brecht was evidently one. A long-time Marxist, Brecht had fled Germany in 1933 for a life in exile in Denmark, then in Sweden and finally in Finland, before emigrating to the United States in 1941. While in exile, Brecht enjoyed a creative boom, penning many of the works that would make his name and through which he expressed his visceral opposition to National Socialism and fascism. Yet it is far too neat to describe Brecht simply as a mouthpiece of Soviet propaganda. Though a convinced communist, he remained rather equivocal about the Soviet Union;

indeed he famously cut short a trip to Moscow in 1935, claiming –
rather disingenuously – that he could not find enough milk and sugar
there to go with his coffee.[45]

In fact, his concerns went deeper and were expressed, privately at
least, late in 1939 around the time of the signature of the Nazi–Soviet
Pact. Like many communist sympathisers across the globe, Brecht
was disillusioned and clearly had little time for the official line, noting
of the pact simply that 'I do not think one can say more than that
the [Soviet] Union is saving itself at the cost of leaving the world
proletariat without watchwords, hope or assistance.'[46] The Soviet invasion of Poland later that month would test his faith still further. In
his journal he raged about

> the stripping of ideological pretences . . . the abandonment of the
> principle that 'the Soviet Union doesn't require a single foot of foreign
> soil', the adoption of all that fascist bullshit about 'blood brotherhood'
> . . . the entire nationalist terminology. This is being spouted to the
> German fascists, but at the same time to the Soviet troops.[47]

It is not inconceivable that this inchoate rage found its way into
Brecht's work; after all, two of his most famous plays, *The Resistible
Rise of Arturo Ui* and *Mother Courage and her Children*, were written at
this time. While both are considered, quite rightly, to be archetypes
of the anti-fascist genre, neither can be construed as uncritically toeing
the Muscovite line. *Mother Courage*, with its critique of profiteering
from war, was written in response to the invasion of Poland in the
autumn of 1939 and is ostensibly and obviously anti-capitalist. Yet
given the circumstances in which Stalin's Soviet Union had entered
that conflict – as an aider, abettor and economic supplier of Hitler's
Germany – it was a critique that might just as plausibly have been
targeted towards Moscow. *The Resistible Rise of Arturo Ui*, meanwhile,
is more unequivocally anti-Nazi: a parody of Hitler's rise, its anti-hero
is a talentless Chicago gangster who is hoisted into power by corrupt
commercial interests and his own ruthless, criminal nature. Yet it is
perhaps instructive that the play was written in March 1941. Brecht
was criticising Hitler in the most brutal, blood-curdling terms – as
'the troubler of this poor world's peace' and 'the lousiest of lice' – at
a time when Stalin and the German leader were still exchanging

pleasantries.[48] Brecht, it seems, never agreed with the 'change of line' dictated by Moscow as a result of the Nazi–Soviet Pact. Indeed, as one scholar has noted, it is tempting to wonder whether he did not harbour 'a lurking suspicion of the similarities' between the two regimes.[49]

From the vantage point of 1939 or 1940, this would not have been an unreasonable conclusion to draw. It was certainly the view of German socialist Rudolf Hilferding, who summed up the feelings of many of the disillusioned when he wrote that the collaboration between Hitler and Stalin had demonstrated that 'there was no fundamental difference between the two'.[50] In truth, there was more to Hilferding's comment than mere fraternal socialist spite. The line emanating from Moscow that autumn came perilously close to advocating a political truce with Nazism, with communist energies instead to be focused on attacking the Western Powers as the true enemies of world revolution. This, certainly, was the tone of one of the foremost German communists in Moscow, Walter Ulbricht. A former joiner and early member of the KPD, Ulbricht had risen to prominence in the interwar years before fleeing into exile upon Hitler's appointment as chancellor in 1933. Once safely ensconced in Moscow, from 1937, he emerged as a convinced and uncompromising Stalinist, and became the leading German representative on the committee of the Comintern. So when he spoke to his countrymen, he did so with considerable authority.

Ulbricht communicated with his communist brethren inside Germany – known as the 'comrades in the country' – primarily via the pages of *Die Welt*, the Comintern's German-language journal. Typical was an article that appeared in February 1940 in which he blamed the war squarely on capitalism and 'big business', and branded British imperialism as more reactionary and more dangerous than Nazi imperialism, indeed as 'the most reactionary force in the world'. Given that the British and French were the most determined to engage in a political crusade against the Soviet Union, he argued, they now superseded the Nazis – who had after all made a pact with Moscow – as world communism's primary opponent. 'The fight for democratic liberties', he wrote, 'cannot be waged in alliance with British imperialism', adding that those who disagreed would 'share responsibility for realising the predatory plans of [the] British and French'. The 'strongest guarantee' for the hindrance of such plans, he concluded, was the German–Soviet Pact.[51]

His was not a lone voice. The Soviet communist newspaper *Izvestia* also put in its penny's worth, ridiculing the West's 'war on Hitlerism' in an editorial, while Ulbricht's comrade Wilhelm Pieck (like him, a later leader of the GDR) went further, criticising the West's war in the most emotive terms as nothing more than an attempt to 'starve Germany and extend the conflict to women and children, the sick and the old'.[52] Even in June 1940, with France and the Low Countries invaded, German communists were still toeing the line of damning the 'imperialist war' and blaming everything on the Western Powers. As the *Rote Fahne* ('Red Flag') – the KPD's official newspaper – cynically explained, it was 'the baleful politics of the ruling classes in England and France, and their social democratic lackeys, that has led to this slaughter'.[53]

Given that the German Communist Party's lines of communication with Moscow were often interrupted and the hierarchy was in utter disarray, the degree to which its domestic membership heeded such convoluted ideological leads is unclear. Moreover, the Gestapo's attentions had scarcely lessened, so many party members preferred to adopt something like a 'holding pattern': waiting for clarity and biding their time until a more favourable, and more easily explicable, political climate developed. A few German communists argued for continued agitation against the Nazi regime, and there were some instances of leafleting in Berlin and elsewhere following the outbreak of the war, but the general trend thereafter was towards inaction. By way of illustration, the monthly average of communist leaflets confiscated by the Gestapo in 1938 was 1,000. In December 1939, it was 277; in April 1940, eighty-two, the level at which it would remain for the rest of the year. Arrests followed a similar pattern, sinking from over 950 in January 1937 to seventy in April 1940.[54] Clearly, German communists were staying their hand. Such was their inactivity, indeed, that an internal SS report from June 1940 noted that within Germany one could 'no longer speak of organised resistance from communist and Marxist circles'.[55] Little wonder that one prominent historian of the period described the German communists of that era as 'the most shameful of Hitler's accomplices'.[56]

For all the clarion calls to compliance with the new line, there were many dissenting voices within the communist movement, not least in

Moscow itself. The primary hotbed of such opinions, paradoxically, was the Hotel Lux in the heart of the Soviet capital, which served as home to hundreds of foreign communists who had come to seek refuge, serve the Comintern, or learn at the feet of their masters. Yet the Lux was not quite the safe haven that it appeared. Many of its residents had already fallen foul of Stalin's purges in the late 1930s, suffering torture, execution or exile to Siberia for their supposed transgressions. At its peak, the purge had cut a swathe through the hotel's guest list, with residents rising each morning in trepidation to enquire who had been taken by the NKVD the previous night. In all, some 170 Lux residents would disappear in this way.[57] By the autumn of 1939, the 600 that remained were the most loyal, and the most desperate, of Stalin's foreign acolytes.

Understandably, then, there were many within the Lux at that time who were willing to go along with Stalin's policy of friendship with Germany without question. Some of them were persuaded by the ideological case: that Hitler could be turned west to defeat Britain and France as an unwitting tool of the Soviets. As one of their number commented on hearing news of the pact: 'Marvellous, marvellous! . . . They should destroy one another . . . that way our job will be easier. Fantastic, marvellous!'[58] Others, motivated more by personal fealty or fear, told themselves that Stalin could 'do no wrong', that his about-turn – however shocking – had to be justified.

Yet there were a few who were unable to square events with their political conscience, and as a result the mood within the hotel soon became fractious. Spanish communist Castro Delgado rose late on the morning of 24 August 1939, and when he reached the bus stop for the trip to Comintern headquarters, he was unaware of the signature of the pact the previous night. 'The scene I saw at the bus stop was different from that on most days', he later recalled:

> Today people didn't pile on board to get a seat. They stood in groups on the sidewalk and talked animatedly. Some were almost shouting. I looked at one and then another. No one noticed me. I said 'good morning' and no one answered. Everyone continued to talk, gesticu- lating and waving their arms. I was the only one who wasn't talking and gesticulating.[59]

Like many of his fellows, Delgado was torn. He told himself that 'Stalin never errs'; yet as a Spaniard, he could not forget the civil war and his anti-fascist principles. 'From Almeria to Guernica,' he wrote, 'from Badajoz to Barcelona I hear the word "but".'[60] Disbelief was a common reaction. Another Spaniard recalled being 'stupefied' by the news that morning: 'We had to rub our eyes to assure ourselves that we were in fact reading *Pravda*.'[61]

Ruth von Mayenburg experienced a similar emotion. As an Austrian communist, she had undertaken a number of espionage visits to Nazi Germany in the mid-1930s before transferring her activities to the Comintern. She was predictably astonished by the pact, writing that it was 'as though the clock on the Kremlin tower stopped', but she justified the measure to herself on the grounds of tactical necessity, realpolitik.[62] Only later did her emotional response resurface. 'It was actually shameful,' she said of the pact, 'and we weren't able to overcome this feeling of shame for a long time.'[63]

For those in the upper echelons of the Soviet hierarchy, grim experience dictated that it was unwise to question a policy already made – Stalin's decision, they knew, was final. This strict conformity was demonstrated by the account of the writer Ilya Ehrenburg, who had himself had such grave concerns about the pact that he sank into a deep depression after it was announced and struggled to feed himself for several months.[64] Returning to Moscow from Paris in the summer of 1940, Ehrenburg was keen to share his belief that the Germans were committed to attack the Soviet Union, but he found few willing to engage in that conversation, while the press continued to laud friendly Soviet–German relations. He was shocked when he tried to air his concerns with a deputy commissar, Solomon Dridzo-Lozovsky, who merely 'listened to me absent-mindedly, without looking at me and with a melancholy expression'. When Ehrenburg challenged his apparent nonchalance, the commissar replied: 'Personally, I find it very interesting. But you know we have a different policy.'[65]

Ordinary Soviet citizens – denied the benefits of foreign travel or a thoroughgoing 'political education' – were often simply bewildered. After all, they had been told for years that fascism was the Soviet Union's primary enemy, and that Hitler's Germany was the nefarious outside power that eyed Soviet territory, and in the service of which 'traitors' had conspired against Stalin. As factory director Victor

Kravchenko recalled: 'The big treason trials, in which Lenin's most intimate associates perished, had rested on the premise that Nazi Germany and its Axis friends . . . were preparing to attack us.' Moreover, he explained, Hitler's villainy had become an article of faith for everyone in the USSR: 'Soviet children played games of Fascists and Communists; the Fascists, always given German names, got the worst of it every time . . . In the shooting galleries the targets were often cut-outs of brown-shirted Nazis flaunting swastikas.'[66]

Far from being just another foreign arrangement, therefore, the Nazi–Soviet Pact signified a complete reversal of the entire foreign and ideological policy of the Soviet Union, and as such was utterly baffling. Kravchenko was most eloquent in recording his feelings at the time. The pact, he wrote in his memoir, streaked 'meteorlike across our horizon and crashed headlong into the minds and consciences of the party membership', leaving all of them 'groggy with disbelief'. 'Not until we saw newsreels and newspaper pictures showing a smiling Stalin shaking hands with von Ribbentrop', he recalled, 'did we begin to credit the incredible.'[67] Explaining the news to party cells in factories and offices was an unenviable task. As one young communist discovered, the audience sat 'bewildered and silent', while 'nobody – not even our political director – could offer any explanation'.[68]

The vast majority of Soviet citizens were no less confused, some even mistaking the announcement for some sort of practical joke. Their sense of bewilderment was perhaps heightened by the rapidity with which the tone of public and cultural life in the Soviet Union shifted after the signature of the pact. From one day to the next, the newspapers stopped criticising Nazi Germany, and instead began lauding German achievements. As Kravchenko noted:

> The libraries, similarly, were purged of anti-Fascist literature. The Society for Cultural Relations with Foreign Countries instantly discovered the wonders of German *Kultur*. Visiting Moscow on business, I learned that several exhibits of Nazi art, Nazi economic achievements and Nazi military glory were on view or in the process of organization . . . In fact, everything Germanic was in vogue.[69]

The Soviet film industry was similarly cleansed. The films *Professor Mamlock* and *The Oppenheim Family* – dramas highlighting the Nazi persecution of the Jews – were unceremoniously withdrawn from circulation. The most famous example of this cultural purge is the case of the Sergei Eisenstein masterpiece *Alexander Nevsky*, which had been released in December 1938 and was still circulating in Soviet cinemas as the ink dried on the pact less than a year later. Retelling the story of the eponymous Russian hero, who famously defeated the invading Teutonic Knights in the mid-thirteenth century, the film served an obvious propaganda purpose, appealing to Russian nationalism and containing graphic scenes of atrocities committed by the German invaders. For those cinemagoers who were beguiled by the film's subtlety, the message was spelled out in a scene in which a crowd of Russian peasants are presented with evidence of the invaders having tortured their womenfolk: 'The German is a beast!' They cry in response, 'We know the German!'[70] Once those same Germans became Moscow's allies in 1939, such a prejudicial screen depiction was deemed unacceptable and the film was swiftly withdrawn. But it may have been too late: it was estimated that, in the first six months of circulation, *Alexander Nevsky* had already been seen by some 23 million Soviet citizens.[71]

Of course, any political or cultural lead had to come from the very top, and Stalin had been quite correct when he stated that 'public opinion in our country will have to be prepared slowly for the change in our relations that this treaty is to bring about.'[72] In the cultural sphere, at least, measures were rather half-hearted, however. Aside from a few exhibitions and the withdrawal of anti-German films such as *Alexander Nevsky*, little else of note was attempted. In the short term, radio programmes were altered, with the anti-German items being replaced by those that projected a more positive image. Eisenstein, meanwhile, was given the chance to redeem himself by staging a production of Richard Wagner's *Die Walküre* at the Bolshoi, which premiered in November 1940.[73] The performance received rave reviews, with *Pravda* praising the 'genius' of Wagner and hailing the work as the 'richest legacy of the great German composer'.[74]

In the political sphere, the Soviet regime was a little more proactive, setting up 'agitation points' in public parks and squares, where party representatives would attempt to explain the new policy and answer questions. At one such point in a Moscow park in mid-September 1939, an elderly man expressed the widespread concern that the Germans would not stop at Poland and would keep going east. In response, the party spokesman declared that there were assurances in place so that this would not happen, but according to an eye-witness was otherwise vague and unconvincing.[75]

Such initiatives evidently did not last long. As Khrushchev recalled:

> For us to have explained our reasons for signing the treaty in straight-forward newspaper language would have been offensive, and besides, nobody would have believed us. It was very hard for us – as Communists . . . – to accept the idea of joining forces with Germany. It was difficult enough for us to accept this paradox ourselves. It would have been impossible to explain it to the man in the street.[76]

For many Soviet citizens, then, the old concerns were barely assuaged, only silenced. As the poet Konstantin Simonov complained: 'They were still the same fascists, but we could no longer write or say aloud what we thought of them.'[77]

A few, it seems, took the new climate of positivity towards Germany literally and began to express admiration for the Nazis or for Hitler personally. The younger generation, for example, had a far from universally negative view of the Third Reich, with some praising Germany's higher standard of living, or applauding its persecution of the Jews. Hitler, too, was praised as charismatic, as the archetypal 'strong man' who 'fears no one, recognises no one, and does as he pleases'. Indeed, NKVD and Communist Party sources even reported finding swastikas daubed on Muscovite walls.[78]

For others, meanwhile, the disillusionment engendered by the Nazi–Soviet Pact proved to be contagious, spilling over into a growing distrust of their own side. Like in the West, one explanation that emerged was to stress the supposed convergence and similarity between communism and Nazism that the pact appeared to symbolise. As one wit put it, Hitler and Stalin 'have agreed simply that there should be no leaders of the opposition and no parliaments. Now all that is needed is for Hitler to transfer from fascism to socialism, and Stalin from socialism to fascism.' Another quip doing the rounds that autumn in Moscow had Hitler and Ribbentrop submitting applications to join the Communist Party, while Stalin considered whether to accept them.[79]

As the Soviet Union expanded westwards, in concert with the Germans, that critical minority grew increasingly shrill, questioning the invasion of Finland, or even extending sympathy to those in eastern Poland who had now become Soviet citizens. 'There they had their own little houses, cows, horses, and land, felt themselves to be the boss,' one opinion ran, 'now they'll go hungry'. Unsurprisingly, an internal party memorandum that winter noted the existence among the population of 'unhealthy and sometimes directly anti-Soviet feelings bordering on counter-revolutionary conversations'.[80] Clearly Stalin would not be having things all his own way.

If Stalin struggled to take his people with him, so did Hitler. The first source of criticism was from his international allies and sympathisers. There was a widespread feeling that the Nazi regime had been morally damaged by its association with Stalin – a sentiment that was even expressed by *The Times* of London.[81] The Portuguese, for instance, were reportedly angered by the pact and by Germany's affection for its new partner. Hungary, too, was unimpressed and its people evidently found it 'difficult to reconcile at such short notice their professed friendship for Germany with their long-standing hatred of Bolshevism'. Only the Budapest pro-Nazi newspaper *Magyarság* applauded the pact as 'a new world record in clever diplomacy'.[82]

In Italy, Mussolini faced a dilemma. Although he feared the prospect of war, he was nonetheless concerned that he would be left out of any windfall of benefits, and so was minded to give his sanction to German plans. His foreign minister, Count Ciano, meanwhile, was more principled in his opposition, seeing in the pact with Moscow a betrayal of the very foundations of Rome's alliance with Berlin. Ciano was right: the Nazi–Soviet Pact was a clear violation of the terms of the secret protocol to the Anti-Comintern Pact, which stipulated that 'without mutual consent' neither signatory would conclude political treaties with the USSR. He therefore confronted Mussolini, demanding that he not go along with the Germans. In his diary, he gave a flavour of the conversation. 'You, Duce,' he wrote,

> cannot and must not do it . . . The Germans, not ourselves, have betrayed the alliance in which we have been partners, and not servants. Tear up the [Axis] pact. Throw it in Hitler's face and Europe will

recognise in you the natural leader of the anti-German crusade . . .
Speak to the Germans as they should be spoken to.[83]

But Ciano's pleas fell on deaf ears. Embittered and disillusioned, he
could only vent his feelings in his diary. 'The Germans are treacherous
and deceitful', he wrote. 'Could there ever be a more revolting
scoundrel than von Ribbentrop?'[84]

The Japanese were similarly dumbfounded, seeing in the pact not
only a public betrayal of their agreement with Berlin and Rome, but
also a dramatic deterioration in Japan's geostrategic security. If Stalin
now had a friendly frontier to the west, they would argue, what was
stopping him from turning towards the east and threatening Japanese
possessions in Manchuria? Indeed, such was the disquiet in Tokyo that
the government of Hiranuma Kiichirō, which had wrestled with the
idea of an anti-Soviet alliance with Germany, collapsed in acrimony.
Even the Japanese ambassador in Berlin, Hiroshi Oshima, a long-time
friend of both Germany and Ribbentrop personally, saw the pact as
a betrayal and tendered his resignation.[85]

Neither did Hitler find much succour among his ideological sympathisers. In Britain, there was nobody supporting Hitler once war broke
out beyond the lunatic fringe of those such as Unity Mitford, who
shot herself in the head in Munich on the outbreak of hostilities,
and William Joyce, who washed up in Berlin as the propagandist 'Lord
Haw-Haw'. Even the British fascist leader Oswald Mosley stated
publicly that 'any Englishman who does not fight for Britain is a
coward'. Fearing that the war would ruin the British Empire, Mosley
had hoped that Britain could avoid involvement and so had previously
adopted a pacifist, anti-war line, with the slogan: 'Why cut your throat
today to avoid catching a cold tomorrow?' But when war came in
September 1939, he nonetheless urged his followers to 'do nothing to
injure our country, or to help any other power'.[86]

Most of the pro-German British right followed Mosley's lead. 'The
Link', for instance, which had been established to 'promote Anglo-
German friendship' in 1937, closed its doors. Though unrepentant, its
pro-Nazi and anti-Semitic founder, Admiral Sir Barry Domvile,
explained: 'Naturally, we closed down on the outbreak of war; that
was essential, the King's enemies became our enemies.'[87] 'The Right
Club' ostensibly followed suit. Another pro-Nazi society, founded by

MP Sir Archibald Ramsay, it also closed down official operations with the outbreak of war, although a number of Ramsay's followers continued leafleting and bill-posting well into 1940.[88]

Only in the United States did Hitler briefly find a modicum of international sympathy. There, the pro-Nazi 'German American Bund', which had been founded in 1936 and was made up almost exclusively of German émigrés, was unabashed in seeking to project a positive view of its homeland and cheerleading for Hitler. Though its activities would peak early in 1939, with a rally at Madison Square Garden in New York attended by some 20,000 members, the events of that autumn would propel the organisation into a rapid decline. In a curious parallel to the fate of the American Communist Party, the Bund's leader, Fritz Kuhn, was convicted on fraud charges soon after the outbreak of the war in Europe and its national secretary followed suit, convicted for perjury, the following year. With that, the organisation swiftly disintegrated.

Domestically, too, Hitler faced considerable opposition. Like Stalin, he had the challenge of contradicting years of propaganda and often deeply ingrained prejudices and fears about his new treaty partner. Nazism had emerged, in part at least, as a response to the rise of the Bolsheviks, and had largely defined itself as a national counterpoint to the perceived evils of 'Judaeo-Bolshevism'. With anti-communism an item of faith for many Nazis, the pact was bound, at the very least, to raise a few eyebrows.

Among his inner circle, of course, Hitler could effectively defend the move by the force of his personality, or by appealing to realpolitik. If Goebbels had any reservations about the new arrangement, he did not share them with his diary. On the day of the pact's signature, he was as effusive in private as his minions were in public, writing that 'the announcement of the Non-Aggression Pact with Moscow is a world sensation!'[89] Others were less convinced, however. The party ideologue Alfred Rosenberg was one of those who were strongly opposed to the new alignment. When he first heard of the pact, he recorded his fury in his diary:

the trip of *our* minister to Moscow; an act of moral disrespect towards our 20-year struggle, towards our Party Rallies, towards Spain . . . About 4 years ago, the Führer said in my presence . . . that he would

not make a deal with Moscow, because it was impossible to forbid the
German people to steal and at the same time make friends with thieves.

He finished the entry snorting with derision: 'Apparently the Soviets
have already booked a delegation for the Nuremberg Rally.'[90] It was
a theme that Rosenberg would return to a few days later. Though
Hitler had clearly gone to considerable lengths to persuade him of
the pact's merits,[91] he was still uneasy. 'I have the feeling', he wrote
in his diary on 26 August, 'that this Moscow-Pact will one day wreak
vengeance on National Socialism. It is not a move made with free
will, but an act of desperation . . . How can we still speak of the
salvation and shaping of Europe, when we have to ask the destroyer
of Europe for help?'[92]

In response to such waverers, Hitler was not above the use of
threats. At Berchtesgaden in August 1939, he defended the pact to his
chiefs of staff, claiming that 'Stalin and I are the only ones who visu-
alise the future. So in a few weeks I shall stretch out my hand to Stalin
at the common German–Russian frontier, and with him undertake to
redistribute the world.' By way of a warning, he added: 'I have given
the command and I shall shoot everyone who utters one word of
criticism.'[93]

One who might have taken such threats seriously was the industri-
alist Fritz Thyssen. A long-time financial and political supporter of
the Nazis, Thyssen had begun to have second thoughts before 1939.
Although he had welcomed the crushing of the left, he had been
increasingly perturbed by the criminality and violence of the SA and
SS. The events of autumn 1939 would prove to be the last straw, not
least the death of his nephew in Dachau and Hitler's chilling declaration in the Reichstag that 'He who is not with me is a traitor, and
shall be treated as such.' Consequently, Thyssen took his family
and began a life of exile in Switzerland. The news of the pact had
troubled him deeply. As he wrote to Göring that September from
his Swiss refuge, he found it 'grotesque' that 'National Socialism has
suddenly discarded its doctrines in order to hob-nob with communism'.
The policy, he argued, amounted to suicide and the only beneficiary
would be the Nazis' 'mortal enemy of yesterday . . . Russia'. Writing
to Hitler the following month, he was no less conciliatory: the pact
and the war, he wrote, meant nothing less than the 'Finis Germaniae'.[94]

Such heretical opinions would not be expressed openly. Public discourse in Germany was uniformly positive about the pact, with German newspapers immediately altering the tone with which they reported Soviet current affairs or Russian culture. Where reporters and editors had once been unable to resist inserting – at the very least – a derogatory adjective or a critical aside, they now reported events with scrupulous even-handedness. On the morning of the pact's announcement, the newspapers seemed desperate to make the case for the new arrangement. Every title carried almost verbatim reports and commentaries, scripted under Goebbels' supervision, rejoicing at the restoration of the 'traditional friendship between the Russian and the German peoples'. In the Nazi Party newspaper, the *Völkischer Beobachter*, Ribbentrop congratulated himself by lauding his achievement as 'one of the most important turning points in the history of our two peoples'.[95] Even the in-house newspaper of the SS, *Das Schwarze Korps*, toed the optimistic line, reminding its readers, in a gallop through Russian and Soviet history, that the Empire of the Tsars had originally been a Germanic state, which had twice 'saved' Prussia and had 'paid dearly' for its enmity with Germany in the First World War. Echoing Ribbentrop, the newspaper concluded that the two countries had always flourished when they were friends, and so looked forward to a new era of collaboration.[96]

With the outbreak of war, the positive attitude continued. The *Völkischer Beobachter* carried extended extracts from Molotov's speech to the Supreme Soviet justifying and lauding the pact. And, following the Red Army's invasion of Poland on 17 September, Soviet military communiqués were given similarly exalted status, with editorial comments dutifully echoing the Soviet line.[97] Rosenberg was predictably disgusted. 'Our press is lacking all dignity', he wrote:

> today they rejoice over the traditional friendship between the German and Russian peoples. As if our struggle against Moscow had been a misunderstanding and the Bolsheviks had been the real Russians all along, with the Soviet Jews at their head! Cuddling up like this is worse than embarrassing.[98]

Cultural content in the newspapers was also swiftly co-ordinated, albeit with a clear preference for Russian subjects over those with a narrower Soviet context. Already on 26 August, for instance, a sympathetic article explored the Russian view of the battle of Tannenberg, the twenty-fifth anniversary of which was about to be marked in Germany. A week later, on 3 September, a whole page of the *Völkischer Beobachter* was devoted to the history of the Kremlin.[99] Similar articles followed, covering such diverse subjects as Russian publishing, history, literature and music. For those who had been raised on a diet of sneering contempt for all things emanating from Moscow, such revelations must have been more than a little disconcerting. In time, *Pravda* and *Izvestia* would be available on Berlin's streets, containing, as one reader recalled, 'a lot of negative stuff about the English and nothing against fascism'.[100]

If one were to believe the American William Shirer, however, Hitler needn't have worried about the popular reaction to the Nazi–Soviet volte-face. According to the renowned radio journalist and commentator, the people of Berlin – though 'still rubbing their eyes' at the news – were at least enthusiastic. 'You may be surprised', he announced to his American listeners,

> but the fact is that they do like [the pact]. Judging from the reaction of the people in the street it is a very popular move . . . I rode around Berlin today on buses, street-cars, the elevated and the subway. Everyone had their head buried in a newspaper. And in their faces you could see they considered that what they read was Good News.[101]

There were certainly many who would have instinctively agreed with Shirer's assessment. After hearing the announcement on the radio, one eye-witness recalled the positive way in which the pact was received. 'Everyone beaming with joy', he recorded. 'Wherever one goes, everywhere people speak excitedly of the Agreement with Russia!'[102] Part of that excitement lay in the erroneous belief that the pact, rather than heralding war, might actually prevent it. But others were less optimistic. In Berlin, the diarist Ruth Andreas-Friedrich reacted with resignation that the tension had finally been broken and war now seemed inevitable. News of the pact, she wrote, had been a 'bombshell', and she was not sure 'whether to heave a sigh of relief or to gasp with horror'. Having long deduced that Hitler wanted his war, she believed that it now seemed he would finally have his wish.

She concluded that an 'end with horror seems almost more bearable to us than horror without end'.[103]

The only uniform reaction to the news, perhaps, was surprise. A Bavarian doctor summed up the thoughts of many when he wrote:

> I just could not believe it, that Hitler had made a pact with the Bolsheviks; with the very same power that – for as long as I could remember – had been evil personified for the National Socialists . . . I began to marvel that the Führer had changed his spots to carry off this amazing diplomatic chess move.[104]

The thoughts of Jewish diarist Victor Klemperer were, understandably, rather darker; the pictures of Ribbentrop shaking hands with Stalin, he wrote, were 'the maddest thing', adding that 'Machiavelli is a babe in arms in comparison.'[105]

Many in the military establishment were similarly dismayed. As intelligence officer Hans Gisevius noted, the army commanders were 'thunderstruck . . . indignant beyond words', adding that 'the vision of Hitler and Stalin walking arm in arm was too much, even for our unpolitical generals'.[106] Colonel General Ludwig Beck, the former Chief of Staff, spoke for many when he expressed his profound disquiet at the new arrangement. In November 1939, he voiced the opinion that Germany's victory over Poland had been diminished by the fact that the 'Russian colossus' had been 'set in motion' westwards in the process.[107]

As General Guderian recalled, Hitler appears to have expected objections from this quarter. Seated next to the Führer at a Reich Chancellery luncheon in late October 1939, after he had been awarded the Knight's Cross of the Iron Cross, Guderian was asked directly 'how the army reacted to the Russian pact'. When the general replied that the soldiers had 'breathed a sigh of relief' as they would not have to fight a two-front war, Hitler stared at him 'in amazement', and he got the distinct impression that the Führer was rather displeased by his answer. Hitler's disappointment, he believed, was because 'he had doubtless expected me to express astonishment at his having ever agreed to sign a pact with Stalin'.[108]

Among the German political class there was also disquiet. Former diplomat Ulrich von Hassell wrote in his diary that he well understood the idea behind the pact – what he called 'using Beelzebub to drive away the Devil' – but he believed that it would be 'regarded by the whole world . . . as proof of the absolute unscrupulousness and lack of principle of Hitler and Stalin'.[109] The final straw for Alfred Rosenberg was when Ribbentrop returned from his second visit to Moscow and proclaimed that the atmosphere in the Kremlin was 'like being among old comrades'. 'That', Rosenberg raged in his diary, 'is just about the most impudent affront that can be inflicted upon National Socialism.'[110]

Such was the discontent in German diplomatic circles that word of it even reached British ears. In the autumn of 1939, the Foreign Secretary, Viscount Halifax, prepared a secret memorandum on German–Soviet relations in which sources in Berlin were cited suggesting that there was 'growing dissatisfaction and disillusionment in Germany – in naval and military circles, among diplomats, on the part of Göring and his entourage, and in the Party – over the Russo-German Pact'.[111] Those sources were not far wrong. On the morning after the announcement of the pact, it was said that the garden of the 'Brown House' in Munich – the Nazi Party headquarters – had been littered with the discarded party badges of disgruntled members.[112] Hitler would later acknowledge that the 'manoeuvre' of the pact with Stalin 'must have appeared to be a rare old muddle' to the convinced National Socialists, but he was confident that the 'about turn' had been accepted 'without misgivings'.[113] He was mistaken. He and his propagandists clearly still had some considerable explaining to do.

To this end, the Nazi state had a number of tools at its disposal. Cinema, ever the bellwether in totalitarian culture, was quickly co-ordinated. Though Nazi film-making had been obsessed with highlighting the 'Bolshevik menace' only months before, the signature of the pact caused it to move seamlessly to showing Germany's eastern neighbour in a more positive light. Typical was the fate of the film *Friesennot*, which had been released in 1935 and was still circulating in Germany in the autumn of 1939. Set in an ethnic German village in the Soviet Union, the film portrays the villagers' brutal persecution at the hands of the Red Army and its political commissars, culminating in a bloodbath and the murder of a local girl who had fallen in love with a Soviet officer. Despite its critical and commercial success – *Friesennot* had even found its way into Hitler's personal film collection – its anti-Bolshevik motifs were profoundly at odds with the change in political climate in 1939, and the film was duly banned in September.[114]

In place of such works, a new programme of films was swiftly commissioned, with themes that were more in tune with the new constellation of power. An obvious subject for cinematic treatment was the nineteenth-century statesman Otto von Bismarck, a hero to German nationalists who had nonetheless been careful to cultivate a healthy alliance with Russia. The film *Bismarck*, which was commissioned by Goebbels personally, appeared in Germany's cinemas in December 1940. Rather more popular, however, was *Der Postmeister*, a tale of doomed love in St Petersburg, adapted from a short story by Pushkin and featuring the former communist Heinrich George in the title role. But, despite receiving rave reviews and winning the 'Mussolini Prize' at the Venice International Film Festival in 1940, *Der Postmeister* enjoyed only a brief heyday. By the following summer it had disappeared from German cinema screens, damned by its sympathetic view of the Russian people.

Pro-Russian activity in other cultural spheres was much less evident. Music was an area in which one might expect to have heard an echo of the new era of Nazi–Soviet friendship, yet little change was apparent. Russian music was not banned in Germany until 1942, but there had been an active campaign to 'Germanise' the Third Reich's cultural output since the mid-1930s, and radio playlists, concert programmes and repertoires all, naturally, tended to reflect and perpetuate that bias. There were exceptions, of course. Soon after the pact was signed Munich Radio marked the occasion by cancelling a scheduled discussion entitled *I Accuse Moscow – the Comintern Plan for World Dictatorship* and replacing it with thirty minutes of Russian music.[115] But beyond such instances, the tone was one of continuity. It is telling, perhaps, that the Berlin Philharmonic devoted concerts during the Third Reich to the music of many foreign lands – including Greece, Bulgaria, Italy, Finland and even Britain – but never to that of Russia.[116] Opera was a little more ecumenical, with works by Glinka, Tchaikovsky, Borodin and Mussorgsky all being performed in Germany during the twenty-two months of the Nazi–Soviet Pact, but these were the exceptions to a solidly Germanic norm.

Germany's vibrant cabaret scene showed similar prejudices, with a few Russian or 'Cossack' choirs circulating, leavening the traditional music-hall fare by offering what one newspaper advertisement described as the 'unique experience' of 'Russian melodies'.[117] One such group, which called itself the 'Ukrainian National Choir', had the misfortune to have been in residence at the Wintergarten music hall in Berlin in June 1941, at the very time that their homeland was being attacked. Their show was cancelled two days after the German inva-sion.[118] The fate of the performers is unknown.

In retrospect, what is surprising is not how little effort was made to propagate a genuine friendship between the Nazis and the Soviets, but that any effort was expended at all. Given the ideological enmity between the two, it is remarkable that cultural exchanges, political education and the might of the respective propaganda machines were all harnessed, at least temporarily, in the interests of improving German–Soviet relations. Of course, as Stalin clearly recognised, any such improvement required sustained effort and engagement; and in the event it got neither. The political will was lacking, on both sides, to make any more than token gestures.

But the domestic reaction to the Nazi–Soviet Pact in Germany and the USSR demonstrated rather well the limitations of propaganda. Though both sides were acknowledged masters of the dark arts of political persuasion, neither could claim any particular success in convincing their respective publics about the sincerity of their partner's new-found benevolence. It may be, of course, that this lack of success was in some sense deliberate, reflecting the temporary, tactical nature of the relationship, and the desire on the part of both regimes not to dilute public distrust of a potentially dangerous enemy. And ideology was not abandoned entirely, of course. Both sides attempted to put an ideological gloss on the pact, in an effort to make events compre-hensible to the faithful. The Germans tried to convince themselves that the two sides were converging, that the Bolshevik excesses of the past had given way to a more nationally minded agenda. The Soviets, for their part, could paint their collaboration with Hitler as a tactical masterstroke in the wider struggle against western imperialism and capitalism.

Yet, regardless of such contortions and convoluted justifications, it must also be considered that, for many of their adherents, Nazism and communism were fervently held creeds, whose principles could not simply be jettisoned at will, irrespective of which way the political wind was blowing. As Harry Pollitt put it, 'I do not envy those comrades who can so lightly go from one conviction to another.' Pollitt refused to recant. Though he continued, after his removal, to campaign publicly for the new line of Rajani Palme Dutt and the Comintern, he did not change his personal view. Indeed, as one account has it, he once attended a communist meeting brandishing a copy of his controversial pamphlet *How to Win the War*, and when challenged exclaimed that he stood by every word of it.[119] Though they might have disagreed about almost everything else, there were doubtless many – fascists and communists alike – who would have applauded such steadfastness.

5

A Rough, Uncertain Wooing

As Winston Churchill would later recall, news of the Nazi–Soviet Pact 'broke upon the world like an explosion'.[1] Secretary of State for War, Leslie Hore-Belisha, struck a similar metaphor, describing the event as 'a complete bombshell'.[2] Strangely, considering their information gathering prowess, Britain's intelligence services had provided little suggestion of any imminent Nazi–Soviet rapprochement. Germany's desire for closer relations with Moscow was known, but it was thought to run counter to Hitler's instincts, and was considered to have found little reciprocity on the Soviet side. Accordingly, a Foreign Office briefing of that very week had judged that a Nazi–Soviet pact was 'unlikely'.[3] If the intelligence community was surprised, the shock for many in Britain beyond those circles was almost palpable. On all sides of the debate, the bitter enmity between the Nazis and the Soviets had been considered as a given, one of the fixed points of political life. Now, overnight, it had apparently been consigned to history. The signature of the pact, then, was one of those rare moments in history where the world – with all its norms and assumptions – appeared to have been turned on its head.

The spectre of those two nefarious regimes now in harness could be a profoundly disconcerting one. For the diarist and politician 'Chips' Channon, it presaged something like an apocalypse. 'Now the Nazis and the Bolsheviks have combined to destroy civilisation', he wrote, 'and the outlook for the world looks ghastly.' MP Harold Nicolson, who had persistently warned of the threat posed by fascism, would have concurred. He confided to his diary: 'I fear it means we are now humbled to the dust.' Veteran diplomat Sir Alexander Cadogan was merely exhausted. Sitting down to dinner on the night that the pact was announced, he mused on its significance but found only weariness: 'These crises really are too tiresome. We can't go on living like this in Europe. There's no point in it.'[4]

Public opinion in Britain was rather less doom-laden and was coloured by a popular respect for the USSR, which was still seen by many in rosy terms as the 'workers' paradise' of Moscow propaganda. A public opinion poll of April 1939 had returned an 87 per cent preference for a military alliance with Moscow, and figures had shifted little by the autumn.[5] Consequently, when news of the pact broke in the UK in August, there was a reluctance among the general public at least to interpret events prejudicially towards the Soviet Union. The opinion most often expressed was that Stalin was merely biding his time, protecting the USSR, and that he would eventually come in on Britain's side.[6]

Beyond that, there was nonetheless a growing certainty of the imminence of war. One British intelligence officer sent a postcard to his wife, on the very day that the pact was signed, warning her: 'I don't want to seem alarmist, but I really think that the Germans will invade Poland this weekend or early next week.'[7] He was not far wrong. The same realisation was summed up rather more pithily in the recollections of Hugh Dundas, an RAF pilot with 616 Squadron, then stationed at Manston on the Kent coast. When he heard the news of the pact, Dundas was sitting with Teddy St Aubyn, an Old Etonian and ex-Guards officer who had been one of the squadron's founders. St Aubyn's reaction was less than gentlemanly: 'Teddy put down his soup spoon and said in a loud, clear voice: "Well that's fucked it. That's the start of the fucking war."' 'I heard his words', Dundas later recalled, 'and knew they were true.'[8]

For all the justified fears, Britain presented an outward face of calm determination to the world in that last week of peace. A leading article in The Times of 23 August was perhaps typical of the stoical mood. It began by withholding judgement on the pact until precise details were known, but expressed doubts that 'the Nazi–Soviet deal would make any material difference to the balance of power either in peace-time or in war'. Nonetheless, it went on, Britain's position was clear: as had been announced by Downing Street, the pact would 'in no way affect [Britain's] obligations to Poland', which had been 'repeatedly stated in public' and which the government was 'determined to fulfil'.

Furthermore, as if to head off the charge that British negotiators had been too half-hearted in their efforts to win the Soviets over, the editorial suggested that 'the consistency and trustworthiness of Russian and of German diplomacy [had] been thrown into graver doubt than ever before'.[9] The clear implication was that the duplicitous Soviets were not worthy treaty partners, and that they were welcome to their new German friends.

Britain, meanwhile, was busy cementing existing relationships. At five o'clock on the afternoon of 25 August, British Foreign Secretary Edward Wood, Viscount Halifax, met with the Polish ambassador, Count Edward Raczyński, in his oak-panelled study in London's Whitehall. Now aged fifty-eight, Halifax had served as viceroy of India and had held a succession of ministerial posts before being appointed Secretary of State for Foreign Affairs early in 1938. He was a striking individual. Immensely tall, with a gaunt frame upon which clothes appeared to hang rather too loosely, he had a starkly receding hairline which seemed to accentuate his height. Calm and rational in character – possessed of an 'Olympian manner',[10] as one biographer put it – he had sad, hooded eyes, a lugubrious expression and a slight lisp.

His opposite number was of a similar stamp. Raczyński came from a Polish aristocratic family whose ancestors had served in both the Saxon and the Prussian courts. A fluent English-speaker who had studied at the London School of Economics, he had been appointed Poland's ambassador to the Court of St James's in 1934. Ten years younger than Halifax, he had a professorial bearing, with a high forehead and wire-rimmed spectacles perched upon an aquiline nose.

The discussion between Halifax and Raczyński was short, lasting about fifteen minutes. At issue was Britain's and Poland's response to the signature of the Nazi–Soviet Pact, which had been announced barely thirty-six hours earlier. Before the two men was a draft treaty, an 'Agreement of Mutual Assistance', which was intended to give permanence to the existing collaboration between the two countries, and reiterate British resolve to assist Poland in the event of German aggression. In truth, the agreement had been under discussion for some time, but had been given added urgency by events in Moscow. It was only a short document – eight articles totalling around 500 words – but it would be highly significant, not least in its provision that should either party 'become engaged in hostilities with a European Power in consequence of aggression by the latter', the other party would lend 'all the support and assistance in its power'. After reading the terms over once more, copies were signed, exchanged and counter-signed; the business was done. The 'war of nerves', Raczyński would later recall, appeared to be drawing to an end. Poland had secured an ally.[11]

An ally of sorts, at least. Although Whitehall was aware that, in the aftermath of the Nazi–Soviet Pact, the Poles might be reckoning with a Soviet invasion as well as a Nazi one, the guarantee was not extended to include Moscow.[12] The British Foreign Office viewed the pact as a fundamentally unnatural arrangement, and so – expecting it to prove temporary – was unwilling to close off a potentially vital link to the USSR by prematurely making her an enemy. Thus, though the treaty mentioned only aggression by an unspecified 'European Power', it was appended by a secret protocol, similarly signed by both parties, which provided clarity. By 'European Power', the protocol explained, the signatory parties understood 'Germany', and in the event of aggression by any other power, they resolved only to 'consult together' on their response. Though this offer was not especially generous, Whitehall mandarins minuted, Polish 'anxiety' was such that it was expected that Warsaw would be amenable.[13]

Although Halifax and Raczyński could not know it, they were giving a grimly ironic echo of the Nazi–Soviet secret protocol, by which the expected dismemberment of Poland had been agreed two days earlier. For the second time in as many days, a treaty was drawn up whose most significant clauses were contained in an unpublished addendum.

When Britain declared war on Germany nine days later, the nation was calm despite London being rattled by an air-raid alert on the very first afternoon. As would become the norm in the months and years to come, the lead was given that day by Churchill, who though not yet prime minister nonetheless did much to frame Britain's war aims and self-image when he spoke in the House of Commons on 3 September. Expressing optimism that there was 'a generation of

Britons' that was 'ready to prove itself' in the coming struggle, he outlined Britain's goals in the war then beginning. 'This is not a question of fighting for Danzig or fighting for Poland', he said. 'We are fighting to save the whole world from the pestilence of Nazi tyranny and in defence of all that is most sacred to man.' A month later, Chamberlain used similar words in outlining British war aims, which were, he said, 'To redeem Europe from the perpetual and recurring fear of German aggression, and enable the peoples of Europe to preserve their independence and their liberties.'[14]

Thus the official British attitude towards Germany was made very clear: it was one of principled and implacable hostility to the evils of Nazi totalitarianism. But, for all the clarity of the British position towards Germany, the attitude – official and unofficial – taken towards the Soviet Union was rather more complex. As much as the British government would wrestle with the question of *how* to take the war to Hitler during the 'Phoney War', it would also have to seriously consider *whether* to also go to war against Stalin.

Public opinion was little help. On the one hand, there were those, like 'Chips' Channon, who saw in Soviet actions that autumn the intrigues of a grand conspiracy. 'Our world . . . is committing suicide', he wrote, 'while Stalin laughs and the Kremlin triumphs.'[15] Yet among the general public there was still widespread sympathy for the Soviets, and a feeling that Chamberlain's government had not done enough to woo Moscow into an alliance that might feasibly have halted Hitler. This complex of sentiments was perhaps best expressed by a civil servant from Hampshire, who confided his feelings on the outbreak of war to the Mass Observation project:

> When I come down to dinner, I'm told that we are at war and that Chamberlain has spoken. I'm glad I missed him. I don't want to hear him say 'God knows I have done my best!' I don't believe it. He could have secured Russian co-operation.

'I'm willing to fight Fascism if necessary', he concluded, but 'if we'd treated Russia decently it wouldn't be necessary'.[16]

The complexities of public opinion and the apparent absurdity of Stalin's new-found friendship with Hitler were a boon for the cartoonists of the British press, who captured the mood rather well that autumn. A common visual theme, adopted by Bert Thomas in the *Evening Standard*, was to show Nazi Germany and the Soviet Union characterised as a gorilla and a bear. In this way, on 18 September – the day after the Soviet invasion of eastern Poland – Thomas showed the two squeezed uncomfortably into a single bed: the bear hunched unhappily, while the gorilla leans over the side to surreptitiously reach for a dagger. At the end of the following month, Thomas returned to the theme, showing the Nazi gorilla bathing in a pool of 'mud and blood' – symbolic of war and the Nazi 'New Order' in Europe – and beckoning the Soviet bear to join him, shouting: 'Come on in – it's fine!'

Perhaps the most famous cartoonist of the period, however, was David Low, a London-based New Zealander, whose satirical representations of Hitler and Mussolini had led to his work being banned in Germany and Italy, and who would earn the honour of appearing on the SS special arrest list in 1940.[17] Adept at baiting the Nazis, he would score a number of hits that autumn, including 'Uncle Joe's Pawnshop' on 2 October, which showed a furtive Hitler and Ribbentrop asking Stalin what he would 'give them' for Nazism; and 'Someone is taking Someone for a Walk', where Stalin and Hitler were depicted arm in arm, tied at the ankle, in a three-legged walk along the 'Eastern Frontier', each with a pistol held behind his back. With such striking images, Low was able to sum up the confusions, fears and absurdities of the age with a visual clarity that few others could match.[18]

Low's most famous cartoon of the period was 'Rendezvous', which was published in the *Evening Standard* on 20 September. It showed Stalin and Hitler meeting amidst the war-torn ruins, bowing deeply and doffing their caps to one another as they exchange pleasantries. 'The scum of the earth, I believe?' says Hitler, while Stalin retorts with: 'The bloody assassin of the workers, I presume?' At their feet, meanwhile, lies the prostrate figure of 'Poland'. The iconic image neatly summed up the prevailing British attitude – that the pact was little more than a cynical short-term arrangement between ideologically opposed enemies.

In British government circles a rather more nuanced view prevailed: a clear-eyed realisation of the need to keep channels of communication open with Moscow, tempered by a visceral fear of Soviet intentions. That ambivalent position was given its first serious test when Soviet forces marched into eastern Poland on the morning of 17 September, thereby making a nonsense of their professed position of 'neutrality' in the war. An editorial in *The Times* the next day was as damning of Moscow as it was uncharacteristically verbose. 'Russian troops crossed the Polish border along the whole front', it announced:

> Only those can be disappointed who clung to the ingenuous belief that Russia was to be distinguished from her Nazi neighbour, despite the identity of their institutions and political idiom, by the principles and purpose behind her foreign policy. The Germans certainly knew better when they judged that the self-denying objects of a peace front would prove pallid and uninviting beside the offer of two Polish provinces at no immediate cost. Germany was to do the murder and Russia was to share the estate.

The editorial concluded on a grimly defiant note:

> Public opinion here is revolted though not in the least dismayed by these cynical exercises in lower diplomacy. Sympathy for Poland, which was warm and eager yesterday, is aflame today . . . We look out upon a world that now has fewer disguises . . . Across the world the line between civilisation and the jungle is drawn.[19]

In Whitehall, meanwhile, the enquiry was made whether the Soviet invasion of Poland would trigger a British declaration of war against the Soviet Union, as the German invasion had done two weeks earlier. Cabinet was reminded by Viscount Halifax, however, of the terms of the secret protocol to the Anglo-Polish Agreement, and the 'understanding' that British assistance would only be triggered in the event of German action. 'On this interpretation', Halifax noted, 'Great Britain was not bound by treaty to become involved in war with the USSR as a result of their invasion of Poland.' For good measure, he added that 'the French Government took the same view'.[20]

Indeed, rather than declaring war on the Soviets, the British were keen to build a connection with Moscow, so as to forestall the spectre of a full-blown German–Soviet alliance. To this end, one bright spark in cabinet even suggested a non-aggression pact, until it was pointed out that such arrangements 'stink somewhat since August 23'.[21] Instead, trade was to be employed as the icebreaker. In the first week of October an agreement was made for the exchange of £1 million of Soviet timber in return for rubber and tin. Other commodities were also considered, including lead, copper, cocoa and machine tools.[22] Yet, though the negotiations were not without success, they were shot through with paranoia regarding Soviet motives and actions. Talks were linked, for instance, to the fate of some sixteen British ships then detained in Soviet ports, while a note was even made of the possibility that the Soviets were acting in bad faith and that they would arrange for their outgoing shipments to be torpedoed by German submarines.[23]

Paradoxically, in the same week as the trade agreement was signed, a memorandum by the British chiefs of staff gave an 'appreciation' of the new strategic situation created by the Nazi–Soviet Pact. It made for sobering reading. Not only could the USSR 'do serious harm to the Allied cause while remaining nominally neutral', it argued, it could also render 'the maximum economic assistance' to Germany, thereby slowing the effects of the British economic blockade. In addition, it warned that the Baltic states and Finland were 'helpless' in the face of Soviet aggression, and that the occupation of Bessarabia was 'quite possible'. This prescient, perceptive memorandum concluded by reminding the British cabinet that 'Russia's abiding aim is to spread world revolution' and suggested that the Nazi–Soviet Pact provided Moscow with a 'golden opportunity' to extend 'Communistic activities throughout the world'.[24]

This was the schizophrenic ambivalence that characterised the British government's attitude towards the Soviet Union that autumn; a fear of Soviet ulterior motives entwined with an even greater fear that a lack of engagement might drive Moscow definitively into Hitler's arms, resulting in a fully-fledged Nazi–Soviet alliance. It was against this complex background that one of Winston Churchill's most famous phrases was coined. In stark contrast to the unequivocally critical attitude that had been struck towards the Germans, Churchill was sympathetic towards the Soviets in a speech which was broadcast by the BBC on 1 October, despite growing evidence that they were rivalling their Nazi allies in their aggressive intentions towards Poland. Soviet actions in invading Poland, Churchill told his listeners, were driven by 'a cold policy of self-interest' but were 'necessary for the safety of Russia against the Nazi menace'. Far from criticising, Churchill was emollient, as indulgent of his potential Soviet ally as he was damning of his German enemy. Russia, he concluded, was 'a riddle, wrapped in a mystery inside an enigma'.[25]

Any fragile equilibrium, however, would be profoundly shaken by Moscow's invasion of Finland – the 'Winter War' – at the end of November 1939. Given that it destroyed any remaining illusions among western ruling elites about the true nature of Soviet intentions, the Winter War served to make a decision on the British position towards the Soviet Union all the more pressing. Already a month before, while Moscow had been ratcheting up the pressure on Finland, some in the British cabinet had begun to consider firmer action towards the Soviets. At the end of October, therefore, at the urging of the British ambassador in Helsinki, Foreign Secretary Halifax had requested a report from the chiefs of staff on the merits and demerits of a British declaration of war on the USSR.[26]

That report returned with a definitive recommendation *not* to declare war on the Soviets, but still the idea did not die. In mid-December, during a discussion about the possibilities of sending material aid to the Finns, it was raised once more, with Halifax again informing the cabinet that he 'had been examining broadly the implications of a conflict between ourselves and Russia', but conceding that he was 'not sure how the matter should be handled'.[27] Halifax certainly faced a conundrum. His intention, as he had stated to a colleague, was to 'drive a wedge' between the Soviets and the Germans, to disrupt the economic and political relationship between them.[28] Yet trade with Moscow had not served its ulterior purpose of bringing about a moderation of Soviet actions, as had been dramatically demonstrated by the Soviet invasion of Finland. Moreover, it was not in Britain's interest to supply a state that was 'benevolently neutral' towards Germany, as it was feared that 'exports to the USSR were probably tantamount to exports to Germany'.[29] However, a declaration of war did not make military or strategic sense, as it would only increase the number of Britain's enemies, while potentially serving to further cement that German–Soviet relationship.

In time, a course of action between those two extremes emerged. While neither of the previous options was discarded entirely, it was suggested that Britain might look to frustrate the relationship by involving the Soviet Union in strategic and economic difficulties, so that she would in turn be 'less able to help Germany'. One strand of this policy consisted of hampering Soviet international trade so as to prevent vital raw materials from falling into German hands, thereby, in effect, extending the British blockade of Germany to include the Soviet Union. So it was that British authorities began intercepting and detaining Soviet vessels, such as the *Selenga*, which was stopped at Hong Kong in January 1940 with a cargo of tungsten, antimony and tin, bound for Vladivostok.[30]

If nothing else, such actions certainly brought the Soviets back to the negotiating table. In March, the Soviet ambassador in London, Ivan Maisky, asked in a meeting with Halifax whether the British government would be willing to resume stalled trade negotiations, and if so whether a first step might be the halting of the interceptions of Soviet ships. Halifax's response was cool, referring disparagingly to the Soviet government's policy of keeping 'the war between the Allies and Germany going, to their own advantage', but he did later raise the question in cabinet as to whether – as part of any possible agreement – the Soviets might be persuaded to restrict their deliveries of oil to Germany.[31] Evidently, the irritant of intercepting Soviet shipping might yet bear fruit.

However, at the same time as these talks were taking place, the British and French were planning something altogether bolder. For a number of years, the vulnerability of the Soviet Union's primary oil-producing region, centred on Baku in the Caucasus, had been well appreciated in the West. Given that it produced fully 75 per cent of the USSR's oil, and was only around 200 km from the Turkish border, Baku was rightly seen as Stalin's Achilles heel.

Thus, when schemes were being considered in London and Paris, in the winter of 1939–40, by which pressure might be brought to bear on Moscow, the idea of targeting Baku once again came to the fore. It was a plan with a curious complex of motivators. In the first instance, those responsible for drawing it up could point to the region's vulnerability to air-raiding, and could speculate on the possible impact that such an attack would have not only on the Soviet economy, but also crucially on that of Nazi Germany. Indeed, the collusion between Moscow and Berlin appears to have triggered a fundamental re-appraisal of British geostrategic priorities. Aware that Germany would now be virtually immune to the traditional British tactic of the blockade, via its economic relationship with the USSR, British planners perceived an urgency to strangle the new joint entity – 'Teutoslavia', as the hawkish Robert Vansittart put it – in its crib. 'We should strike at Russo-Germany', Vansittart told the cabinet in the spring of 1940, 'before it gets too strong.'[32]

French opinion was, if anything, more belligerent. Indeed, France had broadly echoed British actions over previous months, compen-sating for her domestic difficulties by providing London with vital moral support. But Prime Minister Edouard Daladier took a very provocative stance towards the Soviets that winter – outlawing the French Communist Party and expelling the Soviet ambassador, for instance – in part to pre-empt criticism of his failure to adequately help the Finns. Consequently, the idea of attacking the Caucasus was supported by many in the French cabinet, such as the French navy minister César Campinchi, who had optimistically declared that 'if only we could detach Russia from Germany, we should have won the war'.[33] Others were more ambitious still. The French air force officer Paul Stehlin recalled being shown a secret map at air force headquar-ters in Paris that winter, depicting 'two big arrows, one starting from Syria and the other from Finland, meeting east of Moscow'. It was explained to him by the assistant to the chief of staff:

> Russia is now allied to Germany. Accordingly, by attacking it we will deprive Hitler's Germany of its essential resources and also remove the war further from our borders. General Weygand is in command of our troops in Syria and the Lebanon, which will march in the direction of Baku in order to put an end to the oil production there; from there they will proceed towards the north in order to join the armies that will march from Scandinavia and Finland on Moscow.[34]

Astonishingly, it appears the operation in the Caucasus was only a prelude to what the French high command really had in mind.

Yet, beyond these soaring ambitions, there were a number of rather murkier ulterior motives at play, not least a French desire to avoid simply provoking the Germans on the western front, and a British wish for some 'action' to lift the suffocating gloom of the 'Phoney War'. At the root of it all, it seems, was a dose of old-fashioned anti-Bolshevism, a fear of the Nazi–Soviet Pact developing into a genuine alliance, and an assumption that the USSR somehow represented Hitler's 'soft underbelly'. As one French commentator noted in 1940, the perception in French government circles was that Russia 'would collapse from the slightest blow', and that France 'could not beat Hitler until it had crushed Stalin'.[35]

The idea of bombing Baku had already swirled around the British and French governments for some time by the end of 1939, but with the Soviet victory against the Finns in the Winter War in March 1940, it gained renewed traction. At the beginning of the year, a report from the British Air Staff predicted that just a handful of bombers could succeed in rendering the Soviet oil industry lame, thereby hitting Hitler's military production. In early March 1940, the War Office duly approved the construction of the necessary airfields in Turkey[36] and, within the month, a modified Lockheed Electra, belonging to the RAF's Photographic Development Unit at Heston, had made two sorties out of Habbaniya in Iraq to take reconnaissance photographs of the targets. In line with the secret agent's guiding concept of 'plausible deniability', the Lockheed had had its RAF roundel removed and replaced with civilian markings. Similarly its five-man RAF crew were dressed in civilian clothes and carried non-military identification.

Though the first reconnaissance mission passed off without incident, the second – overflying Batumi on the eastern Black Sea coast on 5 April 1940 – attracted the attention of Soviet defence forces. Sighted crossing the Turkish–Soviet frontier, the Lockheed was targeted by flak gunners over the city, before finally being driven off by fighter aircraft of the Red Air Force. As if to underline to importance of the mission, those intercepting Red Air Force fighters were recorded as being German-built Messerschmitt Bf-109s.[37]

The Soviet Union's reaction was not limited to a few Messerschmitts. At the same time that the Lockheed was circling the Caucasus, British emissary Sir Stafford Cripps was in Moscow for talks with Molotov. His mission was primarily concerned with the establishment of a trade deal, but as ever was premised upon the idea of trade as a precursor to an improvement in political relations, with a view to preventing even closer relations between the Soviets and the Nazis. Surprisingly, perhaps, Molotov was very accommodating, indicating to Cripps that the Soviet Union was keen to make a trade and political agreement with the United Kingdom.

The root of Molotov's uncharacteristic bonhomie seems to have been an awareness of Anglo-French plans for Baku and Batumi. How the Soviet authorities gained wind of the plan is unclear, but they were certainly aware of it by early March 1940, when, according to French diplomatic sources, they had been so concerned about the possibility of an air attack on the Caucasus that they had asked the advice of American engineers as to the possible consequences on the ground. The reply was unequivocal. 'As a result of the manner in which the oil fields have been exploited', it said, 'the earth is so saturated with oil that fire could spread immediately to the entire neighbouring region; it would be months before it could be extinguished and years before work could be resumed.'[38] Soon after that opinion was delivered, the Soviet ambassador in London approached Halifax with an offer of trade negotiations. Clearly a Soviet charm offensive was under way to forestall any such belligerent action. As the soldier and diplomat Fitzroy Maclean surmised, the Soviet plan was to sow doubt in Allied minds about the best course of action, and 'by confusing the issue, keep us in play for as long as possible, and thus gain a very necessary respite'. In that process, Maclean added sourly, 'They appear to have found a willing tool in Sir Stafford Cripps.'[39]

Meanwhile, as the Lockheed and her crew returned to Heston, the films were handed over to the RAF Intelligence Section, which analysed the results. In their assessment, which was forwarded to their political masters in mid-April, the analysts concluded that any 'substantial reduction in output of oil from Russia's own resources . . . must lead sooner or later to the complete collapse of the war potential of the USSR'. 'Moreover', they added, 'the repercussions of the dislocation of the Russian oil industry might well prove disastrous for Germany as well.'[40] Soon after, the RAF proposal, whose primary advocate was Air Commodore John Slessor, the Director of Plans at the Air Ministry, was given the name 'Operation Pike'.

Slessor's advocacy was telling. As a veteran airman and the author of the 1937 study *Air Power and Armies*, which proposed a greater degree of collaboration between the army and air force and the use of aerial bombing as a weapon against enemy morale, Slessor was one of the RAF's most senior proponents of the tactical use of air power. He was not alone. In many ways 1940 was the high-water mark of faith in the military potential of aerial bombing: the Luftwaffe's devastating attack on the Spanish town of Guernica, three years earlier, was still fresh in many minds, as was the German bombing of Warsaw the previous year. The belief, expressed by British prime minister Stanley Baldwin in 1932, that 'the bomber will always get through' still held considerable currency; at least until the Butt Report of 1941 exploded the myth of aerial omnipotence, by demonstrating that only one in four RAF crews could drop their munitions within five miles of the target.[41] Operation Pike, then, can be seen in retrospect as an expression of Royal Air Force hubris – a wildly exaggerated confidence in its own abilities.

There were other objections. Many of those who had baulked at the prospect of British military intervention in the Winter War were shocked by the rather offhand and glib way in which an aggressive strike against the USSR was being discussed. The Labour MP Josiah Wedgwood expressed his indignant opposition to an attack on the Soviet Union during a House of Commons debate on the Finnish Crisis in March 1940. 'It is an amazing idea', he said, 'that in the middle of a war with Hitler we should gratuitously take on another war with Russia.'[42] He spoke from personal experience. As a younger man, he had been wounded in another 'peripheral action', the Dardanelles Campaign of 1915, and had participated in a British intelligence-gathering mission to Siberia three years later.

A rather more practical concern was that raised in cabinet by Lord Hankey in January 1940, when he pointed out that the wider objective of hamstringing Germany by hitting the Soviet oil industry was unrealistic. 'Only a trickle' of Soviet oil was reaching Germany, he said, adding – quite correctly – that it was Romania that was 'by far the largest source of oil' for German industry. Though his figures were revised by a subsequent report to cabinet, the gist of his argument was not. In March, Secretary for Mines Geoffrey Lloyd told the cabinet that petroleum exports to that point, from the USSR and occupied eastern Europe into Germany, accounted for only 3 per cent of

Germany's fuel stocks.[43] Hitler's dependence on Soviet fuel, it seems, had been vastly exaggerated.

Despite such objections, planning for Operation Pike continued, until it was overtaken by events and finally shelved when German forces invaded France and the Low Countries on 10 May 1940. Hitler, it seemed, had found his own solution to the tedium of the 'drôle de guerre'.

One counter-argument that puzzlingly does not appear to have occurred to the military and civilian planners of Operation Pike is that of the likely strategic consequences of any such action. Generally, the proposed attack on the USSR was given the broader rationale of disrupting Stalin's relationship with Hitler, but the idea that any such attack might have had the opposite effect, and might have actually strengthened the Berlin–Moscow connection, does not appear to have arisen. Similarly, little intellectual effort seems to have been expended on the issue of what might have happened if Operation Pike had succeeded beyond Slessor's wildest dreams and led to the destabilisation of the USSR. In that event, the most likely benefactor would not have been the Western Powers, but rather Hitler, who would have been free to march east unopposed and take control of those same Caucasus oilfields for himself.

It remains an open question how the prospect of blatant aggression against the Soviet Union might have been received by the wider British public, which persistently viewed the USSR in general and Stalin in particular much more positively than did the political and military elite. In the summer of 1939, for instance, shortly before the outbreak of the war, a questionnaire for Mass Observation, the official network established to keep government informed of public opinion, asked contributors to rank the world leaders for whom they had the greatest respect, and the nations that they would 'prefer the British nation to collaborate with'. The results would have surprised many among the ruling class, with the Soviet Union ranking fourth among the nation's potential allies, close behind France and above Poland; Stalin even ranked second as a 'respected' leader, behind Roosevelt.[44]

It seems that by the winter of 1939, those assessments were essentially unchanged despite the nasty surprise of Stalin's collaboration with Hitler. Though the same questionnaire exercise was not repeated until 1941, it is clear from the anecdotal evidence gathered by Mass

Observation that a positive view of the Soviet Union still prevailed. In the first half of 1940, public opinion was optimistic that the Soviet Union would ultimately enter the war on the Allied side, with even those who were instinctively anti-Communist recognising the need for co-operation with Stalin.[45]

In the summer, as France fell and Britain was imperilled, that positive view of the Soviets barely changed, despite Moscow's repeated expressions of support for Hitler. In early July, for instance, opinion in Nottingham expressed a decrease in anti-Soviet feeling and the curious desire to 'accept Russian help', even though none was actually being offered.[46] Even the Soviet annexation of the Baltic states, Bessarabia and Northern Bukovina that summer did nothing to alert the majority of the British people to Stalin's aggressive, expansionist intentions. Indeed, an opinion from Wales, in July 1940, merely expressed the plaintive hope that 'Russia will be helpful to us in her own time.'[47]

Only with the start of the Battle of Britain did a degree of realism begin to emerge. Given that Britain was now fighting for her very life, it was perhaps inevitable that a shift in opinion should be discernible, away from an expectation of assistance from outside and towards a cussed self-reliance. By August 1940, therefore, although outright hostility to the Soviet Union was seldom expressed, there was a growing awareness that expecting help from Moscow was 'wishful thinking', and even that the Soviet Union was simply 'playing her own game'.[48] Yet, despite that gradual shift in public opinion, there was none of the outright fear that infected the British military and political establishment about the ideological threat that the Soviet Union still posed. Stalin's credit, though profoundly dubious, evidently still held good with large numbers of ordinary Britons.

Of course, the power that Britons most desperately wanted to have onside in 1940 was the USA. Yet, in that tumultuous summer, Roosevelt's America was still determined to keep Europe, and all its troubles, very much at arm's length. For all Roosevelt's high-flown rhetoric about the need to defend democracy against tyranny, and to 'quarantine aggressors', he had proved unable to challenge an isolationist domestic consensus which – though broadly supportive of the British and French – was deeply wary of renewed European entanglements. US Congress had passed four Neutrality Acts in the late 1930s, forbidding American involvement in foreign conflicts and imposing an embargo on arms sales to belligerent nations. Once war arrived in Europe in 1939, Roosevelt had duly reasserted American neutrality, but had nonetheless sought gently to nudge American opinion towards a qualified support of Britain, even securing a revision of the Neutrality Act, permitting foreign powers to purchase war materiel from the US on a 'cash & carry' basis.

To their credit, Roosevelt and his administration were generally as clear-eyed and critical of the Soviets as they were of the Germans, seeing the two very much as totalitarian cousins, a view which had been amply confirmed by the signature of the Nazi–Soviet Pact. Indeed, the opinion of the Soviets held by some in the US State Department and diplomatic service was downright damning. The American ambassador in Moscow, Laurence Steinhardt, for instance, employed some distinctly undiplomatic language in referring to his hosts. The Soviets, he explained, 'need us a great deal more than we need them and as the only language they understand is the language of force, I think it high time we invoked the only doctrine they respect'. Steinhardt's colleague, assistant military attaché Joseph Michela, was even more outspoken, denouncing the 'ruling hierarchy' of the USSR as 'ignorant . . . cunning, shrewd, cruel and unscrupulous', with policies 'based on expediency alone'.[49]

Roosevelt himself, at one remove from the somewhat febrile atmosphere of the Moscow embassy, was rather more cautious, wary of exacerbating the ongoing conflict and of driving Stalin further into Hitler's embrace. Thus he resisted labelling the USSR as a belligerent nation after their invasion of Poland in mid-September 1939. Similarly, he accepted the Soviet military expansion into the Baltic states the following month at face value, choosing to interpret it as an anti-German move rather than the subjection of three sovereign independent states.[50]

Such tactical caution would be difficult to maintain, especially when the Soviet invasion of Finland in November appeared to give definitive proof of Stalin's perfidy. Roosevelt declared the United States to be 'not only horrified, but thoroughly angry' after the Soviet attack and even considered breaking off relations with Moscow. 'People are asking', he wrote on 30 November, 'why one should have anything to do with the present Soviet leaders, because their idea of civilisation and human happiness is so totally different from ours.'[51] In response, he would issue condemnations, calls for restraint and restrict raw-material sales to the Soviets, but he stopped short of supplying the Finns, even though the decision amounted – according to the Finnish ambassador – to signing Finland's death warrant.[52]

Finland so hardened Roosevelt's attitude that he increasingly shared the critical view of his Moscow embassy, and began to warn of the perils of the joint 'Soviet–German' domination of Europe. In a speech to a pro-Soviet audience in February 1940, for instance, he angrily described the USSR as 'a dictatorship as absolute as any other dictatorship in the world', which had 'allied itself with another dictatorship' and had 'invaded a neighbour so infinitesimally small that it can do no conceivable harm to the Soviet Union'. To boos and catcalls from his audience, Roosevelt persisted with his attack, ridiculing the idea that the USSR might evolve into 'peace-loving, popular government' as 'unadulterated twaddle based on ignorance'.[53] For the moment, at least, the Soviet Union was evidently viewed in Washington not as part of the solution, but – like Hitler's Germany – as part of the problem.

Such assessments were to change, however. By the summer of 1940, with Britain and France facing the real prospect of defeat at German hands, the American attitude towards Germany hardened still further, while that towards the Soviet Union grew a little more relaxed, with Undersecretary of State Sumner Welles being instructed by Roosevelt to open discussions with the Soviet ambassador, Konstantin Oumansky. Though the talks achieved little of substance, their importance as a gesture should not be underestimated. Roosevelt was beginning to prepare the ground for a possible British collapse, and was feeling his way towards a necessary rapprochement with Moscow.[54]

For the British, meanwhile, something more than gestures was required. On 15 May, in a message to Roosevelt, Churchill had described Britain's need for US ships to help secure her Atlantic supply lines as a matter of 'life and death'. Two months later, he was even more imploring. 'Mr President', he wrote, 'with great respect I must tell you that in the long history of the world this is a thing to do *now*.'[55] The French were similarly insistent. In June 1940, with his forces buckling under German pressure, premier Paul Reynaud made a final appeal to Roosevelt, requesting that American troops be sent to assist France in her hour of need.

Roosevelt's response was less than immediately dynamic. In an election year, he preferred to steer a moderate course, keen not to be outflanked by his Republican opponent, Wendell Willkie, on foreign policy. His reply to Reynaud, therefore, was a study in emollient non-committal. Though he declared himself 'deeply moved' by Reynaud's message, and lauded the 'magnificent resistance' of British and French forces, Roosevelt made no firm commitments beyond the assurance that his government was 'doing everything in its power to make available to Allied governments the material they so urgently require'.[56] Though those efforts would bear fruit in time – in the 'Destroyers for Bases' Agreement of September 1940, and ultimately in the Lend-Lease Act from March 1941 – from the perspective of the summer of 1940, America was still some distance from being the 'arsenal of democracy' that it would later declare itself to be. For the time being at least, Britain was alone.

It was against this background that Britain was faced with a rather curious episode, which neatly demonstrated the strangely altered circumstances in which the world found itself in 1940. Though most on the right of British politics had hurried to confirm their patriotic credentials upon the outbreak of war in 1939, a few hardened anti-Semites around the disbanded 'Right Club' had continued their clandestine efforts to secure a negotiated peace with Nazi Germany. As part of that effort, contact had been made with a young cipher clerk at the American embassy in London, Tyler Kent, who had begun to take a particular interest in the correspondence passing between Churchill and Roosevelt. As an 'isolationist' and someone who had worked in the US embassy in Moscow, Kent was suspected by the FBI of harbouring sympathies for the Soviets; yet in the curious new constellation of 1940 he soon found himself assisting those who were profoundly pro-Nazi in their outlook. Through a 'White' Russian intermediary, Anna Wolkoff, Kent made contact with the Right Club and began passing them details of the secret correspondence by which Churchill was attempting to bring Roosevelt into the war, in the hope that by publicising such contacts both parties would be embarrassed and American involvement in the European war could be prevented.

Pro-Soviet interests, it seemed, had momentarily meshed perfectly with those of the pro-Nazis.

Unfortunately for both parties, this unholy liaison had already attracted the attention of MI5 and the conspiracy was swiftly wound up when Wolkoff and Kent were arrested in May 1940; a search of Kent's flat revealed 1,500 secret documents that he had copied from American diplomatic correspondence. Tried for violating defence regulations, the two were sentenced to ten and seven years' imprisonment respectively.[57] In the aftermath, fears of the existence of a pro-German 'fifth column' in Britain led to the extension of the powers of internment without trial – the infamous 'Defence Regulation 18B' – and the arrest of many of those on the extreme right, including Oswald Mosley and the Right Club leader Archibald Ramsay.

Defence Regulation 18B was a typically British compromise. Part of a raft of over a hundred emergency regulations decreed in late August 1939, in response to the Nazi–Soviet Pact and the imminence of war, it was in essence an updating of the old Defence of the Realm Act of 1914, allowing for preventive detention of those thought to be a danger to national security. Its wording specified those who might be considered as suspects, including those 'of hostile origins or associations'; those who 'had acted prejudicially to public safety or the defence of the realm'; or those who were members of organisations that were subject to 'foreign influence or control' or whose leaders had 'sympathies with the system of government' of an enemy power.[58]

Of course, such a broad definition could theoretically apply just as much to Mosley's British Union of Fascists (BUF) as it could to Harry Pollitt's Communist Party of Great Britain (CPGB). Yet, in practice, Regulation 18B was applied almost exclusively to those on the right; indeed, of the 1,600 or so British subjects detained under the ruling, about 75 per cent were from the BUF, representing almost the entire active party membership.[59] The only CPGB member so interned was a Yorkshire shop steward, John Mason, who was arrested in July 1940 for allegedly attempting to undermine industrial production.[60] This asymmetry was noted at the time, and Mosley himself cried foul, insisting that the extended application of Regulation 18B in the summer of 1940 was a direct consequence (and condition) of the Labour Party's entry into government.[61] Away from the conspiracy theories, it is clear that many in British government circles were well aware of the potential risk to national security posed by the hard left, but were unwilling to act for fear of the hostile reaction that any such clampdown might provoke, as was demonstrated by the furious public response to a BBC decision in February 1941 not to employ CPGB supporters.[62] Clearly, while the Soviets were being courted abroad, it made little sense to persecute their supporters at home.

In these trying circumstances, with American support not yet secured, a return to a policy of negotiation with the Soviets must have appeared sensible in Whitehall, and the man chosen for the task was Sir Stafford Cripps. A rather humourless socialist and devout Marxist, Cripps had been expelled from the Labour Party for his advocacy of a 'Popular Front' against fascism and had publicly defended the Soviet Union's invasions of both Poland and Finland. Consequently, he must have appeared to the British establishment to have been the ideal candidate to sweet-talk Moscow. He also had a promising track record. As we have seen, he had visited the Soviet Union for impromptu talks with Molotov in February 1940, during the course of which he had gained the impression that the Soviets were 'apprehensive' about their relationship with Germany and were keen for some rapprochement with Britain.[63] So, though doubts were expressed in cabinet about his political reliability, Cripps was duly dispatched to Moscow in late May 1940, with a narrow remit for trade negotiations, being swiftly upgraded to ambassador following Soviet accusations of *lèse-majesté*.

Cripps' optimism swiftly wilted, however. His first interview with Molotov was decidedly chilly and he was obliged to report that, despite his requests, no further meeting was granted for another ten days thereafter – the classic diplomatic snub. Moreover, the realisation began to dawn on him that the Soviets were minded to maintain their benevolent relationship with Germany; and far from being keen on a realignment of their foreign policy, they were apparently only interested in securing a few additional supplies and using the prospect of British negotiations as a lever on Berlin. Back in London, Foreign Office mandarin Sir Orme Sargeant was grimly realistic:

> I am sorry for Sir S. Cripps, who is now entering the humiliating phase which all British negotiators in Moscow have to go through when they

are simply kept waiting on the doormat until such time as the Soviet Government consider it desirable, as part of their policy of playing off one Power against the other, to take notice . . . Stalin has meanwhile got Sir S. Cripps exactly where he wants him, that is to say, as a suppliant on his doormat holding his pathetic little peace offerings of tin in one hand and rubber in the other. Stalin hopes to be able to counter any German browbeating and nagging by pointing to Sir S. Cripps on the doormat, and threatening to have him in and start talking with him instead of with the German Ambassador.[64]

Cripps' left-wing convictions, far from endearing him to his Soviet hosts, may also have proved an obstacle. As Churchill confessed after the war:

we did not at that time realize sufficiently that Soviet Communists hate Left Wing politicians even more than they do Tories and Liberals. The nearer a man is to Communism in sentiment, the more obnoxious he is to the Soviets, unless he joins the Party.[65]

Cripps, it seems, may have been the wrong choice after all. As the Foreign Office noted, it would have had more success in Moscow if it had sent 'a rather rude duke'.[66]

Nonetheless, Cripps persevered, and on 1 July he was granted an audience with Stalin to present a personal message from Churchill. France having now fallen, Churchill was anxious to reiterate Britain's position and to ask Stalin to reconsider his. 'Germany became your friend almost at the same moment as she became our enemy', he wrote. Now that the military situation had changed, Churchill wanted to make it plain that it remained Britain's policy to save herself from German domination and to liberate the rest of Europe. And, while he conceded that only the Soviet Union could judge whether Germany's bid for hegemony constituted a threat to its interests, Churchill reassured Stalin that the British government was prepared to discuss any of the problems that had been created by German aggression.

Stalin's response gave little away. He was said to have been 'formal and frigid' during the meeting, ignoring Cripps' tentative probing and delivering no direct reply to Churchill's message. If he was concerned by the strategic shift that Hitler's defeat of France had clearly caused, he certainly did not let it show. Indeed, it was during this 'severely frank discussion' that Stalin made his rather clumsy comments about opposing Britain's desired preservation of 'the old equilibrium' in Europe, thereby appearing to welcome the seismic impact that Hitler's aggression had wrought.[67] Far from mourning France's fall, therefore, Stalin seemed to celebrate it.

Cripps was left in little doubt that Stalin was wedded to his German alignment and that there would be no major shift in Soviet foreign policy without substantial concessions from the British side. This, he feared, was most unlikely, not least because he believed that Britain in truth had 'not the slightest desire to work with Russia' and ingrained British hostility to the USSR had in fact contributed to driving Stalin into Hitler's arms.[68] As if it were not difficult enough, Cripps' faith in his task was tested still further by the release of documents captured by the Germans in Paris relating to Operation Pike, the aborted Allied plan to bomb the Soviet oilfields.[69] Britain's embarrassment, it seemed, was complete.

In an attempt to break the resulting impasse, Cripps' next approach sought to add some genuine substance to the well-meaning rhetoric, in what he saw as a 'last opportunity' to shift Moscow in London's direction. Building on conversations both with Molotov and with his political masters in Whitehall, Cripps presented a revised proposal on 22 October, which amounted in many ways to a mirror image of the arrangement that the Soviets had come to with Hitler the year before.

Under its terms, Britain offered what might be called a reset of its relationship with Moscow. It promised to treat the USSR on a par with the United States, consulting with the Soviet government on questions of post-war organisation, and ensuring Moscow's participation in the future peace conference. In addition, Britain pledged to refrain from entering into anti-Soviet alliances, on condition that Moscow abstained from hostile action either directly or by internal agitation. Furthermore, the British government agreed to recognise the de facto sovereignty of the USSR over those areas gained under the pact with Hitler: the Baltic states, Bessarabia and Northern Bukovina, and eastern Poland. Trade between the two countries was also to be developed to the widest possible extent, with particular emphasis placed on supplying those items that the USSR required for its defence. In return, the Soviet Union was obliged to maintain the same 'favourable neutrality' in its relations with Britain that it did with Germany. Lastly, London and Moscow would sign a pact of non-aggression.[70]

The Soviet response was less than enthusiastic, stymied no doubt by the fact that Molotov was in Berlin in mid-November 1940 to discuss a possible reset of the eminently more fruitful Soviet–German relationship. Matters were also not helped by the fact that details of the approach were leaked to the international press, and the story duly appeared – to profound embarrassment in Whitehall – in the *News Chronicle* on 16 November 1940, and in *The Times* two days later. Though Cripps angrily suspected the Foreign Office of being the source of the leak, it had actually come from the Soviet embassy in London, doubtless timed to put maximum pressure on the Germans by highlighting Moscow's ongoing discussions with the British.[71]

In the absence of any formal Soviet reply, it was left to the veteran ambassador in London, Ivan Maisky, to articulate Moscow's concerns. To him, the proposals aroused 'surprise and irritation'. The surprise was because he believed that the British position lacked any realistic foundation: Britain simply had little of any value to offer, he said; even recognition of Soviet sovereignty in the Baltic and elsewhere was scarcely a novel development. His irritation, meanwhile, stemmed from the perceived arrogance of the proposal, the idea that Britain could somehow dispense its post-war benefices to a grateful world. 'Does the British Government imagine itself to be something like the Apostle Peter', Maisky asked mockingly, 'who holds in his hands the keys to Paradise?'[72]

Clearly London would have to work considerably harder, offer much more of substance, or think more laterally, if it were to win Moscow over. As Maisky put it to Halifax some days later: 'Believe me . . . we are tired of your good intentions, we can only be convinced by your good deeds.'[73] The British proposal would be formally rejected on 1 February 1941.

With that, many in Whitehall were content to concede that there was little mileage to be had in further approaches. Britain had made its best offer and had been rebuffed; 'it was up to the Russians', said

one mandarin, 'to make the next approach'.[74] Yet, Cripps was unde-
terred and, in early April, submitted a memorandum to Molotov's
deputy, Andrei Vyshinsky, which hinted at the new direction that he
thought British policy might take, raising the spectre of London
making peace with the Germans. Cripps, formerly a hardened apolo-
gist for Soviet actions, had begun to doubt that the Soviets were
entirely honourable in their negotiations and worried that they, too,
were merely 'playing' with the British. His experience of negotiating
with Stalin and his acolytes, it appeared, had convinced him that the
best way to deal with the Soviets was to take a firm line – more 'rude
duke' than devout Marxist. And much to Whitehall's amusement, he
was now pushing London to adopt a policy of toughness towards
Moscow rather than one of conciliation. In his memorandum to
Vyshinsky, therefore, Cripps indulged in some mealy-mouthed sabre-
rattling of his own, warning that:

> it was not outside the bounds of possibility, if the war were protracted
> for a long period, that there might be a temptation for Great Britain
> to come to some arrangement to end the war on the sort of basis
> which has again recently been suggested in certain German quarters.[75]

Whether Vyshinsky fully grasped his meaning or not, Cripps evidently
believed that one way of exerting pressure on Stalin was to threaten
to negotiate with Hitler.

For all its fantasy and verbosity, Cripps' memorandum certainly had
an effect. For one thing, the chilly reception that he was already
experiencing in Moscow cooled still further. Generally snubbed by
Molotov and forced to deal with his deputy, Vyshinsky, Cripps now
found himself cast out altogether. His memorandum, it seemed, had
so irritated the Soviets that they were now terminally distrustful of
him, seeing him as unpredictable and unorthodox, lacking the delicacy
required for the task.[76] Such was Moscow's rejection of him, indeed,
that the Soviet ambassador in London, Maisky, became the preferred
channel for subsequent communication. Despite his commitment and
endeavour, Cripps appeared to have failed entirely. By his own admission, he was left with 'nothing to do . . . no chance of influencing
events one way or the other'.[77]

★   ★   ★

Thus, by the spring of 1941, Britain was as estranged from the Soviet Union as it had been in the autumn of 1939. Negotiation had failed, trade talks had failed, flattery had failed, even flagrant if unrealistic sabre-rattling had failed. Stalin was sticking by his pact with Hitler, and Churchill's Britain was alone in a geopolitical wilderness.

Part of the reason for that failure, of course, was that Britain had precious little to offer that might tempt the Soviets away from their tactical accommodation with the Nazis. Platitudes, goodwill and vague expressions of future support could scarcely compete with the very real territorial and material benefits that Stalin had already accrued courtesy of his relationship with Berlin. In addition, the Foreign Office made sense of its failure to woo the Soviets with the reasoning that the distrustful, unnatural relationship between Stalin and Hitler was so riven by mutual suspicion that neither party would be brave enough to disavow it. 'Neither dictator', one memorandum noted, 'dare turn away lest the other stab him in the back.'[78] It is an image that might have come from a David Low cartoon.

Regardless of Whitehall's assumptions, it was clear that there was a fundamental ideological obstacle – on both sides – to any sort of rapprochement. As numerous asides and marginal comments in the British files show, the political establishment in Whitehall never seriously saw the USSR as a possible ally, rather only ever as a potential enemy to be guarded against and tactically exploited if possible. It was arguably this fundamental inability to seriously contemplate an amicable arrangement with Moscow that had led to flights of fantasy such as Operation Pike.

For their part, the Soviets were similarly blinkered by their own ideology. Unwilling to view Britain as anything other than the arch-imperialist, their long-term ideological opponent, they would be fundamentally unable to seriously contemplate any arrangement with London, even had the latter been able to offer anything of substance. To a large extent, therefore, and despite the efforts of Stafford Cripps and others, the story of Anglo-Soviet relations prior to the summer of 1941 was very much one of 'never the twain'.

Most seriously perhaps, the suspicion and paranoia resulting, on both sides, from these failed negotiations contributed to making the Anglo-Soviet relationship almost as difficult as it could have been, in practice achieving little but driving Stalin further into Hitler's embrace. This counterproductive aspect was fully appreciated at the time by Cripps: 'it was all so mad', he said, to see the Soviet Union 'literally being pushed into the arms of Germany'.[79] It would take the catastrophe of the Nazi invasion of the USSR in June 1941 to alter that self-defeating dynamic.

6

Oiling the Wheels of War

On the last day of May 1940, the citizens of Leningrad would have spotted a peculiar sight. Amid the unremitting greyness of a Baltic late spring day, a German heavy cruiser was being towed into a shipyard on the western edge of the city. There was no bunting, no military band and little ceremony. No mention was made of the arrival in the Soviet press; instead *Izvestia* and *Leningradskaya Pravda* reported the Anglo-French collapse at the other end of the European continent. Consequently, the huge grey monster attracted little attention as it was nudged and cajoled into place by puffing black tugs. Nonetheless, its arrival was an event of profound significance.

The ship in question was the *Lützow*. Named in honour of Ludwig Freiherr von Lützow, one of the Prussian heroes of the German wars of liberation who had raised a militia in 1813 to fight alongside the Russians against the French, she had been constructed in Bremen and launched in July 1939. As one of the *Admiral Hipper* class of heavy cruisers, she was larger and heavier than Germany's famed 'pocket battleships': over 200 metres from stem to stern with a displacement of just under 20,000 tons.

In their finished form, the *Admiral Hipper* cruisers were formidable vessels. Powered by three Blohm & Voss steam turbines, they boasted a top speed of thirty-two knots and carried a crew of over 1,300. Armament was provided by an array of weapons, with the main battery consisting of four eight-inch twin gun turrets, each weighing approximately 250 tons, with a range of around thirty-three kilometres. The most famous of the class would be the *Prinz Eugen*, which entered service in August 1940 and came to prominence with its role in the sinking of HMS *Hood* in 1941 and the audacious 'Channel Dash' of the following year. Despite numerous attacks from Allied forces, the

Prinz Eugen would be the only one of Germany's large surface vessels to survive the entire war.[1]

For all the impressive pedigree, what the few Leningraders watching events in 1940 would have noticed was that the *Lützow* had not been finished. In fact, despite her sleek lines and impressive size, she looked rather unlike a warship, with little finished superstructure above first-deck level and only two of her four turrets completed. Below decks she was similarly incomplete, with no secondary anti-aircraft armament and, crucially, no propulsion system. Indeed, if the time taken to fit out her sister ships was any guide, the *Lützow* would not be ready for commissioning for at least another year.

Despite such shortcomings, the delivery of the *Lützow* to the Soviets was a remarkable event. For one thing, the *Admiral Hipper* class had originally been devised by German engineers to meet the threat posed by the Soviet *Kirov* class of cruiser, which had been first launched in 1936.[2] So, if nothing else, there was a certain irony in the *Lützow*'s delivery to Leningrad. Moreover, the German navy was not exactly awash with large surface ships. Alongside its four battleships – the *Bismarck*, the *Tirpitz*, the *Gneisenau* and the *Scharnhorst* – it possessed only two smaller 'pocket battleships' of the *Deutschland* class – the *Deutschland* and the *Admiral Scheer* – the third of that class, the *Graf Spee*, having been scuttled in the South Atlantic the previous winter. Beyond that, there were only the five heavy cruisers of the *Admiral Hipper* class. And, of these, the *Blücher* had been sunk a few weeks earlier, when she had succumbed to shellfire in Oslofjord during the Norwegian campaign; the *Seydlitz* and the *Prinz Eugen* were still unfinished, and the *Lützow* was now being handed over to the Soviets, thus leaving only the *Admiral Hipper* in German service. In the circumstances, many Germans would have seen the delivery of the *Lützow* as an act of foolhardy generosity.

Officially, however, the transfer of the *Lützow* to the Soviets was trumpeted as a significant step in the improvement of Nazi–Soviet relations. All the more so as it was only the headline transaction in a burgeoning commercial relationship between the two, which had accompanied the signature of the Nazi–Soviet Pact the previous August. Indeed, as the *Lützow* was eased into her berth at the Baltic shipyard, German and Soviet representatives were busy finalising a host of commercial deals in Moscow and Berlin covering the supply of all manner of raw materials and finished goods. To those few Leningraders watching, the *Lützow* must have seemed symbolic of a new age of détente and co-operation between Europe's two primary totalitarian powers. In truth, however, she would become a symbol of a relationship whose rich potential, mired in mistrust and political machinations, would never be realised.

The idea of economic co-operation and trade between Germany and Russia was nothing new, of course. Indeed, the two were remarkably well suited, with raw-material rich Russia, keen to industrialise, a natural complement to the industrial powerhouse of Germany, ever hungry for raw materials. Since the late nineteenth century, German industrialists had been mesmerised by the prospect of tapping into Russia's vast mineral resources, while Russia's leaders had long sought outside technological help for their own industrialisation drive. Hence, many on both sides foresaw a mutually beneficial arrangement beckoning if the political hurdles could be overcome.

The relationship had stuttered somewhat in the ideologically charged atmosphere after the First World War, but the two countries had maintained economic relations, of sorts, throughout the interwar period, which had blossomed into full-blown collaboration when political and strategic circumstances had aligned. One such blossoming occurred with the Treaty of Rapallo in 1922, when Germany and Soviet Russia shocked the world by concluding a bilateral agreement. With both states effectively excluded from the 'community of nations' – one as a discredited ex-enemy, the other as a feared revolutionary – the two pariahs found common ground for a strategic and economic arrangement. Rapallo caused consternation in Allied capitals, but its wider significance has been rather exaggerated. It was as much a symbolic gesture – a joint 'thumbing of the nose' at London and Paris – as it was an expression of practical policy. It was not a formal alliance, or a declaration of neutrality, or a non-aggression pact. Rather it was a marriage of strategic convenience, a temporary expedient in a hostile world, that was intended as much to impress other potential suitors as to signify a genuine meeting of minds. As Churchill noted at the time, Russia and Germany merely shared a 'comradeship in misfortune'.[3]

Consequently, Rapallo's headline political terms were rather conventional: the two signatories agreed to renounce all mutual territorial and financial claims and to normalise their diplomatic relations with one another. Its economic aspect, however, was more eye-catching, with both sides granting 'most favoured nation' status to each other, and promising mutual co-operation in meeting their economic needs. The follow-up Treaty of Berlin of 1926 went further, extending a 300 million Reichsmarks credit facility to the Soviet Union, backed by German banks. Though it had been forged in a moment of political adversity, the German–Soviet relationship proved remarkably resilient, lasting into the early 1930s, long after the strategic rationale that had spawned it had disappeared. Indeed, by 1932, the Soviet Union was taking 47 per cent of her imports from Germany – the same percentage as in 1914 – and receiving fully 72 per cent of her machinery imports from German firms.[4]

With Hitler's advent to power in January 1933, the relationship with the USSR naturally began to change. Hitler had made his career out of baiting the Bolsheviks abroad and German communists at home, yet he did not hurry to kill off the relationship immediately, and even renewed the Treaty of Berlin with Moscow in May 1933. In truth, however, and quite aside from ideological concerns, the economic relationship with the Soviet Union no longer served German interests as clearly as it had done a decade earlier, and so it was allowed to wither. For one thing, Hitler had made a strategic decision to prioritise autarky, and began reorienting German industry away from exports and towards domestic production for rearmament and infrastructure. For another, the relationship with the Soviets was seen as much less vital from the German perspective, especially as barely 6 per cent of German imports came from the Soviet Union, while only 10 per cent of German exports went in the other direction,[5] and those exports had to be funded by a raft of complex credit and loan agreements. While Germany had more reliable trading partners elsewhere, trading with the Soviets was scarcely worth the effort.

Yet, though the political relationship between Moscow and Berlin descended into rancour in the mid-1930s, the economic connection was nonetheless kept alive. On the Soviet side, the head of the Soviet trade mission to Berlin, David Kandelaki, arranged a number of meetings with the minister of economics, Hjalmar Schacht, in 1935 and 1936, in which he not only argued for a rejuvenation of the German–Soviet economic relationship, but also unsuccessfully floated the idea of a general normalisation of relations between the two countries.[6] Kandelaki was certainly no maverick; well connected and a Georgian like Stalin, it has been suggested that he acted as Stalin's own special envoy, seeking to bypass traditional diplomatic channels to build bridges between Moscow and Berlin.[7] Doomed to failure by the prevailing political winds, however, he was recalled to Moscow in April 1937, where he would share the grim fate of many of his fellows. Arrested in September of that year in the Great Purge, Kandelaki would be executed in July 1938. Ironically, it was almost certainly his contacts in Berlin that spelled his end.

Yet, Kandelaki was not alone in his ambitions, and despite his earlier failure, there were a few in German diplomatic and government circles – the so-called 'Easterners' – who were persistent advocates of a political and economic arrangement with the Soviet Union. One of these was Karl Schnurre, a diplomat and legal expert who from 1936 was head of the Eastern European Economic Section of the German foreign office. Schnurre's position – which was shared with a number of others, such as the German ambassador in Moscow, Schulenburg – was that supplies of Soviet raw materials were of such vital import- ance to Germany's continued economic health that she should be willing to put up with the attendant irritations, and even make substan- tial political concessions in order to secure them.

Schnurre was certainly not wrong. Germany by 1939 was still broadly dependent on imports for almost all her raw materials: 80 per cent of her rubber, 60 per cent of her oil, 60 per cent of her iron ore, and 100 per cent of her chrome and manganese had to be imported. The Soviet Union, meanwhile, was the world's largest producer of manga- nese, in second place in chrome production and the third largest source of crude oil and iron ore.[8] Clearly, as many among the 'Easterners' had maintained, Nazi Germany and the Soviet Union were a very good fit economically – if only the political antipathies could be assuaged.

The primary difficulty for Schnurre was that – for the early part of his work, at least – he was very much swimming against the tide, advocating a practical, economic arrangement when the ruling elites of both states were too busy fulminating against each other to contem- plate any collaboration. Like Kandelaki before him, Schnurre found that as long as the political benefits of mutual antipathy outweighed the economic benefits of co-operation, he would find little purchase for his arguments.

By 1939, however, the political constellation was beginning to shift. Frustrated by what he perceived as western 'meddling' at Munich in September 1938, and alarmed by reports of growing Anglo-French rearmament, Hitler increased the pace of his strategic planning. At home, this meant a renewed focus on an already burgeoning armaments sector. Since 1933 military-related production in Germany had risen from 1 per cent of GDP to 20 per cent, but this was to be a mere prelude to the programme unveiled in October 1938.[9] Domestic armaments production was to be tripled overall, Göring announced, with Luftwaffe capacity to increase fivefold to over 20,000 aircraft, and the Kriegsmarine to be swiftly raised to a position of superiority over the Royal Navy. In addition, accelerated investment was ordered to make up for shortcomings in Germany's transport infrastructure. It was, Göring concluded, 'a gigantic programme, compared to which previous achievements are insignificant'.[10]

In foreign affairs, Hitler was no less ambitious. Perversely, he had drawn the opposite conclusion from the West's showing at Munich from that arrived at by Stalin. Where the Soviet leader had seen a baleful foreshadowing of a German alliance with the West, Hitler had concluded that the Western Powers, having spurned all his advances, were now his implacable opponents. Seeing the prospect of war with Britain and France now as inevitable, Hitler started planning for conflict sooner rather than later – by 1940–41 at the latest – while his perceived advantage in men and materiel still held good.[11]

Such vast strategic plans required a rethink of economic priorities. The German economy had already been transformed under the Nazis. From the post-depression doldrums of the early 1930s with 6 million unemployed, Nazi armaments and public-works programmes had produced near-full employment by 1938. Yet, by the autumn of that year, the breakneck economic growth was beginning to stall, as an economy geared primarily towards rearmament and domestic consumption created huge inflationary pressures. The *New York Times* reported in September 1938 that 'alarming' inflation was looming for the German economy, stating that the amount of money in circulation was 40 per cent higher than it had been the previous year,[12] which revealed that the Reichsbank had been managing the early stage of the crisis by simply printing money. By the end of the year – just as Hitler was announcing his intention to triple armaments production – the Reichsbank announced that it faced a cash-flow deficit of 2 billion Reichsmarks,[13] and advised a renewed concentration on exports as the urgent remedy.

Hitler did not take kindly to such interventions by the 'dismal scientists' of the Reichsbank, and sacked its director and genius behind Nazi Germany's economic recovery, the venerable Hjalmar Schacht, in response. But he was nonetheless forced into some concession to his critics. In a keynote speech on 30 January 1939, on the sixth anniversary of the Nazi seizure of power – a speech best known for his 'prophecy' that a return to war would lead to the 'annihilation of the Jewish race' in Europe – he gave his answer. After questioning the 'sagacity' of the 'world economic scholars', whose diagnoses, he complained, never agreed, Hitler conceded that a shift to exports in the German economy was, after all, necessary: 'We must export in order to be able to purchase food from abroad. Since these exported goods use up raw materials which we do not possess, this means we must export yet more goods to secure these raw materials for our economy.' Consequently, Hitler admitted, Germany was compelled 'by dire necessity' to 'export, or perish'.[14] At the same time, the urgent need for imports was highlighted by a number of official studies which concluded that Germany would be unable to wage a major war without access to Soviet resources.[15] This, almost verbatim, was what the 'Easterners' in the German foreign office had long argued. Perhaps now they would be given their head.

Of course, the decision had not yet been made; politics still held the whip hand over economics. Yet behind the scenes, the economic conditions for any possible Nazi–Soviet deal were being worked out; indeed, they were already clear in their essentials by the end of 1938.[16] What followed, then, was an elaborate dance, punctuated by procrastination, intransigence and occasional spats, in which Soviet and German economic negotiators haggled and horse-traded, waiting for a favourable political wind. Only in mid-July 1939, as the clouds of war were already darkening over Europe – and when Karl Schnurre finally received his Soviet counterpart, Evgeny Babarin, for high-level discussions in Berlin – did the talks begin in earnest.

By this point, Hitler was in a hurry. In his haste to expand Germany's frontiers, his occupation of the 'rump' Czech lands and his sabre-rattling against Poland, he had painted himself into something of a strategic corner, from which only an arrangement with the Soviets appeared to offer a coherent exit. The economic aspects of any possible deal, of course, were still secondary but were rapidly gaining in significance. Not only were the old arguments about the benefits of access to Soviet raw-material reserves more relevant than ever, but they were amplified by the acute awareness on the German side that any outbreak of war with Britain would see the use of the traditional weapon of the blockade, which had gravely hampered Germany's war effort in the First World War, severely undermined morale and cost many thousands of civilian lives.[17] Hitler knew that the supply of Soviet foodstuffs in the event of war would effectively circumvent the best efforts of the Royal Navy to starve Germany into submission.

For its part, the Soviet Union could benefit enormously from access to German technology. In its efforts to industrialise in the interwar years it had often struggled to fund its own technological development or bring in the best innovations from abroad. An arrangement with Germany, it was thought, would help to solve those problems, providing not only vital military hardware, but also precision engineering equipment, such as turbines and lathes, and the latest optical and metallurgical technology. It was testament to the importance of this economic aspect that the Commercial Agreement was made an essential precondition of any wider political pact with Hitler's Germany.[18] Yet despite the potential benefits that the alignment with Berlin held for him, Stalin firmly believed that he held the trump cards, and consequently – through delays and procrastination – drove a very hard bargain. The agreement, when it came, would be largely on Soviet terms.

On 20 August 1939, three days before the Nazi–Soviet Pact, a commercial agreement was finally signed between Berlin and Moscow. The Soviet Union committed to supplying 180 million Reichsmarks of raw materials to Germany, in return for a German commitment to provide 120 million Reichsmarks of industrial goods. In addition, a credit line of 200 million Reichsmarks was extended to Moscow, backed by the German government, with an effective interest rate of 4.5 per cent over seven years, which was to be repaid in raw-material shipments from 1946.[19] Little wonder that Molotov would laud the treaty as better than 'all previous agreements', adding that 'we have never had any equally advantageous economic agreement with Great Britain, France, or any other country'.[20] In principle at least, the economic treaty with Nazi Germany was as good as it got.

So while the world reeled in August 1939 from the revelation of the political pact between Moscow and Berlin, negotiators from the two sides began hammering out all those aspects of the Commercial Agreement that were unclear or unsatisfactory, endeavouring to turn the principle of economic collaboration into a practical reality. It was not an easy task. For all the bonhomie on show, mutual suspicions and bad faith persisted, not least due to the speed with which German forces overran Poland that September. Consequently, the wording of the agreement was pored over, analysed and reinterpreted, and figures and prices were proposed, rejected and amended. All the while, the German side, having run the greater political and military risk, expected concessions from the Soviets; Stalin's negotiators, however, perceiving that they had the upper hand, steadfastly refused to compromise. If this was the honeymoon period, it did not augur well for the success of the marriage.

As the gruelling negotiations dragged on into the winter, there were some moments of levity, at least in retrospect. On 27 September, for instance, a bemused Schnurre was inadvertently given the red-carpet treatment on arrival at Khodynka airfield in Moscow, after Ribbentrop's plane had been delayed. Though this was an accurate assessment of who was the 'brains' on the German side, it would certainly not have pleased Ribbentrop, who was eternally sensitive to any perceived slight. Some weeks later, Schnurre's return to Moscow proved similarly problematical, as he was incorrectly reported in the Soviet press as 'Ambassador Baron von Schnurre', despite the fact that he was neither an ambassador nor a baron, and had been a regular visitor to Soviet government circles over the previous five years.[21] It is unclear whether the Soviets were trying to flatter or to ridicule him.

Most bizarre of all, perhaps, was the Soviet economic mission which toured Germany in late October 1939, essentially to draw up a shopping list of German military and technological wares required by Moscow. 'Shopping list', in fact, was the appropriate term. When the forty-five-strong Soviet delegation arrived – all decked out in brand-new brown coats, hats and yellow shoes – each of them carried empty suitcases to accommodate the myriad consumer goods unavailable at home. Once they got down to work, other peculiarities quickly manifested themselves, not least an inveterate suspicion of their German counterparts. According to the later memoir account of one of their number, Lieutenant General and Vice-Minister of Aviation Alexander Yakovlev, the Germans were generous and 'genial hosts', putting the Soviet delegation up in the best hotel in Berlin, the Adlon, and treating them to a number of tours and displays of equipment. Yakovlev recalled with incredulity – his memory doubtless coloured by post-war sensibilities – that 'they smiled at us, shook our hands, paid us compliments, and tried to create an atmosphere of friendship and sincerity'.[22] He went on to describe a meeting with his counterpart, General Ernst Udet, and Hermann Göring at the Johannisthal airfield outside Berlin, where a demonstration of German materiel was held:

> In strict order, as though on parade . . . twin-engine Junkers-88 and Dornier-215 bombers; single-engine Heinkel-100 and Messerschmitt-109 fighters, Focke-Wulf-187 and Henschel reconnaissance planes, a twin-engine Messerschmitt-110 fighter, a Junkers-87 dive bomber, and other types of aircraft. The crews – pilots and mechanics – stood rigidly at attention by each airplane.[23]

Yakovlev recalled Udet taking the head of the Soviet delegation, Ivan Tevossian, up for a turn in a Fiesler 'Storch' reconnaissance plane, before making a 'splendid landing, stopping exactly where it had started from'. When Tevossian expressed his satisfaction, Göring presented the plane to him as a gift. As Yakovlev wrote of the display: 'Everything was impeccably organised and made rather a good impression . . . We returned to the Adlon strongly impressed by what we had seen.'[24]

Not everyone in the group was quite so impressed, however. General Dmitry Gusev, for instance, appeared to believe that the Germans were taking them for fools and were only showing obsolete items. After all, he queried: 'how could they show us the true state of their air force equipment?' On reflection, Yakovlev, too, was uneasy, concerned strangely by the 'candidness with which the most secret weaponry data had been revealed to us'. He would later suggest that the Germans seemed to be more interested in intimidating their guests with their military power than anything else. However, when these complaints were passed on to their host, Ernst Udet, he was indignant, replying: 'I give you my word as an officer. We've shown you everything; if you don't like what you saw, don't buy. We are not pressuring you – do what you think best.'[25]

Yet although his comment arguably said more about the attitudes of the Soviets than those of the Germans, Gusev had a point. For all the affability of their hosts, the Soviet delegation was *not* being shown the true state of German technology. As interpreter Valentin Berezhkov recalled, precautions were put in place to prevent members of the Soviet delegation from seeing things that were *verboten*. For his part, Berezhkov was sent to the Krupp factory at Essen to oversee the construction of the outstanding main turrets intended for the *Lützow*, yet the area was separated off from the rest of the factory by a thick tarpaulin curtain, leaving so little space that the Krupp engineers could barely work. Berezhkov was thus prevented from even seeing the remainder of the workshop.[26]

Sensitive air technology was similarly shielded from view. Despite touring the country and visiting countless sites – including BMW in Munich, Messerschmitt in Augsburg, Junkers in Dessau, Focke-Wulf in Bremen and Arado, Henschel and Siemens in Berlin – the Soviet delegation was not shown either the Focke-Wulf 190, which was then in development, or the new jet engine technology that was being prepared by BMW and Junkers. Moreover, a measure of disinformation was employed. Great claims were made by the Germans for the Heinkel He-100 fighter, for instance, which, despite having vied for the air speed record earlier that year, was known to be dogged by design glitches and consequently had not even been accepted for operational use by the Luftwaffe.[27]

Perhaps sensing that their German partners were not being entirely open, the Soviet naval delegation was especially demanding, arriving with a lengthy list of requests, including inspecting the battleship *Scharnhorst*, the heavy cruiser *Admiral Hipper*, a minelayer, a destroyer and a type VIIB U-boat. Indeed, Soviet requests seemed to grow almost exponentially, including everything from torpedo fuses and detonators to binoculars and radios – as well as many items that the Germans did not even have. Interestingly, the German naval attaché in Moscow was not accorded reciprocal privileges.[28] Little wonder, perhaps, that one German admiral concluded that the entire process was merely a cover for a campaign of Soviet espionage.[29]

Negotiations in other spheres were just as fraught and complex. While the various Soviet delegations were perusing German wares, German businessmen streamed to Moscow to open talks of their own, many of them ending up hopelessly entangled in Soviet red tape and achieving little except provoking a suspension of trading applications, and further eroding an already fragile trust. Meanwhile, the civil servants and bureaucrats attempted to thrash out a mutually acceptable agreement, and it was far from easy.

Believing that the relationship was far more critical to the German side than to their own, the Soviet negotiators drove a very hard bargain, demanding huge amounts of the most advanced German technology, while obstructing their own reciprocal deliveries. The Germans were shocked, for instance, when they received a forty-eight-page list of Soviet demands at the end of November 1939 – including everything from cruisers to fighter aircraft, artillery pieces to complete industrial plants[30] – amounting to a massive 1.5 billion Reichsmarks. Moreover, Soviet negotiators were working to turn the original agreement upside down, by demanding German finished items *in advance* of their own supply of raw materials, while at the same time invoking every obstacle possible to hinder German requests, inflating prices on a whim or arguing that infrastructure or rolling stock were insufficient to handle the volumes required. Indeed, senior German negotiator Karl Ritter was obliged to invoke the positive spirit of the Nazi–Soviet Pact, 'fully approved by Stalin', in an effort to persuade the Soviets to return to those original terms as the basis for their talks.[31] In a later memorandum, Ritter was more critical, noting: 'Negotiations are not proceeding favourably. Both in general and in detail, the other side is not showing the gratitude that should result from the new political situation. Instead they are trying to get all they think they can.'[32] If the Germans had imagined that they could easily tap into the Soviet Union's vast natural resources, they were sorely mistaken.

In fact, some on the German side began to tire of the endless negotiations and exorbitant Soviet demands. Ribbentrop delivered a rebuke to the Soviet ambassador in Berlin, Alexei Shkvartsev, reminding him that 'Germany is at war', and adding that 'everything humanly possible has been done [from the German side] and beyond that one could not go'.[33] Others were less conciliatory. The German military was growing frustrated with the 'voluminous and unreasonable' demands from the Soviets, and the negotiators, Ritter and Schnurre, increasingly had to contend with objections and refusals from their own side.[34] Rumours of German discontent even reached the ears of the American chargé in Berlin, who reported back to Washington that German officials were 'less sanguine' about the relationship with the Soviets than they had been hitherto.[35]

This proved something of a crisis for Nazi Germany, not least because the much-vaunted supplies from the USSR, which it had been promised would circumvent the feared British blockade, were scarcely materialising. Indeed, if American journalist William Shirer was to be believed, the Germans were already adopting some peculiar measures to reassure the public, with supplies of butter and flour from Slovakia and Bohemia being falsely labelled as 'Made in Russia', so as to demonstrate the supposed benefits of the Soviet relationship.[36]

Meanwhile, behind the public-relations facade, German urgency – if not desperation – was increasing. Hitler had been making preparations for the campaign in the West against Britain and France since November 1939, and yet he was still receiving only a trickle of the vital supplies that he had expected from the Soviet Union. In oil, for example, Germany required 60,000 tons per month from the USSR just to maintain its own stocks, but was so far receiving only a fraction of that figure. Similarly, German grain supplies were increasingly perilous, with a 1.6 million-ton shortfall expected for 1940, even under optimal conditions, and assuming a full quota of Soviet deliveries.[37] Far from oiling the wheels of Hitler's war machine, it seems, Soviet supplies were threatening to be a serious hindrance.

Given the looming crisis, the 'big guns' were brought into play: Hitler stressing to his acolytes the necessity for accommodation with the Soviets, while Ribbentrop endeavoured to bring Stalin into the talks, writing to him directly in early February 1940 to request that the USSR fulfil the promise 'given during the September negotiations . . . that the Soviet government was willing to support Germany during the war'.[38] Remarkably the appeal worked; Stalin vowed to take Ribbentrop's views 'into consideration' and within days negotiators in Moscow were finalising details of a new German–Soviet Commercial

Agreement. The USSR now agreed to supply 650 million Reichsmarks of raw materials over the following eighteen months, two-thirds of it within the first year, in return for Germany supplying the same value of military and industrial hardware over the following twenty-seven months to May 1942, with two-thirds of that total falling due within the first eighteen months. The figures involved were certainly considerable. Combined with the earlier Credit Agreement of August 1939, the Commercial Agreement tied the economies of Nazi Germany and the USSR closely together, committing each to around 800 million Reichsmarks of business in the first two years.[39]

The reception, on both sides, was suitably positive. The Soviet press – which had given a rather cool reaction to the original August 1939 agreement – was enthused, praising the February 1940 deal as being of 'great economic and political significance' and providing 'for the future development of co-operation between the USSR and Germany'.[40] Stalin gave his own assessment in the final phase of talks, stating that 'The Soviet Union sees this not merely as a normal treaty for the exchange of goods, but rather as one of mutual assistance.'[41] The Nazi press concurred, hailing the new agreement as 'more than a battle won, it is quite simply the decisive victory' in combating the British blockade.[42] German negotiators were no less effusive. Karl Schnurre minuted to the foreign office in Berlin that the revised agreement represented 'the first great step towards the economic programme envisaged by both sides'.[43] Gustav Hilger, meanwhile, recalled in his post-war memoir that the Commercial Agreement had signified 'a door to the East . . . opened wide, and British efforts at an economic blockade of Germany . . . considerably weakened'.[44]

The various lists of commodities and products appended to the Commercial Agreement are highly instructive and appear to confirm Hilger's assessment. The Soviet Union, for instance, committed to supply 1 million tons of feed grains, 900,000 tons of petroleum, 800,000 tons of scrap and pig iron, 500,000 tons of phosphates and 500,000 tons of iron ore. In addition, lesser amounts were stipulated of platinum, chromium ore, asbestos, sulphur, iridium, iodine, glycerine, albumin, tar, lime and numerous other products.

In return, the items to be supplied by the Germans were set out in four separate lists. The first of these – concerning military equipment – ran to forty-two typewritten pages, encompassing everything from submarine periscopes and hydrographic instruments to complete tanks and aircraft, including five Messerschmitt Bf-109Es, five Messerschmitt Bf-110Cs, two Junkers Ju-88s, two Dornier Do-215s, five half-tracks, two Fa-226 helicopters and one 'fully equipped' Panzer III. Most surprisingly, perhaps, the Soviets also ordered ten Heinkel He-100 aircraft – more than any other single model – evidently convinced by the spurious claims of their German counterparts that it really was superior to the Bf-109.[45] In addition, numerous engines and spare parts were demanded, including 1,500 spark plugs, 10,000 piston rings, thirty propellers and myriad other items including chemical warfare equipment, artillery pieces, armoured vehicles, gun sights, optical instruments and various types of bombs and ammunition.[46]

Additional lists covered sundry military and industrial supplies, including equipment for the mining, chemical and petroleum industries, turbines, forges, presses, cranes and machine tools. Beyond that, 146 excavators were listed, as well as locomotives, generators, diesel engines, steel tubing and a number of ships, including a 12,000-ton tanker, which was to be delivered 'promptly'. A final list outlined those items in which the Soviets expressed 'an interest' for possible future purchases, 'depending on conditions', including plants for coal-hydrogenation, vulcanisation and synthetic rubber production.[47] In essence, the Soviets were demanding from Germany nothing less than the short-cut to an advanced military-industrial economy.

One of the first items on the Soviet 'shopping list' was the heavy cruiser, now referred to by the Germans as the 'ex-*Lützow*'. As with many other categories, the negotiations that led to the sale of the *Lützow* had been rather tortuous. The Soviets had first requested the ship in early November 1939, along with the similarly unfinished *Seydlitz*. Then, at the end of that month, the stakes had been raised further when another *Hipper*-class cruiser, the *Prinz Eugen*, and the plans for the battleship *Bismarck*, were added to the list of Soviet demands. Unsurprisingly, the matter was passed on to Hitler, who vetoed the sale of the *Seydlitz* and the *Prinz Eugen*, and agreed to the sale of the *Bismarck* plans only on condition that they would not be permitted to fall into the 'wrong' (i.e. British) hands. With a green light for the sale of the *Lützow*, the two sides could begin haggling over price. An initial suggestion from Göring of 152 million Reichsmarks, nearly twice what construction had cost, was dismissed by the Soviets out of hand.[48] But by February 1940 the sale of the vessel was included within the Commercial Agreement, in spite of the fact that no price had yet been agreed, suggesting thereby that both sides considered the deal to be as good as done. According to the wording of the agreement, the ex-*Lützow* was 'to be delivered for completion in the USSR': her 'hull and all equipment, armament [and] spare parts' as well as 'complete plans, specifications, working drawings and trial results'. [49]

Thereafter, negotiations on price dragged on until early May 1940, at which point a renewed German proposal of 109 million Reichsmarks for the cruiser and ammunition was immediately met with a Soviet counter-offer of 90 million Reichsmarks. Just as Germany's forces were invading France and the Low Countries that month, it seems her negotiators tired of haggling and agreed to split the difference, fixing a price of 100 million Reichsmarks for the ship, despite the fact that the German side considered that the figure was 'not acceptable from a strictly commercial point of view'.[50] With that, the ex-*Lützow* duly left Bremen, under tow from ocean-going salvage tugs, to arrive in Leningrad at the end of May.

Other German deliveries to the USSR were rather less involved. By the late spring of 1940, after the German campaign in Scandinavia had got under way, Soviet obstructionism eased somewhat and negotiations that previously seemed to have dragged on for months could be smoothed over in a matter of days or weeks. Preparations were then swiftly made for the delivery of many of the other items that had been stipulated in the February 1940 agreement. Many of the aircraft that had been ordered were simply flown via Königsberg direct to Moscow, where the Soviets had laid on full ground support, accommodation, refuelling and meteorological facilities for the incoming crews. Military and industrial items were sent by train as their delivery deadlines, stipulated by the various agreements, fell due. After a sluggish start with the wrangling over terms and payments, German exports to the USSR rose to a monthly total of 15 million Reichsmarks in May 1940, peaking at 37 million Reichsmarks in December.[51]

Soviet deliveries to Germany were theoretically easier to handle, being predominantly bulk cargoes of oil, grain and foodstuffs. However, the Soviet Union's creaking infrastructure did throw up occasional bottlenecks and obstacles, not least at the two main transit points into German-occupied Poland – at Brest-Litovsk and Przemyśl – where a change of rail gauge further complicated matters. Consequently, most of the oil was shipped from the Soviet Caucasus by sea to Varna in Bulgaria and then by rail to Germany, thereby avoiding the problem areas.[52] Nonetheless, Soviet deliveries to Germany rose from a value of around 10 million Reichsmarks per month in the spring of 1940, to peak at nearly ten times that in September of that year.[53]

After initial teething troubles, therefore, German–Soviet trade grew impressively through 1940, with Soviet exports to Germany estimated at 404 million Reichsmarks, over the year, as against a German export figure to the USSR of 242 million Reichsmarks.[54] A glance at German foreign trade figures for 1940 shows that, in the latter half of the year, exports to the Soviet Union consistently amounted to over 60 per cent of monthly totals.[55] At first sight, then, the economic relationship appears to have been delivering what it had promised: providing the Soviet Union with vital examples of the latest precision engineering, with which to continue its ongoing industrialisation programme, while supplying Nazi Germany with essential fuel and foodstuffs for the home front.

Some, indeed, have made even grander claims, suggesting that Soviet supplies made the decisive difference to German forces in their invasion of France and the Low Countries in May 1940. As one author has eloquently suggested:

> Guderian's tanks operated largely on Soviet petrol as they dashed for the sea at Abbeville, the bombs that levelled Rotterdam contained Soviet guncotton, and the bullets that strafed British Tommies wading to the boats at Dunkirk were sheathed in Soviet cupro-nickel.[56]

The truth is rather more mundane. Soviet deliveries of fuel and other military supplies were only trickling into Germany by the early summer of 1940. By May total deliveries of oil had barely topped 100,000 tons, contributing only one-seventh of German oil stocks, with a similar figure for grain of 103,000 tons.[57] Such modest amounts were unlikely to have made much noticeable contribution to the French campaign.

In fact, the wider economic arrangement hammered out between the Nazis and the Soviets was much less influential than the casual observer might imagine. It is easy to be misled by the figure for September 1940, for instance – when German exports to the USSR made up 76 per cent of the monthly total – into assuming that the economic relationship had undergone a step change. Such large percentages are deceptive, however, and are merely evidence that German export trade had virtually collapsed following the outbreak of war, leaving the Soviet Union as practically Berlin's only serious trading partner. Even that export figure for September 1940 was less than a quarter of the total for March of that year, when the last pre-war orders were being fulfilled.[58] Over the year as a whole, German exports to the USSR were decidedly modest, amounting to less than 1 per cent of German GDP.[59] Such figures, though an increase on the immediately preceding peacetime years, were broadly in line with totals from the early 1930s and less than import totals from the USSR for the years 1927–30.[60] For all its promise, then, the much-vaunted Commercial Agreement barely restored the economic status quo that had preceded Hitler.

For the Soviet Union, meanwhile, the relationship was a little more vital, comprising 31 per cent of its total imports for 1940, and contributing to a brief boom in export trade in which exports of oil doubled, grain increased fivefold and the total figure rose by 250 per cent. In 1940 nearly 53 per cent of the USSR's total exports were destined for Nazi Germany.[61]

But, as in the German case, the paucity of trade in the immediately preceding years means that such apparently impressive increases can be deceptive. In truth, the new relationship was barely reaching parity with the volumes of trade that had gone before. Soviet imports from Germany in 1940, for example, were quantitatively less than the annual totals from the decade between 1924 and 1933, while Soviet exports in the other direction fell short of the peak of the period 1926–30.[62] Though the Nazi–Soviet Pact marked a very definite political departure, then, its economic aspects were much less remarkable, hardly matching the volumes of German–Soviet trade that had already existed a decade earlier.

Of course, it wasn't just sheer volumes that were supposed to be decisive, it was also the specifics. The economic relationship was intended to address particular shortcomings, such as the Soviet

(*Left*) 'Ours are better!' Guderian and Krivoshein enjoy the joint Nazi–Soviet parade at Brest, Poland, September 1939.

(*Below*) Soviet and German troops exchange cigarettes and comradely greetings.

(*Above*) Molotov signs the Nazi–Soviet Pact under Stalin's watchful eye, 24 August 1939.

(*Below*) 'I know how much the German nation loves its Führer. I should therefore like to drink to his health.' Stalin and Heinrich Hoffmann share a celebratory toast in the Kremlin.

(*Right*) Harry Pollitt's ill-starred Communist Party pamphlet 'How to win the War', which angered the Kremlin by advocating the defence of Poland.

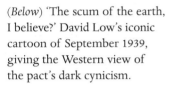

(*Below*) 'The scum of the earth, I believe?' David Low's iconic cartoon of September 1939, giving the Western view of the pact's dark cynicism.

RENDEZVOUS

(*Above*) Hitler announces the German invasion of Poland to the Reichstag
in the Kroll Opera House, 1 September 1939.

(*Below*) Victorious German troops march through the ruins of a Polish village.

(*Right*) Molotov announces the Soviet invasion of Poland on 17 September, in support of the USSR's 'brothers of the same blood'.

(*Below*) A Red Army BT-7 tank trundles through the eastern Polish town of Raków, past the bewildered inhabitants.

(*Above*) The German 6th Army parades before Hitler in the former Polish capital Warsaw, October 1939.

(*Below*) The murderous reality of German rule: an execution in the Polish town of Sosnowiec, autumn of 1939.

(*Above*) The Red Army parades through the Polish city of Lwów, past a portrait of Stalin, September 1939.

(*Below*) The murderous reality of Soviet rule: the corpses of a few of Stalin's Polish victims, exhumed at Katyn in April 1943.

(*Above*) Jews being deported by the Nazis from the city of Łódź in occupied Poland, March 1940.

(*Below*) Replacing them, in theory, were ethnic Germans gathered from the areas ceded to Stalin by the pact. Here *Volksdeutsche* from Bessarabia are loaded onto trains for the journey 'Home to the Reich'.

(*Above*) 'This is how we annihilate the enemies of Soviet power.' A rare photograph of the mass deportation from Soviet-occupied Riga, the Latvian capital, June 1941.

(*Below*) Condemned to 'disappear … like a field mouse'. A deported Polish family from Stanisławów poses in front of their new 'home' in Soviet Kazakhstan. They were among the lucky ones.

(*Above*) The unfinished German heavy cruiser *Lützow* – the 'flag-ship' of the Nazi–Soviet Pact – being towed into Leningrad, May 1940.

(*Right*) The German–Soviet economic relationship – more important to Berlin 'than a battle won'. Here an engineer checks the levels on a consignment of Soviet oil heading for Hitler's Reich, winter of 1940.

(*Above*) Molotov arrives in Berlin in November 1940 to negotiate the next phase of the Nazi−Soviet Pact.

(*Below*) 'Let's divide the whole world!' Hitler and Molotov discuss terms, with Gustav Hilger interpreting, but agreement eludes them.

(*Left*) Goebbels reads Hitler's announcement of the attack on the USSR to the German people. 'I feel totally free', he later wrote in his diary.

(*Right*) Anxious Moscow residents listen to Molotov's radio announcement of the Nazi invasion. 'Our cause is just', he intoned. 'Victory will be ours.'

(*Below*) For many in Moscow's newly annexed territories – such as here near Chișinău in former Bessarabia – the invading Germans were greeted as liberators.

(*Above*) 'The only thing left of the 56th Rifle Division was its number.' Some of the countless thousands of Red Army soldiers who surrendered to the Germans in the opening days of Operation Barbarossa.

(*Below*) A destroyed T-34 tank, one of the few sources of optimism for Stalin in June 1941, and ironically built in large part using German technology.

Local civilians remove a statue of Stalin, only recently erected, in Białystok, Poland, July 1941.

Sikorski (*left*) and Maisky (*right*) sign the Polish–Soviet Agreement, in the presence of Eden and Churchill.

(*Above*) The Lietukis Garage Massacre: the Jews of Kaunas are beaten to death by the Nazis' local collaborators, June 1941.

(*Below*) Victims of the Soviet NKVD, strewn across the prison courtyard in Lwów, awaiting identification by their horrified relatives, June 1941.

The 'Baltic Way' – a human chain that snaked its way through the Baltic republics of the USSR on the 50th anniversary of the Nazi–Soviet Pact – in protest at Stalin's annexation of the three countries, August 1989.

This demonstration, at Šiauliai in Lithuania in August 1989, made the connection brutally clear, showing the three Baltic republics as coffins, with the Nazi and Soviet flags joined over them.

deficiency in precision engineering and Germany's dependence on the world market for essential supplies. For the Soviets, the results were rather mixed in this regard. In some spheres, the benefits from the relationship with Germany are hard to perceive. It is clear from the nonplussed reaction of the Soviet aeronautical delegation to Berlin, for instance, that they were expecting to see far more advanced technology than what they were actually shown. After all, Soviet engineers had already independently developed both a delta-wing aircraft and a functioning prototype jet engine by 1938,[63] so this perhaps explains why their buying delegation was less than wholly impressed when the Germans showed them conventional piston-engined examples the following year.

In other areas, such as precision machine tools, the benefit is much easier to divine. Soviet industry was endeavouring to close the gap on its rival economies via the third Five-Year Plan from 1938 onwards, and the German connection can only have helped in that respect, in spite of the exports of raw materials that it demanded. Indeed, it is very clear that, after plateauing through 1939, Soviet industrial production rose again in 1940, with a couple of sectors – such as high-grade steel – showing particularly impressive increases. Moreover, such advances appear to have saved the Five-Year Plan, which despite a poor start was well on the way to being 'fulfilled and overfulfilled' by the middle of 1941.[64] Though economic historians of the period rarely mention the German connection, it seems plausible to attribute these increases, at least in part, to the influence of the Commercial Agreements.

One area in which a clear – indeed a vital – benefit is perceptible is that of military production. The Soviet tank industry is a salient example. Soviet tank production was in flux in 1940, with the obsolete T-26 and BT series tanks being phased out and production switching to the more modern T-34 and KV models. In addition, a simultaneous expansion of the sector was undertaken, with new plants being built and existing plants being retooled to produce the new models. A natural partner in these processes was German heavy industry, which could provide both the hardware and the know-how to assist; and it was a resource that the Soviets were not shy of exploiting.

Starting in the summer of 1940, Soviet foreign-trade commissar Anastas Mikoyan began submitting sizeable orders with German firms

– such as Reinecker, which had been Europe's largest machine-tool manufacturer in 1939 – for sundry heavy engineering items including mills, forges, presses and cranes. The KV factory at Chelyabinsk alone took over 400 German machining tools, while an order from mid-July 1940 contained a request – worth 11.5 million roubles – for the import from Germany of 117 metal-processing tools, twenty-two presses, forges and a complete bearing assembly plant.[65] The collaboration was not confined to the tank industry. When 'Factory 292' was set up at Saratov in 1941, for the production of the mainstay Yakovlev Yak-1 fighter, it was established with 40 per cent of its machine tools coming from Germany. And when factories were retooled at Kirov and Kharkhov in 1940 for the production of the M-30 and M-40 aero-engines, nearly 20 million roubles was spent on machinery from German suppliers.[66] Total figures and volumes of such orders will probably never be known, but it is surely no exaggeration to say that German engineering was one of the unacknowledged godfathers of the Red Army's later military prowess.

For the Germans, however, the economic advantages brought by the connection with the Soviet Union are rather more difficult to discern. It is often lazily assumed, for instance, that supplies of Soviet fuel were paramount in German thinking. Certainly, the thirst for fuel shown by Hitler's war machine would ultimately prove its Achilles heel, but one should be wary of projecting such problems back to the opening phase of the conflict. Germany went to war in September 1939 with over 2 million tons of oil stocks, and by the start of the campaign against the Soviet Union, in June 1941, that figure had dropped by only about a quarter. Total oil supplies from the Soviet Union, meanwhile, amounted to less than 1 million tons – i.e. less than the monthly German reserve stock, and barely 3 per cent of the USSR's total annual production – over that same period.[67]

More significantly, perhaps, the Soviet Union was not Germany's only source of oil; Hitler's troops confiscated around 1 million tons of French oil stocks following the fall of France in 1940.[68] Romania, too, put its oil wells at Hitler's disposal, and with greater generosity than Stalin did, quickly emerging in 1940 as Germany's most important supplier of crude oil. In the same period that the USSR supplied barely a million tons of oil to Germany, Romania supplied over four times that amount.[69] Every drop would ultimately be crucial, of course, but the idea that Hitler was dependent on Soviet oil between 1939 and 1941 simply does not withstand scrutiny.

It's a similar story with iron ore, essential for the creation of steel. The Soviets supplied Germany with 750,000 tons of it under the terms of the Commercial Agreement of February 1940, a figure far larger than those stipulated for other ores, such as manganese, chrome and copper, though less than 3 per cent of Soviet annual production.[70] Yet Swedish supplies of iron ore to Germany would dwarf those of the Soviet Union. In a memorandum to a German–Swedish trade treaty in December 1939, it was noted that the projected Swedish export of iron ore to Germany in 1940 alone would reach 10 million tons, over thirteen times the total Soviet figure.[71] Germany would get more iron ore from Sweden every month than it would receive from the USSR in over a year.

Rubber is another area of Soviet supply which appears to have fallen short of expectations. The importance of rubber to the modern military should not be underestimated, and Germany's pre-war supply came largely from British-controlled sources in South-East Asia. Once war broke out in 1939 and those sources dried up, Germany hoped to source its rubber via the USSR, with the latter serving as a proxy buyer and transporting the goods to Germany.

In the event, Soviet-sourced rubber would be rather symptomatic of the wider shortcomings of Germany's economic relationship with the USSR. Already at the outbreak of war, Germany was a world leader in the production of synthetic rubber, which was known by the trade name 'Buna' and was being produced in three plants. Heightened wartime demand, projected at around 9,000 tons per month,[72] required alternative resources, mainly the USSR. Yet Soviet-sourced rubber could not make up the shortfall. Soviet deliveries, totalling only 18,000 tons – less than Germany's annual production of synthetic rubber – would barely ease the shortage.[73]

In the circumstances, it is not surprising that German technocrats were keen to expand domestic synthetic-rubber production, so in the winter of 1940 a new state-of-the-art chemicals facility was planned close to the little-known Upper Silesian town of Auschwitz. The resulting 'Buna-Works', and the associated labour camp at Monowitz, or 'Auschwitz III', as it became known, opened in May 1942, with the target production of 25,000 tons per annum.[74] The plant would consume some 600 million Reichsmarks of investment – a similar figure to the export trade associated with the Nazi–Soviet Pact – and around 30,000 lives.[75] One of those who survived Monowitz was the Italian-Jewish chemist Primo Levi, who later in life often recalled his experience of working in the factory:

> Buna is as large as a city; besides the managers and German technicians, forty thousand foreigners work there and fifteen to twenty languages are spoken . . . [It] is desperately and essentially opaque and grey. This huge entanglement of iron, concrete, mud and smoke is the negation of beauty. Its roads and buildings are named like us, by numbers and letters, not by weird and sinister names. Within its bounds not a blade of grass grows, and the soil is impregnated with the poisonous saps of coal and petroleum, and the only things alive are machines and slaves – and the former are more alive than the latter.[76]

One of the few areas where a tangible economic benefit to Germany can be discerned is in the area of foodstuffs. Hitler's paladins were highly sensitive to the issue of food supply, mindful as they were of the morale-sapping experience of the home front in the First World War. Consequently, the Nazi regime was keen to shore up domestic morale by ensuring that food supply was prioritised, which was achieved through the setting of artificially high rationing allocations, and by lifting restrictions on what German troops could bring home from abroad.[77]

In this regard, the supply of Soviet animal feed could play a vital part, helping Germany's farmers to maintain domestic deliveries of meat – an important influence on civilian morale. As a result, the supply of 1 million tons of 'feed grains and legumes' from the Soviet Union was duly included in the February 1940 Commercial Agreement, an estimate that was later revised upwards to 1.5 million tons, with a further million tons anticipated for the second year. Although German reserves remained stable at around 4 million tons for most of 1940, they dwindled rapidly in 1941, such that, by the middle of the year, Germany was effectively reliant on supplies from the Soviet Union.[78] By that point, just as the Germans and the Soviets clashed on the battlefield, it was Stalin's collective farmers who were keeping Hitler's people fed.

From the German perspective, then, the economic aspects of the

Nazi–Soviet Pact were something of a curate's egg, with a few positives arguably outweighed by more serious shortcomings. This, naturally, would have been a profound frustration and disappointment to the Nazi regime, for it is clear that Hitler's negotiators had entertained high hopes of being able to tap into the raw material riches that were promised by the Soviet Union. Realising that ambition, however, had proved to be a rather more difficult prospect.

To some extent, German ambitions were stymied by Soviet nego-tiating methods, which one German participant described simply as 'chicanery'.[79] Exorbitant demands and unrealistically high prices for their own goods were married to constant haggling over the tiniest details, deliberate delays and outright stubbornness. In addition, Soviet negotiators could be bizarrely unpredictable – uncooperative one day, genial the next, leaving their German counterparts often confused and frustrated. This, of course, was doubtless part of the plan, but there were also concrete reasons for such peculiar behaviour.

First of all, mindful perhaps of the fate of many of their fellows in the great purges of the late 1930s, many Soviet functionaries showed a remarkable unwillingness to commit to any proposal or suggestion, for fear that they might be treading on the toes of their superiors. As Germany's negotiator in Moscow, Gustav Hilger, noted in his post-war memoir:

> The negotiations were marked by the chronic suspicion of the Soviet negotiators and by the fear of responsibility even on the part of a Politburo member like Mikoyan; this in part explains the fact that it took four months of active discussions to come to terms.[80]

Lacking a political lead, Soviet negotiators often preferred – whether subconsciously or by design – to allow talks to drift into discussions of minutiae or unreasonable demands, and await direction from the Kremlin.

That direction was usually forthcoming. As one German official noted, the 'extremely difficult' negotiations repeatedly required the 'personal intervention of Stalin to prevent a premature collapse'.[81] Ribbentrop, as we have seen, appealed to Stalin to break the deadlock in the talks for the February 1940 agreement, and Soviet officials did the same to smooth their negotiations. General Yakovlev, for instance, dismayed by the amount of bureaucracy involved in any purchases earmarked by the Soviet delegation to Germany, was relieved to be able to cut through the red tape by cabling Stalin in the Kremlin, who promptly acceded to the request and ordered that no further difficulties were to be made.[82]

For his part, Stalin certainly did not intervene out of altruism. Rather, he very definitely used the economic negotiations as a political tool: a lever with which to exert pressure on his German ally, smoothing matters when he wanted to appear conciliatory, ignoring matters when he did not. For many on the German side, this wider political link to the negotiations was patently obvious. Goebbels gave an example in the summer of 1940. At a time when German–Soviet relations were increasingly strained by the Soviet annexation of the Baltic states, Bessarabia and Northern Bukovina, deliveries from Moscow suddenly began to flow, briefly meeting their quotas. As Goebbels noted in his diary, the connection was clear: 'The Russians are providing us with more than we want', he wrote. 'Stalin is making an effort to please us.'[83]

Believing that he held the stronger hand in the economic relationship with Germany, Stalin was also not shy of seeking to exploit that position in any way he could. His primary weapon in this regard was to demand artificially high prices for Soviet deliveries, while insisting on bargain-basement prices for German products. Soviet negotiators refused to accept the industry standard 'Gulf price' for their oil, for example, insisting instead on a premium of at least 50 per cent, which their German counterparts were obliged to accept. At the same time, the price for German deliveries of coal in the other direction was driven so low that Moscow was able to sell much of it on at a healthy profit.[84]

Another example is that of manganese, which is vital for the creation of steel alloys, and was one of the few commodities that Germany had already sourced from the USSR prior to the war. However, whereas Germany had paid 2.9 million Reichsmarks for 60,000 tons of Soviet manganese in 1938, by 1940 the price for 65,000 tons had risen by 75 per cent to 5.5 million Reichsmarks.[85] For communists, Stalin's negotiators clearly demonstrated a sound understanding of the fundamental workings of capitalism.

In extreme cases, Stalin was not above resorting to more radical methods to get his point across. In September 1940, for instance, Mikoyan expressed his growing frustration at what he saw as German delays in balancing deliveries and a generally unhelpful attitude from her negotiators. Stalin reacted by simply 'turning off' the oil supply, in the expectation that such a move would swiftly cause his German partners to see sense. No new shipments followed for the next two weeks and Soviet supplies for the month dropped to under half what they had been for August.[86]

In his intransigence, Stalin arguably overplayed his hand. For, although he had been Hitler's only viable option in the autumn of 1939, by the summer of 1940 Germany's strategic situation had vastly improved and there were a number of alternative suitors – occupied France, Romania, Sweden – able to supply the Greater German Reich. In the light of that strategic shift, Berlin's perception of the relationship with the Soviet Union began to change as well, and Hitler's economic advisors increasingly began to envisage a European economic area, with Germany at its heart, rather than an increasingly turbulent and unpredictable economic partnership with Moscow.[87] Paradoxically, therefore, the more Stalin intervened, the less influence he would have.

Aside from their capitalist flourishes and heavy-handed responses, the Soviets also had a few grievances of their own. For one thing Stalin appears to have been particularly disquieted by the staggered aspect of the Commercial Agreement – by which Soviet deliveries were balanced by *later* German counter-deliveries – and was perennially worried that the Germans were behind schedule. Indeed, Soviet complaints were constantly aired about supposed German foot-dragging. Valentin Berezhkov recalled one such conversation with Gustav Krupp von Bohlen in Essen in 1940. After complaining about the slow progress of the assembly of the *Lützow*'s guns, and accusing Krupp of 'violating the schedule' for delivery, he was told that 'there are forces beyond our control'. Blaming the war and Anglo-French intransigence, Krupp claimed that he was doing his 'patriotic duty' in supplying the Wehrmacht first of all, but promised to look into the Soviet complaints, and pledged to finish work on the *Lützow* as soon as the *Prinz Eugen* had been completed.[88] This approach was certainly in line with the official instruction from Berlin, that Soviet orders were to be given priority *after* those of the German military, but it is quite possible that it still gave ample scope for procrastination.

The Germans too could raise complaints regarding the progress of the *Lützow*, but on a quite different issue. As Khrushchev related in his post-war memoir, a German rear admiral, Otto Feige, was dispatched to Leningrad with the vessel, to oversee the job of fitting her out. However, Feige soon attracted the attention of the Soviet intelligence service and a 'honey trap' was prepared for him, involving a 'young lovely', an 'indecent pose' and some photographic equipment. Despite the ensuing scandal, Khrushchev claimed, the Soviet secret service failed to recruit Feige, as the brazen rear admiral 'couldn't have cared less'. Hitler, meanwhile, was said to have been most indignant and 'raised a rumpus' with the NKVD chief Lavrenti Beria.[89]

While ideology would undoubtedly have added a certain spice to such confrontations, it was not the primary irritant. There were, in many cases, genuine economic or strategic reasons for either or both sides to feel aggrieved. In the Baltic states, for example, German companies had an estimated 200 million Reichsmarks of investment in 1940, as well as a similar value in export trade in foodstuffs and fuel.[90] However, with the Soviet annexations of that summer, those contacts were effectively severed and the markets and assets lost. Of course, when Berlin had negotiated the Baltic states away in the autumn of 1939, it had done so in the expectation that access to Soviet markets and resources would easily counterbalance such losses, but the reality was that it rarely did.

Berlin was similarly disquieted by developments in Moscow's two newly annexed Romanian provinces, where its existing trade contracts, predominantly for lumber and foodstuffs, were promptly downgraded. Although Molotov had promised to respect German economic interests in the region, he informed Berlin after the annexation that the agreed grain export to Germany from Bessarabia for 1940 was to be reduced by two-thirds.[91] In such instances, Germany got the worst of both worlds: losing stable, reliable trading partners and having to deal solely with Moscow, which was proving to be an increasingly difficult and demanding client.

The frustrations ran both ways, of course. For one thing, Stalin's pride would not allow him easily to assume a subordinate position to Hitler's Germany – as he put it, to become 'Germany's tail'.[92] Yet, beyond that, the Soviets had many similar concerns to the Germans about the loss of their traditional markets and suppliers. By signing the pact with Nazi Germany, Stalin had so isolated himself internationally that Hitler's was almost the only other state that was willing to do business with him. Where 60 per cent of Soviet machinery and technology imports had come from the USA in 1938, for instance, that dwindled to nothing after the signature of the pact and the invasion of Finland late in 1939, with President Roosevelt even imposing a 'moral embargo' on trade with the Soviet Union.[93] The idea that Moscow was simply stringing the Germans along, therefore, intent on a bit of industrial espionage and military pilfering, simply does not correspond to reality. The Soviets had as much involved in the relationship, economically, as the Germans, maybe more so. Indeed, if anything, their intransigence in negotiating with Berlin was as much a symptom of desperation as anything else.

In addition, where Nazi Germany and the Soviet Union were now sharing a border, new points of friction emerged. As the Soviet ambassador in London had confessed to Viscount Halifax in September 1939, German military success had been a 'great surprise' to the USSR, which was now concerned at the prospect of a 'powerful and victorious Germany' as her next-door neighbour.[94] One of the resulting points of friction was the so-called 'Lithuanian Strip', a small parcel of land along the Šešupė river in southern Lithuania, which but for finding itself on the fault line between two totalitarian rivals would doubtless have remained in total obscurity. However, despite being assigned to Germany in the September 1939 Boundary and Friendship Treaty, the strip was annexed wholesale by the Soviets, along with the rest of Lithuania, in the following summer. When the Germans raised the issue in subsequent negotiations, Moscow offered to retroactively purchase the territory for around 16 million Reichsmarks, to which Berlin made a counter-demand of 54 million Reichsmarks, which Moscow duly rejected. As the talks descended into acrimony, Ribbentrop attempted to excise the issue from the wider negotiations, but the spat rumbled on, poisoning already fraught relations as it went.[95]

The squabble over Bessarabia and Northern Bukovina would prove even more divisive. The Soviet occupation of the provinces, in the summer of 1940, caused profound disquiet in Berlin. Though Moscow and Berlin had agreed in 1939 to Bessarabia falling into the Soviet 'sphere of interest', when Stalin came to collect the following summer, his lieutenants demanded nearby Bukovina as well, which had not previously been slated to fall under Moscow's rule, as 'compensation' for historic Soviet losses at Romanian hands.[96]

Stalin's motives were complex. Russia had a long-standing claim to Bessarabia, going back to the Crimean War and beyond, and its annexation provided a vital depth of defence to the port of Odessa, which was only forty kilometres from the old Romanian frontier. But Stalin's overriding motivation was that the annexation extended Soviet influence into the Balkans, with the ultimate ambition – in echo of the nineteenth-century 'Eastern Question' – of establishing Moscow's control over the Bosphorus and the Dardanelles, without which the Black Sea was potentially little more than a Soviet lake.[97]

However, such ambitions ran very much counter to Hitler's desire to preserve the Balkans, and particularly Romania, as his own economic and strategic hinterland. As we have seen, Romanian oil was crucial to Berlin. Hitler would confess to the Finnish leader Marshal Mannerheim two years later that he had 'always feared that Russia would attack Romania in the late autumn of 1940 . . . and occupy the petroleum wells'. Had they done so, he said, 'we would have been helpless': without Romanian oil, Germany 'could not have fought the war'.[98] Yet, beyond that, there was a broader strategic concern: Stalin's move into the Balkans was interpreted in Berlin as a worrying westward shift, a challenge to Germany's continental hegemony.

So, though Berlin did not object in principle to the cession of the Romanian provinces – indeed it urged the government in Bucharest to comply with Soviet demands – it did nonetheless lodge a protest with its Soviet ally. In late June, Ribbentrop wrote a long memorandum to Molotov, via Schulenburg, reminding him that Germany was 'abiding by the Moscow agreements' but that the Soviet claim to Bukovina was 'something new'. Not only did Bukovina present complications regarding the local ethnic German population, he explained, it was also close to Germany's 'very important economic interests' in the rest of Romania, consequently Germany was 'extremely interested in preventing these areas from becoming a theatre of war'. As concerns were raised in Berlin that Moscow was overstepping the limits of the 1939 pact, and unilaterally demanding territories beyond the agreed 'spheres of influence', Ribbentrop's memorandum was something like a warning shot.[99]

Stalin's move south went unchecked, however, and though condoned by Berlin, nonetheless set alarm bells ringing and increased Hitler's determination to ensure his own control over the region. What followed would be an unseemly scramble for the Balkans, in which Romania and Bulgaria would slip from sovereign nations to desperate clients and petitioners.

Romania was the first to implode. Following Stalin's annexation of Bessarabia and Northern Bukovina, the government in Bucharest abandoned its previous policy of uneasy neutrality and actively sought an alignment with Germany, disavowing the Anglo-French guarantee of 1939, abandoning the League of Nations, and finally announcing her desire to join the Axis in mid-July 1940. Such obeisances were not enough to save her from her neighbours, however, as Bulgaria and Hungary both lodged territorial claims, to southern Dobrudja and Transylvania respectively, which were granted following German and Italian arbitration. The subsequent, and arguably inevitable, collapse of King Carol's government – with the king himself fleeing into a life of exile – ushered in a tense alliance between a pro-German senior general, Ion Antonescu, and the home-spun fanatics of the Romanian fascist movement, the Iron Guard. At the end of all that, shorn of its disputed territories and in political ferment, Romania slipped definitively into the German orbit. Bulgaria would be next.

By the late summer of 1940, the German–Soviet relationship was in trouble. Strategically, the two appeared to be on a collision course. The mood of collaboration of late 1939 had shifted increasingly to one of confrontation, with growing suspicions on both sides that the other was acting in bad faith. Typical in this regard, perhaps, was an NKVD assessment, drawn up for the first anniversary of the pact in 1940, which came to the following stark conclusion: 'Intoxicated by victory, the German Government together with the Italians and without the consent of the USSR, violated the agreement of 23 August 1939 by deciding the fate of the Balkan peoples.'[100] The irony, and the root of the problem, was that Berlin could just as easily have accused Stalin of the very same thing.

In economics, too, the relationship was faltering. Despite the not-inconsiderable benefits that had accrued for both sides over the previous year or so, both Moscow and Berlin were feeling dissatisfied. The Germans were frustrated that the connection with Moscow was not bearing the rich fruit that had been expected, and were well aware that other sources, such as occupied France or Romania, were proving more bounteous than the USSR. The Soviets, meanwhile, knew that their relationship with Germany, turbulent at best hitherto, was in need of recalibrating, to acknowledge the huge changes that the intervening year of warfare had brought. Trade, which had been regarded by both sides as an essential component of the political arrangement, had become merely an indicator of a deeper malaise.

Even the ex-*Lützow*, grimly symbolic of the relationship, was in difficulties. At the end of September 1940, though only two-thirds completed and moored in her dock in Leningrad, the ship was formally incorporated into the Red Navy and given the name *Petropavlovsk*, commemorating a Russian victory against the British and French in the Crimean War. However, in a microcosm of the wider problems, the tentative co-operation on board the ship between German and Soviet crew and engineers had all but collapsed, with interminable haggling effectively paralysing any genuine progress on finishing the vessel. The Soviets requested that their training be carried out in Russian, for instance, with specialist officers being sent to German factories for instruction. They also demanded that a Red Navy training detail should be permitted to serve aboard the *Admiral Hipper*.[101] Unsurprisingly, the German authorities refused. Then, when an article appeared in the Soviet newspaper *Izvestia* in October 1940 outlining the historical background of a number of Soviet warships, including the *Petropavlovsk*, the vessel's German origins were not mentioned.[102] A cynic might have surmised that the Nazi–Soviet Pact was already being airbrushed out of history.

In such circumstances, it naturally fell to Ribbentrop, as one of the progenitors of the Nazi–Soviet alignment, to attempt to revivify it. In mid-October, he addressed Soviet concerns with a letter sent to Stalin personally, in which he advocated inviting Molotov to Berlin for talks preparatory to a revision of the pact through a new 'delimitation of mutual spheres of influence'.[103] Stalin was evidently relieved by the invitation, smoothing a number of ongoing squabbles before replying with the hope that relations between the two would thereby be improved.[104]

Molotov, meanwhile, was thoroughly briefed. His primary goal was not necessarily to secure an agreement, as the Berlin talks were seen by Moscow merely as the opening bout of a new round of negotiations;

rather it was to divine Germany's 'real intentions' and the possible role for the USSR envisaged in Berlin's 'New Europe'. Furthermore, he was to ascertain what Hitler foresaw as their spheres of interest both in Europe and in the Near and Middle East. Most importantly, however, Molotov was to express Moscow's dissatisfaction with developments in Romania and address wider Soviet security concerns in the Balkans. 'The main topic of the negotiations', he was told by Stalin, was to be 'Bulgaria', which 'must belong by agreement with Germany and Italy to the USSR's sphere of interests, on the same basis as had been done by Germany and Italy in the case of Romania'.[105]

Clearly some tough negotiations were in the offing. But it is telling that Stalin's instructions to Molotov still stressed the principle of working in concert with Nazi Germany to achieve the Soviet Union's strategic goals. For all the bluster and opprobrium, it appears that – from Moscow's perspective at least – the Nazi–Soviet Pact still had some mileage left in it.

7

Comrade 'Stonearse' in the Lair of the Fascist Beast

The weather did not provide a positive omen for Molotov's arrival in Berlin. Leaden skies and lashing rain welcomed the Soviet foreign minister to Hitler's capital. Yet aside from the elements, the greeting extended was warm enough, with the platforms and ticketing hall of the vast Anhalter station festooned with Soviet flags and bouquets of pink and red flowers. The welcoming party was similarly extravagant, with an honour guard of the Wehrmacht, standing to immaculate attention in the rain outside the station, while inside the platform was thronged with senior representatives of the Nazi state and military, including Ribbentrop and Army Supreme Commander Field Marshal Wilhelm Keitel, all with their crimson-lined uniform greatcoats buttoned up tight against the November chill.

Molotov, meanwhile, had had a rather comfortable, if lengthy, journey. He had departed from Belorussky station in Moscow three evenings previously, in a special 'European-designed' train, with a pistol in his pocket and an entourage of more than sixty people, including sixteen security guards, a physician and three personal servants.[1] His journey across the western Soviet Union and newly annexed Lithuania had given him ample time to contemplate his task: that of ascertaining Germany's strategic intentions and, if possible, negotiating a follow-up to the Nazi–Soviet Pact.

If he had ever imagined that it would be an easy job, Molotov was perhaps reminded of the very real difficulties that persisted between Nazi Germany and the Soviet Union by an incident at Eydtkuhnen on the German–Soviet border in East Prussia. The small town marked the extreme eastern end of the German rail system and the point where travellers from the east were obliged to change trains to the standard-gauge European network. However, in the highly charged atmosphere of 1940, with Europe's two major totalitarian powers vying for supremacy, simply changing trains became a very political act. German diplomat Gustav Hilger discovered this early on in the journey. He had travelled with Molotov's entourage from Moscow to act as an auxiliary interpreter in Berlin, and had asked one of the senior members of the Soviet party, NKVD Deputy Commissar Vsevolod Merkulov, to remind him where the change of trains took place. Puzzlingly, Merkulov replied: 'We shall change trains at such a place as will be designated by the chairman of the Council of People's Commissars.' Bemused, Hilger attempted to argue that the location of the rail terminus was not within the gift even of Molotov, but to no avail, and eventually he had to console himself by making a mental note of the absurd ends to which the Soviet Union's 'excessive secrecy and stupid subordination' could lead.[2]

Once Molotov's train arrived at Eydtkuhnen, another incident served to highlight the political tensions. The interpreter, Valentin Berezhkov, was woken by the sound of an argument on the platform and hurried to investigate. Interpreting between the Soviet train driver and a German official, he learned that the official was insisting that the Soviet delegation had to transfer to another train – as per regulations – while the driver claimed that he had been told to take the train directly to Berlin. Though the technical problem could be solved by changing the train's bogies, the official still insisted that the carriages were too large to ride on standard German lines. However, after much measuring and heated discussion, it was agreed that two German saloon carriages would replace the larger Soviet examples. Berezhkov would later note in his memoirs that the German carriages were 'very comfortable' with 'an excellent bar and restaurant . . . salons fitted with radios' and even 'vases of fresh roses in the compartments'. However, he added sourly, 'it was not concern for our comfort that made the Germans so stubborn in insisting that we should change trains. Undoubtedly their carriages were not only equipped with a fine bar, but with a fine lot of bugging apparatus too.'[3]

Whatever the truth of that assumption, Molotov's train sped onwards to Berlin, arriving in the German capital at 11.05 a.m. on 12 November. There, Molotov and his immediate entourage alighted on to the packed platform of the Anhalter station. In their Soviet suits

and felt homburg hats they cut rather incongruous figures among the
myriad military uniforms, like a group of provincial accountants who
had inadvertently alighted at the wrong station. They were welcomed
by Ribbentrop, who gave a short address, and were introduced to the
waiting dignitaries, Molotov doffing his hat extravagantly in greeting.
Moving outside, through the packed ticket hall, the group processed
past the guard of honour, while a military band struck up the Prussian
'Presentation March', in preference to the Soviet anthem, the
'Internationale', which, it was feared, might induce some sympathetic
Berliners to join in.[4]

Though not unimpressive, Molotov's reception was a low-key affair;
Goebbels described it with uncharacteristic terseness in his diary as
'cool'.[5] The poor weather may well have dampened Berlin spirits, and
the Nazi authorities might have feared encouraging their citizens to
wave the hammer and sickle, but nonetheless the effort expended for
Molotov appears to have bordered on the bare minimum: no cheering
crowds were organised and, beyond the Anhalter station, few Soviet
flags were in evidence. Interpreter Paul Schmidt certainly noticed the
difference between Molotov's arrival and other state visits, noting that
ordinary Berliners were completely silent on the streets in the heart
of the capital – the 'Via Spontana', as he sarcastically called it – in
contrast to the usual reception, when cheering and flag-waving were
organised by party functionaries.[6] Furthermore, it is suggested that
Goebbels squashed Ribbentrop's idea of an additional honour guard
of SA men to greet the Soviet minister.[7] Even the newsreel coverage
was minimalist, comprising barely two minutes of that week's
programme; surprisingly, French cinema audiences learned more
about Molotov's visit than those in Germany did.[8] The contrast to the
elaborate reception organised for the visit of the Japanese foreign
minister, Yōsuke Matsuoka, six months later is highly instructive.

Molotov would later claim to have no recollection of his arrival in
Berlin,[9] let alone whether he felt that he was being snubbed. After being
driven through the 'half-empty streets'[10] of the German capital, however,
he would doubtless have been cheered by his arrival at the Bellevue
Palace, the Third Reich's 'guest house' for visiting dignitaries. 'Guest
house' was, in fact, something of a misnomer. Bellevue Palace had
originally been built in 1786 as a summer residence for Prince Augustus
Ferdinand of Prussia. Located in central Berlin, between the Tiergarten

and the banks of the river Spree, it was an elegant neoclassical palace which had just undergone a 14 million Reichsmarks renovation and expansion at the hands of architect Paul Baumgarten, whose other credits included the Minoux villa in Wannsee, made infamous by the eponymous conference that would take place there in 1942. Beautifully presented, with over 130 rooms – including four self-contained luxury apartments, as well as guest bedrooms, conference halls and offices – the palace comprised a main central building and three perpendicular wings. Its exterior was complemented inside by countless paintings, tapestries, sculptures and items of furniture, most of which had come from the collection of the former diplomat Willibald von Dirksen, and included works by Titian and Tintoretto.[11] It was all very impressive, as Valentin Berezhkov testified:

> A long avenue of limes led to the entrance. Inside we were amazed at the ostentation of the rooms. Everywhere we could smell the delicate scent of roses coming from the bouquets which stood in tall porcelain vases in every corner. The walls were decorated with tapestries and paintings in heavy gilt frames. There were statuettes and cases of the finest porcelain standing all around in exquisitely carved cabinets . . . The furniture was antique and the servants and waiters were garbed in gold-braided livery. All this lent the hotel an air of ceremonial pomposity.[12]

After settling in, the Soviets enjoyed an opulent lunch served by white-gloved staff and overseen by a 'tall, grey-haired *maître d'hotel* . . . who silently conducted proceedings with nothing more than a barely noticeable gesture or look'. Thereafter, Molotov's party climbed back into their Mercedes limousines and made their way to Wilhelmstrasse for the first round of talks. En route, there were now small crowds of Berliners watching proceedings on the streets; some of them dared to wave as the cars passed.[13]

Even to those accustomed to the political contortions of the previous year or so, the sight of the Soviet foreign minister in Berlin for talks with Hitler must have seemed like a strange mirage. Yet, for all the apparent unreality of the scene, the meeting was no chimera. It had been called for hard-headed political reasons: to repair the fraying relationship between Berlin and Moscow and renegotiate the Nazi–Soviet Pact.

When he had written to Stalin a month earlier to extend the invitation, Ribbentrop had expressed the hope that the relationship with the Soviet Union might be established 'on a broader basis' through a 'demarcation' of their respective interests.[14] The neutral tone of the letter belied the tension of its author. Berlin had grown increasingly frustrated by its Soviet partner: the economic relationship had not brought the expected windfall of raw materials, and Stalin had shown his continued European ambitions by annexing territory beyond the line agreed in August 1939. From the German perspective, some sort of reckoning with Moscow was in the offing.

For his part, meanwhile, Molotov did not feel that he owed the Germans anything. Echoing the prevailing Soviet view, he was coming to Berlin not as a supplicant or a junior partner; rather he was negotiating from a position of strength. The Soviet Union, he believed, was very well placed. It had expanded its territory and advanced its economic position, and while its rivals were fighting one another in western Europe, it was at peace. As Politburo member Andrei Zhdanov noted in the late autumn of 1940, the Anglo-German war gave the USSR the opportunity to 'go about its business' undisturbed.[15] Molotov, like many of his confederates in Moscow, believed that while Germany was militarily engaged in the west, it was scarcely in any position to dictate terms to its eastern partner. Clearly, the discussions were not going to be easy.

The first meeting was held at the foreign-ministry building on Wilhelmstrasse.[16] There, Ribbentrop and Molotov sat down together, with their respective interpreters and Molotov's deputy, Vladimir Dekanozov, at a small round table to open discussions. Ribbentrop worked particularly hard to show his most obliging side to his guests, according to Schmidt; so smiling and affable, he claimed, that his regular political partners would have 'rubbed their eyes in amazement'. Molotov, meanwhile, was as inscrutable as ever. A notoriously difficult negotiating partner, he was untroubled by concepts such as charm or politeness. Wasting no superfluous words, he rarely allowed his 'poker face' to slip.[17] Clearly it was not for nothing that he had earned himself the nickname of 'Stonearse'.

What followed might have reminded Molotov of interminable

meetings in the Kremlin. Ribbentrop got matters under way. As one who never tired of hearing himself speak, Hitler's foreign minister launched into a lengthy monologue, in an 'excessively loud voice', about how 'no power on earth could alter the fact that England was beaten' and that it was it was only a matter of time before she would 'finally admit her defeat'. Germany, he said, was 'extraordinarily strong' and so 'completely dominated its part of Europe' that the Axis powers were not considering how they might win the war, 'but rather how rapidly they could end the war which was already won'.

Given that Ribbentrop evidently considered that the war was as good as over, he moved seamlessly to the issue of dividing up the spoils of the soon-to-be-defunct British and French empires. Echoing his master's voice, he opined that the time was right for a broad delineation of 'spheres of influence' between the Soviet Union, Germany, Italy and Japan. Molotov's interest would doubtless have been piqued by this phrase, but he would have been bemused by what followed. A wise policy, Ribbentrop suggested, was that each power should direct its expansion southwards, thereby avoiding points of possible friction. Thus Italy was already expanding to the southern coast of the Mediterranean in North and East Africa, he explained, Japan was pushing south into the China Sea and the western Pacific, and Germany – having defined her sphere of influence with the USSR – was to seek her *Lebensraum* in Central Africa. Would the Soviet Union, Ribbentrop wondered aloud, not 'also turn to the South' for the 'natural outlet to the open sea' that was so important to her? Momentarily confused, Molotov interrupted Ribbentrop's flow to ask to which sea he was referring. After another lengthy discourse on the benefits of the Nazi–Soviet Pact, the Reich foreign minister replied, asking whether 'in the long run the most advantageous access to the sea for Russia could not be found in the direction of the Persian Gulf and the Arabian Sea'?[18] Molotov said nothing and merely stared back at Ribbentrop, as inscrutable as ever.

Unfazed, Ribbentrop pressed on with his monologue, diverting into a brief though rambling foray into the subject of Turkey, a topic he knew was close to Soviet hearts. As a sop to Moscow, he advocated reopening the 'Straits Question' via an Axis-sponsored revision of the Montreux Convention, which since 1936 had regulated military and civilian traffic through the Bosphorus and the Dardanelles and recognised

Turkish control of both areas. Still Molotov studiously kept his counsel. Ribbentrop wound up his exposition with an airy summary, dangling the idea of some Soviet alignment with the Tripartite Pact and floating the prospect of another visit to Moscow to discuss matters further. Tellingly, however, he stopped short of any concrete proposals, restricting himself instead to an outline of 'the ideas which the Führer and he had in mind'.[19]

In response, Molotov was as laconic as Ribbentrop had been loquacious, agreeing that an exchange of ideas 'might be useful' and asking for clarification on a couple of points: the significance and purpose of the Tripartite Pact and the precise meaning of the phrase the 'Greater East Asian Sphere', which had arisen in the preparatory conversations. He was right to query them. But in response, Ribbentrop was less than entirely enlightening. The Greater East Asian Sphere, he admitted, was 'new to him, too' and had 'not been defined to him either'. So he could offer little explanation beyond the unconvincing assurance that it had 'nothing to do with the vital Russian spheres of influence'. Explaining the Tripartite Pact would have done nothing to ease Ribbentrop's discomfort. Though not explicitly anti-Soviet, the pact – which had been signed by Germany, Italy and Japan only two weeks before in Berlin – had nonetheless grown out of the Anti-Comintern Pact of 1936, which *had* been directed against Moscow. The new agreement pledged co-operation between the three powers in the establishment and maintenance of the 'New Order' in Europe and East Asia, forming the basis of the 'Axis'. Predictably, perhaps, Ribbentrop soothed his embarrassment by suggesting that the Soviet party might like to break for a late luncheon.[20]

In the hour or so that Ribbentrop had spoken, Molotov had asked only three brief questions; Dekanozov had said nothing at all. Paul Schmidt believed that Molotov was 'keeping his powder dry', preserving his strength for the main event with Hitler later that day.[21] However, it may also be that he recognised that he needed to speak to the organ grinder rather than the monkey.

After lunch, Molotov got his chance. Chauffeured into the austere neoclassical courtyard of the new Reich Chancellery, past an honour guard of the SS-Leibstandarte, he was led through the polished marble halls, 'lined by people in various kinds of uniform'. Berezhkov suspected that the visitors were deliberately taken by the most circuitous route, so as to impress upon them the size and grandeur of the building. When they finally reached the door to Hitler's office, a last piece of political theatre was enacted:

> Two tall blond SS men in black tightly belted uniforms with skulls on the caps clicked their heels and threw open the tall, almost ceiling-high doors with a single well-practised gesture. Then, with their backs to the door jambs and their right arms raised, they formed a kind of arch, through which we had to pass to enter Hitler's office, a vast room that was more like a banqueting hall than an office.[22]

Seated at his desk, Hitler hesitated for a moment then rose to greet his visitors. He moved with 'small, rapid steps' before stopping in the centre of the room and raising his arm in the Nazi salute 'bending his palm unnaturally'. Then, Berezhkov recalled, 'still without a word, he came up close and shook each one of us by the hand. His palm was cold and moist to the touch, and his feverish eyes seemed to bore through you like gimlets.'[23] As one of his entourage would later recall, it was Hitler's habit to silently hold a newcomer's gaze for a time by way of a test of their mettle[24] and it seems from this account that he might have tried this method with his Soviet visitors. Molotov, however, was apparently unmoved and later merely noted Hitler's 'surprisingly gracious and friendly manner'.[25]

After the formalities, the small group, joined again by Ribbentrop, Schmidt and Hilger, got down to business seated in the armchairs at one end of Hitler's office. As before, it began with a monologue. Hitler stated his goal of continued 'peaceful collaboration' between the Soviet Union and Germany, and stressed the 'considerable value' that had already accrued to both countries through their connection. However, he added – alluding to the points of friction that had arisen between the two – neither country could expect to get everything it wanted from the relationship, and in war Germany had been compelled to react to events, to 'penetrate into territories remote from her and in which she was not basically interested politically or economically'. Consequently, one had to look towards a settlement of European relations after the war, in 'such a manner that, at least in the foreseeable future, no new conflict could arise'. To this end, Hitler outlined Germany's viewpoints, stressing a need for *Lebensraum*, colonial expansion in Central Africa and certain raw materials – the supply of which would be safeguarded 'under all circumstances' – and finally her determination not to permit unnamed 'hostile powers' to establish military bases 'in certain areas'.[26]

In response to this catalogue of vagueness, Molotov finally stirred himself. He had eagerly agreed with much of what Hitler had said up to this point, concurring on the need for Germany and the Soviet Union to 'stand together', and chiming with his host on the 'intolerable and unjust' situation that the 'miserable island' of England should own 'half the world'.[27] However, he wanted specifics; as Schmidt recalled, 'he wanted the i's dotted'.[28] Taking the initiative, Molotov gave a brief survey of the benefits gleaned by both sides from the German–Soviet agreement, then moved on to the essential business of his visit. He asked Hitler, first of all, if the letter of the pact was still being honoured with regard to Finland. Before the Führer could answer, he went on, demanding to know the significance of the Tripartite Pact? And what role would the USSR be given in it? And what of Soviet interests in the Balkans and the Black Sea region? It would interest the Soviet government, he said, to know the precise form of Hitler's 'New Order' in Europe, and what the boundaries of the so-called Greater East Asian Sphere might be.[29] According to Schmidt, 'the questions hailed down on Hitler. No foreign visitor had ever spoken to him in this way in my presence.'[30]

Hitler was taken aback. Berezhkov claimed that the effect of this tirade on him was 'like a cold shower' and that he 'could not disguise his confusion'. For Schmidt, however, Hitler was 'meekness and politeness itself' and he noted with praise that the Führer did not 'jump up and rush to the door', as he had been known to do during previous difficult negotiations.[31] Rather, it seems, he calmly explained the principle behind the Tripartite Pact, stressing the importance of Soviet co-operation, and reassured Molotov that the USSR was 'by no means . . . to be confronted with a fait accompli'. Though momentarily mollified, Molotov calmly restated his questions, pushing for more detail and demanding that matters must be 'more closely defined'. With that, it seems, Hitler decided that he had had enough. He looked at his watch and drew the meeting to a close, stating that discussions should be postponed 'in view of a possible air-raid alarm'.[32] So, in his first day of talks in the German capital, Molotov had already endured many hours of negotiations, yet he was no nearer to finding an agreement with his hosts; indeed, the two sides barely seemed to be reading from the same script.

That evening, the strains were already beginning to show. Molotov and his entourage repaired to the Bellevue Palace to inform Stalin of the day's proceedings by telegram. Berezhkov, as part of his remit as interpreter, was obliged to type up his notes and was just about to begin dictating to a secretary when Molotov appeared in the doorway, stuttering with alarm: 'What d-d-do you think you are doing? How many pages have y-y-you already transcribed?' Ripping the still-blank pages from the typewriter, Molotov reminded him: 'Consider yourself lucky. Can you imagine how many ears might have heard what Hitler and I spoke about one-on-one?' Fearing that the rooms of the Bellevue were bugged, the pair disappeared into Molotov's bedroom, where they worked on the transcript in strict silence, passing scribbled notes to one another to address queries. Berezhkov knew he had had a lucky escape. People had been shot for less.[33]

After the telegram had been sent to Moscow, Molotov was driven to the Kaiserhof Hotel, close to Hitler's Chancellery, for a small reception hosted by Ribbentrop. Though the event was amiable enough, the political differences between the two sides were soon mirrored in other spheres. According to Molotov's later recollections, he grilled the hapless deputy Führer, Rudolf Hess, on the structure of the Nazi Party. 'Do you have a party programme?' he asked. 'How could it be a party without a programme?' 'Do you have party rules?' he demanded, though he claimed he knew that the Nazis had neither. He went on 'tripping up' Hitler's deputy, asking if the Nazi Party had a constitution.[34] Hess, it seems, had not expected a Soviet inquisition.

Neither was Hitler spared scrutiny. As Molotov would later recall, the Führer's puritanical eating habits were swiftly made manifest. 'The war is on', he told Molotov, 'so I don't drink coffee now because my people don't drink coffee either. I don't eat meat, only vegetarian food. I don't smoke, don't drink liquor.' Molotov was bemused at such abstemiousness. 'I looked', he said, 'and it seemed a rabbit was sitting next to me eating grass.' He was not minded to join his host in self-denial. 'It goes without saying', he boasted, 'that I was abstaining from nothing.'[35]

If Molotov had momentarily felt elated by such exchanges, he was soon brought back down to earth upon his return to the Bellevue. There, at around midnight, Stalin's response to his earlier telegram had arrived, and he spared his foreign minister few criticisms. He was especially angered by a passing comment that Molotov had made to Hitler that the 1939 agreement was 'exhausted'. Stalin was concerned that such a formulation might lead the Germans to conclude that the non-aggression pact had fulfilled its purpose, when in fact it was important to append further treaties to that agreement. Far from being defunct, Stalin reminded his minister, the Nazi–Soviet Pact still represented the fundamental basis of Soviet–German relations.[36]

The following morning, over breakfast at the Reich Chancellery, Goebbels got a close look at Molotov and his entourage for the first time. He would later confide his observations to his diary. The Soviet foreign minister, he wrote, 'made an intelligent, astute impression, very reserved . . . one gets almost nothing out of him. He listens attentively, but nothing more, even with the Führer.' Essentially, he noted, Molotov was little other than 'an outpost for Stalin, upon whom everything depends'. Goebbels was even less complimentary about Molotov's entourage. 'Very average', he noted sourly of the assorted advisers, translators and NKVD commissars, 'not a single man of calibre. As if they wanted to thoroughly confirm our insights into the nature of Bolshevik ideology.' He went on:

> One can't have a sensible talk with any of them. Fear of each other and an inferiority complex are written on their faces. Even an innocuous chat is as good as impossible. The GPU [secret police] is watching. It's terrible. In their world life is no longer worth living.

Goebbels drew his own political conclusions: 'Our association with Moscow must be governed by pure expediency. The closer we get politically, the more distant we become in spirit and world view. And rightly so.'[37]

Despite such increasingly apparent differences, the meeting on that second day proceeded in a similar vein to that which had gone before, with both sides essentially talking past one another, but without particular rancour or controversy. Hitler kicked off proceedings by returning to the issue that Molotov had raised the previous evening.

Against Molotov's assertion that Germany was violating the existing Nazi–Soviet agreements by stationing German troops in Finland, Hitler countered that Germany had 'no political interest there' and had 'lived up to the agreements' by not occupying any territory that was within the Soviet sphere of influence, which – he added testily – could not quite be said for the Russian side. Lengthy, inconclusive discussions followed, with German actions in Finland contrasted with Soviet actions in Bukovina, about which, Hitler complained, there had been 'not a word . . . in the agreements'.[38]

When Molotov claimed that matters such as Bukovina were 'irrelevant' to the wider relationship, Hitler showed a flash of irritation. 'If German–Russian collaboration was to show positive results in the future', he said, 'the Soviet Government would have to understand that Germany was engaged in a life and death struggle, which she wanted to conclude successfully.' Consequently, there were a number of economic and military prerequisites which Germany wanted to secure and which 'did not conflict with the agreements with Russia'. He assured Molotov that 'If the Soviet Union were in a similar position', Germany would 'demonstrate a similar understanding for Russian needs'. Stressing the benefits of united German–Soviet action, Hitler stated that there was 'no power on earth which could oppose the two countries' if they fought side by side.[39]

Molotov agreed with that sentiment, but, sticking doggedly to his theme, demanded a clarification of what he called the 'Finnish Question'. Criticising the presence of German troops in Finland, he launched into a stinging rebuke of German actions in the region, ignoring Hitler's protests that he had 'always exerted only a moderating influence' on the Finns. Molotov pressed his case, asking for definitive recognition from Hitler that Finland lay in the Soviet sphere of influence and that Moscow had the same freedom of action in dealing with Helsinki as she had enjoyed in her dealings with the Baltic states.[40] Hitler was evasive in response, denying any political ambitions in the region, but stressing repeatedly that war in the Baltic was to be avoided at all costs. Such a war, he warned, would put 'a strain on German–Russian relations with unforeseeable consequences'.[41] Hitler then suggested that they move on to more important problems.

Finally Hitler had managed to drag talks around to his favoured subject, the imminent collapse of the British Empire. 'Thus far', he said, 'a minority of 45 million Englishmen had ruled 600 million inhabitants of the British Empire.' But he was soon to 'crush' that minority. What would be left thereafter, he bragged, would be a 'gigantic world-wide estate in bankruptcy of 40 million square kilometres', which naturally gave rise to 'world-wide perspectives'. A key issue, therefore, was to decide what the USSR's participation should be in the 'solution of these problems', and to this end Hitler advocated the creation of a 'coalition' of Spain, France, Italy, Germany, Japan and the USSR, to partition that 'bankrupt estate' between them.[42] According to Molotov, Hitler's ambition was unlimited: 'Let's divide the whole world', he said.[43]

Molotov, however, was unmoved by such wide vistas of possibility and although he agreed that it was time to come to a broader agreement between the USSR and Germany, he first wanted to 'discuss . . . a problem closer to Europe': Turkey. Part of his brief for the Berlin talks had been to air Moscow's traditional concerns regarding the Straits, and its related ambitions towards Turkey and Bulgaria. What would Germany say, Molotov asked, 'if Russia gave Bulgaria, that is, the independent country located closest to the Straits, a guarantee under exactly the same conditions as Germany and Italy had given to Rumania?' Hitler initially sought to dodge the question – mentioning the same possible revision of the Montreux Convention that had been floated by Ribbentrop the previous day – but when pressed he grew irritated, snapping that he was unaware that Bulgaria had requested any such guarantee.[44]

Molotov persevered, however, reiterating that the USSR had 'only one aim' in this regard, that of securing control of the Straits to prevent enemy attack via the Black Sea, and stating that agreement with Turkey and the 'guarantee' to Bulgaria would 'alleviate the situation'. Tiring of the Führer's platitudes, he restated the question, asking Hitler directly – as 'the one who was to decide on the entire German policy' – what position Germany would take with regard to a Soviet guarantee to Bulgaria. Again Hitler avoided the question, saying that he would have to consult with Mussolini, as Bulgaria was of only peripheral interest to Berlin. However, he added in a barbed aside, if Germany were looking for sources of friction with the Soviet Union, 'she would not need the Straits for that'.[45]

In his memoir of the Berlin meetings, Paul Schmidt repeatedly employed boxing metaphors, with Hitler's and Molotov's discussions described as 'the main event' , for instance, or the talks on that second day as an 'exchange of blows', with Molotov's questions raining down and Hitler ducking them as best he could.[46] To stretch the analogy somewhat, one could suggest that Hitler was 'saved by the bell'. Though he tried one last time to wrench the conversation around to the subject of the imminent disintegration of the British Empire, Molotov would not be deflected; as the Soviet minister would later recall, 'I persisted. I wore him down.'[47] Consequently, Hitler glanced again at his watch and suggested that, given the possibility of an RAF raid, the talks should be brought to a close. After all, he added, 'the main issues' had 'probably been sufficiently discussed'.[48]

According to Valentin Berezhkov, it seems that Hitler was not yet so exasperated with Molotov that he could not muster up a few last pleasantries. As he showed his guest to the door of his office in the Reich Chancellery, he made a surprising suggestion. 'Stalin is undoubt-edly a great man,' he said, 'an historical personality . . . I too flatter myself with the hope that I shall go down in history. Therefore, two statesmen like us ought to get together and I am ready for such a meeting to take place as soon as possible.' In this, Hitler may well have been attempting to employ Ribbentrop's trick of appealing to the very top to ease difficult negotiations; or perhaps his curiosity had indeed been piqued by the Nazi–Soviet relationship. Either way, Molotov was nonplussed. He merely promised to convey the sugges-tion to Stalin, said his goodbyes, and left.[49]

That evening, Molotov threw a farewell reception in the Soviet embassy on Unter den Linden. It was a lavish affair, made all the more glamorous by the opulent tsarist-era decor of the building, as well as a few more modern additions. As Paul Schmidt recalled: 'Under Lenin's gaze, whose bust decorated the embassy, all the finest of Russia's produce – above all caviar and vodka – was presented. No capitalist or plutocratic banqueting table . . . could have been more impressively laden.'[50] In spite of the language barrier, the atmosphere was most convivial, with both sides drinking to each other's health, almost à la Russe. But when Molotov proposed a toast to his German counterpart, Ribbentrop could barely reply before the RAF crashed the party and the air-raid siren wailed into life. As the guests hurriedly departed, Ribbentrop escorted Molotov the short distance to Wilhelmstrasse, and to his own bunker beneath the Reich foreign ministry, where they could continue their discussions.

Gamely, Ribbentrop attempted to put some flesh on to the very bare bones of the agreement suggested by Hitler and explain his conception of a possible 'joint policy of collaboration between Germany and the Soviet Union' and how it might be reconciled with the provisions of the Tripartite Pact. To this end, he produced a draft agreement from his pocket, which he thought might form the basis of any future nego-tiations. In three rather anodyne paragraphs, the draft expressed the mutual desire to establish natural boundaries, the willingness to extend their collaboration to other nations, and the undertaking to respect one another's spheres of influence.[51]

True to form, Ribbentrop suggested that the agreement should be appended by not one, but two secret protocols. The first of these would establish the territorial aspirations of the four powers. Japan's wishes were still to be clarified, but Ribbentrop explained that Germany's aspirations would centre on Central Africa, Italy's on North and North-East Africa, and the Soviet Union would focus its expansion 'in the direction of the Indian Ocean'. With the second protocol, Ribbentrop proposed recognising Soviet ambitions in south-eastern Europe by promising a concerted effort by the signatory powers to persuade Turkey to allow a revision of the Straits Convention, in line with Soviet interests.[52] Ribbentrop concluded his proposal with an offer to convene a foreign ministers' conference at which all relevant questions could be discussed and finalised, and advocated a Soviet rapprochement with Japan, stating that the latter was eager for a 'broad understanding' with Moscow.

He then invited Molotov to respond. In his own recollection of the discussion, Ribbentrop painted a picture of an affable final meeting in which Molotov assured him that he would discuss the possible Soviet accession to the Tripartite Pact with Stalin, while Ribbentrop promised to raise the issue of the German–Soviet relationship with Hitler, as he put it, 'to find a way out of the difficulties'.[53] The official record gives a little more detail, however. Molotov, it seems, was certainly cheered by the prospect of an understanding with Japan, but was determined not to be seduced by nebulous German promises of 'jam tomorrow' at the expense of British India. In response to Ribbentrop's offer of turning south towards the Indian Ocean, therefore, he instead listed a succession of European matters in which the Soviet Union demanded to have her say: the Straits, Bulgaria, Romania, Hungary, Yugoslavia, the future of Poland, the issue of Swedish neutrality, the Kattegat and the Skagerrak at the mouth of the Baltic, and the still-unresolved 'Finnish Question'. Ribbentrop was flustered and obfuscated valiantly, sometimes defending German actions and sometimes claiming that he would have to consult with others before answering. But he kept coming back to his 'decisive question': whether the 'Soviet Union was prepared to co-operate with us in the great liquidation of the British Empire'.[54]

The RAF's raid on Berlin that night was a relatively short one. According to Churchill, it had been deliberately timed to coincide with Molotov's presence in the German capital. 'Though not invited to join in the discussion', the British prime minister later joked, he 'did not wish to be entirely left out of the proceedings'.[55] It is possible, of course, that this is an example of Churchill rewriting history to suit his purposes, but it is certainly clear that the raid started very early, with the siren sounding shortly after half-past eight in the evening, and that the centre of the city was targeted.[56]

As Molotov and Ribbentrop discussed their division of the world beyond the bunker, therefore, they would most certainly have heard the ongoing cacophony of the air raid, particularly the undulating wail of the sirens and the outgoing firing of Berlin's flak-batteries. In such circumstances, Ribbentrop's repeated assertions that the British were finished and that the war against Britain had 'already been won' must have seemed a trifle premature. According to Stalin, Molotov halted Ribbentrop's boasts with a well-aimed riposte, asking that if Britain really is defeated, 'why are we in this shelter, and whose are those bombs that fall?'[57] Ribbentrop was finally silenced; he had no answer.

The following morning, as Molotov and his entourage left the German capital, the same Wehrmacht honour guard was drawn up in the square outside the Anhalter station as had been present two days before, and the same train – complete with its German saloon and restaurant cars – raised steam beneath the huge glass and steel frame of the station canopy. Yet this time, there were few fanfares and only Ribbentrop appeared to see his Soviet counterpart off.[58] It would be their last meeting.

★　　★　　★

Despite the apparent finality of Molotov's departure from Berlin, there was little sense in the immediate weeks thereafter that a die had been cast. In fact, Molotov was rather pleased with himself and, at a party thrown for his return to Moscow, was described by an eye-witness as 'swollen-headed and puffed-up'.[59] He had good reason for satisfaction. Having rebuffed German efforts to deflect the USSR southwards and firmly stated the Soviet Union's strategic ambitions in Europe, he had carried out the task outlined for him by Stalin to the letter. As far as Moscow was concerned, the negotiations were expected to continue. The Berlin talks were merely the opening stage in that ongoing process.

Hitler, meanwhile, was not quite so sanguine. He had become increasingly exasperated with his Soviet partner as the year had progressed and was clearly beginning to think that the connection with Moscow had run its course and that a final reckoning with Bolshevism was in the offing. More seriously, he was also under the impression that continued British resistance was somehow being spurred by Stalin. As the chief of the army high command, General Franz Halder, noted in his diary, the issue at the front of Hitler's mind that summer was Britain's puzzling unwillingness to make peace, despite facing apparently insuperable odds. Hitler's answer to that conundrum was that Churchill was holding out in 'some hope of action on the part of Russia'[60] and with this assumed nexus, the issue of 'what to do' with the Soviet Union had begun to climb the agenda. On 22 July, for instance, Hitler was recorded by General Halder as stating that 'the problem of Russia must be dealt with', and that 'We must begin thinking about this.' This was a sentiment that Hitler would reiterate before his generals at the Berghof on 31 July, giving those present a brief rundown of his views on the main operations involved in the 'Destruction of the power of Russia'.[61]

This is the exchange that is traditionally taken as the moment when Hitler made his unalterable decision to attack the Soviet Union. Yet that interpretation is rather too neat. After all, as any politician would attest, an order for preparatory planning is not the same thing as an irrevocable decision; and as we know, Hitler was a supreme opportunist, who had made his career reacting to events rather than committing himself, long in advance, wholeheartedly and conclusively to a specific policy. Moreover, as General Walter Warlimont noted, the planning that followed this meeting was initially rather desultory and half-hearted, resulting in 'no carefully thought-out plan as a basis for action'.[62]

It makes better sense, therefore, to view Hitler's July order to prepare for an attack on the Soviet Union as part of a multi-track policy, with the military option a back-up to a diplomatic approach that had not yet been abandoned. Certainly, at the time of the July conference at the Berghof, the meeting with Molotov still lay more than three months in the future. And though the Berlin summit was engineered primarily by the Russophile 'Easterners' of the German foreign office, who had got wind of Hitler's growing belligerence towards Moscow and sought to bring Molotov to Berlin to smooth tensions, one should not imagine that Hitler was completely disingenuous in his negotiations.

Hitler, clearly, was still considering all possibilities. Indeed, two weeks before Molotov's arrival, he had sent a letter to Stalin personally, in an attempt to enrol his help in the war against the British, raising the prospect of a joint division of the empire's spoils. 'If the plan succeeds', Halder wrote in his diary, 'we could go all out against Britain.'[63] Another option was aired by the 'Easteners' of the German embassy in Moscow, to be circulated among the upper levels of the foreign ministry. As the senior official Ernst von Weizsäcker noted, within Wilhelmstrasse at least, the idea of a military attack on the USSR – far from being fixed – was not considered especially favourably. After all, there were other ways to ensure Moscow's subjugation, not least that of containing the USSR and allowing it to slowly collapse:

> It is argued that without liquidating Russia there will be no order in Europe. But why should it not stew next to us in its damp Bolshevism? As long as it is ruled by bureaucrats of the present type, this country has to be feared less than in the time of the tsars.[64]

Even as Molotov was being shuttled around Berlin on that rainy Tuesday, Hitler was issuing a war directive reviewing the various strategic possibilities available to him. His short paragraph on 'Russia' is instructive: 'Political discussions for the purpose of clarifying Russia's attitude in the immediate future have already begun', he wrote, yet, 'regardless of the outcome of these conversations, all preparations for the East for which verbal orders have already been given will be continued'.[65] As much as the military planning then ongoing, therefore, the Berlin talks formed part of a multi-track German effort to neutralise the Soviet Union and leave Germany as the undisputed master of all of Europe.

This is made further evident by the deal that Molotov was offered in the German capital. Hitler clearly wanted Stalin's Soviet Union out of Europe, unable to meddle in Balkan affairs, or in those of the Baltic Sea or of the Bosphorus. By attempting to turn the USSR south, to direct her ambitions towards the Indian Ocean and the 'bankrupt' British Raj, he would not only achieve that goal but also lure the Soviet Union into conflict with the British, thereby destabilising the USSR and rendering any putative Anglo-Soviet rapprochement impossible. In all, it was a rather ingenious solution to the predicament that Hitler imagined that he faced, achieving both his strategic ambitions in one fell swoop. The Berlin negotiations, therefore, should not be seen as a bizarre charade, or a diplomatic veneer to hide preparations for war; rather they were a genuine – if cynical – exchange of views between two treaty partners. Indeed, a couple of days after Molotov's departure, on 18 November, General Halder noted in his diary that the 'Russian operation' had apparently been pushed into the background.[66] The negotiated solution, it seems, was still very much on the table.

But Stalin was not inclined to take the deal that was on offer. Like generations of Russian statesmen before him, he was intent on Moscow spreading *westwards*, and – as Molotov's discussions revealed – his ambition was most certainly not limited to those areas that had already fallen under his control. Indeed, Molotov's mention of the Kattegat and the Skagerrak in the final round of negotiations must have rung alarm bells in the Reich Chancellery. Far from being satisfied with the return of her recent irredenta in Poland and the Baltic, and with the promise of vague gains in British India, it appeared that Moscow was intent on pushing even further westwards.

This, then, was the strategic vision that would underpin Stalin's formal response to Ribbentrop's suggestion that the Soviet Union might join the Tripartite Pact. Delivered by Molotov to the German ambassador in Moscow, Schulenburg, on the evening of 26 November, the statement was essentially a reiteration of the position that had been outlined in Berlin two weeks before. If it were to accept the draft of a four-power pact, the Soviet government imposed four conditions. Firstly, a German withdrawal from Finland, with recognition that the country belonged to the Soviet Union's sphere of influence. Secondly, Molotov demanded the conclusion of a mutual-assistance pact between the USSR and Bulgaria and the establishment of Soviet military bases within range of the Bosphorus and the Dardanelles. Thirdly, recognition was demanded that the area of the southern Caucasus 'in the general direction of the Persian Gulf' was a 'centre of the aspirations' of the USSR. Lastly, Moscow stipulated that Japan renounce her rights to coal and oil concessions in northern Sakhalin. It was certainly an ambitious list, demonstrating not only that the Soviet Union retained her European ambitions, but also that she had further demands relating to Persia and Japan. Molotov closed the discussion by stating that he would 'appreciate a statement of the German view'.[67] None would be forthcoming.

Though Stalin's response would prove a severe setback for the advocates of a negotiated solution, it was not yet the end of the story. Indeed, in December Ribbentrop claimed to have discussed the Soviet proposal with Hitler. He advised agreement, stating that if Stalin were to join the Tripartite Pact, then Germany would be in an excellent position to neutralise the USA and further isolate Britain, forcing the latter to the negotiating table. The prospects for success, he claimed, 'would be better than after Dunkirk'. According to Ribbentrop's account, Hitler was not entirely against the idea. Though he raised concerns about Finland, and about permitting any extension of Soviet influence into Romania and Bulgaria, he did not reject the plan out of hand. Indeed, Ribbentrop considered that a compromise with Stalin was a possibility: 'We have already achieved a lot together [with Russia]', Hitler told him, 'perhaps we will be able to bring this about too'.[68]

For the moment, Hitler could comfort himself with the thought that Soviet ambitions in Europe were still mainly theoretical, expressed in abstract demands and diplomatic requests. His relationship with Moscow, therefore, was strained, but it was not yet moribund. Before the end of 1940, however, the clash between his own 'world view' and that of his Soviet partner would become blatantly apparent.

Hitler's decision would be made for him by events at an obscure conference, in Galați, Romania.

The International Danubian Commission was the sort of regional organisation whose proceedings rarely troubled international affairs. For the previous eight or so decades it had met periodically, and in various iterations, to regulate traffic on the Danube and provide a forum for neighbouring powers to negotiate their differences. But by 1940, that which had once been a rather parochial affair had become the plaything of Europe's totalitarian dictatorships, with Germany and the Soviet Union – the latter now a 'Danubian Power' – vying for supremacy.

When the conference convened in late October 1940, tensions, which had been stoked over that most tumultuous of summers, were running high. Germany, already exercising a dominant role both in the region and at the conference table, was determined to maintain that position and ensure the effective exclusion of the Soviet Union. Moscow, on the other hand, saw the conference as the ideal arena in which to flex its muscles and realise its new Danubian role. The importance of the mission was underlined by the choice of Arkady Sobolev, Molotov's deputy, to head the Soviet delegation; he then undertook something of a Balkan tour, stopping in Sofia to charm King Boris and personally inspecting the Bulgarian–Romanian border at Ruse, before proceeding to Galați on the Danube for the conference.

Once under way, the meeting essentially saw a rehearsal of many of the arguments that were aired by Molotov in Berlin in November, with Sobolev demanding – among other things – mooring rights in the Danube delta and a joint Russo-Romanian administration of the area, and complaining about Italian participation. Unsurprisingly, perhaps, debate swiftly degenerated into stalemate and by mid-December negotiations had stalled entirely, with Berlin expressing its 'astonishment' at the heavy-handed tactics of the Soviets and complaining of the 'irreconcilable' positions of the two sides.[69] If Hitler had harboured any remaining doubts about Soviet ambitions in the Balkan region, then the proceedings of the Danubian Commission conference would have provided him with a useful corrective. More than Molotov's visit to Berlin the previous month, more than the sometimes tortured economic negotiations, more than the perpetual squabbling over Finland, the Danubian conference represented the first serious breach in Nazi–Soviet relations.

Berlin's frustrations are understandable. To the German mind, it had been her soldiers who had engineered the great military victories of 1939 and 1940, and her statesmen who had propelled Nazi Germany to a position of unchallenged superiority on the continent of Europe. The Soviet Union, in contrast, had gained everything she had over the same period, directly or indirectly, through her collaboration with Berlin. Germany had run the risks alone, but the Soviets had reaped a sizeable share of the rewards. Seen in this way, the continued Soviet insistence on a role in Europe, whether on the Danubian Commission or as a player in Baltic or Balkan affairs, was little more than bare-faced cheek. Small wonder, perhaps, that Hitler was becoming exasperated.

The Führer's primary complaint against Moscow, therefore, was not ideological, it was strategic. The turn against the Soviet Union is habitually described almost exclusively in ideological terms: as the expression of a long-held and barely suppressed anti-Bolshevik preju-dice. There is something in this, of course. Anti-Bolshevism was one of the primary articles of faith of every self-respecting Nazi, and racial-political justifications were certainly swift to come to the fore once the decision for war had been made. But strategic and geopolitical concerns still held sway over ideology, as indeed had been the case when the Nazi–Soviet Pact had been signed in the late summer of 1939. Though both sides had held their noses when they made common cause, both had recognised the enormous practical advantages that the pact promised. Now, as their partnership was beginning to falter, it was strategic concerns rather than ideology that still played the dominant role.

Consequently, it was only in December, when Moscow's insistence on its perceived European role was once again expressed at the Danubian Commission conference, when the Soviet response to Ribbentrop's Berlin proposals had been received, and when the prospects for a negotiated solution appeared to have been exhausted, that Hitler finally made his irrevocable decision to attack Stalin. This nexus is made abundantly clear from the timing of events. The Danubian Commission conference finally collapsed on 17 December, with a fist-fight breaking out between the Italian and Soviet delegations.[70] The very next morning Hitler issued his Directive No. 21, ordering his forces to prepare 'to crush Soviet Russia in a rapid campaign'.[71] With that, the death knell of the Nazi–Soviet Pact was sounded – and 'Operation Barbarossa' was born.

8

Riding the Nazi Tiger

On 23 December 1940, the Soviet Union's senior Red Army men descended on a snow-bound Moscow. They were there to attend the annual military conference, where members of the high command and other dignitaries would expound on the state of the Soviet Union's defences and the Red Army's degree of readiness.

The conference was to be held in the People's Commissariat for Defence, an elegant, strangely crenelated complex, not far from Red Square, which was one of the curiosities of interwar Moscow. Designed by the doyen of Stalinist architects, Lev Rudnev, and completed in 1938, the Commissariat for Defence was an uneasy combination of Italian Renaissance and modernist influences, with stucco walls, brutal bas reliefs of stylised tanks and an elaborate central tower sporting red stars instead of clock faces. Rudnev was himself very much the rising star of Soviet architecture, having completed the monumental Frunze Military Academy in Moscow in 1937 – also with a decorative tank motif – and the massive Government House in distant Baku. In time, his star would rise still further, and his career would be crowned by his post-war authorship of the iconic Moscow State University building, as well as its unloved Polish cousin, the Warsaw Palace of Culture.[1]

In the winter of 1940, however, it was Rudnev's Renaissance-brutalism that played host to the high-command conference. It was bitterly cold that winter, with a December record low of –38.8°C being recorded in Moscow earlier in the month, but Muscovites were doubtless distracted by the usual diet of industrial statistics and war reports that filled the pages of *Pravda*. They would have been thrilled, for instance, by news of the increased production of tractors, and by plans for larger and faster escalators to be installed in the Moscow metro. Elsewhere, the Moscow district Komsomol conference was attracting attention, as was a heated debate which was raging between the critics about a new production of Flaubert's *Madame Bovary*, playing at the Kamernyi Theatre with Alisa Koonen in the lead role.

Naturally, military matters also dominated the press, with *Pravda* devoting a whole page each day to war reports from western Europe. The reciprocal air-raiding between the Luftwaffe and the RAF was soberly reported, with 'exceptionally intensive' German raids on Liverpool and Manchester counterbalanced by British raids on Berlin and the Ruhr.[2] Churchill was reported as making a direct radio appeal to the Italian people, recalling the traditional friendship between the two nations and blaming the war on Mussolini. Hitler, meanwhile, was said to have made a Christmas visit to the western front, touring positions on the French coast.[3]

Yet, although the average Muscovite reading *Pravda* could glean much information about the world around them that December, they would have searched in vain for references to the high-command conference taking place beneath their very noses. Such was the sensitivity of the meeting that it was evidently thought prudent to conceal it from public view. So, while it was reported that Marshal Timoshenko presented awards to young people at the Komsomol conference, the real reason for the marshal's presence in the capital was not betrayed.

For all the reflexive secrecy, the high-command conference was to be very significant. In contrast to previous years, Stalin had ordered the conference's remit to be expanded to cover all aspects of Red Army doctrine, organisation and training; consequently invitations had been sent out, not only to the members of the high command, but also to many others, including the commanders of the military districts, as well as numerous army, divisional and corps commanders. In all, some 270 senior officers of the Red Army and Red Air Force were expected to attend.[4] Although Stalin himself did not grace the meeting with his presence, his Politburo confederate Andrei Zhdanov attended in his stead and reported proceedings to his master every evening. In spite of this, according to one participant, the conference had something of a holiday atmosphere: 'results . . . were generally satisfactory', he recalled, 'and we were in a cheerful and confident mood'.[5]

The conference consisted of only six presentations, covering topics such as military training, offensive operations, the war in the air and the role of the infantry, with each one lasting up to two hours, to be followed by an extensive, open-ended discussion. Chief of the General Staff, General Kirill Meretskov, got proceedings under way with an examination of the Red Army's combat and command training preparations. The previous year, he explained, had provided a 'complex international environment' in which the Imperialists had fought among themselves and had sought, without success, to draw the Soviet Union into their conflict. In addition, he suggested that the Red Army had gained much precious experience from what he euphemistically called the 'march westward' into the Baltic states and the 'provocation' of the Finnish War. Yet, despite such positives, he believed that the war had nonetheless revealed 'major shortcomings' in organisational, operational and tactical matters, with all levels of the military requiring substantial modernisation if the Red Army was to serve its political masters and be ready at any moment to 'take the field'.[6]

Later speakers revealed deeper failings. Delivering his presentation 'On the Nature of Offensive Operations', General Georgy Zhukov made an impassioned plea that the Red Army should learn from the military successes of the previous eighteen months and adopt something akin to a strategy of blitzkrieg. Recent wars, he said, had demonstrated the utility of the sudden, bold and co-ordinated use of air power, airborne troops and concentrated armour: the defeat of the Japanese at Khalkhin Gol in August 1939, for example, had shown the vital importance of air superiority, tactical surprise and of flanking manoeuvres. Neatly sidestepping the lessons of the Finnish debacle, Zhukov moved on to analyse the German successes of 1939–40, which, he suggested, were due to their 'close interaction' between infantry, air and mechanised forces, and the key element of surprise, enabling deep devastating thrusts into enemy lines. Only in this way, he concluded, by the use of 'energetic, decisive and bold offensive operations', could the Red Army 'complete the tasks of the revolution'.[7]

In his post-war memoirs, Zhukov was upbeat about the favourable reception that his paper received and praised the conference for recognising the 'chief trends' in modern warfare and the pressing reality of German military might.[8] Yet such reminiscences were rather rose-tinted. In fact, Zhukov had come in for some hefty criticism from his colleagues, with one commentator, Lieutenant General Filipp Golikov, warning pointedly against 'exaggerating the success of foreign armies'.[9]

Of course, Zhukov's opinions shouldn't have been remotely controversial: after all he was only advocating that the Red Army should adopt the 'best practice' that had been demonstrated to have been successful elsewhere. Some of his rivals, certainly, perceived an implied slight of their own abilities in his thesis, but there was more to it than that. For one thing, the Soviet high command in 1940 was no ordinary, objective body of men; rather it was an uneasy amalgam of the 'political generals' who had Stalin's ear, and less able commanders promoted as a consequence of the purges, with a minority of pure military men, like Zhukov, attempting to navigate a course between them. As a result of such tensions, as Khrushchev would later recall, the high command was 'like a kennel of mad dogs', with all of those present 'tearing at each other's throats'.[10]

In this febrile atmosphere, Zhukov's advocacy of a Soviet variant of blitzkrieg was akin to rolling a hand grenade under the conference table, as it came very close to the theory of 'deep operations' that had been espoused by Marshal Mikhail Tukhachevsky in the mid-1930s and had, for a time, been official Red Army doctrine. Tukhachevsky, however, had been one of the most prominent victims of the Soviet purges; exposed as an alleged German agent, his interrogation file spattered with his own blood, he had been executed in 1937. Advocating his ideas, therefore, regardless of their military merits, could be construed as a profoundly political – even heretical – act.

Notwithstanding such concerns, however, the argument for more offensive military planning carried the day. Another general, Dmitry Pavlov, presented a companion piece to Zhukov's in his examination of the 'Use of Mechanised Forces in Offensive Operations', in which he argued for the development of concentrated, massed tank units along the German model, rather than their piecemeal use in infantry support, as the French had attempted earlier in the year.[11] Lastly, after a few more presentations, Marshal Timoshenko once again took the floor for a rousing closing address, in which he, too, advocated the adoption of a more offensive mindset: 'defence is not the decisive means of defeating the enemy', he said, 'only attack can achieve that'.[12] He ended by calling for increased political education for Red Army soldiers, so that they might demonstrate their 'boundless loyalty to the party of Lenin' and be better prepared to 'defend their socialist motherland'.[13] With that, the conference was brought to a close.

Though the conference participants did not yet know it, the martial spirit that they were invoking would be required sooner than they imagined. Stalin had been kept abreast of the numerous rumours that had emanated from Nazi Germany over the previous months, the private speeches and aired frustrations of senior Nazi personnel. Indeed, even before Hitler had given the order for Operation Barbarossa, the new Soviet ambassador in Berlin, Vladimir Dekanozov, had received an anonymous tip-off about the Führer's aggressive intentions.[14] It would have come as no surprise, therefore, when a document landed on Stalin's desk on 29 December – in the middle of the high-command conference – claiming that 'high military circles' in Germany had informed a Soviet agent that 'Hitler has given the order to prepare for war with the USSR.' 'War will be declared', it went on, 'in March 1941.'[15]

Confirmation was sought from the Soviet military attaché in Berlin, and sources were checked and rechecked. Circumstantial corroboration was given by NKVD intelligence reports about German troop transfers in occupied Poland, the erection of barracks and fortifications, and the precipitate rise from late 1940 in border incidents along the German–Soviet frontier. An intercepted telegram from Tokyo to the Japanese embassy in Bucharest even suggested that the German army had 'completed its full deployment' and was 'confident of an easy victory'.[16]

Stalin was unnerved. In the discussions that followed the conference, he was cold and unusually ill-humoured; Mikoyan even thought that he had become 'unhinged'.[17] As his policy of riding the Nazi tiger began to unravel, it was becoming clear that he would need all the military capability that his high command could give him.

Yet if Stalin thought his task would be easy, he was wrong. In the first weeks of the new year, two war games were 'played' in Rudnev's Defence Commissariat, in which Zhukov fought his rival Pavlov, first as the Soviet defender and then as the western attacker. During the debrief that followed, Stalin was treated to a disconcerting insight into the mind of one of his senior generals, which demonstrated the difficulty he faced in reforming the Red Army.

Grigory Kulik was one of the few Soviet marshals to have survived the purges, yet his resistance to any technological or doctrinal innovation within the Red Army made him such a buffoonish liability that his survival can only be attributed to his closeness to Stalin. Kulik was a bullying incompetent who sported a fashionable 'Hitler moustache' and seemingly yearned for the simplicity of an earlier soldiering age. He railed against the idea of armoured warfare, which he denounced as 'degenerate fascist ideology', deplored the development of the Katyusha rocket (favouring the horse-drawn gun), and described anti-tank artillery as 'rubbish'.[18] Yet in spite of such antediluvian attitudes, he had been promoted to the post of deputy defence commissar, implausibly with responsibility for overseeing artillery development.

As if Stalin needed any more evidence of Kulik's startling incompetence, he got it at the debrief that followed the war games. While Stalin's mood was not improved by a rather bumbling, evasive presentation from Meretskov on the games themselves – which Zhukov had decisively won – Kulik's intervention did nothing to help. Raging against mechanisation, Kulik stubbornly espoused the use of horsepower for the military, complaining that the utility of tanks had been grossly exaggerated, before concluding that 'for the time being, we should refrain from forming tank and mechanised corps'.[19] He finished, embarrassing himself further, by showing his ignorance of basic procurement requirements. Stalin was uncharacteristically tolerant in his response. He reminded Kulik that 'victory in war will be won by the side that has more tanks and more highly motorized troops',[20] before adding ominously: 'the government carries out a program of mechanizing the armed forces, introduces the engine into the army, and Kulik comes out against the engine. It is as if he had come out against the tractor and the combine and supported the wooden plough.'[21] It sounded like a death sentence.

Strangely, Kulik remained in his post, at least in the short term. Stalin had only recently ordered the general's wife to be kidnapped and murdered for an unrelated indiscretion, so it is just possible that this stayed his hand.[22] Nonetheless there were to be significant changes, most notably the promotion of Zhukov to the post of chief of the general staff of the Red Army. Despite the challenges that Kulik personified, therefore, Zhukov's appointment signalled a step in the right direction.

One of Zhukov's first actions as commander-in-chief was to oversee the promulgation of the revised Red Army mobilisation plan, known as MP-41, in mid-February. Given that the plan had been in preparation since the previous summer, the extent of Zhukov's direct influence must be doubted, but he certainly would have approved its main points, including the doubling of Red Army manpower to over 8 million, two-thirds of whom would be stationed in the western military districts; and the stipulation that fully ninety divisions (nearly a third of the planned total) would be armoured or motorised. In addition, that February saw the establishment of three 'front' headquarters – the 'north-western', the 'western' and the 'south-western' – on the USSR's western border.[23] Clearly, the Red Army was well aware of the threat that it might face.

That threat was indeed substantial. The strategic plan that Hitler and his generals had agreed foresaw three separate army groups – North, Centre and South, totalling over 3 million men – which would strike east into Soviet territory, enveloping and destroying the defending forces. It was expected that the Red Army would even aid their cause by standing and fighting – rather than effecting a headlong retreat – as German planners considered that the Soviets could ill afford to lose those most developed and industrialised regions such as the Baltic states, Ukraine and Leningrad. With its army destroyed and its western, industrial heartlands and main cities conquered and occupied, the reasoning ran, the Soviet Union would surely collapse.

What was more, it was already clear by that spring that any coming conflict with the Soviet Union would not be fought according to the accepted norms of warfare. In a supplement to Hitler's earlier 'Barbarossa Directive', issued in mid-March 1941 by Army Supreme Commander, Field Marshal Keitel, the rules were laid down for the expected German administration of the occupied Soviet Union, with an outline of the 'special tasks' that were to be assigned to Himmler's SS – tasks which were 'determined by the necessity to settle the conflict between two opposing political systems'.[24] Behind the euphemisms there lurked wholesale slaughter.

Stalin, meanwhile, preferred to err on the side of caution and – though he was thoroughly informed about the German threat – opted to stick to diplomatic methods, convinced that the military build-up and the rumour-mongering were little more than a Nazi negotiating tool: an attempt to exert psychological pressure as a prelude to the resumption of talks. Indeed, he essentially shared Molotov's outlook, demonstrated in Berlin the previous autumn, that the Soviet Union was in a position of strength in its relationship with Nazi Germany, and that while Hitler was engaged in the west against the British, he would have to be mad to attack the USSR.[25]

In addition, Stalin had a rather peculiar view of the German military, attributing to them far more independence of thought and action than was actually the case. In this, he was doubtless influenced by the experience of the First World War, in which the German kaiser himself had been sidelined by the growing influence of the military, with the army duumvirate of Field Marshal Hindenburg and General Ludendorff effectively running Germany as a 'silent dictatorship' from 1916 onwards. Mindful of this, perhaps, Stalin appeared to trust the German military even less than he trusted Germany's politicians, perceiving them to be more hawkish than their political masters. This developed into an almost morbid fear, on Stalin's part, of provoking the Wehrmacht: an obsessive unwillingness to do anything that might be construed as an aggressive or anti-German move, for fear that the military might react and thus drag the politicians in Berlin unwillingly into war.[26] 'We must not respond to the provocations of the German military', Stalin explained, according to his interpreter. 'If we show restraint, and ignore the provocateurs, Hitler will understand that Moscow does not want any problems with Germany. He will then take his generals in hand.'[27] In this, Stalin was thoroughly mistaken, as – if anything – the reverse was true. It was a misperception that would have grave consequences. Zhukov would soon see evidence of this for himself. When, in March 1941, he submitted a revision of the MP-41 plan, which – though it was still essentially defensive in character – requested the call-up of Red Army reservists, Stalin regarded it as a potentially provocative gesture and refused the request.[28]

Despite Stalin's objections, the Soviet western military districts were not entirely silent in the spring of 1941. As early as the previous summer, Red Army reinforcements had been brought into the area, taking the total deployment to fifteen divisions in Finland, twenty in the Baltic states, twenty-two in occupied Poland and thirty-four in Bessarabia. Further units to the immediate rear of these brought the Red Army force facing the Germans in 1940 to ninety rifle divisions, twenty-three cavalry divisions and twenty-eight mechanised brigades.[29] In March, Zhukov succeeded in pushing through a limited call-up of reservists,[30] but the time frame was vague and of the 250 Red Army divisions planned to be under arms in the western districts by that summer, many would inevitably be under-strength and ill-supplied.[31]

A similar picture prevailed with the Soviet Union's system of fortifications in the west. Since the mid-1920s, the USSR had been constructing a network of defences along its western border: the *ukreplinnye raiony*, or 'fortified areas', known colloquially as the 'Stalin Line'. However, with the addition of the territories gained in alliance with the Germans in 1939–40, those incomplete defences now lay some 300 or so kilometres east of the new Soviet frontier. Consequently, in the summer of 1940, a new network of defences was begun further west, snaking through the newly gained territories from Telšiai in Lithuania, via eastern Poland to the mouth of the Danube in Bessarabia. It would later be given the unofficial name of the 'Molotov Line'.

Like its predecessor, the Molotov Line was not a single complete line of fortifications; rather it was to consist of interlocking systems of earthworks, concrete bunkers and other strongpoints, utilising natural barriers wherever possible, to channel any invading force into areas where Red Army units could be concentrated. It was certainly ambitious, with nearly 4,500 installations planned to span the 1,200 km from the Baltic to the Black Sea, requiring the work of around 140,000 labourers.[32]

However, up until the summer of 1940, those efforts had been very half-hearted, with the decommissioning of the older Stalin Line being carried out in a rather leisurely, piecemeal way, while work on the new Molotov Line to the west had not yet begun, despite a flurry of instructions. The fall of France in June 1940 gave some impetus to the programme, but even then there were serious practical problems, due mainly to the USSR's profound infrastructural and logistical shortcomings. Even the short-term fix of stripping out the fittings of the Stalin Line for use further west was stymied because the guns installed in the older line were often not compatible with the casemates of the new fortifications.[33]

Yet despite such difficulties, it is clear that there was little sense of urgency apparent until the early months of 1941. Part of that might have been tactical in origin: though the Mannerheim Line in Finland had thoroughly proved its worth in the Winter War, the Maginot Line had fared much less well in 1940 and so had done little to make the case for static fortifications. Yet by February 1941 there was a palpable shift, with various meetings, edicts and directives ordering an acceleration of the construction on the Molotov Line, allocating 10 million roubles to the project and giving responsibility for it to the former chief of staff, Boris Shaposhnikov.[34] Thus prioritised, there was an upsurge in activity, and by April 1941 the number of fortified areas under construction in the western Soviet Union was equal to the total number that had been built in the decade before 1939,[35] with a special focus being given to the approaches to Kiev and, tellingly, to the area between Grodno and Brest in eastern Poland – the historic 'Road to Moscow'.[36] Yet, in spite of all that, an official report in the spring of 1941 arrived at the sombre conclusion that 'overwhelmingly' such defences were 'not militarily ready'.[37]

For his part, Stalin's focus in those months tended to be elsewhere, preferring to concentrate on diplomatic avenues rather than the potentially provocative preparations being carried out by the military. His approach was essentially to utilise the economic relationship to appease Germany as far as was possible, in the belief that Hitler's sabre-rattling was purely a tactical ruse. In this, he was guided by his understanding of the materialist fundamentals of Marxism, expecting that Hitler's antipathy could be 'bought off' by economic benefits. Moreover, he was already very well accustomed to using his economic connection with Germany as a bellwether of the wider relationship, smoothing matters when he wanted to court Germany, halting deliveries altogether when he wanted to show who was in charge. This pattern would become most marked in the early months of 1941.

Economic negotiations between the two sides had stuttered on, occasionally peaking in the run-up to a headline agreement, or dwindling almost to nothing. As was not uncommon, the talks had stalled again in the autumn of 1940, partly because the two sides were some way apart and partly as it made sense to await the outcome of Molotov's visit to Berlin. However, in the aftermath a curious shift became evident. In late November 1940 the normally sober German negotiator, Karl Schnurre, was describing negotiations as 'quite cordial' and praising what he called the 'surprising indication of goodwill on the part of the Soviet government'.[38] Accordingly, a Tariff and Toll Treaty was signed between the two on 1 December 1940.

Somewhat trickier, however, were the broader talks regarding 'Year Two' of the economic relationship, which included a number of points on which the two sides were seemingly as far apart as ever. Yet even here, although there were inevitably conflicts, the Soviets demonstrated an uncharacteristic willingness to compromise; agreeing to compensation terms over the 'Lithuanian Strip', for example, and promising to meet property claims for those *Volksdeutsche* who had emigrated from their newly gained western districts. The German negotiators were delighted and attempted one evening to drink as much of the revised grain quota (in its distilled form) as they possibly could:[39] they were literally drunk with their success. Sobriety restored, the final points of a new treaty were hammered out in the month that followed, and on 10 January 1941, a new German–Soviet Border and Commercial Agreement was signed in Moscow. It was, Schnurre enthused, 'the greatest [economic agreement] Germany had ever concluded'. His colleague Karl Ritter concurred, praising it as 'the largest contract ever between two states'.[40] Given all that had gone before, every bone of contention, every tit-for-tat squabble and every failed compromise, a Soviet concession such as this can only have had a tactical motive behind it. Having rejected Germany's offer of the previous autumn, Stalin felt obliged to appease Hitler, and so was using economics to effect some sort of political rapprochement.

It is worth clarifying that neither side was yet labouring in the knowledge of an 'inevitable attack' in June 1941. The Soviets, for their part, were receiving a growing volume of evidence of a German build-up and of German intentions, but Stalin was still confident that diplomatic manoeuvres could deflect any crisis, postponing a possible showdown into 1942 or beyond. His negotiators, therefore, while mindful of the political need to throw a concession or two Berlin's way, certainly did not yet feel that they were bartering for the USSR's life. In that sense, therefore, the tone of negotiations was still largely in line with what had gone before.

The German side was similarly unencumbered by coming events. Like many of his fellow 'Easterners', Schnurre – although ignorant of the order for an attack – was well aware of the broad anti-Soviet shift in Berlin and sought to use the economic relationship as an argument to the contrary. Hence, once the new treaty was signed he travelled to Berlin to preach the gospel of economic co-operation with the Soviets, proclaiming that the treaty provided the 'solid foundation for an honourable and great peace for Germany'.[41] While the majority of senior Nazis nodded sagely, large sections of German industry and bureaucracy went into overdrive to fulfil Soviet orders, before which only Wehrmacht orders were given priority.[42] Not even the Italians were given such favourable treatment. Such was the German commitment, indeed, that deliveries to the Soviets in the first half of 1941 alone – over 150 million Reichsmarks – would exceed those from the three years prior to the pact.[43] It is not clear whether this was part of a deliberate campaign of deception, but it is perhaps more plausibly explained as a symptom of a communication failure between Hitler and the German foreign office, where the latter was responsible for most of the lower-level negotiations and tended to be much less anti-Soviet in outlook than its political master. Whatever its precise origin, it would nonetheless prove expensive to Germany, so much so that Hitler ordered that details of the shipments to the USSR were not to be publicised.[44]

Up until March 1941 at least, Stalin's diplomatic 'game' with Germany had progressed quite favourably. Despite the hiccups of France's precipitate defeat of the previous summer, and of Molotov's inconclusive visit to Berlin the previous autumn, he had remained confident that he could keep Hitler on a tight leash. That confidence would be profoundly shaken in the weeks that followed.

One of the key battlegrounds in the diplomatic chess game had been the Balkans. Bulgaria and Turkey had loomed large for Molotov in his talks in Berlin, not only as the two held the key to the Straits – and thereby to one of Russia's perennial strategic interests – but also as the erection of obstacles to German expansion in the Balkans would serve to frustrate Hitler's more ambitious plans. However, in the aftermath of Molotov's visit, that Balkan policy had begun to unravel. In quick succession in the weeks that followed, Hungary and Romania had adhered to the Tripartite Pact, thereby falling definitively into Germany's 'sphere of influence'. By early March 1941, Bulgaria had finally followed suit, spurning Soviet overtures in the process. Stalin suddenly faced the uncomfortable prospect of Soviet influence being excluded from the Balkans altogether. With Turkey resolutely neutral, only Yugoslavia remained as a potential ally.

By late March 1941, Yugoslavia was completely isolated. Surrounded on all sides by Axis-aligned countries, it was hamstrung domestically by internal ethnic divisions, and militarily unprepared to resist outside aggression. Hitler's terms for accession to the Tripartite Pact, articulated during numerous meetings with Yugoslav leaders earlier that spring, were comparatively generous, meanwhile, extending to a guarantee of territorial integrity and an assurance that Belgrade would not be required to provide military assistance or be used for stationing Axis troops.[45] Unsurprisingly, perhaps, Prince Regent Paul agreed, sending his emissaries to Vienna to sign the agreement on 25 March 1941.

Scarcely was the ink dry on the Yugoslav accession to the Axis, however, than Paul was overthrown in a bloodless military coup, forced into exile and replaced as premier by the former chief of the general staff, General Dušan Simović. The coup – which had been sponsored by the British Special Operations Executive (SOE) and applauded by *Pravda* in Moscow – broadly reflected the majority anti-Axis attitude in the country, bringing thousands of ordinary Yugoslavs, predominantly Serbs, out on to the streets in protest at German machinations and in support of an alliance with the Soviet Union.[46] Sensing an opportunity to shore up his faltering position in the Balkans, Stalin moved fast, seeking to dampen anti-German rhetoric in Belgrade while opening negotiations in the hope that an expression of solidarity with Yugoslavia would checkmate Hitler's expansion. The result would be the Soviet–Yugoslav Treaty of Friendship and Non-Aggression, signed in Moscow in the early hours of 6 April.

If Stalin thought that this would deter his ally from a fresh adventure, however, he was wrong. Even as the treaty was being signed, Hitler's Luftwaffe was already preparing its attack on Belgrade, code-named 'Retribution'. Outraged by the coup, Hitler had ordered Yugoslavia to be hit 'with merciless brutality' – no 'diplomatic inquiries' were to be made, 'no ultimatum presented'.[47] That morning, heavy air raids heralded a military occupation and the collapse of Yugoslavia itself, with Croatia declaring itself independent even before Belgrade fell less than a week later on 12 April.

Stalin had been comprehensively outplayed: brute force had defeated his guile. Almost before it had been announced, his new treaty with Yugoslavia had been shown to be a dead letter; Goebbels even mocked

him for 'waging war with bits of paper'.[48] Stalin's influence in the
Balkans was now virtually extinguished, and with that German domination of the continent of Europe was all but complete. If he had
thought that he could bring Hitler back to the table via diplomacy
and economic sleight of hand, he was obliged to think again, and
he was running out of alternatives. For Stalin, the fall of Belgrade
marked the moment at which the active appeasement of Hitler began
in earnest.

His first opportunity presented itself that same month, just as the
Yugoslav debacle was drawing to a close, when the Japanese foreign
minister, Yōsuke Matsuoka, passed through Moscow while returning
to Japan after a visit to the German capital. Talks with the Japanese
had already rumbled on inconclusively for some time, but recent
events had given them renewed impetus. A Soviet rapprochement
with Tokyo had been advocated by Ribbentrop the previous autumn
in Berlin, so Stalin naturally saw it as a way of improving his stock
with Hitler. Moreover, Japan had been a co-founder of the Axis and
had been at war with the USSR barely eighteen months previously,
so any agreement with Tokyo had to be beneficial. Consequently, a
neutrality pact was signed in the Kremlin on 13 April, pledging 'peaceful
and friendly relations . . . mutual respect' and neutrality in the event
of conflict with a third party.[49]

Convinced that he had pulled off a veritable coup – what Matsuoka
would later describe as 'diplomatic Blitzkrieg'[50] – Stalin was in
exuberant mood and even appeared at Moscow's Yaroslavsky railway
station to wave off his new partners, something that he had never
done before. Somewhat the worse for wear following an impromptu
breakfast banquet and the inevitable rounds of toasts, he embraced
the Japanese delegation warmly, while Molotov staggered about
shouting communist slogans. Matsuoka himself could barely stand
and almost had to be carried to the train. What was most significant,
perhaps, was what happened when Stalin spotted the distinctive,
towering figure of Hitler's deputy military attaché, Hans Krebs, on
the platform. 'German?' he asked, to which Krebs stood to attention
in affirmation. 'We've been friends with you', Stalin exclaimed after
slapping him jovially on the back, 'and we'll remain friends with you.'[51]
It was clearly as much a wish as a statement of fact. But the wider
significance of the new pact was not lost on Goebbels in Berlin, who

crowed in his diary that the Russo-Japanese treaty was 'marvellous and for the moment extremely useful', before adding that 'It seems that Stalin has no desire to make the acquaintance of our German Panzers.'[52]

A week later Stalin had another opportunity to flutter his eyelashes in Berlin's direction. After an evening at the Bolshoi on 20 April, the senior members of the Politburo retired to the Kremlin, with the head of the Comintern, Georgi Dimitrov, in attendance. There, Stalin gave forth on the prospects for world communism in general, and the role of the Comintern in particular. It was a speech that would shock many of those present.

The Comintern's role in fostering international communist revolution was, naturally, not uncontroversial outside the Soviet Union and came to be particularly loathed by communism's opponents on the right, such as Hitler. The Nazis had railed against the Comintern as an 'international conspiracy', and even sought to make the Reichstag Fire trial of 1933 into an indictment of the Comintern itself, by placing the organisation's regional leaders – including Georgi Dimitrov – in the dock alongside the supposed arsonist, the hapless Dutch communist Marinus van der Lubbe. Three years later, the German–Japanese Anti-Comintern Pact was explicitly directed against the organisation, which was described in the preamble as a 'threat to the general peace of the world'.[53]

Now, however, in the spring of 1941, Stalin had clearly come to believe that the revolution's 'handmaiden' had become something of a liability. With Dimitrov present, he criticised the Comintern as an 'obstacle' and advocated allowing national communist parties to be independent of it, so as to be able to adapt to their own local conditions. The Comintern, he implied, belonged to yesterday; today, national tasks must have priority.[54] No time was wasted. Already the following day Dimitrov was hard at work rewriting the new terms for admission to the Comintern; he made no mention in his diary of what he thought of the shift. Stalin also demanded that the usual communist slogans should be replaced by more nationally inspired ones for the coming May Day celebrations.[55] With one eye on Berlin, it seems, communism itself was being detoxified.

All the while, intelligence reports continued to pour into Moscow, which were collated and presented to Stalin by the head of military intelligence, the same Lieutenant General Golikov who had criticised Zhukov a few months earlier. Golikov's report of 25 April, for instance, concluded that Germany had as many as one hundred divisions massed on the USSR's western frontier, with an additional fifty-eight in Yugoslavia and seventy-two elsewhere in Europe.[56] In addition, over the previous three weeks, there had been eighty recorded German violations of Soviet airspace.[57] Such raw data was added to the various human intelligence reports that had begun to come in from Soviet agents – such as Richard Sorge in Tokyo, Anthony Blunt in London and Arvid Harnack in Berlin – all of which pointed to a growing German threat.

It is possible that Stalin also got wind of a speech that Hitler gave to over 200 of his senior military personnel on 30 March in the Reich Chancellery, in which he outlined his reasoning for the coming conflict. Hitler began his two-hour speech with an extensive review of the war and its historic antecedents, addressing the vexing question of why Britain continued to fight and the prospect of an American entry. Then he moved on to his main subject: that of the coming conflict with the Soviet Union. Firstly, he explained, Germany had a moral justification for the attack, as Stalin had 'gambled on Germany's bleeding to death' in the autumn of 1939. Moreover, only the defeat of the Soviet Union, 'the last enemy factor in Europe', would clear the way for Germany to 'solve the continental problem finally and thoroughly'. He was espousing nothing less than German hegemony over the entire continent.[58]

But the war against the Soviet Union would be no ordinary conflict, Hitler warned: it was to be a 'struggle between two opposing ideologies'. Bolshevism was an 'asocial criminal system' which was enormously dangerous. 'Everywhere. In Latvia, Galicia, Lithuania [and] Estonia' the crimes of the Soviet commissars had demonstrated that they could only behave in 'an Asiatic way'.[59] Consequently, there could be no place for 'soldierly comradeship with the enemy'. Instead, Hitler said, this was to be 'a war of annihilation': the Red Army was not only to be defeated in the field, it was to be exterminated.[60] If any of those generals present were still labouring under the illusion that Nazi Germany was an ally of the Soviet Union, this was to be a final wake-up call.

By late April 1941, then, Stalin would have been clearly aware that his relationship with Hitler had moved into a new, more challenging phase, demanding increased concessions and more exaggerated gestures. But, crucially, he still did not believe that war was coming, and he was growing increasingly impatient with those who tried to persuade him of anything different. But, while he would continue to appease his German counterpart, he simultaneously sought to demonstrate the USSR's preparedness to meet an attack.

So just as Soviet negotiators were pushing for solutions to long-stalled disputes with the Germans, and floating the possibility of increasing raw material deliveries, Stalin was inviting the German military attaché and other senior personnel on a trip to the Urals and western Siberia to visit the factories producing the most modern Soviet tanks and aircraft, particularly T-34s and the Petlyakov Pe-8 long-range bomber. According to Nicolaus von Below, Hitler's Luftwaffe adjutant, there could be 'no doubt' from this visit that the USSR was 'arming on a grand scale'.[61] At the same time, Soviet agents in the German ministries of aviation and economics began to spread the opinion that war against the Soviet Union would be a catastrophe for the Nazi leadership.[62] Stalin clearly did not want any underestimation of the enormity of the decision for war.

A week or so later, Stalin had another chance to impress the Soviet Union's martial preparedness upon the outside world. On 4 May, he had himself appointed by the Politburo as chairman of the Council of People's Commissars. It was a largely symbolic change – previously Stalin's official position had simply been that of general secretary of the Communist Party – but with this appointment, he effectively became head of state, formally concentrating power in his own hands. He was thereby sending a message of determination and resolve, demonstrating 'absolute unity in the work of the leadership' during 'the present tensions'.[63]

The following day, he made his first speech in his new capacity as Soviet premier, to an audience of 2,000 military academy graduates and senior military personnel, gathered in the Andreevsky Hall of the Great Kremlin Palace. Introduced by Timoshenko, Stalin spoke without a script for around forty minutes, addressing the current difficulties. The Red Army had learned much, he said, from the Finnish War and the war in the west: 'We possess a modern army, equipped with the latest weapons. We have tanks of the first order, which will break through the front.'[64] The Red Army, he explained,

> is very different from the way it was . . . It's much larger and better equipped. It has grown from 120 to 300 divisions. One third are mechanized, armoured divisions . . . Our artillery has been transformed, with more cannon and fewer howitzers . . . We didn't have mortars and now we do; until recently we lacked anti-aircraft artillery and now we have a decent amount.[65]

The Germans, he said, had 'become conquerors', shifting from the task of reversing the Treaty of Versailles to that of waging aggressive war. Their army was 'dizzy with success', but Stalin reminded his listeners that 'there is no invincible army in the world . . . and, from a military point of view, there is nothing special about the German army with regard to its tanks, artillery or air force'.[66]

Yet he acknowledged that war was now likely. In the reception that followed the speech, Stalin extrapolated on Soviet policy in reaction to an external threat. Intoxicated by the moment – and perhaps by the inevitable round of toasts – he may have said more than he had meant to: 'Defending our country', he stressed, 'we must act offensively. From defence to go to a military doctrine of offensive actions. We must transform our training, our propaganda, our agitation, our press in an offensive spirit. The Red Army is a modern army, and a modern army is an offensive army.'[67]

According to one eyewitness account, Stalin was even more explicit. Responding to an ill-judged toast from a general, who had praised the leader's policy of peace, an enraged Stalin waved away the applause:

> This general has understood nothing. He has understood nothing. We Communists are not pacifists; we have always been against unjustified wars, against imperialistic wars for dividing up the world, against slavery and exploitation of the workers. We have always been for just wars for freedom and independence, for revolutionary wars to free the people from the colonial yoke, for the most just war to defend the socialist Fatherland. Germany wishes to destroy our socialist state, which the workers won under the leadership of Lenin's Communist Party. Germany wishes to destroy our great Fatherland, Lenin's Fatherland, the results

of October, wipe out millions of Soviet people and enslave those who are left. Only a war with fascist Germany and a victory in that war can save our Fatherland. Raise your glasses and drink to the war, to aggression in that war, and to our victory in that war.[68]

With that, it was reported, Stalin drained his drink and sat down, while his audience stood in silence.

Understandably, the speech and the toasts that followed have proved highly controversial. At the time, it was given fairly wide coverage, with extensive front-page reports appearing both in *Pravda* and *Izvestia* the following day, the former with a large full-width photograph of Stalin addressing the ranks of academy graduates.[69] Though the broad theme of the speech – that of the readiness and competence of the Red Army – was outlined in the press, rather unusually a verbatim text was not reproduced, and the subjects of the informal toasts that followed were not reported, so rumours duly swirled around Moscow about precisely what had been said. Indeed, no official record of the speech exists to this day, so details of its contents have to be pieced together from a number of sometimes unreliable eyewitness accounts.[70] This unusual secrecy has led to some wild speculation, and the speech became a key piece of evidence in the dubious suggestion that Stalin was himself planning a pre-emptive strike against Hitler in the summer of 1941.[71]

Yet it is more plausible to see the speech as proof not of any supposed offensive plan, but rather as a vital component in Stalin's *defensive* armoury.[72] At the very least, this was Stalin giving a pep talk to new military academy graduates, telling them that the Red Army was making good progress and that they had nothing to fear from any enemy. But by his show of brazen, sabre-rattling confidence and his conscious inflation of the Red Army's strength and capability, Stalin may well have also been seeking to deter Hitler. As one account has put it, Stalin's speech had very clearly 'been prepared for export'.[73] Barely a week later, however, Stalin's new-found confidence – or belligerence – would be tested anew, and in a rather unexpected way.

On the night of 10 May 1941, the pilot of a Luftwaffe aeroplane – a Messerschmitt Bf-110 – bailed out over Eaglesham in the Scottish lowlands, south of Glasgow. Coming to earth in a farmer's field, he identified himself as Hauptmann Alfred Horn when apprehended by a farm labourer, and was promptly taken to a nearby cottage, where he was offered a cup of tea. In due course, 'Hauptmann Horn' would be exposed as Rudolf Hess, Hitler's deputy, apparently on a mission to negotiate peace with Britain.

Hess's precise intentions in flying solo to Britain in the middle of a war are still contentious, not least the rather fraught issue of whether he was lured and with whom he was intending to negotiate. He brought few concrete proposals with him, beyond the broad idea that Britain should give Germany a free hand in Europe, and in return Germany would leave Britain to its empire. Interrogated and sounded out by a number of senior British figures – foreign office advisor Ivone Kirkpatrick and former foreign secretary Sir John Simon most prominent among them – his grand plan quickly foundered between the Scylla of German arrogance and the Charybdis of British intransigence. Hess would be interned in Britain for the remainder of the war: a sorry figure, increasingly viewed as a crank or a lunatic, even by his own former comrades in Germany. As Joseph Goebbels exclaimed in his diary: 'It is all too stupid. A fool like [Hess] was the Führer's deputy. It is scarcely conceivable.'[74]

The British had clearly arrived at the same conclusion. And, although they evidently believed there was nothing to be gained by negotiation, there was nonetheless an obvious propaganda coup to be scored by Hess's arrival and captivity. Churchill, who attached little importance to the Deputy Führer's escapade, was minded to play the affair with a straight bat, making only a public statement of the facts surrounding the case. But he was persuaded otherwise by the Whitehall mandarins, who saw it as too good an opportunity to miss. Consequently, only the barest details were made public while a whispering campaign was begun through covert channels, with the intention not only of unnerving Hitler and undermining German morale, but also of stoking Soviet anxieties about what the Hess mission might signify.[75]

The British had long wanted to try to detach Stalin from his partnership with Berlin, seeing such a course of action as a prime weapon in the struggle against Hitler. But they had been perennially frustrated by their inability to make any headway in Moscow. As Alexander Cadogan, permanent undersecretary at the Foreign Office, noted bitterly, diplomacy towards the USSR was 'completely hamstrung' as 'unless you can (a) threaten (b) bribe it you can do nothing, because Russia has (a) no fear of us whatever and (b) we have nothing to offer her'.[76] The Hess affair, however, appeared to provide a way out of the impasse, giving the British an opportunity, by adroitly 'managing' the story, to exert a favourable influence on Stalin. The line that was spun to Moscow, therefore, was that Hess's flight was a symptom of a split in the Nazi Party, with the purists (represented by Hess) displeased by Hitler's collaboration with the Soviets and eager to clear the way – by securing British neutrality – for a final reckoning with communism. By stressing Nazi perfidy and the probability of an attack, it was hoped that Stalin could be turned against his former partner in crime and that the Nazi–Soviet Pact could be fatally undermined.

This plan, though not entirely wrong-headed, was nonetheless fundamentally flawed. Not only did it underestimate the extent of Stalin's paranoia, it also failed to recognise that his distrust of British motives was just as great as his fear of German intentions. As the archetypal 'imperialist power', Britain held a special place in Soviet demonology, particularly as it had taken the lead in the Allied intervention against Soviet rule in the Russian Civil War of 1918–19 and Churchill himself had famously said at the time that Bolshevism was a baby that should be 'strangled in its cradle'.[77] Clearly, any story emanating from British sources was to be treated with the utmost circumspection.

The information on Hess came to the Soviets via a number of channels, among them the British ambassador to Moscow, Stafford Cripps, and the 'Cambridge spy' Kim Philby, as well as the extensive Soviet intelligence network. It was fairly thin on detail and most of it was managed in some way by Whitehall. Yet, rather than indicating a split in the Nazi Party, the message that Stalin and his cohorts duly gleaned was that Hess, and by extension Hitler, was trying to woo the British and that if Moscow was not careful it could find itself facing the Nazis alone. As Khrushchev noted in his memoirs, the idea of Hess's flight being unauthorised by Berlin was unthinkable.[78] In addition, the news that Sir John Simon had been involved in the debriefing of Hess would have worried Moscow deeply; after all, Simon was viewed by many on the left as one of the architects of appeasement, an avowed 'Man of Munich'. Stalin would have been forgiven for wondering whether another round of appeasement was in the pipeline.

In fact, he thought it was much more serious than that: for Stalin the Hess episode represented a dangerous anti-Soviet conspiracy. In a speech to the party's Central Committee some days after Hess arrived in Britain, he outlined his thoughts on the subject: 'On the one hand,' he said, 'Churchill sent us a personal message in which he warns us about Hitler's aggressive intentions . . . and on the other hand, the British meet Hess, who is undoubtedly Hitler's confidant, and conduct negotiations with Germany through him.' The only obvious answer for Stalin was that the British wanted to provoke a war between Russia and Germany. 'When Churchill sent us his personal warning', he explained, 'he believed that we would activate our military mechanism. Then Hitler would have a direct and fair reason to launch a preventive crusade against the Soviet Union.'[79]

So, rather than galvanising Stalin in his dealings with Hitler, as London had wanted, the leak of the Hess story did the opposite, confirming Stalin's pathological distrust of the British as eternal meddlers and dissemblers. The imminent threat, Stalin concluded, came not from the Germans, but from the British.[80] As he explained to Zhukov: 'Don't you see? They are trying to frighten us with the Germans, and to frighten the Germans with us, setting us against one another.'[81]

Thus, while the Hess episode deepened Stalin's suspicion of the outside world, beyond that it altered little. Golikov's intelligence reports for May still gave an accurate assessment of the German military build-up on the Soviet western frontier – on 5 May it was estimated at 102–7 divisions, on 15 May 114–19, and on 31 May 120–2[82] – but this was dismissed by Stalin as disinformation or an attempted provocation. Indeed, by this point, Stalin was growing so impatient with his subordinates that they increasingly tended to submit their reports 'in fear and trepidation'.[83] Golikov, meanwhile, was learning to present a deliberately ambiguous reading of his information, so as not to earn Stalin's displeasure. On 15 May, for instance, he chose to focus his report on those German forces earmarked for action against the British in the Middle East and Africa, rather than those massing on the Soviet border.[84]

Nonetheless, military preparations continued. In mid-May, mindful of Stalin's recent call for a more offensive attitude, Zhukov revised the Red Army's war plan to include a proposal for a pre-emptive strike against the Germans. The so-called 'Zhukov Plan' argued that it was 'necessary not to give the initiative to the German command' and advocated an attack on the Wehrmacht 'at that moment when it is still at the deployment stage and has not yet managed to organise a front'. It ended with a request that Stalin might permit a 'timely mobilisation'.[85]

That permission would not be forthcoming. Indeed, some have doubted whether Stalin even saw the Zhukov Plan at all. At the same time, defensive preparations continued. By midsummer 1941 around 2,000 strongpoints had been completed along the Molotov Line, of which around half were armed and equipped. In addition, all of the 'fortified areas' were ordered to be brought up to combat strength as soon as possible.[86] In mid-May Zhukov succeeded in securing a 'partial mobilisation', with reservists being called up, and over 50,000 troops from the Caucasus and other interior districts of the Soviet Union being relocated to the western frontier areas. 'Train after train began to arrive', the general recalled in his memoirs. 'It was gratifying. The apprehension that in the event of war we would have no troops in depth was dispersed.'[87] The sobering truth, however, was that many of those new cadres lacked officers and basic materiel and would be no match for the battle-hardened Wehrmacht.

In economic affairs, too, the same pattern of behaviour that had characterised the early months of 1941 continued into May and June. Just as the Germans had stepped up their deliveries to the Soviets over the previous few months, so the Soviets followed suit, with Stalin using economics to appease Hitler as best he could. From April to June alone, the Soviet Union delivered over half a million tons of grain, nearly a third of the total promised. In addition new contracts were agreed in April: for 982,500 tons of oil, 6,000 tons of copper, 1,500 tons of nickel, 500 tons of zinc and 500 tons of molybdenum.[88]

May was similarly bountiful, with 14 per cent of the total value of Soviet exports to Germany being transacted that month alone, and the usual squabbles over pricing and terms curiously absent. Such was the Soviet enthusiasm for trade in the early summer that the German infrastructure on the western side of the border in occupied Poland – already overburdened as it was by the enormous military preparations – was unable to cope with the increased volume, and hundreds of wagons containing grain, fuel, metal ores and other raw materials were backed up on the Soviet side of the frontier.[89]

It is telling that by June, when the Germans had all but halted reciprocal deliveries, Stalin still did not appear to be unduly worried. On the 13th, for instance, Admiral Kuznetzov reported to him that spare-part deliveries for the cruiser *Petropavlovsk* (the ex-*Lützow*), which was still being fitted out in Leningrad, had mysteriously stopped. In response, Stalin asked no further questions and raised no concerns. 'Is that all?' he asked.[90]

Given the apparent alacrity with which the Soviets were still fulfilling their economic liabilities, one might have imagined that less hawkish opinions were being voiced in Berlin's corridors of power. Certainly, this had long been the position of the 'Easterners' in the German foreign office – such as Karl Schnurre and Ambassador Schulenburg – but others now joined their chorus, most notable among them the finance minister Lutz Schwerin von Krosigk, who argued that Germany would certainly lose out in the event of war, due to the inevitable dislocation and destruction. Schnurre went further, suggesting that the Soviet desire to appease Berlin was such that additional economic demands could be made, even beyond the scope of the existing agreements.[91] Why make war when the Soviets were already willing to deliver almost everything that was requested? Why slaughter the cow that you want to milk?

There were shortcomings to this argument, however. For one thing, in their zeal to avoid conflict, Schnurre and others painted an excessively rosy picture of Soviet 'fulfilment'. There were still areas of the relationship in which Moscow was less than entirely forthcoming, and it was fully expected in Berlin that as soon as any crisis had passed Stalin would revert to his old obstructionist ways.

But, however much he might once have understood the complexities of the economic relationship with the USSR, by 1941 Hitler had moved on to much more seductive motivators, such as ideology and geopolitics. Indeed, he had so tired of those warning of economic doom following his planned invasion of the Soviet Union that in the spring of 1941 he complained to Göring that 'from now onwards' he was going to 'stop up his ears' so that he wouldn't have to 'listen to any more of that talk'.[92] Like many of his more ideologically minded countrymen, Hitler was by this stage motivated more by his prejudices than by hard facts. To his mind, Stalin was devious, a 'cold-blooded blackmailer' waiting for his opportunity to spread communism westwards.[93] Only war against the Soviet Union, he believed, would decide the vital question of hegemony in Europe, and it was a war that Germany had to win. Goebbels elaborated on his master's strategic thinking in his diary, after a meeting in the Reich Chancellery that June. 'We must act', he wrote. 'Moscow intends to keep out of the war until Europe is exhausted and bled white. Then Stalin will move to bolshevise Europe and impose his own rule. We shall upset his calculations with one stroke.'[94] With such grand concepts at stake, the minutiae of economics found little purchase.

Hitler also needed the coming campaign against the Soviets to help solve the population problems that he had stored up for himself in eastern Europe. The process of ethnic reorganisation in occupied Poland, which had been embarked upon in the winter of 1939, had thus far proceeded only fitfully, its progress hindered by the exigencies of war and the lack of any coherent overarching plan. Indeed, by the winter of 1940, a renewed impatience among senior Nazis was forcing the question of 'resettlement' back up the political agenda.

In the first instance, the issue of the fate of the *Volksdeutsche* 'liberated' from eastern Europe following the Nazi–Soviet Pact still had to be satisfactorily addressed. Over the second half of 1940, Poles and Jews had been deported en masse from the Warthegau, into the General Government to make way for the *Volksdeutsche* arriving from Volhynia, the area of south-eastern Poland annexed by Stalin. In March 1941, Nazi propaganda would boast that over 400,000 'Poles and Jews' had already been 'resettled'.[95] This process, though rather chaotic and hampered by logistical shortcomings, as well as official disappointment over the ethnic 'quality' of some of the new arrivals, nonetheless sparked something of a 'deportation fever' in Nazi circles, as many regional potentates elsewhere sought to follow suit. As a result, late in 1940, some 70,000 'undesirables' – including Jews, criminals, homosexuals and the mentally ill – were deported into Vichy France from Alsace and Lorraine, which had been annexed by the Reich. A further 6,000 Jews were deported west from the regions of Baden and the Saarland in October, making these the first '*Gaue*' of Nazi Germany to be officially declared *Judenfrei*, or 'Jew-free'.[96]

Following the lead of Baden and the Saarland, the gauleiter of Vienna, Baldur von Schirach, now petitioned Hitler directly to request permission to deport 60,000 Viennese Jews. Permission granted, he began the action in February 1941, deporting 5,000 unfortunates to the district of Lublin, south-east of Warsaw, before logistical difficulties forced a halt to the operation.[97] Though large-scale deportations of Jews from the Reich would not begin until October 1941, the Vienna 'Aktion' provided a sinister portent of what was to come.

Those affected were brought, by night, to the Aspang station in Vienna and loaded into passenger wagons. All heads of households had already signed away their remaining property and possessions to the German Reich and had declared that they were being deported of their own volition. After a lengthy journey to rural Poland, the deportees – many of them urbane, cultured Viennese – were astonished by the conditions that they found. It was little other than a slow death. As one desperate deportee wrote home: 'You can imagine what our prospects are; no source of income whatsoever! I can only say to you that it would have been better if they had put us up against the wall in Vienna and shot us. It would have been a good death, but we have to die in misery.'[98]

Some of Germany's allies were similarly enthusiastic about ethnic cleansing. In Romania, still reeling from the territorial losses and the ensuing political collapse of the previous year, tensions were running particularly high, and it was widely believed that the nation's Jews were primarily responsible for the catastrophe. Consequently, the country's native fascist movement – the Iron Guard, which had been elevated into government the previous autumn – was waiting for an opportunity to settle scores with its perceived foe. That chance came in January 1941, when the Guard revolted against its government partners and embarked on a three-day rampage, venting its anger upon the Jews of Bucharest. The results shocked even those who had been hardened to Romania's recent crises and atrocities. 'The stunning thing about the Bucharest bloodbath', one commentator noted, 'is the quite bestial ferocity of it . . . ninety-three persons were killed on the night of Tuesday the 21st. It is now considered absolutely certain that the Jews that were butchered at Straulesti abattoir were hanged by the neck on hooks normally used for beef carcasses.'[99] Such violence was a grim foretaste of what would follow across much of eastern

Europe, particularly in those areas that had been annexed by Moscow, and were 'liberated' by the Germans in the war against the Soviet Union. Throughout the region, blameless Jewish populations would be forced to pay the blood price for nearly two years of Soviet rule.

In Berlin, meanwhile, the deportations of recent months were brought to a halt in the spring of 1941. Frustrated that their previous efforts had achieved little beyond the shunting of unwanted peoples into the General Government, from late 1940 onwards senior Nazis began talking rather Delphically of a future 'settlement of the Jewish question' through deportation to a territory 'yet to be determined'. That territory was the Soviet Union.[100] Deporting Europe's Jews into former Soviet territory made logistical and ideological sense; after all, it was an easier solution than the previous suggestion – that of shipping them to Madagascar. In addition, it was seen as a fitting destination, neatly encapsulating the Nazi belief in the link between Jewishness and communism. In the meantime, however, all further deportations were to be shelved, pending the expected destruction of the USSR.

Just as the Nazis were pondering their own programme of 're-settlements', the Soviets were planning a new deportation of their own. Over the previous two years, the Soviet occupation of eastern Poland, the Baltic states, Bessarabia and Northern Bukovina had been followed by a swift Sovietisation, with the rapid co-ordination of all administrative infrastructure, a thoroughgoing land reform and the deliberate targeting of all those belonging to the old political elite. Now, fresh impetus was given to consolidating the new territories and rooting out further potential sources of opposition from within the native populations.

Of course, Soviet repression and persecution of those who dared to transgress had continued apace. In Bessarabia, it was said that after only six months of Soviet occupation, the prisons were already so full that barracks were used to house those who had been arrested.[101] Conditions and treatment were predictably brutal. In Lithuania, Juozas Viktoravičius was arrested in April 1941 for criticising the Soviet system. After two weeks in the cells, he was questioned by the NKVD for the first time. Placed in chains, beaten and sexually abused, he fainted twice during a forty-five-hour interrogation. When he was finally returned to his cell, nobody recognised him.[102] Elsewhere no less imaginative methods were employed. As one Bessarabian victim of the NKVD recalled: 'Not only did they interrogate you but they also beat you like a dog. Their basements were filled with water and they would hold you in there, upside down, for hours. From time to time they would even touch you with electric wires.'[103]

Now, in a new phase of repression, the Soviet apparatus reverted to the time-honoured tactic of targeting entire classes of otherwise innocent people, in the belief that by their mere existence they posed a threat to Soviet power. A document drawn up by the head of the NKVD in Lithuania, Alexander Guzevičius, in the winter of 1940 listed some of the groups that were believed to constitute a 'pollution' of the Lithuanian Soviet Socialist Republic:

a) All former members of anti-Soviet political parties, organisations and groups: Trotskyists, rightists, socialist revolutionaries, Mensheviks, social democrats, anarchists, and the like.

b) All former members of the national chauvinist anti-Soviet parties, organisations and groups.

c) Former gendarmes, policemen, former employees of the political and criminal police and of the prisons.

d) Former officers of the tsar, Petliura and other armies.

e) Former officers and members of military courts.

f) Former political bandits and volunteers of the White and other armies.

g) Persons expelled from the Communist Party and Komsomol for anti-party offences.

h) All deserters, political emigrants, re-emigrants, repatriates and contrabandists.

i) All citizens of foreign countries, representatives of foreign firms, employees of offices of foreign countries, former citizens of foreign countries.

j) Persons having personal contacts and maintaining correspondence with abroad, foreign legations and consulates, Esperantists and philatelists.

k) Former employees of the departments of ministries.

l) Former workers of the Red Cross.

m) Religionists, sectants and active members of religious communities.

n) Former noblemen, estate owners, merchants, bankers, commercialists, shop owners, owners of hotels and restaurants.[104]

Clearly, the Soviet net was to be cast extremely wide. In practice the numbers caught in that net far exceeded those who actually met the criteria, as, across the Baltic states, family members were considered guilty by association. In Latvia, for instance, Augusts Zommers was arrested because of his membership of the local National Guard, the *Aizsargi*; however, his wife and daughter were also labelled as 'socially dangerous'. His daughter, Ina, was only five years old.[105] By one NKVD estimate, fully one in seven Lithuanians was included on a list of so-called 'unreliable people'.[106]

Having identified their opponents, the Soviet authorities in the newly annexed republics then moved to eliminate these groups in the early summer of 1941, mindful of the growing threat on the western frontier and the pressing need to preserve political control in any coming crisis. Three previous waves of deportations had already been inflicted upon eastern Poland, so by the early months of 1941 the Soviet authorities were well versed in the practicalities of swiftly identifying, arresting and removing large numbers of people. The procedures to be followed in deporting these enemies of the Soviet state were laid down in the so-called 'Serov Instructions', issued by the deputy commissar of the NKVD, Ivan Serov, in early June 1941. Throughout, Serov ordered, deportations were to be carried out calmly, without panic and excitement. Persons to be deported were identified in the first instance by a *'troika'* of local Communist Party and NKVD operatives; they would be apprehended at their homes at daybreak, and they and the premises were to be thoroughly searched, with any offending items – counter-revolutionary materials, weapons or foreign currency – being listed and confiscated. The victims would then be informed that they were to be deported to 'other regions' of the Soviet Union, and that they were permitted to take with them household necessities – clothes, bedding, kitchen utensils and a month's supply of food – not exceeding a total weight of 100 kilograms. Separate trunks or packing cases were to be labelled with the Christian name, patronymic and surname of the deportee, as well as the name of their home town or village. Once prepared, they were to be transported to the local railway station, where the male heads of families were to be separated from the others. After a railway carriage was loaded – an estimated capacity of twenty-five persons per wagon was given – the doors were to be locked. The entire process from arrest to entrainment should be completed, Serov ordered, in under two hours.[107]

For all the calm and clinical precision demanded by Serov, the experience of deportation was a terrifying one. The operation began in Bessarabia on the night of 12 June, continued across the three Baltic republics two days later, and concluded with a further deportation affecting the north-eastern region of occupied Poland from 14 to 20 June 1941. Those affected were woken in the early hours by the arrival of arrest parties, usually a couple of local militiamen accompanied by Red Army or NKVD personnel. In Latvia, Herta Kaļiņina's experience was typical: 'Everyone was woken by a loud knocking at the door. Accompanied by soldiers, a Russian man and a rather distant neighbour of ours barged into the room. They ordered us to pack as many things as we could and said that we had to go and live somewhere else.' There was no sympathy for their plight. When her father asked the men what he had done to hurt anyone, he was told: 'You are a class enemy and we are going to annihilate you.'[108]

In the confusion, few had time to prepare for the ordeal that was to follow. In some cases, arresting officers assisted by advising the deportees that they would need warm clothing and a good supply of food, but most were much less helpful. In Estonia Aino Roots was given only a quarter of an hour to organise her three small children:

> We had to get ready so quickly that all I had time for was to pull a coat over my nightgown. I had bare legs, shoes and nothing on my head . . . One of the men kept screaming that we only have fifteen minutes! What can you do in fifteen minutes? . . . So I went to Siberia wearing just a nightgown, like a madwoman, with a coat over it.[109]

When the guards had gathered together those on their lists, the deportees were loaded on to trucks. In Poland Maria Gabiniewicz recalled casting a last glance homewards as the NKVD truck pulled away: 'The vehicle began to roll. One more look at our home, the buildings, the fields, and the path we knew so well leading up to the hill . . . where we loved to walk and play. Mother blessed everything that remained behind with the sign of the cross.'[110]

As if they were not already distressed enough, a new shock awaited many of the deportees when they reached the railway stations, and learned that the male heads were to be separated from their families, with the accompanying fiction that they were required to travel in separate carriages to 'prevent embarrassment'. For many women, it was the last sight they would have of their menfolk. When one deportee later asked the whereabouts of her husband, the guards just laughed at her.[111]

Conditions aboard the trains were extremely primitive. Wooden cattle wagons were used, similar to those employed in the three earlier Polish deportations of 1940, with barred windows, a few bare wooden bunks and a hole in the floor to serve as a toilet. Rather than the official capacity of twenty-five people, each one would contain around forty deportees, and their possessions, meaning that cramped, forced intimacy quickly became the norm. As Latvian Sandra Kalniete remembered:

> natural functions had to be taken care of right there in the car . . . it was humiliating. Especially for the girls and women, who, from modesty, could not force themselves to go to the dark, repulsively smelling hole . . . The prisoners sat hunched on their bunk beds or on their belongings in the middle of the car. Their despondency inter-rupted by wailing and weeping.[112]

To make things worse, the trains were often obliged to wait, under guard, for several days until they were filled. As one eyewitness of the Bessarabian deportation recalled:

> I remember a lot of soldiers, screaming, crowds and wagons filled with tormented people lying all at sixes and sevens, each one: men, women, children, clinging to their belongings . . . All different people were there: young clerks, shopkeepers, prostitutes and teachers, one thing united them: no one knew what would happen, and all of them were crying because they were so frightened and desperate.[113]

Some deportees were given buckets of water by their guards, but others received nothing beyond the supplies brought by locals or concerned friends. While they waited, and as the trains began their journey, some of the deportees threw notes and letters out of the wagons in a desperate attempt to let their friends and loved ones know of their fate. Remarkably, Estonian Robert Tasso's letter reached his mother: 'Based on what we have seen so far', he wrote, '[we] are very deeply worried. After all, no one knows when their turn will come. But we hope for the best, and that hope must sustain us . . . Be strong, and don't grieve for me.'[114]

Once under way, conditions in the carriages deteriorated still further as the trains trundled eastwards, in some cases taking as long as six weeks to reach their destination. Food and water were scarce, dependent it seems on the whim of the Red Army guards: some supplied water and bread at each stop, while others merely threatened their prisoners and told them that as criminals they did not deserve anything. As one deportee recalled, medical care was non-existent: 'the dead were buried by the railroad tracks when the train halted', she said. 'For we were nobody.'[115] The stress of the deportation was hard to bear. As one Estonian woman recalled:

> the entire experience left me numb, as if I had gone mad! It was all unreal. We were like living corpses. We moved, but our minds didn't work. We were starved and sleepless, because there was no place to sleep . . . the children were so little they couldn't understand what was happening. Little Jaan cried and said 'Bad soldier, go away from the door, Jaani wants his daddy.' How could I explain anything to him? At night he would say that he wants to go home to his own bed. I said that we could not. We had to stay there till the end.[116]

Little Jaan would not survive the journey.

For some parents, it was all too much. One Latvian woman became convinced that all of them would be executed and, tortured by her anxiety, killed her three small children and herself with a razor blade. When the Red Army guard was called, he merely crossed the four names off his list, while carefully avoiding stepping in the spreading pool of dark blood at his feet.[117]

Arrival at their destination did not bring an end to the deportees' tribulations. A grim existence in a labour camp was the norm, and for those who survived, it was the start of what was often a lifelong exile. In this way, Stalin 'cleared the decks' on his western frontier, purging those from the newly absorbed territories who were considered to be possible sources of German-inspired sabotage or subversion, or simply 'anti-Soviet elements'. In the process, 34,260 Lithuanians, 15,081 Latvians and 10,205 Estonians were deported to Siberia, Kazakhstan and other inhospitable corners of the Soviet interior.[118] An additional 29,839 are thought to have been deported from Bessarabia,[119] as well as an estimated 200,000 in the fourth and final deportation from eastern Poland.[120] The majority of these deportees would never see their homelands again.

By June 1941, then, Stalin was in little doubt that he was staring down the Nazi barrel. Although he had tended to close his ears to the increasingly insistent news of German preparations, his actions of the previous months demonstrated that he was most certainly not unaware of the growing threat on his western frontier. Yet he had hoped that by appeasing Berlin he could buy time to see out the summer and effectively postpone any German attack until the following year. As he would later confess: 'I did not need any warnings. I knew war would come, but I thought I might gain another six months or so.'[121] Stalin also expected that any hostilities would be preceded by some demands, negotiations and an ultimatum from Berlin. Until that happened, he reasoned, his brinkmanship had not yet edged to the brink.

In addition, Stalin was inextricably linked to the Nazi–Soviet Pact. The negotiations of August 1939 had marked the first time that he had directly involved himself in foreign-policy matters, personally conducting the negotiations and setting the terms. As the German naval attaché in Moscow noted, Stalin was 'the pivot of the German–Soviet collaboration';[122] all correspondence passed over his desk. The pact was widely seen as Stalin's idea, his brainchild, his 'signature policy'. Therefore, it was politically difficult for him to disavow the agreement; there was no scapegoat who could be sacrificed, no one else at whom the finger of blame might be pointed. This goes some way to explaining Stalin's stubborn intransigence; it may be that he saw his own fate intertwined with that of the pact.

Facing the cacophony of rumours in mid-June, Stalin was finally obliged to act. He drafted a communiqué which was to be carried, via the TASS news agency, in every Soviet newspaper on 14 June and broadcast to the masses via public address. It began by outlining the 'widespread rumours of an impending war between the USSR and Germany' which had circulated in 'the English and foreign press'. It was alleged, the text went on, that Germany had made 'territorial and economic demands' of the Soviet Union which the USSR had declined and that as a result the two sides were preparing for war. This was an 'obvious absurdity', the TASS communiqué declared: Germany had addressed no demands to the Soviet Union, and no negotiations were taking place. Moreover:

> according to the evidence in the possession of the Soviet Union, both Germany and the USSR are fulfilling to the letter the terms of the Soviet–German Non-Aggression Pact, so that in the opinion of Soviet circles the rumours of the intention of Germany to break the Pact and to launch an attack against the Soviet Union are completely without foundation.[123]

Aside from the criticism of London, this was a rather desperate attempt to persuade Berlin to publicly concur with the Soviet statement: to induce some sort of commitment in kind from Hitler, a denial of belligerent intent perhaps, or even an opening of the long-awaited negotiations. It was, as Molotov would later admit, very much 'a last resort'.[124] The problem was that it was met only with an echoing silence from the German side.

On the home front Germany was not entirely silent, however. According to the diarist Ruth Andreas-Friedrich, the rumour that Stalin himself was coming to Berlin for talks ran 'like wildfire' through the German capital on the following day, 15 June. She heard it first from her milkman, who added the detail that 200 women had been set to work sewing Soviet flags. A neighbour then repeated the story, stating that the Soviet leader was arriving in the next few days 'by special armoured train'. After Molotov's appearance in the capital the previous autumn, it must have seemed plausible, but Andreas-Friedrich was unimpressed, particularly when she claimed to have found the origin of the fable: Ribbentrop's office.[125]

Back in Moscow, the evidence for an imminent attack was still piling up. On 16 June, the commissar for state security, Vsevolod Merkulov, forwarded new information to Stalin – from the NKVD's agent 'Starshina' (Harro Schulze-Boysen) within the German air ministry

– stating that the final order for the attack on the Soviet Union had been given. Exasperated, Stalin's reply was definitive. 'Tell the "source" in the Staff of the German Air Force to fuck his mother', he scrawled back to Merkulov. 'This is no source, but a disinformer.'[126]

Two days after that, it was Zhukov's turn to feel Stalin's wrath. On 18 June, he and Timoshenko attended a three-hour meeting with Stalin in the Kremlin, in which they explained the current situation on the western frontier and asked Stalin to allow them to place the Red Army in 'full military readiness'. Stalin, however, grew increasingly irritated as Zhukov spoke, tapping his pipe on the table in frustration. Finally, as Timoshenko recalled, he exploded with rage, shouting at Zhukov: 'And what, have you come to scare us with war, or do you want a war, as you are not sufficiently decorated or your rank is not high enough?' When Zhukov then backed down, Timoshenko persisted, but Stalin would have none of it. 'It's all Timoshenko's work', he told the assembled guests of the Politburo, 'he's preparing everyone for war. He ought to have been shot.' Stalin went on: 'You have to realize that Germany on her own will never fight Russia. You must understand this.' And, as he left the room, he fired a last Parthian shot: 'If you're going to provoke the Germans on the frontier by moving troops there without our permission, then heads will roll, mark my words.'[127] With that, he slammed the door behind him.

By the day before the expected attack, there was no ignoring the mounting evidence. The staff of Moscow's German embassy had already been evacuated, along with their families and their belongings; paperwork had been reported burnt in braziers in the courtyard. Further messages had been received from London, from America, and from Richard Sorge in Tokyo. Closer to home, Polish women are reported to have shouted across the border on 15 June that the Soviets should expect war within a week, while an upsurge in spies, saboteurs and defectors crossing the frontier appeared to confirm that prediction. One Soviet border commander noted what he called the 'growing insolence of the Hitlerites', as German sentries now began to turn their backs on their Red Army counterparts, where they had previously been known to stand to attention and salute.[128] In Romania, meanwhile, wild rumours were circulating, claiming not only that a joint German–Romanian attack was imminent, but also that lists of functionaries had been drawn up to be appointed in Bessarabia, and that the National Theatre was rehearsing plays to be staged in Chișinău after its liberation from Soviet rule. It was said that the Romanian leader, General Antonescu, wanted to enter the city on 27 June, a year to the day since the province had been lost.[129]

In all, it has been claimed that, in the ten days before 22 June, Soviet intelligence was informed of the invasion from forty-seven different sources.[130] One of the last of those was Alfred Liskow, a Wehrmacht soldier and communist sympathiser, who swam the river Bug on the night of 21 June to warn the Red Army that an attack along the entire front had been scheduled for dawn the following morning. After midnight, Zhukov phoned through to the Kremlin to advise Stalin of the new claims. The dictator was unimpressed, however, and ordered that Liskow was to be shot for his disinformation.[131]

Only three hours later, the German ambassador, Friedrich-Werner von der Schulenburg, telephoned Molotov's office in the Kremlin to arrange a meeting. He had already had a torrid night. Earlier in the evening, he had been summoned by Molotov to explain German violations of Soviet airspace. The interview became a grilling. 'Why had the German embassy staff left Russia?' he was asked. 'Why had the German government not responded to the TASS communiqué?' Unable to glean any answers, Molotov had complained that 'there was no reason for the German government to be dissatisfied with Russia'.[132] Now, a few hours after that meeting, Schulenburg was hurrying to see Molotov once again. This time he was authorised to provide an official response.

The ambassador solemnly read the telegram that had recently arrived from Berlin, carefully skipping the litany of accusations that prefaced its main message. It was 'with the deepest regret', he told Molotov, that he had to announce that the German government felt itself obliged to take 'military measures' in response to the build-up of Soviet troops on the frontier. He took care to mention his own 'utmost efforts' to preserve 'peace and friendship', but he conceded that he believed that 'it meant the beginning of war'. Molotov was aghast. Stammering with disbelief, he tried to explain the troop concentrations away, before complaining that Berlin had not presented any demands to the Soviet government. 'Why', he asked, 'did Germany conclude a pact of non-aggression, if she so easily breached it?' The attack, he exclaimed, was 'a breach of confidence unprecedented in history . . . Surely we haven't deserved that.' Schulenburg, who had been one of the primary architects of the German–Soviet relationship, could only shrug in response.[133]

9

No Honour among Thieves

Just before dawn, on Sunday 22 June 1941, the code word 'Dortmund' was transmitted to German units stationed on the border with the Soviet Union. With that, on the stroke of 3.15 a.m., the assault began. All along the 1,300 km frontier, from the Baltic to the Black Sea, an intense artillery bombardment prefaced the massed advance of 3 million men, accompanied by thousands of tanks and aircraft, across the line that had once been dubbed the 'Boundary of Peace'. In some places, at strategically vital river crossings or fortified guard posts, the attack was preceded by guile. At Koden, near Brest, for instance, Soviet sentries on a bridge over the river Bug were called out by their German counterparts to discuss 'important business' and then machine-gunned.[1] Elsewhere, elite teams of 'Brandenburger' commandos, deep behind the Soviet border, cut telephone lines or disabled radio masts to hamper the Red Army's response. Along most of the front no ruse or deception was necessary, however, and the guns simply opened fire, heralding the largest invasion in the history of warfare. The Nazi–Soviet Pact had run its course.

Perfectly timed to coincide with Schulenburg's resigned shrug in Moscow, Soviet ambassador Vladimir Dekanozov was summoned to the German foreign ministry in Berlin. There, he and his interpreter, Valentin Berezhkov, were met by Ribbentrop, looking 'puffed and purplish, his eyes clouded, the eyelids enflamed'. 'Could he be drunk?' Berezhkov wondered. When Ribbentrop began, he left little doubt as to the answer to Berezhkov's speculation. Raising his voice, he gave a rambling account of alleged Soviet violations of German territory and airspace, and accused Moscow of harbouring the intention to 'stab the German people in the back'. Accordingly, he concluded, 'German troops had crossed the border into the Soviet Union.' After vainly protesting Moscow's innocence, Dekanozov and Berezhkov were escorted from the foreign ministry. As they left, Ribbentrop hurried after them and in a hoarse whisper told them that he had disagreed with the decision to invade and that he had tried to dissuade Hitler. 'Tell Moscow I was against the attack', he said. Returning to the Soviet embassy on Unter den Linden, they turned on the radio to hear what Moscow was saying about the offensive then raging. To their surprise, they heard only the morning callisthenics spot, as usual, followed by mundane news items about agriculture and hard-working labourers. They wondered if Moscow even knew what was going on.[2]

A couple of hours later, Hitler announced the attack to his own people. At 5.30 a.m. Goebbels read the Führer's declaration from his office in the propaganda ministry, to be broadcast simultaneously across all radio stations. 'Weighed down with heavy cares,' he began, reading Hitler's words, 'condemned to months-long silence, the hour has now come when at last I can speak freely.' What followed was a study in Nazi sophistry, as Hitler recast the history of the war to date as a tale of Anglo-Soviet machinations to encircle Germany. The Nazi–Soviet Pact, he suggested, had been his effort – undertaken 'only with great difficulty' – to undo that encirclement, but its success had only been fleeting: London's 'Mr Cripps', he said, had been sent to Moscow to restore the relationship, and Stalin thereafter began his 'menacing' expansion westwards into the Baltic states and Bessarabia. In response, Hitler had kept his own counsel, and had even invited 'Herr Molotoff' to Berlin for talks, but such was the Soviet Union's 'miserable betrayal' of the pact that he was now obliged to act against the 'Jewish Anglo-Saxon warmongers'. Consequently, he had decided to 'lay the fate and future of the German Reich and our people in the hands of our soldiers'.[3] For Goebbels, reading the declaration was 'a solemn moment' when one could 'hear the breath of history'. But it was also a liberation: 'The burden of many weeks and months falls away', he wrote in his diary. 'I feel totally free.'[4]

Churchill felt a similar emotion. He had spent the night at Chequers, the prime minister's country residence in leafy Buckinghamshire, where he had dined the previous evening with Foreign Secretary Anthony Eden and the new American ambassador, John Winant. The party were awoken on the Sunday morning by news of the German attack, producing – as Churchill's private secretary, Jock Colville, recalled – a 'smile of satisfaction' on the faces of all three.[5] Eden received the message accompanied by a large celebratory cigar on a silver salver. Putting on a dressing gown and hurrying to Churchill's room, he savoured the relief – if not the cigar – and the two discussed what was to follow.[6] Churchill was not surprised by the news. It merely 'changed conviction into certainty', he later recalled, adding 'I had not the slightest doubt where our duty and our policy lay.'[7]

Some 1,500 miles to the east, meanwhile, Moscow was in denial, lulled into a curious calm. Strangely, that very morning, *Pravda* had reprinted Lermontov's famous poem about the battle of Borodino, which spoke of Moscow burning at French hands in 1812:

> Say, uncle, why in spite of clashes
> You gave up Moscow burnt to ashes,
> And yielded to the foe.[8]

It was not some peculiar presentiment of war that caused the publication, however, it was the looming anniversary of the poet's death.[9] The Soviet capital was in ignorance of the war raging far to the west. Indeed, when reports first came in of the German attack, Red Army troops were instructed not to resist. On the vital south-western front, for instance, General Dmitry Pavlov had ordered that while 'provocationist raids by Fascist bandits were likely', there was to be no response: the attackers were to be captured but the frontier was not to be crossed. It was an order that clearly came right from the very top. When Zhukov telephoned Stalin early that morning to ask for permission for Soviet forces to return fire, he was told: 'Permission not granted. This is a German provocation. Do not open fire or the situation will escalate.'[10] Blinded still by his faith in the pact and his expectation of the long-awaited negotiations with Berlin, Stalin was staying the Red Army's hand.

Arriving in Moscow that hot, sunny Sunday morning, Admiral Nikolai Kuznetsov recalled that the Soviet capital was resting peacefully, apparently unaware that 'a fire was blazing on the frontiers'. Entering the Kremlin, he noticed that everything looked as it would do on any normal Sunday; the guard saluted smartly, and there was 'no evidence of anxiety . . . Everything was silent and deserted.' He imagined that the Soviet leadership must have gathered somewhere else to confer, so returned to the Defence Commissariat. 'Has anyone called?' he asked an aide. 'No', he was told. 'No one has called.'[11]

In fact, for all the apparent lack of reaction, Stalin had not been idle. Having conferred with Molotov and other members of the Politburo early that morning, he had issued a new directive, authorising Soviet forces to attack the invader 'with all means at their disposal', and had ordered the removal of countless factories as well as 20 million people from the area adjacent to the front. In addition, he had responded to Hitler's betrayal in the most effective way he knew: with terror, ordering NKVD chief Lavrenti Beria to secure Moscow by flooding it with agents, arresting over 1,000 Muscovites and foreigners suspected of 'terrorism, sabotage, espionage, Trotskyism' and sundry other offences.[12] Yet, for all the momentous developments, Stalin evidently found it hard to adapt to the new situation. According to Comintern chief Georgi Dimitrov, he complained that day that the Germans had attacked 'like gangsters' without first presenting any demands, or an ultimatum, confounding his expectations.[13]

Stalin also delegated to Molotov the task of addressing the Soviet people – possibly because he did not wish to be associated with the ongoing catastrophe, possibly because it had been Molotov who had signed the treaty with Germany. Either way, it was his foreign minister's clipped, nasal voice that the Soviet people heard announce the outbreak of war over the radio and public address systems later that day. Echoing the sense of injured innocence of his superior, Molotov described the German attack as 'perfidy unparalleled in the history of civilized nations', referring repeatedly to the Nazi–Soviet Pact, and to the absence of any German complaints:

> The attack on our country was perpetrated despite the fact that a treaty of non-aggression had been signed between the USSR and Germany, and that the Soviet Government most faithfully abided by all provisions of this treaty.
>
> The attack upon our country was perpetrated despite the fact that during the entire period of operation of this treaty, the German Government could not find grounds for a single complaint against the USSR as regards observance of this treaty.

Warming to his task, Molotov stressed Soviet innocence of any border violations and the 'unshakeable conviction' that the forces of the Soviet

Union would 'deal a crushing blow to the aggressor'. The 'bloodthirsty Fascist rulers of Germany', he went on, had 'enslaved the French, Czechs, Poles, Serbs, Norway, Belgium, Denmark, Holland, Greece, and other nations', neglecting to mention that the Soviet Union had been similarly rapacious. Nonetheless, he vowed that 'the Red Army and our entire nation will once again wage victorious war for the fatherland, for our country, for honour and for liberty'. Mendacious to the last, Molotov claimed that Soviet casualties numbered 'over 200 persons'. He closed by providing the line that would become one of the mottos of the German–Soviet war: 'Our cause is just', he solemnly intoned. *'Pobeda budet za nami'* – 'Victory will be ours.'[14] It was a competent performance, but no more. Stalin told his underling, rather cruelly, that he had sounded 'a bit flustered'.[15]

Soon after, Stalin left the Kremlin for his dacha at Kuntsevo, outside Moscow. It was only at 9.15 that evening that he finally dictated 'Directive No. 3', which ordered the Red Army not only to 'hold firm' and 'destroy' the enemy, but also to cross the Soviet frontier in pursuing their foe.[16] The problem was that, by that time, the Red Army was already in headlong retreat.

It had not taken long that morning for Soviet forces to realise that the German attack was not a mere provocation. Swiftly overrun in its forward positions, the Red Army was being slaughtered where it stood, outgunned and outfought by an enemy who was better equipped, better trained and better led. On average, it has been calculated, a Red Army soldier died every two seconds that day.[17] In the chaos of the attack, entire units simply disappeared: consumed in the maelstrom of explosions or crushed into the sun-baked earth.

At the end of the first day, the remains of the 10th Army regrouped at its new headquarters. A few hours earlier, it had consisted of six infantry divisions, six armoured divisions, two cavalry divisions and three artillery regiments; now its stragglers possessed little more than two tents, a few tables and a telephone.[18] Others had even less. As one Soviet commander would later confess, 'the only thing that was left of the 56th Rifle Division was its number'.[19] The Red Air Force, meanwhile, had been destroyed on the ground, with few pilots even getting airborne to engage the Germans. On the first day alone, the Luftwaffe claimed to have destroyed nearly 1,500 Soviet aircraft.[20] It was almost certainly an underestimate. As Hitler's Luftwaffe adjutant would write a couple of days later: 'The ease of our victories along the whole front came as a surprise to both Army and Luftwaffe. Enemy aircraft were parked in neat rows on their airfields and could be destroyed without difficulty.'[21] When he received the news, Stalin was incredulous: 'Surely the German air force didn't manage to reach every single airfield?' he asked his minions. The affirmative response sent him into an impotent rage.[22]

For Soviet ground forces it was a similar story. Despite the tenacity and bravery of its soldiers, the Red Army was, for the most part, simply overwhelmed. Already at the end of that first day – as Stalin was finally calling on his troops to throw out the invaders – some German spearheads were over fifty miles beyond the former frontier. Isolated pockets of Soviet resistance were surrounded and neutralised, as German armoured columns swept on eastwards, penetrating deep into the rear areas, disrupting communications and support efforts, in a classic demonstration of blitzkrieg. After two days, the capital of the Lithuanian Soviet Republic, Vilnius, fell to the Germans: a week after that the Latvian capital, Riga, the Byelorussian capital, Minsk, and the western Ukrainian city of L'vov (the former Polish Lwów) had also fallen. By that time, some German units had advanced over 250 miles from their starting positions.[23] Already, almost all the lands gained under the pact had been lost.

One of the only sources of optimism for Stalin in those opening days was the performance of his new breed of tanks, the T-34 and the heavier KV. Though fewer than 1,500 of these models were available to the Red Army in June 1941, they came as an unwelcome surprise to German forces, who had grown accustomed to enjoying battlefield superiority. Wehrmacht anti-tank crews quickly discovered that their weapons, especially the standard 37 mm gun, were ineffectual against them; one crew claimed to have hit a T-34 twenty-three times without destroying it.[24] Panzer crews, meanwhile, were similarly alarmed to note that the main gun of the new Soviet tanks was highly effective, and could inflict serious damage on their vehicles before they were even within range. As one German account recalled:

The KV-1 and KV-2 . . . were really something! Our companies opened fire at about 800 yards, but it remained ineffective. We moved closer and closer to the enemy, who for his part continued to approach us unconcerned. Very soon we were facing each other at 50 to 100 yards. A fantastic exchange of fire took place without any visible German success. The Russian tanks continued to advance, and all armour-piercing shells simply bounced off them.[25]

Unsurprisingly, German field commanders were soon beginning to speak of 'tank terror' among Wehrmacht troops.[26] Yet despite such fears, the Axis advance was scarcely halted: there were too few T-34s and KVs to make a serious difference on the battlefield, and too few of those available had crews experienced or well trained enough to exploit their temporary advantage.[27]

Some of the strongpoints that briefly offered resistance were those centring on the fortifications of the Molotov Line, such as at Kunigiškiai in Lithuania or Rava-Russkaya near L'vov.[28] A German field report that summer would record sixty-eight artillery casemates, 460 anti-tank emplacements and 542 machine-gun installations, the majority with accompanying bunkers and anti-tank earthworks.[29] Though incomplete and overwhelmed, the defences of the Molotov Line were clearly not just a paper tiger. A similar, if more antiquated, example was the fortress at Brest, the town where the Nazis and the Soviets had jointly paraded to mark their conquest of Poland in 1939. Built in the mid-nineteenth century by the town's then Russian occupiers, the fortress was a formidable construction, once considered impregnable. Spread across the confluence of the river Bug and a tributary to the west of the town, it formed a huge complex of barracks, ravelins, moats and casemates, with walls five feet thick and space for a garrison of up to 12,000 soldiers.

Ironically, the sector of the German front facing Brest was under the command of General Heinz Guderian, who had taken the salute with the Soviets there in September 1939. 'I had already captured the fortress once, during the Polish campaign', Guderian wrote in his post-war memoir. 'I now had the same task to perform a second time, though in more difficult circumstances.' As he recalled, 'The fortifications at Brest were out of date, but . . . the [rivers] and water-filled ditches made them immune to tank attack.'[30] Such was Guderian's concern about the fortress, indeed, that he asked that an infantry corps be placed under his direct command for the crucial assault.

The Germans attacked the fortress on the morning of 22 June. Subjected to a massive artillery bombardment from the outset, followed by an infantry advance and finally an aerial assault, its 7,000-strong Red Army garrison fought bravely, with around 2,000 Soviet soldiers paying with their lives, while others held out for a week, finally succumbing on 29 June. One Red Army officer, Major Pyotr Gavrilov, even managed to avoid capture, hiding out in the fortress's cellars, until he was finally apprehended on 23 July, a full month after the beginning of Barbarossa.[31] Remarkably, he would survive the war.

By that time, Guderian was already 250 miles to the east, narrowly avoiding another uncomfortable reminder of recent history. In mid-July, his 2nd Army was near the towns of Zhlobin and Rogachev in eastern Byelorussia, when it faced an unsuccessful counter-attack by the Soviet 25th Mechanised Corps, under the command of Major General Semyon Krivoshein, with whom Guderian had shared a platform in Brest in 1939.[32] Though neither appears to have realised it, the two were probably no more than a few kilometres apart across the battlefield. One must assume that Krivoshein's earlier offer to Wehrmacht officers, to 'visit him in Moscow' after the defeat of the British, no longer stood.

In fact, reminders of the Nazi–Soviet Pact were all around. Considering the extent of the German–Soviet economic relationship in the opening phase of the Second World War, it is inevitable that that connection should have played a significant role in the Barbarossa campaign. As we have seen, it is sometimes wrongly suggested that Soviet supplies made the decisive contribution to the German campaign in the west in the summer of 1940: that the Panzers racing for the French coast near Abbeville were 'running on Soviet fuel'. As much as this contention does not fit the Nazi offensive of 1940, it fits rather better to that of 1941: German tanks racing to take Minsk, or encircle Kiev, were to some extent dependent on Soviet oil supplies – statistically speaking, one in every eight of them was indeed 'running on Soviet fuel'.[33]

The same partial dependency ran the other way. The T-34s and KV heavy tanks that had given the Germans such a momentary fright in the summer of 1941 had rolled off production lines that had themselves been set up largely using imported German machinery – lathes, cranes, forges and mills. That recent co-operation was perceptible in other aspects as well. As one economic historian has memorably expressed it:

> German soldiers fed by Ukrainian grain, transported by Caucasus oil, and outfitted with boots made from rubber shipped via the Trans-Siberian railroad, fired their Donets-manganese-hardened steel weapons at their former allies. The Red Army hit back with artillery pieces and planes designed according to German specifications and produced by Ruhr Valley machines in factories that burned coal from the Saar.[34]

Some would even complain that the German–Soviet co-operation had not gone far enough. Colonel General of the Red Air Force Alexander Yakovlev would later ruefully note that his buying delegation had been offered the Ju-87 Stuka dive-bomber during one of their visits to Germany but had rejected it. 'Why throw money down the drain?' they had concluded. 'It's slow, obsolete.' That assessment had certainly not been wrong – after all the Stuka had been badly mauled by the RAF the previous summer during the Battle of Britain – but it had nonetheless proved itself to be highly effective when enjoying air superiority, as it did over the eastern front in 1941. It was an irony that was not lost on Yakovlev: 'In the first days of the war', he recalled, 'these "obsolete, slow" machines caused us incalculable calamities.'[35]

A salient example of the interconnection between the Soviet and German military machines in that brutal summer is that of the ex-*Lützow*, the *Petropavlovsk*. Having languished for over a year in the shipyards of Leningrad, the unfinished German battleship was inevitably pressed into service in the battle for the Soviet Union's second city. Though she was not yet seaworthy, the vessel nonetheless had four of her eight main 203 mm guns installed, and thus could be used as a floating battery when the Wehrmacht approached the city in late August. So it was that, on 7 September, the *Petropavlovsk* – built by German labour in Bremen – bombarded approaching German troops, firing around 700 German-made shells, each one weighing 122 kilograms. Ten days later, German artillery in turn found their range and hit the cruiser with fifty-three rounds, causing her to be beached, bow first, in the coal harbour.[36] It was a fitting end to a vessel that had come to be symbolic of the tortured relations of the Nazi–Soviet Pact.

Such were German successes against the Soviets that summer that it seemed to confirm Hitler's prediction that 'You only have to kick in the door and the whole rotten structure will come crashing down.'[37] And in fact, in the early days of the German invasion, Soviet rule began to look distinctly fragile, both at the front and behind the lines. In those regions recently annexed by the Soviets, local populations were predictably hostile. Across all three Baltic states, popular risings against Soviet rule preceded the arrival of the Germans, who were greeted as liberators despite the fact that they were just as inimical towards the idea of national independence as the Soviets had been.[38] As one Estonian eyewitness recalled:

> The German troops were at first met with great enthusiasm. The horrors of the red regime were over now. Many men, especially those whose family members had been killed or deported, went into the German army of their free will. They wanted to take revenge on the communists.[39]

In Latvia, meanwhile, morale among local units incorporated into the Red Army was predictably bad; desertions were common, and some units even turned their guns on their former masters.[40] Hostility to the Red Army was not confined to the Baltic states. As one Soviet soldier fighting in the city of L'vov recalled, the locals there 'were as likely to spit in a Soviet soldier's face as they were to offer him directions'. A Red Army general had a similar experience when his staff car broke down near Kovel in western Ukraine. A crowd of about twenty locals gathered, he wrote, but 'no one was saying anything. No one offered to help', they just 'smirked maliciously at us'.[41]

Even far behind the lines, there was disquiet. In Moscow there was a spate of panic buying, a run on the banks and a stand-off at a food plant degenerated into a violent confrontation. Although many keen young men volunteered to fight, and a general mood of Russian patriotism prevailed, there was nonetheless genuine discontent in evidence, with sometimes long-standing resentments against the collectivisation, or the terror, finally being aired.[42] One Muscovite claimed that it was just as well that the war had started, as life in the Soviet Union had become so unbearable that 'the sooner it was all over the better'. Another said that 'at last we can breathe freely. Hitler will be in Moscow in three days and the intelligentsia will be able to live properly.'[43]

What was worse for Stalin was that some, even beyond the border areas, were actively welcoming the invaders. As one German officer noted near Vitebsk in Byelorussia:

> I was astonished to detect no hatred among [the local people]. Women often came out of their houses with an icon held before their breast, crying: 'We are still Christians. Free us from Stalin who destroyed our churches.' Many of them offered an egg and a piece of dried bread as a 'welcome'. We gradually had the feeling that we really were being regarded as liberators.[44]

More worrying still for Stalin was the apparent disintegration of Soviet forces in those opening days of the campaign. Facing the full force of the blitzkrieg, the Red Army was in disarray, with surviving troops often fleeing eastwards alongside columns of similarly leaderless refugees. In some cases, officers attempting to stem the panic and restore order were shot by their own troops.[45] One soldier recalled his experience of the constant shelling, the din of battle and the orders that never arrived. Finally, he decided to leave his post, and taking a small group of men with him set off eastwards on foot. 'There was no one to help with advice or supplies', he remembered. 'None of the men had ever seen a map.'[46] They would walk without a break for forty-eight hours.

It was not only the ordinary soldiers who were seeking a way out; Marshal Grigory Kulik was also looking to flee. After his buffoonish intervention in the high-command conference earlier in the year, the fleshy fifty-year-old had arrived at the front on 23 June in a leather flying suit and goggles, seeking to rally what was left of the 10th Army. However, when disaster loomed, he ordered his men to follow his lead in shedding their uniforms, disposing of their documents and adopting peasant dress. After burning both his marshal's uniform and his flying suit, he fled east on a horse-drawn cart.[47]

Once again, Kulik would escape with his life. But given the scale of the disaster unfolding on the western frontier, discipline clearly had to be restored swiftly. One way that this was achieved was via the reintroduction, in late June, of so-called 'blocking units': NKVD troops tasked with preventing unauthorised withdrawals from the front, with extreme force if necessary. From its role in the purges, the NKVD was already widely feared. As one Red Army colonel recalled, the mere sight of the cornflower-blue cap of an NKVD man could be enough to transform the most hardened soldier into a nervous babbling wreck, desperately protesting his innocence.[48] Now the NKVD was given the task of 'leading the fight against deserters, cowards and alarmists'. They had the authority to shoot suspects on the spot, and anyone behind the front lines who could not adequately explain their presence fell under immediate suspicion.

According to some accounts, Stalin too required a certain stiffening of his resolve. Though he had handled most of the opening week with exemplary vigour – working all hours to co-ordinate the desperate Soviet response – by the time of the fall of Minsk on 28 June, he had seemingly reached the end of his tether. Minsk, indeed, was grimly symbolic. Not only was it the capital city of the Soviet Republic of Byelorussia and a major population centre, it was also fully 300 km from the frontier – thereby demonstrating the scale of the Red Army's collapse – and lay on the traditional 'Road to Moscow', less than 700 km from the capital. If they could continue that rate of advance, Hitler's troops would be arriving in Moscow within two weeks.

Unsurprisingly, this realisation appears to have momentarily shaken Stalin's confidence. On the evening of 28 June, when news of Minsk's fall reached him, Stalin was reportedly furious, storming out of his office when his demand for an update from the front was met with impotent shrugs. That same night, according to Zhukov, Stalin twice visited the Defence Commissariat, where he reacted violently to bad news and caused an unseemly spat between himself, Timoshenko, Zhukov and Beria, with the latter threatening that the NKVD might have to intervene to restore the army's martial spirit.[49] No longer able to contain his fury, Stalin shouted at Zhukov: 'What is the General Staff for? What is the Chief of Staff for, if during the first days of war he loses his head, is not in communication with his forces, doesn't represent anyone and doesn't command anyone?'[50] In the aftermath, a mood of resignation took hold of the Politburo, with many, including Stalin, 'very depressed' by the night's events. Later, as he left the Defence Commissariat, Stalin gave voice to his darkest fears. 'Everything's lost', he said. 'I give up. Lenin founded our state and we've fucked it up.' It was said that he cursed all the way to his dacha at Kuntsevo.[51]

The suspicion that Stalin had some sort of breakdown in the opening weeks of the war has been a remarkably persistent one. It first emerged with Khrushchev and his 'Secret Speech' of 1956 – as part of a successful attempt to discredit the once-revered dictator – and has been retold, regurgitated and embellished by biographers and commentators ever since. Some publications still confidently assert that Stalin was absent for fully ten days, during which the Soviet Union was effectively 'leaderless'.[52] This idea is no longer taken very seriously. An analysis of the visitors' book in Stalin's Kremlin office, for instance, has demonstrated that there was no hiatus in appointments in that first week, with Stalin absent from the Kremlin for only two days – 29 and 30 June – during which time he chaired meetings elsewhere. Whether at his dacha, at the Defence Commissariat or in the Kremlin, Stalin barely stopped.[53]

Yet the image of Stalin, unshaven, sulking at his dacha, visited by a cowering coterie of Politburo officials who beg him to resume his duties, is nonetheless a highly seductive one. In its most elaborate form, the story has Molotov, Mikoyan, Beria and Voroshilov entering the house, where they confront Stalin, who was 'thinner . . . haggard . . . gloomy', and 'turned to stone' when he saw them. According to one account, the dictator was rambling about Lenin. 'If he could see us now', he lamented, bewailing what destiny had visited upon 'those to whom he entrusted the fate of his country'. It was also claimed that he had been 'inundated with letters' from ordinary Soviet citizens 'righty rebuking us'. Finally, it is said, he addressed his acolytes with the wary, suspicious question: 'Why have you come?'[54] as though Stalin feared that he himself was about to be purged.

While the episode is most likely a post-war invention, it is a tale that has a certain logic. For one thing, Stalin had signed far too many death warrants to have been ignorant of the fate meted out to those who were perceived to have failed, transgressed or stepped out of line. Yet beyond that, there was also every reason for him to have indulged in a spot of genuine 'mea culpa' introspection. After all, he had himself been a prime mover in formulating the policy which had led to the Nazi–Soviet Pact and he had taken a personal hand in the negotiations with Ribbentrop; more than any other Soviet policy, perhaps, that of rapprochement with Germany carried Stalin's imprimatur. Moreover, once that relationship had begun to sour, it had been Stalin who had stopped his ears to the Cassandra-like prophecies of an imminent German attack; and, worse still, it had been Stalin who had refused to bolster the Red Army's defences to the west, leaving the 'Road to Moscow' insufficiently guarded.

Though we can now dismiss the wilder idea of a sulking Stalin spending days *hors de combat* at his dacha, the suggestion that he might yet have endured a bout of uncertainty and reflection is still very persuasive. The fall of Minsk symbolised the wider disaster not only for the USSR, but for Stalin personally. It was arguably the gravest crisis that he would ever face, the moment at which his misjudgement was thrown into sharp relief. Only a dictator of his brutal determination – and one with the absolute power that he had arrogated for himself – could have survived it.

Whatever the truth of the dacha episode, Stalin reappeared in the Kremlin on 1 July. That same day, he was appointed chairman of the State Defence Committee, which would be directly responsible for the prosecution of the war with Germany. Two days later, he spoke to the Soviet people, by radio, for the first time since the German attack. 'Comrades! Citizens! Brothers and sisters!' he began haltingly, but with uncharacteristic warmth. 'Men of our army and navy! I am addressing you, my friends!' What followed was essentially a call to arms, a plea to all Soviet peoples to 'rise in defence of our native land' and to show 'unexampled valour' in combating their 'most malicious and most perfidious enemy – German fascism'. He reminded them that there were 'no invincible armies and never have been', and predicted, stretching history a little, that Hitler's Wehrmacht 'will be smashed, as were the armies of Napoleon and Wilhelm'.

Naturally, perhaps, alongside this rousing rallying cry, Stalin felt obliged to offer a defence of his earlier policy of collusion with Germany. 'It may be asked', he said, 'how could the Soviet government have consented to conclude a Non-Aggression Pact with such treacherous fiends as Hitler and Ribbentrop?' It had not been an error, he answered piously; no 'peace-loving state' could turn down a treaty with a neighbour. Indeed, the Soviet Union had gained a 'definite advantage' from the pact, Stalin claimed, by securing 'peace for a year and a half and the opportunity of preparing its forces to repulse fascist Germany should she risk an attack'.[55]

In addition to such rhetorical flourishes, Stalin needed a scapegoat for the debacle of the opening week of the war, and he found one in General Dmitry Pavlov, commander of the western front. Pavlov had evidently been overwhelmed by the course of events, hamstrung by the speed of the German advance and the disintegration of his own forces. Increasingly, it had seemed to his subordinates, he was issuing unrealistic orders, trying to justify his own existence, to 'show Moscow that something was being done'.[56] Yet by the end of June, with Minsk having fallen, Pavlov had lost most of his force – including twenty divisions, totalling around 400,000 men, taken prisoner by the Germans in just one vast encirclement battle. Arrested and taken to Moscow, along with most of his staff and subordinates, he was accused of 'panic-mongering', 'dereliction of duty' and 'cowardice', and slated for execution.[57] Pavlov refused to go quietly, however, repudiating his confession and, in a final rebuke to Stalin, making it quite clear where he thought the blame for the disaster lay. 'We are here in the dock', he said, 'not because we committed crimes in time of war, but because we prepared for this war inadequately in time of peace.'[58] One of the Red Army's most gifted generals was shot in the head, his body dumped in a municipal landfill.

Such actions were not particularly unusual. Indeed it is rather telling that the person whom Stalin saw most often during the opening weeks of the war was Lavrenti Beria, the head of the NKVD.[59] Alongside Pavlov, a number of other commanders were charged with treason and made to pay personally for the Red Army's failings, including Lieutenant General Aleksandr Korobkov, commander of the 4th Army, and Major General Stepan Oborin, commander of the 14th Mechanised Corps. The arrests were quite arbitrary, arranged more or less by quota, as had been done during the Great Purge. Stalin's order required simply that one front commander, one chief of staff, one chief of communications, one chief of artillery and one army commander were to be arrested and charged; any specific transgression or offence was immaterial. The unfortunate Korobkov, for instance, had performed no worse than his colleagues, but was merely the only army commander who could be found on the day of the order.[60] In addition, a further 300 or so Red Army commanders would be executed later in the year, as German forces neared Moscow, *pour encourager les autres*.

Given such levels of brutality against his own loyal generals, Stalin could scarcely be expected to show any compassion to his perceived political opponents. On the day after the German invasion, Beria's deputy, Vsevolod Merkulov, instructed his subordinates in the areas threatened by the invasion to check their prisoner holdings and 'compile lists of those whom you deem necessary to shoot'.[61] The instruction was clarified the following day by Beria, who ordered that all prisoners convicted or even accused of counter-revolutionary activity, sabotage, diversionism or anti-Soviet activity were to be executed.[62] The NKVD jailers did not need telling twice. While ordinary criminals were sometimes released, and others were successfully evacuated to the Soviet interior, the looming chaos of the German attack made evacuation seem a rather perilous and unreliable way of dealing with Moscow's political enemies, a point that had been grimly demonstrated by the unhappy fate of two transports of the last mass deportation from the Baltic states, which had simply disappeared in the chaos of the blitzkrieg.[63] From the NKVD's perspective at least, the most responsible option for the remaining prisoners was execution.

Consequently, in countless locations, the incoming Germans found evidence of killings and massacres of those people whom the departing NKVD had not wanted to take with them and could not afford to leave alive. At Tartu in Estonia, for instance, some 200 political prisoners were shot and dumped in the prison yard and in a nearby well.[64] At Rainiai in western Lithuania, about eighty prisoners were driven out to a local forest on 24 June, where they were tortured and abused before being executed. The victims were so badly mutilated that more than half of them could not be identified.[65] At Chişinău, in what had once been Bessarabia, the garden of the former NKVD headquarters was found to contain the corpses of some eighty-five prisoners, all with their hands and feet tied and shot in the back of the head.[66]

In the former Polish eastern regions, annexed by Stalin in 1939, it is estimated that at least 40,000 prisoners – Poles, Ukrainians, Byelorussians and Jews – were confined in overcrowded NKVD prisons by June 1941. As elsewhere, some were released, others evacuated, but around half would not survive.[67] The worst massacres were in L'vov, where around 3,500 prisoners were killed across three prison sites, and at Lutsk (the former Polish Łuck), where 2,000 were murdered. But almost every NKVD prison or outpost saw a similar action – from Sambor (600 killed) to Czortkov (Czortków) (890), from Tarnopol (574) to Dubno (550). In most cases, the methods employed were similar: prisoners would be brought to the prison yard in batches of forty or so and simply machine-gunned. Where time was short, NKVD troops would do the killing in the cells, firing through the observation holes, or merely tossing in hand-grenades and locking the door. Any survivors were then bayoneted or battered to death.[68] One eyewitness of the killings at Lutsk recalled: 'Blood flowed in rivers, and body parts flew through the air.'[69]

Total figures for those executed by the NKVD in the wake of the German invasion are unclear, and will probably never be known for sure, but a few tentative figures may be suggested. In Latvia, for instance, over 1,300 corpses would later be unearthed from the grounds of the NKVD prison and other locations, while a further 12,000 individuals were unaccounted for.[70] For Lithuania, the figure of 1,000 murdered by the NKVD in June 1941 has been suggested.[71] In Estonia, meanwhile, a figure of 2,000 has been estimated for those civilians killed either by the NKVD or in fighting with the withdrawing Red Army.[72] An analysis of recent Soviet data gives a total of 8,700 Poles executed by the NKVD in June 1941, though other investigations suggest a figure around three times that.[73] Charting a course between the hyperbole and the denial is not easy, but it should be borne in mind that in many cases the dead from that period find no reference in the official Soviet record. Given that one respected historian has given a total figure of 100,000 for prisoners executed by the NKVD in former eastern Poland alone, one might assume a significantly larger figure for the total across all of the Soviet borderlands.[74]

Just as the NKVD had eliminated their perceived class enemy, so the SS and its allies were exterminating their perceived racial enemy. Indeed, in the opening phase of the invasion, there could be a link between the two processes. Though Hitler's SS and *Einsatzgruppen* had genocidal designs of their own upon crossing the German–Soviet frontier, in a few places anti-Soviet feeling was running so high that they had little difficulty in inspiring local paramilitaries to take the lead in targeting those who were deemed responsible – the Jewish populations.

One of the most infamous examples was the 'Lietukis Garage

Massacre' in Kaunas, Lithuania, which took place on 27 June 1941. One German eyewitness recalled coming across a crowd of people 'cheering and clapping . . . mothers lifting their children to get a better view', so he decided to push his way through to take a look. What he witnessed there, he said, was 'probably the most frightful event that I had seen during the course of two world wars'. A local man – nick-named 'the Death Dealer' – was dispensing mob justice to those considered 'traitors and collaborators':

> On the concrete forecourt of the petrol station a blond man of medium height, aged about twenty-five, stood leaning on a wooden club, resting. The club was as thick as his arm and came up to his chest. At his feet lay about fifteen to twenty dead or dying people. Water flowed continu-ously from a hose washing blood away into the drainage gully. Just a few steps behind this man some twenty men, guarded by armed civil-ians, stood waiting for their cruel execution in silent submission. In response to a cursory wave the next man stepped forward silently and was then beaten to death with the wooden club in the most bestial manner, each blow accompanied by enthusiastic shouts from the audience.[75]

Another German watching events that day was astonished by the behaviour of the crowd, women and children included, who applauded every time the man beat one of his helpless victims. When it was all over, he recalled, the 'Death Dealer' put down his club, picked up an accordion and played the Lithuanian national anthem.[76]

In Lithuania alone, it is thought that some 2,500 Jews were slaugh-tered by their neighbours in similar bloody pogroms in the opening weeks of the German–Soviet war.[77] In eastern Poland, at least thirty towns saw pogroms against the local Jews as soon as the Soviets departed.[78] In many cases, anti-Semitism merged with anti-Soviet senti-ment, and unfortunate Jewish victims were forced to sing Red Army songs or hymns to Stalin as part of their public humiliation. In Kolomyia (the former Polish Kołomyja), Jews were rounded up and forced to pull down the statue of Stalin which had been erected in the centre of the town in 1939.[79] A particularly gruesome example of the treatment meted out to local Jewish populations was what happened in Boryslav, once the south-eastern Polish town of Borysław, where the incoming German commander gave locals twenty-four hours in which to 'avenge themselves'. In the horrors that followed, Jews were rounded up by a militia and herded to the former Soviet prison in the town, where they were forced to exhume and clean the corpses of those Poles and Ukrainians who had been murdered by the NKVD and buried in the prison grounds. One eyewitness recalled:

> I found myself in the middle of a huge courtyard. Everywhere there were bodies. They were terribly distorted and their faces were unrecognisable. It stank of old blood and rotting flesh. Next to the corpses stood Jewish men with wet cloths in their hands, to wipe away the blood . . . They keenly washed the decaying bodies. Only their eyes were feverish – crazed with fear.[80]

Their grim work done, the unfortunate Jews were then shot or beaten to death by the mob, their bodies in turn flung into the mass graves that they had so recently exhumed. It is estimated that 250 people were murdered in Boryslav that day, before the German authorities put a stop to the slaughter. The numbers killed elsewhere in similar atrocities will probably never be known.

These hideous actions were, in part, a way for a minority among local populations to curry favour with the incoming occupier, an attitude that has been aptly described as 'anticipatory obedience'.[81] It has also been plausibly argued that such horrors were not as spontaneous as they might have appeared, and that the incoming SS commanders actively sought to instigate pogroms and massacres, but – initially at least – preferred to allow local auxiliary units to do the dirty work. As the commander of *Einsatzgruppe* A, Walter Stahlecker, would note:

> The attempts at self-cleansing on the part of anti-Communist or anti-Semitic elements in the areas to be occupied are not to be hindered. On the contrary, they are to be encouraged, but without leaving traces, so that these local 'vigilantes' cannot later say that they were given orders or political concessions.[82]

But these factors alone do not adequately explain such atrocities, as they ignore the role played by the ingrained hatred that many in the

Baltic states and elsewhere had for the NKVD and the Soviet Union. Of course, most NKVD, Soviet administrative staff, and even Communist Party members would have already fled, but the commonly perceived association of Soviet communism with Jewry meant that it would be local Jewish populations who bore the brunt of popular anger.

As they invaded the Soviet Union, the Nazis actively sought to propagate that conflation of Jewishness and communism. Of course, it made no difference that the connection was mythical. Though some of the region's Jews had indeed welcomed the arrival of the Red Army, they had collectively benefited little from their annexation into the Soviet Union, and had suffered disproportionately from the resulting waves of arrests and deportations. In Latvia, for instance, Jews had made up around 5 per cent of the total population, but had numbered at least 12 per cent of those deported by the Soviets in 1941.[83] Nonetheless, a twisted ideology and guilt by association demanded that they would be made to pay for Soviet crimes.

In many places, the new occupiers consciously sought to make the link, therefore, publicly blaming NKVD killings on the Jews, forcing Jews to carry out the exhumations of NKVD victims, and targeting recruitment efforts for local auxiliary units towards those who had had relatives killed or deported by the Soviets.[84] Yet the Nazis might well have felt that they were, to some extent, pushing against an open door. The Kaunas 'Death Dealer', for instance, though unnamed, was said by eyewitnesses to have lost his parents to an NKVD murder squad only two days earlier.[85] In nearby Latvia, a policeman recalled a public exhumation, organised by the Germans:

> The day was hot, the corpses had been under for at least a week and they exuded an intolerable stench. I had never seen such horror before or since; I vomited from the stench and the sight. The purpose of the display was to create hatred against the Communists, an incentive that we Latvians actually did not need.[86]

Latvia had scarcely any history of anti-Semitism prior to the trauma of 1939–41; indeed it had even been a destination for some Jews fleeing the Third Reich, including the Russian-born scholar Simon Dubnow. Yet in 1941 and beyond, it became the scene – like its Baltic neighbours – of some of the most hideous atrocities in which local units, such as the infamous Arajs Kommando, would play a significant role. It seems clear that the Soviet occupation – with its informers, its collaborators, its denunciations and its persecutions – had so poisoned already fragile community relations that, even without Nazi encouragement, some sort of bloody reckoning was almost inevitable. In this regard, the example of Estonia is instructive. There, the small Jewish population that had remained in the country in 1941, numbering just under 1,000, was swiftly exterminated once the Germans arrived. Yet as many as 5,000 non-Jewish Estonians were also murdered by the local 'Self-Defence Committee' for their supposed collaboration with the Soviet regime.[87] In some places at least, anti-Soviet sentiment was clearly as much of a motivator in the horrors of that summer as anti-Semitism.

Though Barbarossa transformed large swathes of eastern Europe into a vision of the lowest circles of hell, in Germany it ushered in the return of something like normality. It was understandable, perhaps, that Hitler and Goebbels should have felt relieved by the outbreak of war with Stalin's Soviet Union, but strangely it was a sentiment that seems to have been shared by many ordinary Germans, who were evidently tired of the political machinations and the oppressive rumour-laden atmosphere. As the CBS radio correspondent in Berlin, Henry Flannery, explained:

> The war against Russia was the first popular campaign that had been launched. None of the Germans had been able to understand why a treaty should have been made with the Soviets, after they had been the main object of denunciation since 1933. Now they had a sense of relief, a feeling of final understanding. I listened to their conversations around the news-stands and on the subways. I talked with a number of them. For the first time, they were excited about the war. 'Now', they said, 'we are fighting our real enemy.'[88]

The diarist Victor Klemperer would have concurred. Walking in Dresden on the evening of 22 June, he noted the 'general cheerfulness' and 'triumphant mood' of the populace. 'They were dancing in the Toll House', he wrote, 'cheerful faces everywhere. A new entertainment, a prospect of new sensations, the Russian war is a source of new pride for the people, their grumbling of yesterday is forgotten.'[89]

Behind the facade, of course, there were concerns. Many were simply shocked by the news, particularly those who had believed the rumours of the previous week that Stalin was on his way to Berlin for talks. 'We knew it was coming', Berlin diarist Missie Vassiltchikov wrote. 'And yet we are thunderstruck.'[90] Others entertained dark fears about the sheer scale of the new adventure. One Berliner noted glumly that 'Russia has never been suited to lightning wars', adding: 'What's the use of our being in the Urals? They'll just go on fighting beyond the Urals. No, that mouthful is one we can't chew.'[91] Even Himmler's own twelve-year-old daughter, Gudrun, struck a pessimistic tone. Writing to her father on 22 June, she chided: 'It is terrible that we're at war with Russia – they were our allies . . . Still Russia is sooo big, if we take the whole of Russia, the battle will become very difficult.'[92]

Beyond such concerns, however, there was a sense of business as usual. The German Cup Final, for instance, scheduled for the afternoon of 22 June in Berlin, went ahead as planned, with the stadium announcer making only the briefest mention of the titanic struggle then being waged 700 km to the east. As Rapid Vienna midfielder Leopold Gernhardt would later recall, none of the players gave much thought to Barbarossa that day, they were too focused on the match.[93] Those spectators distracted by events elsewhere were at least treated to a classic, with Rapid coming from behind to defeat Schalke 4–3.

For many Germans, therefore, there was little sense at the time of the invasion of the Soviet Union having any transcendent significance, marking the crossing of a Rubicon. Though almost all of them would have known someone who was involved in the invasion – brother, son, father or neighbour – they had already accepted war as the bloody backdrop against which their everyday lives were being played out. Thus the invasion of Stalin's USSR was just another act in the ongoing drama. Indeed, as Ruth Andreas-Friedrich noted in her diary, there was a distinct sense of continuity: 'Our propaganda can pick up where it had to leave off so suddenly in September of 1939', she wrote mockingly. 'United against Bolshevism! Guard Europe from the Soviet menace!'[94]

Germany's communists, meanwhile, felt a profound sense of relief. Barbarossa brought an end to the ideological gymnastics that they had been obliged to perform for so long, and an end to the enforced suspension of their activities. With the Nazi invasion of the bastion of proletarian revolution, they could once again take sides to defend Stalin and world communism, as was their duty. To this end, dormant cells across the country would be revitalised and long-silent agitators would rejoin the fight. The 'imperialist war' waged by Britain and France was now transformed, overnight, into a principled crusade against 'fascist aggression'. From that summer, the German Communist Party (KPD) began publishing its 'Informationsdienst', or 'Information Service', providing tips on how best to disrupt the Nazi war effort, and walls in the big cities were soon defaced by scrawled slogans and crude hand-printed posters. In July 1941 alone, the number of illegal KPD leaflets captured by the Gestapo across Germany rose to almost 4,000, a tenfold increase on the previous month.[95] The unofficial truce observed by Germany's domestic communists had come to an end. Battle had finally been joined.

For their comrades in the Soviet capital, meanwhile, the changes experienced with the outbreak of war were a little more subtle. The vast majority of the Soviet people received the news of the war with a profound sense of shock; some with tears and incredulity, others with a surge of ideological or patriotic fervour. There was also, inevitably, a good deal of anger directed towards the Germans, who were accused by ordinary Muscovites of having cruelly betrayed Stalin and broken faith with the pact. Others blamed the pact itself: 'whoever had faith in Hitler, that Herod?' one asked.[96] Some stopped short of blaming the German people as a whole, however. Molotov had given a lead in his speech, in which he had stated that the war 'had not been inflicted upon us by the German people . . . but by Germany's blood-thirsty rulers', and it was a sentiment that found a ready echo, perhaps due to the influence of two years of positive propaganda about Moscow's pact partners. The idea of ordinary German soldiers as a deadly enemy was one that some evidently found hard to comprehend. 'What have we got to be afraid of?' one man asked his neighbour. 'The Germans are civilized people.'[97] It was a sentiment that would not last.

Paranoia, ever present in Stalin's Soviet Union, naturally increased.

While those who were arrested in Beria's initial clampdown in the capital were carted off to the NKVD's prisons for interrogation, space was made for them by sending the same number of existing inmates off to an uncertain fate in the work camps of the Gulag. New arrivals in Moscow were quick to notice the nervousness. Members of the British military mission, arriving in the capital in their unfamiliar uniforms, were swiftly confronted by an angry crowd after someone suggested that they might be 'parachutists'. Speaking anything but Russian aroused immediate suspicion, one foreign journalist recalled. Another foreigner was dismayed when instructed by a militia-woman to put out his cigarette: she evidently suspected that he was using it to signal to German aircraft.[98]

Other changes were more profound. As well as a reflexive swelling of Russian patriotism and a dogged conviction that Mother Russia would prevail, many were moved by a genuine attachment to Stalin. Whereas the 'Stalin cult' had previously been rather perfunctory and often tainted by fear as a result of the purges, with the German invasion the Soviet people found that they had a leader to look up to. While Molotov's speech on the outbreak of war had been uninspiring, Stalin's had been much more assured, infusing a frightened, bewildered people with new hope, direction and the prospect, however distant, of eventual victory. It was, wrote journalist Alexander Werth, 'a great pull-yourselves-together speech, a blood-sweat-and-tears speech', with Churchill's own wartime orations as 'its only parallel'.[99] The 'Father of Nations' long promised by Soviet propaganda, seemed to have finally emerged.

For Churchill, enjoying a celebratory cigar at Chequers on the morning of the invasion, Barbarossa posed a rather different challenge. Of course, with Hitler's attentions distracted elsewhere, the attack certainly gave Britain a vital breathing space, as General Alan Brooke noted:

> As long as the Germans were engaged in the invasion of Russia there was no possibility of an invasion of these islands. It would now depend on how long Russia could last and what resistance she would be able to put up . . . [but] it certainly looked as if Germany would be unable to launch an invasion of England until October and by then the weather

and winter would be against any such enterprise. It therefore looked as if we should now be safe from invasion during 1941.[100]

Yet beyond that, Barbarossa presented something of a dilemma, particularly with regard to framing Britain's response. According to MP Harold Nicolson, the reception to news of the invasion was mixed. 'Most people in England will be delighted', he wrote in his diary, suggesting that the addition of a new ally was always welcome. But there were also reservations. 'It will have a bad effect on America', he noted, 'where many influential people do not like to see themselves as the allies of Bolshevism [and] it will have a bad effect on Conservative and Catholic opinion here.'[101] There were further caveats. For some, it was considered rather poetic that, after a long period of what Churchill called 'seeming to care for no one but themselves', the Soviets were now eagerly calling for assistance from the capitalist world. As Foreign Secretary Anthony Eden tartly noted, Moscow's great fear was now 'that we would stand inactively watching their life-and-death struggle, as they had watched ours'.[102]

What was more, many did not consider that the Soviet Union would be able to resist Hitler for long. Nicolson reckoned that the Soviets were 'so incompetent and selfish that they will be bowled over at a touch', while General Brooke's more measured assumption was that they would last '3 to 4 months, possibly slightly longer'.[103] Remarkably, the latter opinion was rather optimistic by the standards of the British military establishment. An assessment by the chiefs of staff from mid-June, for instance, concluded that the Red Army suffered from 'inherent failings' and obsolete equipment, and its offensive value was low. Mindful of such shortcomings – and the Red Army's unimpressive showing in the Winter War with Finland – a rapid Soviet collapse was anticipated, with Moscow and Ukraine foreseen as falling to the Germans within as little as six weeks.[104]

Many in Britain still harboured a fundamental distrust of the USSR. The efforts of Sir Stafford Cripps to find some arrangement with Moscow had foundered – as much on British impotence as Soviet intransigence – but beyond that British government and military circles remained profoundly suspicious of Stalin's motives, and many persisted in the view that the USSR was more a potential enemy than a potential ally. The fact that the Soviets had invaded and annexed eastern Poland

and the Baltic states had not been forgotten, neither had the Winter War with the plucky Finns, or the more recent fiasco of the attempt to warn Moscow about Hitler's aggressive intentions. On the very eve of the invasion, Churchill, who was already known for his colourful epithets about the USSR, would coin another one, summing up the ambivalent British attitude rather neatly. Russia, he said, was like a 'formidable crocodile':

> If a crocodile came up on one side of our boat and helped to balance it, so much the better. But you never know with Russia. You give the crocodile a hearty kick and he may be agreeable to you. You give him a pat and he may snap off your leg. We had tried both methods and gained nothing.[105]

Hence Churchill had to execute a precise balancing act. He had to avoid alienating those on the British right who hated the idea of any association with communism, as well as those on the left who craved a full-blown alliance with Stalin. In addition, he wanted to give the Soviets enough encouragement that they would keep fighting, knowing that every month fought on the eastern front would give Britain a vital stay of execution. Above all, perhaps, he had to consider the Americans, whose alliance he valued much more highly than that of Stalin, yet whose public and politicians, he feared, would baulk at any binding commitments to the USSR.

In his own account of events of the morning of 22 June, Churchill implied that his reaction to news of the invasion was more or less spontaneous. 'I spent the day composing my statement', he wrote. 'There was not time to consult the War Cabinet, nor was it necessary.' Yet that impression of spontaneity should be resisted. Churchill had thrashed out the British position over the previous days, with the vital help of Cripps, so as to be able to sail the treacherous course between all of the conflicting interests. The result was a glorious example of Churchillian rhetoric.

In a radio broadcast that same evening, the veteran anti-Bolshevik made his new support for Stalin and the Soviet Union plain. Hitler's invasion of the USSR, Churchill declared, was nothing less than the fourth 'climacteric', the fourth 'intense turning point' in the progress of the war. Hitler – a 'monster of wickedness' and a 'bloodthirsty guttersnipe' – was now carrying his 'work of butchery and desolation' to the vast multitudes of Russia and of Asia, 'grinding up human lives and trampling down the homes and the rights of hundreds of millions of men'. That human catastrophe, Churchill suggested, transcended everything:

> The Nazi regime is indistinguishable from the worst features of Communism. It is devoid of all theme and principle except appetite and racial domination. It excels in all forms of human wickedness, in the efficiency of its cruelty and ferocious aggression. No one has been a more consistent opponent of Communism than I have for the last twenty-five years. I will unsay no word that I've spoken about it. But all this fades away before the spectacle which is now unfolding. The past, with its crimes, its follies and its tragedies, flashes away.

In a strikingly lyrical passage, he implied that it was not communism that was being attacked, but Mother Russia herself:

> I see the Russian soldiers standing on the threshold of their native land, guarding the fields which their fathers have tilled from time immemorial. I see them guarding their homes where their mothers and wives pray – ah yes, for there are times when all pray – for the safety of their loved ones, for the return of the breadwinner, of the champion, of their protector. I see the 10,000 villages of Russia, where the means of existence was wrung so hardly from the soil, but where there are still primordial human joys, where maidens laugh and children play. I see advancing upon all this, in hideous onslaught, the Nazi war machine, with its clanking, heel-clicking, dandified Prussian officers, its crafty expert agents, fresh from the cowing and tying down of a dozen countries. I see also the dull, drilled, docile brutish masses of the Hun soldiery, plodding on like a swarm of crawling locusts.

British policy, Churchill went on with a characteristic flourish, was simple:

> We have but one aim and one single irrevocable purpose. We are resolved to destroy Hitler and every vestige of the Nazi regime. From

this nothing will turn us. Nothing. We will never parley; we will never negotiate with Hitler or any of his gang. We shall fight him by land, we shall fight him by sea, we shall fight him in the air, until, with God's help, we have rid the earth of his shadow and liberated its peoples from his yoke. Any man or state who fights against Nazidom will have our aid.[106]

It was stirring stuff, and deliberately so: 'a masterpiece', according to Harold Nicolson.[107] Churchill had given a decisive line – making a moral case for support of the USSR, yet stopping short of advocating alliance – which would satisfy not only his domestic audience but also his potentially fractious cabinet, and most importantly his American ally. In private, he was less gracious but the message was broadly the same: 'If Hitler invaded Hell', he had told Jock Colville, 'I would at least make a favourable reference to the Devil!'[108]

If Churchill's aim had been to rally the nation around his vague offer of assistance to Stalin's Soviet Union, he succeeded. His speech attracted widespread praise for its deft handling of a ticklish situation. Only a few, it seems, expressed doubts about his sincerity or railed against his supposed hypocrisy.[109] Even British communists – though no friends of Churchill – were assuaged. As the Communist Party's only MP, Willie Gallacher, noted, Churchill's speech had been 'agreeably surprising', and though it did not go quite far enough, he said, 'it went further than [he] expected'.[110]

Indeed, the British Communist Party was one of the natural beneficiaries of the speech. Where they had previously been confined to a rather uncomfortable, unpopular position of opposing the war on the political fringes, now at a stroke British communists were swimming with the mainstream, almost in tune with the Churchillian zeitgeist. In London, the party's Central Committee decreed that the 'imperialist conspiracy against the working class' had now become a 'global crusade against fascism'. Loyal shop stewards were now ordered to ban strikes rather than foment them. In due course, Harry Pollitt would leave the Poplar shipyard where he had been working and resume his position as general secretary of the party – his principled position of 1939 vindicated, the squabbles with Rajani Palme Dutt forgotten, if not wholly forgiven. The Communist Party, once again, had the benefit of a clear, concise, defensible line: that of waging war 'side by side with the Soviet Union' against fascism.[111] The embarrassing ideological gymnastics of the previous two years now over, the party's membership would soon rise to record levels.

The Americans were a little harder to bring on-board. President Roosevelt had long wrestled with America's isolationist instincts, seeking to balance his own domestic approval ratings with his personal conviction of the necessity of involvement in the war against Hitler. Consequently, though he had promised American mothers in October 1940 that 'your boys are not going to be sent into any foreign wars', he was nonetheless persistently nudging American opinion towards outright intervention. By the summer of 1941, he had made considerable strides: Lend-Lease had been signed into law in March of that year, making the US the self-proclaimed 'arsenal of democracy', and the following month American forces had occupied Greenland to protect Atlantic sea lanes. In June, German consular officials in the US had been expelled en masse on charges of espionage.

But whereas the German attack on the Soviet Union ushered in a moment of clarity in London, it did nothing of the sort in Washington, loosing instead a storm of controversy and infighting. While the interventionists around Roosevelt saw it as an opportunity to decisively get behind Churchill against Hitler, others were vehemently opposed to the implication that that meant supporting Stalin. Future president Harry Truman, for instance – then a senator for Missouri – voiced the somewhat Machiavellian suggestion that 'If we see that Germany is winning we ought to help Russia, and if Russia is winning, we ought to help Germany, and that way let them kill as many as possible.'[112] Despite Churchill's high-flown rhetoric, Roosevelt's urgings and the unspeakable slaughter of the new eastern front, Americans did not yet see the Second World War as their fight. It would take the surprise Japanese attack on Pearl Harbor in December 1941 to fully free them from their isolationist scruples.

On 5 July 1941, an unusually strained meeting was held in the British Foreign Office in Whitehall. Arrangements had been so sensitive that intermediaries had been used and a neutral venue had been found. It was even claimed that one of those attending had let it be known that he would be arriving precisely three minutes later than his negotiating partner, so as to clearly demonstrate the difference in their ranks.[113] It was not merely a clash of egos, or the raking over of historic injustices that caused the tension – though both undoubtedly played a part – rather it was the fact that the government of one of those present had recently sought to erase the other's country from the map. But with the sea change occasioned by Operation Barbarossa, the Soviet Union and the Polish exile government were now tasked with restoring something like diplomatic relations.

For its part, the Soviet Union was facing the worst crisis in its history. Hitler's forces had swept all before them that summer, so much so that the USSR itself appeared to be heading for collapse. By the first week of July, when the diplomats sat down together in the comparative comfort of London, most of the western Soviet Union was already in flames. The losses suffered by Stalin's Red Army in the opening two weeks or so of the war were staggering: over 10,000 tanks, 19,000 guns, 4,000 combat aircraft and fully 750,000 soldiers. In addition, almost all of the lands gained in concert with the Germans had already been lost – eastern Poland, Latvia, Lithuania and Bessarabia – with only Estonia still in Red Army hands. More seriously yet, Byelorussia had been occupied, along with much of Ukraine, and the invaders had already advanced 600 km along the 'Road to Moscow'.[114] Those in London would have been forgiven for wondering if the USSR would still exist by the time the negotiations were completed.

Poland's future was also in doubt. Now wholly occupied by the Germans – its government in exile in Britain – it endured a shadowy existence which, were it not for the collective memory of 123 years of foreign occupation prior to 1918, might have been considered terminal. Of course, the outbreak of war between the two powers that had invaded and divided the country in 1939 was to be welcomed, as it held at least the possibility that Poland's suffering might be brought to an end. But Poland's predicament was rather more complex than that. Unlike the British, the Poles had considered themselves to be at war with *both* Hitler's Germany and Stalin's Soviet Union prior to June 1941, and the prospect of now finding an accommodation with the latter was one that few relished. Moreover, Poland itself was not 'at one remove' from the fighting. The Soviet and German occupations had already unleashed unprecedented brutality on their helpless populations, and Polish politicians and military leaders in exile in Britain were acutely aware that the new phase of the conflict had recently raged over the former Polish eastern territories; lands that – for many of them – were very familiar indeed. Far from edging towards its end, therefore, Poland's Calvary just seemed to have entered a new chapter.

So, when the Soviet ambassador to London, Ivan Maisky, sat down in Whitehall to meet the Polish premier, General Władysław Sikorski, the tension was palpable. The plump, avuncular Maisky and the stern, vain Sikorski were in some sense polar opposites. In his later memoir, Maisky was much amused to relate the story of how Sikorski had arrived preceded by an entourage of adjutants, who had swept through the building 'pushing aside those whom they met' and shouting 'The General is coming! The General is coming!' Upon entering the room, Maisky wrote, Sikorski – in full dress uniform – had glanced towards him and 'a slight grimace of surprise, almost of indignation, passed over his face'. He told himself that the general's reaction was due to the 'light-heartedness' of his summer suit, but Sikorski's look of contempt was almost certainly not sartorial in origin.[115]

That chilly disdain rather set the tone for the negotiations that would follow. Sikorski had believed that, given the Soviet Union's new predicament, Poland was entitled to expect that Stalin would cancel the Nazi–Soviet Pact.[116] Indeed, he had been aggrieved that Churchill had not demanded some sort of quid pro quo along these lines, before pledging British assistance to Moscow two weeks earlier. In the circumstances, Sikorski saw that it fell to him to try not only to undo the profound harm that nearly two years of Soviet occupation, persecution and deportation had wrought on his people, but also to secure some guarantee of Poland's future existence. These principles, then, formed the essence of his opening demands to Maisky: the Soviet Union was to formally renounce the Nazi–Soviet Pact and was to free all Polish military and civilian prisoners still held in Soviet jails and the Gulag. In return, normal diplomatic relations would be restored between the two and he would authorise that a Polish army could even be formed from the 300,000 soldiers still thought to be in Soviet hands.[117]

Inevitably, the talks were rather fraught. Sikorski was not above airing a few grievances. 'You hate the Germans as much as we', he said to Maisky during their first meeting, 'you ought never to have made agreement with them in 1939.' In reply, Maisky could only laugh nervously and counter: 'All that is past history.'[118] The negotiators were certainly not helped by the logistics required by holding their discussions in London; Maisky needed to refer back to Stalin regularly and that could require a few days for messages to be passed both ways. Sikorski, too, was obliged to report back to his cabinet, which could be an uncomfortable experience. Consequently, the two of them would hold only two meetings in London in July, thereafter using Anthony Eden as an intermediary, and so were still little closer to agreement when Sir Stafford Cripps and Molotov signed the Anglo-Soviet Agreement – pledging mutual assistance in the war against Hitler – on 12 July in Moscow.

The primary sticking point in London was Poland's frontiers. The two sides, naturally, had rival conceptions of what Poland's – at that point rather theoretical – geographical extent should be. Sikorski suggested that, given the demise of the Nazi–Soviet Pact, the Polish eastern border should revert to that of August 1939. Maisky, meanwhile, was instructed by Moscow to view Poland within what he called her 'ethnographical' limits, which very broadly approximated to the border later agreed by Molotov and Ribbentrop. Though both parties would eventually agree a compromise position – effectively postponing any decision on frontiers to an unspecified later date – the issue would overshadow further talks, becoming a touchstone of Poland's understandably limited trust in its new Soviet partner.

The second obstacle was the issue of the many Poles – civilian and military – still detained in the Soviet Union. Sikorski demanded the release of all Polish prisoners of war and deportees in the USSR as an essential condition of any agreement. But this put Maisky in a difficult position, because to free such prisoners would not only imply that their arrest and deportation had not been legal, but also cast the Soviet occupation of eastern Poland in a very dubious light. He therefore countered that he saw no reason why a Pole convicted of a crime by the Soviets should now have his conviction quashed. To which Sikorski tersely retorted that Poles were regarded as criminals by the Soviets simply for being Polish citizens, and added that for him not to demand their release would be tantamount to accepting that Moscow had a right to judge them. Realising the seriousness of the impasse, Eden, who chaired the meeting, sought to postpone any decision until the broader diplomatic framework had been agreed – as had been done with the issue of frontiers – but neither side was willing to give.[119]

At this point, the talks were close to collapse. Sikorski was faced with a revolt from within his own cabinet, on 25 July, when three ministers resigned in protest at their premier's handling of the negotiations.[120] The British, meanwhile, were eager for agreement, and were desperately trying to reassure both sides while seeking to delay the discussion of all contentious issues until some future undefined date. The British government, as Churchill would later recall, was on the horns of a dilemma. Having gone to war in defence of Poland, he wrote, 'we had a strong obligation to support the interests of our first ally . . . [and] could not admit the legality of the Russian occupation of Polish territory in 1939'. However, in the maelstrom of summer 1941 'we could not force our new and sorely threatened ally [the USSR] to abandon, even on paper, regions on her frontiers which she had regarded for generations as vital to her security. There was no way out.' In consequence, he lamented, 'we had the invidious responsibility of recommending that General Sikorski rely on Soviet good faith in the future settlement of Russian–Polish relations'.[121] As Churchill well knew, the problem for the Poles was that the phrase 'Soviet good faith' was not one that they recognised.

The breakthrough came on 27 July. In his memoir, Maisky predictably praised the 'insistence and flexibility of the Soviet government' in bringing the 'long arguments and acute polemics' to a successful conclusion.[122] Eden credited Sikorski's statesmanship, while acknowledging Britain's role as one of 'patient diplomacy tinged with anxiety for what the future must hold for the Poles'.[123] Cripps, meanwhile, congratulated himself for his extended negotiations with Stalin in Moscow and, crucially, for 'persuading him to grant an immediate amnesty to every Polish citizen detained in this country'.[124] The idea of an amnesty was controversial – and has even been considered an error – but it neatly sidestepped the divisive issue of the legality of the Soviet occupation, allowing the prisoners to be released while the Soviets saved face. It certainly broke the deadlock, but it has rankled with many Poles ever since. How could those many thousands of Poles be 'amnestied', they would ask, when they had committed no crime?

So it was that agreement was finally reached. Crucially, the Soviet Union recognised that the Soviet–German treaties of 1939 had 'lost their validity' regarding territorial changes in Poland. This was not quite the 'null and void' renunciation that Sikorski had wanted, but it was close. In addition, diplomatic relations between the two powers were to be restored and ambassadors exchanged; and a Polish army would be formed on Soviet soil, under a commander appointed by the Polish government in accord with Moscow. As was the fashion, the agreement was appended by two protocols: one public, stating that an amnesty would be granted to all Polish citizens still detained in the USSR once diplomatic relations were restored; and one secret, declaring that all public and private claims to compensation would be postponed until subsequent negotiations.[125]

In essence, the Polish–Soviet Agreement was a classic diplomatic fudge. Like the Nazi–Soviet Pact – whose formal demise it signified – it was an exercise in realpolitik: a strategic necessity, an uneasy marriage of convenience between two parties with a history of conflict, in which most of the contentious points were put off until a later date. The British secured the alliance that they had wanted between their newest ally and the country for which they had gone to war; the Americans had an agreement that they could sell to a domestic electorate that was rightly wary of Soviet intentions; and Stalin had – to some extent at least – re-established his bona fides before the western world, albeit while making few genuine concessions. For Sikorski and Poland, meanwhile, it was probably the best that could realistically have been achieved at the time, even though it left them – as Churchill had feared – almost entirely dependent on Stalin's goodwill.

The Polish–Soviet Agreement was signed, in the Secretary of State's room at the Foreign Office in London, on 30 July 1941. Sikorski and Maisky sat at opposite ends of a long table that was covered with paperwork, blotters and inkwells, Sikorski erect in full dress uniform, Maisky – this time – in a dark pinstripe suit. Eden and Churchill were seated on one side, the latter grinning broadly and treating himself to his trademark Romeo y Julieta cigar. On the other side of the table were photographers and gentlemen of the press, invited to record the event for posterity and for the purposes of Allied propaganda. Surveying the scene was a white marble bust of an earlier British prime minister, William Pitt the Younger, who – according to Churchill's private secretary, Jock Colville – 'looked down rather disapprovingly'.[126]

EPILOGUE

Life After Death

The Nazi–Soviet Pact was clearly an embarrassment for both its signatories, and they subsequently sought to explain it away as best they
could. On 3 October 1941, in Berlin, Hitler gave his verdict. With his
armies embarking on the final push for Moscow, and the Red
Army apparently smashed, he was already envisaging victory over
Stalin and referring to Russia as 'our India'.[1] That evening, in the
cavernous Sportpalast, speaking without notes, he addressed
the assembled masses in a speech broadcast live by radio. 'On 22 June',
he proclaimed, 'the greatest battle in the history of the world started
. . . Everything since then has proceeded according to plan.' German
troops, he said, were

> 1,000 kilometres beyond our frontier. We are east of Smolensk, we are
> before Leningrad and are on the Black Sea. We are before Crimea and
> the Russians are not on the Rhine . . . The number of prisoners has
> now risen to roughly 2,500,000 Russians. The number of captured or
> destroyed guns in our hands is, in round figures, 22,000. The number
> of captured or destroyed tanks in our hands amounts to over 18,000.
> The number of destroyed and shot-down planes is over 14,500. Behind
> our front line is a Russian area twice as large as the German Reich . . .
> four times as large as England.

'The enemy is already broken', he assured his audience, 'and will never
rise again.'

In the circumstances, this was a good time to reflect on the decision
to make a pact with Stalin. It had been difficult, Hitler acknowledged,
'the most bitter triumph over my feelings'. But, he had been betrayed:

You yourselves know best how honestly we observed our obligations. Neither in our press nor at our meetings was a single word about Russia mentioned. Not a single word about Bolshevism. Unfortunately, the other side did not observe their obligations from the beginning. This arrangement resulted in a betrayal which at first liquidated the whole northeast of Europe. You know best what it meant for us to look on in silence as the Finnish people were being strangled, what it meant to us that the Baltic States were also being overpowered.[2]

In private, Hitler was rather more forthright. In a letter to Mussolini on the eve of Barbarossa he gave the strategic rationale behind the coming attack and explained why he was bringing the 'hypocritical performance' with the Kremlin to an end. 'The partnership with the Soviet Union . . . was often very irksome to me', he wrote, 'for in some way or other it seemed to me to be a break with my whole origin, my concepts, and my former obligations. I am happy now to be relieved of these mental agonies.'[3] For Hitler, therefore, the Nazi–Soviet Pact had been an ugly strategic necessity, forced upon him by the West's plans to encircle Germany. Stalin's subsequent betrayal, he claimed, had made its demise inevitable.

The Soviet interpretation was naturally rather different. As we have seen, when he addressed the Soviet people soon after the German invasion, Stalin had stood by the pact, stating that it had not been an error and that the Soviet government could not have declined Hitler's proposal. What was more, he claimed that the USSR had thereby secured eighteen months of peace in which it had had 'the opportunity' to rearm. This rationale, thrown in by Stalin in 1941 almost as an afterthought, quickly became the dominant Soviet explanation.

In the months and years that followed, the pact faded from view, obscured by the more pressing daily concerns of waging the most costly and deadly conflict the world had ever known. Only when the war was over did it come under scrutiny once again. At the Nuremberg International Military Tribunal (IMT), which opened late in 1945 to try the surviving Nazi leaders, the pact and its consequences were also examined. The prosecutors at Nuremberg knew very well that part of the defendants' case would rest on the appeal of *tu quoque* – 'you did it too'. It was an inadmissible defence – arguably more suited to the playground than a court of law – but it nonetheless had the potential to damage the Soviets, whose territorial expansions of 1939–40, under the auspices of the pact, had violated many of the principles that the Western Allies were now seeking to apply to German actions. As one British foreign office advisor predicted, it was inevitable that the Nazi defendants would seek to 'bring out as much Russian dirty linen as they can to mix with their own'.[4] Consequently, given that the Allied prosecutors had no wish to discredit their Soviet ally, the item at the very top of that 'laundry list' – the Nazi–Soviet Pact – was scarcely mentioned in the tribunal's opening statements.

Thereafter, the Soviet legal team fought a desperate action to prevent the pact – and particularly the damning 'secret protocol' – from emerging as evidence. Typical in this regard was an exchange on 21 May 1946, when the defence counsel for Rudolf Hess tried to raise the protocol, but was met with protests by the Soviet chief prosecutor, General Roman Rudenko, who howled that 'we are examining the matter of the crimes of the major German war criminals. We are not investigating the foreign policies of other states.' In any case, Rudenko went on, the protocol was 'a forged document', which was of no value whatsoever.[5] The issue of the pact itself was marginally less sensitive for Moscow. Derided by the Soviet judge Iona Nikitchenko as 'irrelevant' and 'nothing but propaganda', it upset the Soviet team at Nuremberg most when it was suggested, however obliquely, that in signing the pact Stalin might have been fooled or misled by German cunning. In contrast, they argued, the USSR had been fully aware of Germany's nefarious intentions from the very beginning. Clearly, Stalin preferred the charge of cynicism to that of gullibility.[6]

Such chutzpah was only trumped when Soviet prosecutors insisted on having the Katyn massacres added to the Nazi indictment, claiming that the killings were 'one of the most important criminal acts for which the major war criminals are responsible'. Already adept at staging 'show trials' of their political enemies, they demanded that the Soviet investigation into the case should be accepted by the tribunal without demur, and duly produced a Bulgarian pathologist who claimed that the forensic evidence pointed to autumn 1941 as the date of the massacres – i.e. when the region was under German control. To their credit, the British and American judges dismissed the charge, as the Soviets were unable convincingly to attribute the crime to any of the defendants in the dock.[7]

After the pact's brief and rather inconsequential outing at Nuremberg, Stalin's propagandists and prosecutors might have congratulated themselves on a successful exercise in damage limitation. However, the American publication in 1948 of a volume entitled *Nazi–Soviet Relations 1939 –1941* would have shaken their complacency. The book, published by the US State Department, contained transcripts of hundreds of documents seized from German sources at the end of the war, including correspondence, discussions and negotiations as well as the text of the commercial agreements, of the pact itself and the secret protocol. For the first time, it brought the relationship between Moscow and Berlin out of the shadows and into the glare of public scrutiny.[8]

The Soviet response was swift. Later that year, the pamphlet *Falsifiers of History* appeared giving Moscow's case. Personally edited and given its provocative title by Stalin, it had grown out of a series of articles that had appeared in *Pravda*, and was subsequently translated and distributed across the world. It was remarkable because it was the first time that the subject of the pact with Germany had been officially addressed in the Soviet Union since 1941. It was certainly strident stuff. With tempers piqued by the ongoing tensions of the nascent Cold War, *Falsifiers of History* carried the ideological fight to the Soviet Union's enemies, attacking the West for its own complicity in failing to stop German aggression prior to 1939, criticising the Americans for presenting 'a distorted picture of events . . . to slander the Soviet Union' and even denouncing the hapless Finns for being 'in league with the Hitlerites' in the Winter War of 1940.[9] It also provided Stalin's post facto justification for signing the pact. It was all down to western perfidy: to the desire harboured in Paris and London to appease Hitler and turn him eastwards, and the wish of the 'billionaires' of Washington to profit from the ensuing conflagration.[10] 'In August 1939', it stated, 'the Soviet Union did not doubt for a moment that sooner or later Hitler would attack it.' It went on:

> That was why the first task of the Soviet Government was to create an 'Eastern' front against Hitler's aggression, to build up a defence line along the western frontiers of the Byelorussian and Ukrainian Republics and thus set up a barrier to prevent an unhindered advance of the German troops eastward.

This task, the pamphlet explained, necessitated the move of Soviet troops into eastern Poland and the signature of 'pacts of mutual assistance' with the Baltic states: 'Thus the foundation was laid for the Eastern Front.'[11] Clearly, the message Moscow wanted the world to hear was that Stalin's motives in signing the pact with Hitler had been purely defensive.

With that, Moscow's line on the Nazi–Soviet Pact was fixed, but it was still a subject that no Soviet historian dared touch. By the 1960s, however, that had begun to change. Stung by what it viewed as further 'falsifications' emerging from the West, Moscow embarked on a propaganda campaign to wrest the memory of the Second World War away from its ideological enemies – a campaign which one prominent commentator described as 'one of the most audacious enterprises of the Soviet propaganda machine to smother reality'.[12] Remarkably, this effort even extended to a discussion of the Nazi–Soviet Pact, which until that point had been a taboo subject. In the new Soviet histories published in the 1960s, therefore, the pact received a few pages of analysis, albeit with the expected omissions, evasions and justifications. It would be argued, for instance, that Stalin had accepted Hitler's offer solely as a last resort – that otherwise war with Germany would have been inevitable – and that acceptance of the pact brought the USSR numerous advantages.[13]

It was an analysis that even Khrushchev, whose denunciation of Stalin in 1956 had echoed around the world, would loyally parrot. Writing his reminiscences decades after the war, he was still firmly on message: 'We weren't fooling ourselves. We knew that eventually we would be drawn into the war, although I suppose Stalin hoped that the English and French might exhaust Hitler . . . first.' The pact, he wrote, was 'profitable to the Soviet Union. It was like a gambit in chess: if we hadn't made that move, the war would have started earlier, much to our disadvantage. As it was we were given a respite.'[14]

Ever the loyal Bolshevik, Molotov concurred. Speaking some years later he first denied the suggestion that Stalin had trusted Hitler: 'Such a naïve Stalin? No. Stalin saw through it all. Stalin trusted Hitler? He didn't trust his own people! Hitler fooled Stalin? And as a result of that deception Hitler had to poison himself, and Stalin became the head of half the world!' Explaining the pact, he went on, 'We had to delay Germany's aggression, that's why we tried to deal with them on an economic level – export-import.' Stalin, he said, 'wanted to delay the war for at least another half a year, or longer'.[15]

The Soviet Union thus forged its post-war interpretation of the Nazi–Soviet Pact: it was an agreement that had been forced on Stalin by circumstances. Importantly, however, the Soviet leader had not been taken in by Hitler's blandishments and had managed thereby to delay the inevitable Nazi attack, thus saving the USSR from an even worse fate. Naturally, the fate of the millions persecuted, killed and deported by the Soviets from former eastern Poland, the Baltic states and Bessarabia was not permitted to disrupt the rosy narrative. Those territories had been regained by Red Army troops in 1944–5 and were now safely restored to the Soviet bosom, despite the efforts of the few 'nationalists' and 'terrorists' who had briefly disturbed the Pax Sovietica in the first post-war decade. The region's historians and journalists were similarly circumscribed. The pact was a taboo subject, passed over in silence, hidden from view, with even the most minimal mention forbidden to deviate from the strict line dictated from Moscow.

The ultimate taboo, however, was the secret protocol. Though the original document had presumably been destroyed in wartime Berlin, a microfilm copy had been made and had found its way into American hands at the end of the war, after which it was mentioned obliquely at Nuremberg and then published for the first time in 1948. Yet given the lack of an original – and the protocol's embarrassing content – its existence was officially denied by the Soviet Union and the copy that circulated in the West was duly denounced as a forgery, a slander of the Soviet Union and yet another 'falsification of history'.

So when Vyacheslav Molotov was asked in 1983 about a 'secret agreement' signed in 1939 with the Germans, he was adamant that there was no truth in the allegation. 'None whatever', he said. 'There wasn't one?' the journalist repeated. 'There wasn't. No, that's absurd.' The journalist pressed a little more: 'Surely we can talk about it now?' Molotov replied:

> Of course, there is no secret here. In my view these rumours were deliberately spread to damage reputations. No, no, this matter is very clean. There could not have been any such secret agreement. I was very close to this matter, in fact I was involved in it, and I can assure you that this is unquestionably a fabrication.[16]

Molotov certainly had been 'close to' the secret protocol; in fact, he had signed it. Yet he went to his grave in 1986 denying its existence.

Not everyone in the USSR would be so loyal to Stalin's line. Three years after Molotov's death, in 1989, a summer of protests in Moscow's Baltic republics would see a quite different narrative emerging. Taking the spirit of Gorbachev's glasnost and perestroika policies at face value, many among the Baltic peoples had by that time begun to openly rail against Soviet rule. Spurred by exiles and sympathisers who had already named 23 August as 'Black Ribbon Day' and had held rallies in New York, London and elsewhere in protest at human-rights abuses in the Soviet Union, Baltic activists had gathered signatures and made earnest pleas for international recognition of their plight. But, for the fiftieth anniversary of the signature of the Nazi–Soviet Pact, on 23 August 1989, they planned a protest on an unprecedented scale.

On that day, a human chain comprising as many as 2 million people snaked down main roads and byways through the three Baltic republics, linking the three capitals of Tallinn, Riga and Vilnius, a distance of over 500 kilometres. At 7 p.m. they all linked hands, in what would be known as 'the Baltic Way'. It was the largest popular protest that the Soviet Union had ever witnessed. Elsewhere vigils were held, as well as church services and local gatherings. In the centre of Vilnius, 5,000 came together to sing patriotic songs and light candles. Pre-war national flags were flown and black ribbons worn in memory of those who had been victims of Stalin.[17]

For all of them across the three republics, the protest was about human rights, Soviet occupation and the desire for national independence. But the focal point of their grievances was very clearly the Nazi–Soviet Pact. At Šiauliai in Lithuania, for instance, a public demonstration showed three coffins draped in the flags of the pre-war republics, while beside them the swastika and the hammer and sickle were crossed, tied together with a black ribbon. In Estonia and Latvia, meanwhile, banners proclaimed the illegality of the Soviet occupation, or simply carried the date '23 August 1939'. In a communiqué sent to the UN, the central significance of the pact was made clear. With the signature of the Nazi–Soviet Pact, many wounds were inflicted, it stated, and 'some of those wounds are still bleeding'. 'The criminal pact', it went on,

has to be voided! The essence of the Hitler–Stalin Pact and its secret protocols was imperialist division of the spheres of interest between two

great powers. On the basis of this criminal deal, the Soviet Union unilaterally violated all the international treaties concluded with the Baltic
republics, infringed on the historical right of the Baltic nations to self-
determination, presented ruthless ultimatums to the Baltic republics,
occupied them with overwhelming military force, and under conditions
of military occupation and heavy political terror carried out their violent
annexation . . . The Hitler–Stalin Pact is still shaping the Europe of today.

In the aftermath, the Soviet authorities made a few token arrests,
complained about the 'nationalist, extremist groups' and their 'anti-
Soviet agendas', and rebuked the local authorities for failing to take
action to break up the protests.[18] Beyond a few well-intentioned
international comments, little changed, but the Baltic peoples were
emboldened, encouraged to push again for independence.

Aside from the obvious political challenge that the Baltic Way
posed, it was also an intellectual one. After decades of exercising a
total control over information within the USSR, the realities of
Gorbachev's new era meant that the Soviet view no longer went
unchallenged in the realm of ideas. The same was true of history,
where Stalin's traditional 'defensive' narrative of the Nazi–Soviet Pact
was increasingly being brought into question. Forced by events into
a more honest reassessment of its own past, Moscow established an
official commission to investigate the circumstances of the Nazi–
Soviet Pact, and in particular the question of the existence of the
secret protocol.[19] In December 1989, the commission duly reported
in the affirmative declaring that there 'could not be the slightest
doubt' that the protocol existed.[20] The Congress of the People's
Deputies of the Soviet Union[21] then passed a resolution in support
of its findings.

Other revelations followed. In the spring of 1990, after decades of
official denial, the Soviet state finally acknowledged the responsibility
of its secret police forces in carrying out the Katyn massacres, adding
a rather hollow-sounding expression of its 'profound regret'.[22] The
Soviet monolith was cracking. And, just as Soviet control over eastern
Europe had collapsed with spectacular suddenness that very winter,
so it would begin to unravel at home as well. When it did in 1991, it
would be the Baltic states that were the first to head for the exit,
spurred in large measure by the injustices of five decades earlier.[23]

Rarely, it seemed, had high politics and dark history been so closely entwined.

In early April 2009, the European Parliament in Brussels considered a resolution proposing that 23 August was henceforth to be recognised as the European Day of Remembrance for the Victims of Stalinism and Nazism. Drawing on the earlier Prague Declaration, tabled by the Czech government and co-signed among others by the former Czech president Václav Havel and the later German president Joachim Gauck, the resolution vowed 'to preserve the memory of the victims of mass deportations and exterminations'. It was passed by a large majority. 'Better late than never', said one Estonian MEP during the debate, adding: 'We owe our parents and grandparents a firm parliamentary message, and that is what we have produced today.'[24]

Of course there were dissenting voices. Thirty-three members of the European Parliament abstained in the vote and forty-four voted against the resolution. One of the latter was a Greek communist who waxed indignant, in an impassioned written submission, against the 'indescribably vulgar' juxtaposition of the Nazi and Soviet regimes, which thereby advocated 'acquitting fascism, slandering socialism and exonerating imperialism of the crimes which it committed and is committing today'.[25] A few others concurred. One British journalist, for instance, criticised the vote as 'an unpleasant effort by many Baltic and central European politicians to equate Stalinism and Nazism',[26] ignoring the glaringly obvious point that those who had experienced both horrors were perhaps best-placed to make the judgement.

Russia, too, cried foul, with 53 per cent opposing the resolution in one opinion poll and only 11 per cent in favour. According to another survey, Russian popular opinion considered that the European Parliament's decision had been adopted to 'undermine Russia's authority' and to 'diminish its contribution to the victory over fascism'.[27] A few weeks later, the then Russian President, Dmitry Medvedev, established a 'Presidential Commission to Counter Attempts to Falsify History', along with accompanying legislation that enabled transgressors to be fined or imprisoned for up to five years. The new body, one of its members vowed, would 'ensure the Russian view prevails'.[28] Any worrying sense of déjà vu was only heightened by the

presence on the commission of prominent members of the Russian
military and the FSB, the successor to the Soviet-era KGB.

Nonetheless, on 23 August that summer – the seventieth anniversary
of the Nazi–Soviet Pact – the first European Day of Remembrance
for Victims of Stalinism and Nazism was solemnly marked in the
Baltic states and in Sweden. In subsequent years, the commemorations
would spread. Wreathes would be laid, flags would be raised and
prayers would be offered across central and eastern Europe, from
Poland to Crimea, and from Estonia to Bulgaria. It was a small victory,
perhaps, but a significant one. The Nazi–Soviet Pact had come out of
the shadows. It was no longer forgotten; no longer taboo. It was an
essential part of the narrative

APPENDIX

Text of the Nazi–Soviet Non-Aggression Pact

The Government of the German Reich and the Government of the Union of Soviet Socialist Republics desirous of strengthening the cause of peace between Germany and the USSR, and proceeding from the fundamental provisions of the Neutrality Agreement concluded in April 1926 between Germany and the USSR, have reached the following Agreement:

Article I. Both High Contracting Parties obligate themselves to desist from any act of violence, any aggressive action, and any attack on each other, either individually or jointly with other Powers.

Article II. Should one of the High Contracting Parties become the object of belligerent action by a third Power, the other High Contracting Party shall in no manner lend its support to this third Power.

Article III. The Governments of the two High Contracting Parties shall in the future maintain continual contact with one another for the purpose of consultation in order to exchange information on problems affecting their common interests.

Article IV. Neither of the two High Contracting Parties shall participate in any grouping of Powers whatsoever that is directly or indirectly aimed at the other party.

Article V. Should disputes or conflicts aries between the High Contracting Parties over problems of one kind or another, both parties shall settle these disputes or conflicts exclusively through friendly exchange of opinion or, if necessary, through the establishment of arbitration commissions.

Article VI. The present Treaty is concluded for a period of ten years, with the proviso that, in so far as one of the High Contracting Parties does not advance it one year prior to the expiration of this period, the validity of this Treaty shall automatically be extended for another five years.

Article VII. The present treaty shall be ratified within the shortest possible time. The ratifications shall be exchanged in Berlin. The Agreement shall enter into force as soon as it is signed.

Done in duplicate, in the German and Russian languages.

MOSCOW, 23 August 1939

For the Government of the German Reich:
v. Ribbentrop

Plenipotentiary of the Government of the USSR:
V. Molotov

Secret Additional Protocol

Article I. In the event of a territorial and political rearrangement in the areas belonging to the Baltic States (Finland, Estonia, Latvia, Lithuania), the northern boundary of Lithuania shall represent the boundary of the spheres of influence of Germany and USSR. In this connection the interest of Lithuania in the Vilna area is recognized by each party.

Article II. In the event of a territorial and political rearrangement of the areas belonging to the Polish state, the spheres of influence of Germany and the USSR shall be bounded approximately by the line of the rivers Narew, Vistula and San.

The question of whether the interests of both parties make desirable the maintenance of an independent Polish State and how such a state should be bounded can only be definitely determined in the course of further political developments.

In any event both Governments will resolve this question by means of a friendly agreement.

Article III. With regard to Southeastern Europe attention is called by the Soviet side to its interest in Bessarabia. The German side declares its complete political disinterest in these areas.

Article IV. This protocol shall be treated by both parties as strictly secret.

Moscow, 23 August 1939.

For the Government of the German Reich:
v. Ribbentrop

Plenipotentiary of the Government of the USSR:
V. Molotov

Notes

Prologue: A Meeting on the Boundary of Peace   *pp 5-12*

1   Vasily Laskovich, quoted in Yuri Rubashevsky, 'Radost byla vseobshaya i triumfalnaya' in *Vercherniy Brest*, 16 September 2011, archived at http://www.vb.by/article.php?topic=36&article=14200.
2   Bronisława Predenia, quoted in Tadeusz Czernik, at http://tadeuszczernik.wordpress.com/2011/07/26/wspomnienia-z-ziemi-brzeskiej-bronislawa-predenia/.
3   Quoted in Vasily Sarychev, 'v poiskach utrachennogo vremeni' in *Vercherniy Brest*, archived at http://www.vb.by/sarychev/content/75/main.php.
4   Heinz Guderian, *Panzer Leader* (London, 1952), p. 81.
5   'Kriegstagebuch des Generalkommandos XIX AK über den Feldzug in Polen' in United States National Archives and Record Administration, Microfilm Series T-314, roll #611, frame numbers 665–93, p. 126 (hereafter 'XIX Corps War Diary').
6   Georg Schmidt-Scheeder, *Reporter der Hölle* (Stuttgart, 1977), p. 95.
7   XIX Corps War Diary, op. cit., pp. 168–9.
8   Romuald Bulas, quoted in Sarychev, op. cit.
9   XIX Corps War Diary, op. cit., p. 179.
10 Guderian, op. cit., pp. 81–3.
11 Janusz Magnuski & Maksym Kolomijec, *Czerwony Blitzkrieg. Wrzesien 1939: Sowieckie Wojska Pancerne w Polsce* (Warsaw, 1994), p. 72.
12 Quoted in Sarychev, op. cit.
13 German eyewitness account from a 1939 postcard, reproduced at http://riowang.blogspot.com/2009/09/brest-nazi-soviet-military-parade-23_25.html.
14 Quoted in Sarychev, op. cit.
15 Quoted in ibid.
16 Quoted in ibid.

17   Quoted in ibid.
18   Quoted in ibid.
19   Quoted in ibid.
20   Semyon Krivoshein, *Mezhdubure* (Voronezh, 1964), p. 261.
21   Quoted in Sarychev, op. cit.
22   Krivoshein, op. cit., p. 261.
23   Ibid., pp. 260–1.
24   Schmidt-Scheeder, op. cit., p. 101.
25   See, for instance, *Deutsche Allgemeine Zeitung*, 25 September 1939, p. 4.
26   See the German newsreel transmission of 27 September 1939, at http://www.youtube.com/watch?v=uDIqzJgZNHM.
27   Frowein article quoted in Fundacja Ośrodka KARTA, *September 1939* (Warsaw, 2009), p. 44.

1 *The Devil's Potion*

1   Paul Schmidt, *Statist auf diplomatischer Bühne* (Wiesbaden, 1984), p. 441.
2   Heinrich Hoffmann, *Hitler was my Friend* (Barnsley, 2011), p. 105.
3   Peter Kleist, *Zwischen Hitler und Stalin, 1939–1945* (Bonn, 1950), p. 55.
4   Hoffmann, op. cit., p. 105.
5   Anthony Read & David Fisher, *The Deadly Embrace* (London, 1988), p. 248.
6   Johnnie von Herwarth, *Against Two Evils* (London, 1981), p. 165.
7   Schmidt, op. cit., p. 442.
8   Hans Baur, *Hitler's Pilot* (London, 1958), p. 95.
9   Adolf Hitler, *Mein Kampf* (London, 1939), p. 539.
10   Hitler's speech to the Nuremberg Party Congress, 13 September 1937, quoted in Max Domarus, *Hitler, Speeches and Proclamations, 1932–1945*, Vol. II (London, 1992), pp. 941–2.
11   *Pravda*, 16 September 1937, No.256 (7222), p.1 editorial.
12   *Working Moscow*, 1 December 1936, No.275, reporting a speech by V. M. Molotov, and 2 December 1936, No.276, reporting a speech by N. S. Khrushchev. Herostratus was a character from fourth-century-BC Ephesus who sought fame by burning down a temple.
13   Norman Davies, *White Eagle, Red Star: The Polish–Soviet War, 1919–20* (London, 2003), p. 29.
14   Hitler, op. cit., pp. 533, 536–7.
15   Hoffmann, op. cit., p. 107.
16   Schmidt, op. cit., p. 443.
17   Baur, op. cit., pp. 97–8.
18   Ibid., pp. 98–9.

19 Hoffmann, op. cit., p. 105.

20 Baur, op. cit., pp. 95–6.

21 Kleist, op. cit., p. 56.

22 Gustav Hilger & Alfred G. Meyer, *The Incompatible Allies* (New York, 1953), p. 309.

23 Joachim von Ribbentrop, quoted in Rudolf von Ribbentrop, *Mein Vater: Joachim von Ribbentrop, Erlebnisse und Erinnerungen* (Graz, 2013), pp. 225, 228.

24 This is the inference drawn by Gustav Hilger, in Hilger & Meyer, op. cit., p. 301.

25 Ibid.

26 *Documents on German Foreign Policy 1918–1945* (hereafter '*DGFP*'), Series D, Vol. VI (London, 1956), No. 73, pp. 85–7.

27 Cited in Ian Kershaw, *Hitler 1936–1945* (London, 2000), p. 164.

28 The text of the British Guarantee is in E. L. Woodward & R. Butler (eds.), *Documents on British Foreign Policy 1919–1939*, Third Series, Vol. IV (London, 1951), p. 552. The best discussion of the subject is G. Bruce Strang, 'Once more unto the Breach: Britain's Guarantee to Poland, March 1939' in *Journal of Contemporary History*, Vol. 31, No. 4 (1996), pp. 721–52.

29 D. C. Watt, *How War Came* (London, 1989), p. 185.

30 Quoted in Hans-Bernd Gisevius, *To the Bitter End* (Boston, 1947), p. 363. Though the English edition of Gisevius translates Hitler's curse as 'a stew that they'll choke on', 'a devil's potion' is closer to the original German, so is retained here.

31 Domarus, op. cit., Vol. III (London, 1997), pp. 1524–34.

32 D. C. Watt, 'The Initiation of the Negotiations Leading to the Nazi–Soviet Pact: A Historical Problem', in C. Abramsky (ed.), *Essays in Honour of E. H. Carr* (London, 1974), pp. 164–5.

33 Alfred Rosenberg's Diary, United States Holocaust Memorial Museum, p. 269. www.ushmm.org.

34 Quoted in Richard Overy, *Interrogations* (London, 2001), p. 320.

35 Adam B. Ulam, *Expansion and Coexistence: Soviet Foreign Policy 1917–73* (New York, 1974), pp. 257–9.

36 Jane Degras (ed.), *Soviet Documents on Foreign Policy*, Vol. III (New York, 1978), p. 318.

37 Ibid., p. 320.

38 Sir Stafford Cripps to the Foreign Office, 16 July 1940, National Archives, London, FO371/24846, f.10 N6526/30/38.

39 Text from Albert Weeks, *Stalin's Other War: Soviet Grand Strategy, 1939–41* (Oxford, 2002), pp. 171–3.

40 See Sergej, Slutsch, 'Stalins "Kriegsszenario 1939": Eine Rede die es nie gab' in *Vierteljahrshefte für Zeitgeschichte*, Vol. 52, No. 4 (2004), pp. 597–635.

41 Quoted in Ivo Banac (ed.), *The Diary of Georgi Dimitrov, 1933–1949* (New Haven, 2003), p. 115.

42 Cited in Richard Raack, *Stalin's Drive to the West, 1938–1945* (Stanford, 1995), p. 24, with the full text of the conversation quoted at http://www.lituanus.org/1965/65_2_02_KreveMickevicius.html.

43 Fridrikh I. Firsov, Harvey Klehr & John Earl Haynes, *Secret Cables of the Comintern, 1933–1943*, (New Haven & London, 2014), p. 248.

44 Felix Chuev & Albert Resis (eds.), *Molotov Remembers: Inside Kremlin Politics* (Chicago, 1993), p. 8.

45 Jeffrey Herf, *The Jewish Enemy: Nazi Propaganda During World War II and the Holocaust* (Harvard, 2006), pp. 97–8.

46 Documents quoted in Albert Resis, 'The Fall of Litvinov: Harbinger of the German–Soviet Non-aggression Pact' in *Europe-Asia Studies*, Vol. 52, No. 1 (2000), pp. 34–5.

47 Z. Sheinis, *Maksim Maksimovich Litvinov: revoliutsioner, diplomat, chelovek* (Moscow, 1989), pp. 363–4, in Aleksandr Nekrich, *Pariahs, Partners, Predators: German–Soviet Relations, 1922–1941* (New York, 1997), p. 109.

48 Simon Sebag Montefiore, *Stalin: The Court of the Red Tsar* (London, 2003), p. 34.

49 Ibid., p. 206.

50 D. C. Watt, quoted in Chuev & Resis (eds.), op. cit., p. xix.

51 Ibid., p. 192.

52 Michael Bloch, *Ribbentrop* (London, 1992), p. 207.

53 *DGFP*, Series D, Vol. VII (London, 1956), No. 180, p. 189, Ribbentrop circular, 22 August 1939.

54 *SSSR-Germania 1939. Dokumenty i materialy o sovetsko-germanskikh otnosheniiakh v aprele-sentiabre 1939 g.* (New York, 1983), p. 23, quoted in Nekrich, op. cit., p. 115.

55 *DGFP*, Series D, Vol. VI, op. cit., No. 56, p. 63.

56 Elke Fröhlich (ed.), *Die Tagebücher von Joseph Goebbels*, Part 1, Vol. 7 (Munich, 1998), p. 75.

57 Quoted in Anthony P. Adamthwaite, *The Making of the Second World War* (London, 1977), p. 220.

58 Cited in Frank McDonough, *Neville Chamberlain, Appeasement and the British Road to War* (Manchester, 2010), p. 174.

59 *British Foreign Policy*, 3rd Series, VI, Appendix V, quoted in A. J. P. Taylor, *English History 1914–1945* (Oxford, 1965), p. 447 fn.

60 Taylor, op. cit., p. 448.

61 On this, see Davies, op. cit.

62 Text of negotiations reproduced in Adamthwaite, op. cit., pp. 218–19.

63 Charles Bohlen, *Witness to History, 1929–1969* (New York, 1973), p. 86.

64 *DGFP*, Series D, Vol. VII, op. cit., No. 56, p. 64. Ribbentrop to Schulenburg, 14 August 1939.

65 *DGFP*, op. cit., No. 62, pp. 68–9. Weizsäcker to Schulenburg, 15 August 1939.

66 Ribbentrop, op. cit., p. 224.

67 *DGFP*, op. cit., No. 88, p. 99. Schulenburg to Weizsäcker, 16 August 1939.

68 Herwarth, op. cit., p. 162.

69 See, for instance, *DGFP*, op. cit., Nos. 125 & 132, pp. 134, 149, 19 and 20 August 1939.

70 Fröhlich (ed.), op. cit., p. 71.

71 Alexander Werth, *Russia at War 1941–1945* (London, 1965), p. 66.

72 *DGFP*, op. cit., No. 142, p. 157. Hitler to Stalin, 20 August 1939.

73 *DGFP*, op. cit., No. 159, p. 168. Schulenburg to Moscow, 21 August 1939.

74 Albert Speer, *Inside the Third Reich* (London, 1970), p. 234.

75 V. N. Pavlov, quoted in Laurence Rees, *World War Two Behind Closed Doors: Stalin, the Nazis and the West* (London, 2008), p. 10.

76 Vladimir Karpov, *Marshal Zhukov: Ego soratniki i protivniki v dni voĭny i mira* (Moscow, 1992), p. 124.

77 Ibid.

78 Ribbentrop, op. cit., p. 228.

79 Nicolaus von Below, *At Hitler's Side: The Memoirs of Hitler's Luftwaffe Adjutant, 1937–1945* (London, 2004), p. 28.

80 Döhring, quoted in Rees, op. cit., p. 17.

81 Herwarth, op. cit., p. 165.

82 Andor Hencke, 'Die deutsch-sowjetischen Beziehungen zwischen 1932 und 1941', unpublished protocol held at the Institut für Zeitgeschichte, Munich, MA 1300/2, p. 11.

83 Quoted in Nekrich, op. cit., p. 121.

84 *DGFP*, op. cit., No. 213, pp. 227–8.

85 Read & Fisher, op. cit., p. 252.

86 *DGFP*, op. cit., Nos. 228–9, pp. 245–7.

87 Derek Watson, *Molotov: A Biography* (Basingstoke, 2005), p. 170.

88 Chuev & Resis (eds.), op. cit., p. 12.

89 Hencke, op. cit., p. 13.

90 Ibid.

91 Hoffmann, op. cit., p. 109.

92 Hencke, op. cit., p. 13.

93 Herwarth, op. cit., p. 165.

2 Bonded in Blood

1 Mihail Sebastian, *Journal 1935–1944* (Chicago, 2000), p. 230.
2 Terry Charman, *Outbreak 1939: The World Goes to War* (London, 2009), pp. 54, 55, 59.
3 Diarist Vivienne Hall, quoted in ibid., p. 56.
4 Quoted in Michael Bloch, *Ribbentrop* (London, 1992), p. 250.
5 Heinrich Hoffmann, *Hitler was my Friend* (Barnsley, 2011), pp. 112–13, and Alan Bullock, *Hitler and Stalin: Parallel Lives* (London, 1991), p. 685.
6 Hoffmann, op. cit., pp. 113–14.
7 Quoted in Hugh Trevor-Roper (ed.), *Hitler's War Directives 1939–1945* (London, 1964), p. 38.
8 Nikita Khrushchev, *Khrushchev Remembers* (London, 1971), p. 111.
9 Quoted in Simon Sebag Montefiore, *Stalin: The Court of the Red Tsar* (London, 2003), p. 276.
10 Adam Ulam, *Expansion and Coexistence: Soviet Foreign Policy 1917–1973* (New York, 1968), p. 279.
11 *Documents on German Foreign Policy 1918–1945* (hereafter 'DGFP'), Series D, Vol. VII (London, 1956), No. 193, p. 205.
12 John Lukas, *Forgotten Holocaust: The Poles under German Occupation, 1939–1944* (Lexington, 1986), p. 3.
13 Christopher Browning, *The Origins of the Final Solution* (London, 2004), p. 29.
14 Lukas, op. cit., p. 3.
15 Jochen Böhler, *Zbrodnie Wehrmachtu w Polsce* (Kraków, 2009), pp. 106–16. Jochen Böhler, *Auftakt zum Vernichtungskrieg: Die Wehrmacht in Polen 1939* (Frankfurt am Main, 2006), p. 106.
16 Szymon Datner, *55 Dni Wehrmachtu w Polsce* (Warsaw 1967), pp. 114–17.
17 See, for instance, Ribbentrop telegram to Schulenburg, 15 September 1939, at http://avalon.law.yale.edu/20th_century/ns072.asp.
18 Steven Zaloga, *Poland 1939* (Oxford, 2002), p. 80.
19 *DGFP*, Series D, Vol. VIII (Washington DC, 1954), No. 63, pp. 60–1.
20 Ibid., No. 80, pp. 79–80.
21 Text in *Sprawa polska w czasie drugiej wojny światowej na arenie międzynaodowej. Zbiór dokumentów* (Warsaw, 1965), pp. 83–4. Translated by Sebastian Palfi.
22 Tomasz Piesakowski, *The Fate of Poles in the USSR 1939–1989* (London, 1990), p. 36.
23 Olaf Groehler, *Selbstmörderische Allianz: Deutsch-russische Militärbeziehungen, 1920–1941* (Berlin, 1992), p. 116.

42-73

24 David G. Williamson, *Poland Betrayed: The Nazi–Soviet Invasions 1939* (Barnsley, 2009), p. 119.

25 Jan Gross, *Revolution from Abroad* (Princeton, 1988), pp. 21–3.

26 Janusz Bardach, *Man is Wolf to Man* (London, 1998), p. 19.

27 Jan Gross, *Neighbours* (Princeton, 2001), p. 43.

28 Adolf Hitler, *Mein Kampf* (London, 1939), p, 539.

29 Groehler, op. cit., p. 136.

30 Williamson, op. cit., p. 123.

31 Piesakowski, op. cit., p. 38. See also case file of the Institute of National Remembrance, Warsaw, available at http://www.ipn.gov.pl.

32 Halik Kochanski, *The Eagle Unbowed: Poland and the Poles in the Second World War* (London, 2012), p. 80.

33 Richard Hargreaves, *Blitzkrieg Unleashed: The German Invasion of Poland 1939* (Barnsley, 2008), pp. 263–4.

34 Groehler, op. cit., p. 121.

35 Gross, *Revolution*, op. cit., p. 10.

36 See Sergej Slutsch, '17. September 1939: Der Eintritt der Sowjetunion in den Zweiten Weltkrieg' in *Vierteljahrshefte für Zeitgeschichte*, 48 (2000), pp. 228–30.

37 F. B. Czarnomski, quoted in Williamson, op. cit., p. 126.

38 Hargreaves, op. cit., p. 201.

39 *Izvestia*, 20 September 1939.

40 Quoted in Slutsch, op. cit., p. 231. Translated by the author.

41 Quoted in Robert Conquest, *Stalin: Breaker of Nations* (London, 1991), p. 224.

42 Gustav Hilger's reminiscences quoted in Ingeborg Fleischhauer, 'Der Deutsch-Sowjetische Grenz-und Freundschaftsvertrag vom 28. September 1939' in *Vierteljahrshefte für Zeitgeschichte*, 39 (1991), p. 458.

43 Kochanski, op. cit., p. 96.

44 Andor Hencke, quoted in Laurence Rees, *World War II Behind Closed Doors* (London, 2009), p. 33.

45 See Browning, op. cit., pp. 31–3.

46 Alexander B. Rossino, *Hitler Strikes Poland: Blitzkrieg, Ideology and Atrocity* (Kansas, 2003), p. 234.

47 On the AB Aktion, see Timothy Snyder, *Bloodlands* (London, 2010), pp. 146–50.

48 Keith Sword, 'The Mass Movement of Poles to the USSR, 1939–41', in Keith Sword, *Deportation and Exile: Poles in the Soviet Union, 1939–48* (Basingstoke, 1994), pp. 6–8.

49 Author interview with Mr Czesław Wojciechowski, London, 8 September 2011.

50 Grzegorz Hryciuk, 'Victims 1939–1941: The Soviet Repressions in Eastern Poland', in Elazar Barkan, Elizabeth A. Cole & Kai Struve (eds.), *Shared History, Divided Memory: Jews and Others in Soviet-Occupied Poland, 1939–1941* (Leipzig, 2007), pp. 182–3.

51 Quoted in Jan Gross, 'The Sovietisation of Western Ukraine and Western Byelorussia', in Norman Davies & Antony Polonski (eds.), *Jews in Eastern Poland and the USSR, 1939–46* (London, 1990), p. 72.

52 Niall Ferguson, *The War of the World* (London, 2006), p. 418. In truth, it is the acronym of its title: 'Narodnyy Komissariat Vnutrennikh Del'; 'People's Commissariat for Internal Affairs'.

53 Quoted in Anna Cienciala, Natalia Lebedeva & Wojciech Materski (eds.), *Katyn: A Crime without Punishment* (New Haven, 2007), p. 120.

54 Stanisław Swianiewicz, quoted in Allen Paul, *Katyn, Stalin's Massacre and the Triumph of Truth* (DeKalb, IL, 2010), p. 107.

55 Quoted in Janusz K. Zawodny, *Death in the Forest* (London, 1971), p. 110.

56 Snyder, op. cit., p. 137.

57 On the methods employed at the various Katyn sites, see Cienciala et al. (eds.), op. cit., pp. 122–36.

58 Figures quoted in ibid., p. 168.

59 Snyder, op. cit., pp. 149–50.

60 Phillip T. Rutherford, *Prelude to the Final Solution: The Nazi Program for Deporting Ethnic Poles 1939–1941* (Kansas, 2007), p. 211.

61 Mrs J. K., quoted in Mark Mazower, *Hitler's Empire: Nazi Rule in Occupied Europe* (London, 2008), p. 82.

62 Browning, *Origins*, op. cit., p. 51.

63 Hans Frank, *Das Diensttagebuch des deutschen Generalgouverneurs in Polen 1939–1945* (Stuttgart, 1975), p. 104.

64 Quoted in Mark Spoerer, *Zwangsarbeit unter dem Hakenkreuz* (Stuttgart, 2001), p. 48.

65 Ulrich Herbert, *Hitler's Foreign Workers* (Cambridge, 1997), p. 84.

66 Berliner Geschichtswerkstatt (ed.), *Zwangsarbeit in Berlin 1940–1945* (Berlin, 2000), p. 74.

67 Robert Gerwarth, *Hitler's Hangman: The Life of Heydrich* (London, 2011), p. 143.

68 Christopher Browning, *Remembering Survival* (London, 2010), p. 26.

69 Gerwarth, op. cit., p. 158.

70 Schulenburg telegram to foreign office, Berlin, 17 December 1939, quoted in Hans Schafranek, *Zwischen NKWD und Gestapo* (Frankfurt am Main, 1990), p. 62.

71 Chaim Kaplan diary, quoted in Saul Friedländer, *The Years of Extermination: Nazi Germany and the Jews, 1939–1945* (London, 2007), p. 45.

72 Friedländer, op. cit., p. 150.

73 Ibid., p. 104.

74 Piesakowski, op. cit., p. 50, quoting the original NKVD deportation orders.

75 Cienciala et al. (eds.), op. cit., p. 121.

76 Testimony of Wiesława Saternus, in Teresa Jeśmanowa (ed.), *Stalin's Ethnic Cleansing in Eastern Poland* (London, 2008), p. 131.

77 Quoted in Piesakowski, op. cit., pp. 55–6.

78 Gross, *Revolution*, op. cit., p. 209.

79 Kochanski, op. cit., p. 134.

80 Author interview with Mr Mieczysław Wartalski, London, 8 September 2011.

81 Gross, *Revolution*, op. cit., p. 215.

82 Author interview with Mr Henryk Wieksza, Berkhamsted, 17 August 2011.

83 Sword, 'Mass Movement', op. cit., p. 20.

84 Wartalski author interview, op. cit.

85 Gross, *Revolution*, op. cit., p. 218.

86 Sword, 'Mass Movement', op. cit., p. 27.

87 Quoted in Gross, *Revolution*, op. cit., p. 222.

88 Zbigniew Siemaszko, 'The Mass Deportations of the Polish Population to the USSR, 1940–1941', in Keith Sword (ed.), *The Soviet Takeover of the Polish Eastern Provinces 1939–41* (London, 1991), p. 225.

89 Revised figures are in Kochanski, op. cit., p. 137, and a more thorough statistical breakdown can be found in Hryciuk, in Barkan, Cole & Struve (eds.), op. cit., pp. 184–99.

90 Correspondence with Professor Norman Davies, December 2013.

91 *DGFP*, op. cit., No. 419, p. 489, Memorandum by State Secretary Weizsäcker, 5 December 1939.

92 Browning, *Remembering*, op. cit., p. 27.

93 Video testimony of Wilhelm Korn, held by Yad Vashem archive and available at http://www.youtube.com/watch?v=Z61GKpqccxI.

94 Valdis Lumans, *Himmler's Auxiliaries: The Volksdeutsche Mittelstelle and the German National Minorities of Europe, 1933–1945* (London, 1993), p. 18.

95 Ibid., p. 163.

96 Khrushchev, op. cit., p. 141.

97 Quoted in Gross, *Revolution*, op. cit., p. 206.

98 Quoted in Yosef Litvak, 'The Plight of Refugees from the German-Occupied Territories', in Sword (ed.), *Soviet Takeover*, op. cit., p. 66.

99   Sword, 'Mass Movement', op. cit., p. 16.
100   Ibid., p. 18.
101   Siemaszko, op. cit., p. 224.
102   Gross, *Revolution*, op. cit., p. 226.
103   This is cited ibid., p. 207, and a variation of it is played out in Andrzej Wajda's film *Katyn* (2007).
104   Quoted in Gross, *Revolution*, op. cit., p. 50.
105   Peter Raina, *Gomułka: Politische Biographie* (Cologne, 1970), pp. 22–3.
106   Norman Davies, *God's Playground: A History of Poland*, Vol. 2 (Oxford, 1981), p. 452.
107   Ibid., p. 545.
108   Ribbentrop memorandum to Schulenburg, 26 November 1939, quoted in Schafranek, op. cit., p. 58.
109   Ibid., pp. 67–9.
110   Margarete Buber-Neumann, *Under Two Dictators* (London, 2008), p. 143.
111   Airey Neave, *They Have their Exits* (Barnsley, 2013), p. 16.
112   The National Archives, Kew, London, Official MI9 Camp Report, ref: WO 208/3281.
113   Experience of Private R. Berry of the 1st Battalion Duke of Cornwall's Light Infantry, MI9 Report 3311931, at www.conscript-heroes.com.
114   Clare Mulley, *The Spy who Loved* (London, 2012), p. 90.
115   Khrushchev, op. cit., p. 124.
116   Valentin Berezhkov, *At Stalin's Side* (New York, 1994), pp. 271–4.
117   Slutsch, op. cit., p. 234.
118   On 'Basis Nord', see Tobias R. Philbin III, *The Lure of Neptune: German–Soviet Naval Collaboration and Ambitions, 1919–1941* (Columbia, SC, 1994), pp. 81–117.
119   Quoted in Rees, op. cit., p. 69.
120   See Tom Frame, *HMAS Sydney: Loss and Controversy* (Rydalmere, NSW, 1993).
121   Philbin, op. cit., p. 141.
122   Quoted in Rees, op. cit., pp.75–6.
123   Ibid., p. 77.
124   Quoted in Alexander Werth, *Russia at War: 1941–1945* (London, 1964), p. 89.
125   Ibid.

3 *Sharing the Spoils*

1   Andor Hencke, 'Die deutsch-sowjetischen Beziehungen zwischen 1932 und 1941', unpublished protocol held at the Institut für Zeitgeschichte, Munich, MA 1300/2, p. 21.

2   Molotov–Selter negotiations quoted in Albert Tarulis, *Soviet Policy towards the Baltic States: 1918–1945* (Notre Dame, 1959), p. 150.

3   'Minutes of the Estonian–Soviet Negotiations for the Mutual Assistance Pact of 1939', *Litanus*, Vol. 14, No. 2 (1968), p. 4.

4   Ibid., p. 5.

5   Ibid., p. 14

6   Ibid., p. 18.

7   Felix Chuev & Albert Resis (eds.), *Molotov Remembers: Inside Kremlin Politics* (Chicago, 1993), p. 9.

8   Stalin quoted in Tarulis, op. cit., p. 154.

9   Alfred Erich Senn, *Lithuania 1940, Revolution from Above* (New York, 2007), p. 20.

10 Romuald Misiunas & Rein Taagepera, *The Baltic States: Years of Dependence 1940–1980* (London, 1983), pp. 15–16.

11 *Documents on German Foreign Policy, 1918–1945* (hereafter 'DGFP'), Series D, Vol. VIII (Washington DC, 1954), No. 113, pp. 112–13.

12 Alfred Rosenberg's Diary, United States Holocaust Memorial Museum, p. 297. www.ushmm.org.

13 *DGFP*, op. cit., No. 213, p. 238.

14 Valdis Lumans, *Himmler's Auxiliaries: The Volksdeutsche Mittelstelle and the German National Minorities of Europe, 1933–1945* (London, 1993), p. 160.

15 Arved Freiherr von Taube, quoted in Richards Olavs Plavnieks, '"Wall of Blood": The Baltic German Case Study The Baltic German Case Study in National Socialist Wartime Population Policy, 1939–1945', MA Thesis, University of North Carolina at Chapel Hill, 2009, p. 36, fn 73.

16 Dr Wolfgang Wachtsmuth, quoted in ibid., p. 37, fn 77.

17 *Himmler's Auxiliaries*, Lumans, op. cit., p. 160.

18 Werner von Glasenepp, quoted in Plavnieks, op. cit., p. 39, fn 83.

19 Nikita Khrushchev, *Khrushchev Remembers* (London, 1971), p. 135.

20 *DGFP*, op. cit., Nos. 232 & 240, pp. 255, 267.

21 Quoted in William R. Trotter, *A Frozen Hell: The Russo-Finnish Winter War of 1939–1940* (Chapel Hill, 2000), p. 18.

22 Quoted in Robert Edwards, *White Death: Russia's War on Finland 1939–40* (London, 2006), p. 106.

23 Philip Jowett & Brent Snodgrass, *Finland at War 1939–1945* (Oxford, 2006), p. 6.

24 Trotter, op. cit., p. 34.
25 See Stéphane Courtois, *The Black Book of Communism: Crimes, Terror, Repression* (Cambridge, MA, 1999), p. 198.
26 Trotter, op. cit, p. 40.
27 Ibid., p. 72.
28 Edward Ward, *Despatches from Finland* (London, 1940), pp. 54–5.
29 Trotter, op. cit., pp. 169–70.
30 Ward, op. cit., p. 63.
31 Bair Irincheev, *War of the White Death* (Barnsley, 2011), p. 117.
32 Quoted in Eloise Engel & Lauri Paananen, *The Winter War* (London, 1973), p. 103.
33 On Häyhä, see Roger Moorhouse, 'The White Death', in John L. Plaster (ed.), *The Sniper Anthology* (London, 2012), pp. 1–14.
34 Quoted in Martin Gilbert, *Second World War* (London, 1989), p. 42.
35 Quoted in Roy Jenkins, *Churchill* (London, 2001), p. 567.
36 *Daily Sketch*, 22 December 1939, quoted in Edwards, op. cit., p. 232.
37 Statistics from former defence minister Juho Niukkanen, quoted in Engel & Paananen, op. cit., pp. 153–7.
38 Seppo Myllyniemi, 'Consequences of the Hitler–Stalin Pact for the Baltic Republics and Finland', in Bernd Wegner (ed.), *From Peace to War: Germany, Soviet Russia and the World, 1939–1941* (Oxford, 1997), p. 86.
39 Khrushchev, op. cit., p. 136.
40 Frederick Taylor (trans. and ed.), *The Goebbels Diaries, 1939–1941* (London, 1982), p. 59.
41 Quoted in *DGFP*, op. cit., No. 526, p. 651.
42 Heinz Boberach (ed.), *Meldungen aus dem Reich: 1938–1945* (Herrsching, 1984), Vol. III, pp. 514, 524.
43 Ulrich von Hassell, *The Ulrich von Hassell Diaries, 1938–1944* (London, 2011), p. 61.
44 Hugh Gibson (ed.), *The Ciano Diaries: 1939–1943* (New York, 1946), pp. 174–5.
45 *DGFP*, op. cit., No. 423, p. 494, 6 December 1939.
46 Max Domarus, *Hitler: Speeches and Proclamations, 1932–1945*, Vol. III (London, 1997), pp. 1896–7.
47 Taylor (trans. and ed.), op. cit., p. 46.
48 Tobias R. Philbin III, *The Lure of Neptune: German–Soviet Naval Collaboration and Ambitions, 1919–1941* (Columbia, SC, 1994), pp. 129–31.
49 German foreign-office sources, quoted in Gerd Überschär, *Hitler und Finnland: 1939–1941* (Wiesbaden, 1978), p. 91.
50 Khrushchev, op. cit., p. 137.
51 Trotter, op. cit., p. 216.
52 Ibid., p. 220.

53 David Kirby, *Finland in the Twentieth Century* (London, 1979), p. 128.

54 Trotter, op. cit., p. 263.

55 Khrushchev, op. cit., p. 139.

56 *Izvestia*, 1 November 1939.

57 Valdis Lumans, *Latvia in World War II* (New York, 2006), p. 80.

58 Leonas Sabaliūnas, *Lithuania in Crisis: 1939–1940* (London, 1973), p. 158.

59 *Select Committee on Communist Aggression*, Vol. III (Washington DC, 1954), p. 232.

60 The root of the confusion is the Select Committee proceedings of 1954, which published the text of the Serov Instruction but labelled it as 'Order 001223'. The majority of writers and historians on this issue since have repeated the error.

61 Ivo Banac (ed.), *The Diary of Georgi Dimitrov 1933–1949* (New Haven & London, 2003), p. 120.

62 *Select Committee*, op. cit., p. 241.

63 Lumans, *Latvia*, op. cit., p. 85.

64 *Select Committee*, op. cit., p. 318.

65 Misiunas & Taagepera, op. cit., pp. 17–18, and Myllyniemi in Wegner (ed.), op. cit., p. 87.

66 A. A. Gromyko & B. N. Ponomareva (eds.), *Istoriya vneshney politiki SSSR*, Vol. I (Moscow, 1980), p. 393.

67 Alex Danchev & Daniel Todman (eds.), *War Diaries 1939–1945: Field Marshal Lord Alanbrooke* (London, 2001), p. 59.

68 See Karl-Heinz Frieser, *The Blitzkrieg Legend* (Annapolis, 2013).

69 *Izvestia*, 16 May 1940.

70 *Select Committee*, op. cit., p. 319.

71 *Pravda*, 28 May 1940, quoted in *Select Committee*, op. cit., p. 241.

72 *Select Committee*, op. cit., p. 242.

73 Ibid., pp. 322–9, and Senn, op. cit., p. 93.

74 The Masḷenki and Kaleva incidents are reported in German diplomatic sources: *DGFP*, Series D, Vol. IX (Washington DC, 1956), Nos. 439 & 458, pp. 574–5, 589.

75 Gabriel Gorodetsky, *Grand Delusion: Stalin and the German Invasion of Russia* (New Haven & London, 2001), p. 25.

76 Quoted in Sandra Kalniete, *With Dance Shoes in Siberian Snows* (Riga, 2006), p. 43.

77 Original is at the Museum of Occupation, Riga: http://www.e-okupaci-jasmuzejs.lv/#!/lv/eksponats/0328.

78 *DGFP*, op. cit., No. 533, p. 688.

79 Quoted in Misiunas & Taagepera, op. cit., pp. 25–6.

80 V. Stanley Vardys, 'The Baltic States under Stalin: The First Experiences,

1940–41', in Keith Sword (ed.), *The Soviet Takeover of the Polish Eastern Provinces 1939–41* (London, 1991), p. 277.

81 Cited in Misiunas & Taagepera, op. cit., p. 27.

82 Figures from the Museum of Occupation, Riga, 9 October 2012.

83 Figures quoted in Vardys, in Sword (ed.), op. cit., p. 278, and Misiunas & Taagepera, op. cit., p. 28, fn. 28.

84 Khrushchev, op. cit., p. 131.

85 Misiunas & Taagepera, op. cit., p. 41, and Lumans, *Himmler's Auxiliaries*, op. cit., p. 170.

86 *DGFP*, op. cit., No. 465, pp. 595–6.

87 *DGFP*, Series D, Vol. X (London, 1957), No. 219, p. 286.

88 *DGFP*, Series D, Vol. IX, op. cit., No. 451, p. 583.

89 Elke Fröhlich (ed.), *Die Tagebücher von Joseph Goebbels*, Part 1, Vol. 8 (Munich, 1998), p. 233.

90 John Hiden, Vahur Made & David J. Smith (eds.), *The Baltic Question during the Cold War* (London, 2008), p. 39.

91 Quoted in Dennis J. Dunn, *Caught Between Roosevelt & Stalin* (Kentucky, 1997), p. 118, and Sumner Welles text is displayed in the Museum of Occupation, Riga.

92 Florin Constantiniu, *O istorie sinceră a poporului român* (Bucharest, 2008), p. 361.

93 Nicholas Constantinesco, *Romania in Harm's Way, 1939–1941* (New York, 2004), p. 136.

94 Quoted in Jane Degras (ed.), *Soviet Documents on Foreign Policy*, Vol. III (London, 1953), pp. 458–9.

95 Quoted in Constantiniu, op. cit., p. 364.

96 Constantinesco, op. cit., p. 149.

97 Quoted in Ioan Scurtu & Constantin Hlihor, *Anul 1940: drama românilor dintre Prut si Nistru* (Bucharest, 1992), p. 85.

98 Quoted in Dinu Giurescu, *Romania in the Second World War* (New York, 2000), p. 24.

99 Lyn Smith (ed.), *Forgotten Voices of the Holocaust* (London, 2006), p. 91.

100 Khrushchev, op. cit., p. 145.

101 Quoted in Degras (ed.), op. cit., p. 465.

102 Quoted in Constantinesco, op. cit., p. 150.

103 Misiunas & Taagepera, op. cit., p. 25.

104 On the Sovietisation of the Baltic states, see ibid., pp. 25–40.

105 Kalniete, op cit., p. 47.

106 Peep Varju, 'The Destruction of the Estonian Political Elite during the Soviet Occupation', in *History Conference of the Estonian Memento Association* (Tallinn, 2007), p. 33.

107   Museum of Occupation, Riga.

108   Leonas Sabaliūnas, *Lithuania in Crisis: Nationalism to Communism, 1939–1940* (London, 1972), p. 204.

109   Bronis J. Kaslas, 'The Lithuanian Strip in Soviet–German Diplomacy, 1939–1941' in *Journal of Baltic Studies*, Vol. 4, No. 3 (1973), p. 217.

110   Alan Palmer, *Northern Shores* (London, 2005), p. 343.

111   Quoted in Joseph Pajaujis-Javis, *Soviet Genocide in Lithuania* (New York, 1980), p. 36.

112   Arvīds Lasmanis, quoted in Astrid Sics (ed.), *We Sang Through Tears: Stories of Survival in Siberia* (Riga, 1999), p. 140.

113   Vieda Skultans, *The Testimony of Lives: Narrative and Memory in Post-Soviet Latvia* (London, 1998), p. 188.

114   Figures quoted in Toomas Hiio, Meelis Maripuu & Indrek Paavle (eds.), *Estonia 1940–45: Reports of the Estonian Commission for the Investigation of crimes Against Humanity* (Tallinn, 2006), p. 328, Artis Pabriks & Aldis Purs, *Latvia: The Challenges of Change* (London, 2013), p. 27, and Vardys, in Sword (ed.), op. cit., p. 286.

115   Ion Constantin & Valeriu Florin Dobrinescu, *Basarabia în anii celui de al doilea război mondial: 1939–1947* (Iaşi, 1995), p. 215.

116   Pajaujis-Javis, op. cit., p. 27.

117   Hiio, Maripuu & Paavle (eds.), op. cit., p. 309.

118   Ibid., p. 312.

119   Andrei Brezianu & Vlad Spânu, *Historical Dictionary of Moldova* (London, 2007), pp. 46–7.

120   Menachem Begin, *White Nights* (Tel Aviv, 1977), p. 81.

121   Anthony Read & David Fisher, *The Deadly Embrace* (London, 1988), p. 488.

122   Gorodetsky, op. cit., p. 33.

123   Read & Fisher, op. cit., p. 489.

124   Fröhlich (ed.), op. cit., pp. 196–7, 205.

125   Taylor (trans. and ed.), op. cit., p. 124.

4 Contortions

1   Kevin Morgan, *Harry Pollitt* (Manchester, 1993), p. 96.

2   *Daily Worker*, 23 August 1939, p. 3.

3   Ivo Banac (ed.), *The Diary of Georgi Dimitrov: 1933–1949* (New Haven & London, 2003), p. 114.

4   *Daily Worker*, 2 September 1939, p. 3.

5   Harry Pollitt, *How to Win the War* (London, 1939), *passim*.

6   Douglas Hyde, *I Believed* (Adelaide, 1950), p. 68.

7   Quoted in Nigel Jones, *Through a Glass Darkly: The Life of Patrick Hamilton* (London, 1991), p. 219.

8   Francis King & George Matthews (eds.), *About Turn: The British Communist Party and the Second World War* (London, 1990), p. 91.

9   Quoted in King & Matthews, op. cit., pp. 69–70.

10 Ibid., pp. 73–7, *passim*.

11 Ibid., pp. 86–7.

12 Ibid., pp. 91–3, *passim*.

13 Ibid., pp. 197–209, *passim*.

14 'Communist Split', *The Times*, 12 October 1939, p. 10.

15 George Orwell, 'London Letter', 3 January 1941, in Peter Davison (ed.), *Orwell and Politics* (London, 2001), pp. 101–2.

16 Adolf Hitler, *Mein Kampf* (London, 1939), p. 538.

17 Eric Hobsbawm, *Interesting Times* (London, 2002), p. 153.

18 Norman Mackenzie & Jeanne Mackenzie (eds.), *The Diary of Beatrice Webb*, Vol. IV, 'The Wheel of Life' (London, 1985), pp. 438–40.

19 Ibid., p. 441.

20 Dorothy Sheridan (ed.), *Among You Taking Notes . . . The Wartime Diary of Naomi Mitchison 1939–1945* (London, 1985), p. 40.

21 Quoted in Hyde, op. cit., p. 69.

22 Mackenzie (eds.), op. cit., pp. 444–5.

23 Hyde, op. cit., p. 71.

24 James Eaden & David Renton, *The Communist Party of Great Britain since 1920* (Basingstoke, 2002), p. 75.

25 Quoted in Angus Calder, *The Myth of the Blitz* (London, 1991), p. 79.

26 Victor Gollancz, *Where are You Going?* (London, 1940), pp. 1–2.

27 Ibid., p. 30.

28 Robert Gellately, *Lenin, Stalin and Hitler: The Age of Social Catastrophe* (London, 2007), p. 359.

29 Earl Browder, *Whose War Is It?* (New York, 1939), pp. 7–8, 13.

30 Fraser Ottanelli, *The Communist Party of the United States* (New Brunswick, 1991), p. 198.

31 James G. Ryan, *Earl Browder: The Failure of American Communism* (Tuscaloosa, AL, 1997), p. 182.

32 See George Watson, 'Hitler and the Socialist Dream' in the *Independent on Sunday*, 22 November 1998, at http://www.independent.co.uk/arts-entertainment/hitler-and-the-socialist-dream-1186455.html.

33 Kingsley Martin, 'The Man of Steel' in *The New Statesman and Nation*, 9 December 1939.

34 Henry Brailsford, quoted in George Watson, 'The Eye-Opener of 1939' in *History Today*, August 2004, p. 51.

109 – 141

35 Nigel West, *MI5: British Security Service Operations 1909–1945* (London, 1981), pp. 254–5.

36 From a declaration of the French 'Bureau Politique', quoted in Edward Mortimer, *The Rise of the French Communist Party 1920–1947* (London, 1984), p. 281.

37 Adam Rajsky, *Nos Illusions Perdues* (Paris, 1985), p. 64: English text from Wolfgang Leonhard, *Betrayal: The Hitler–Stalin Pact of 1939* (New York, 1989), pp. 110–11.

38 François Furet, quoted in Gellately, op. cit., p. 358.

39 Leonhard, op. cit., p. 115.

40 Mortimer, op. cit., p. 292.

41 Quoted in Allan Merson, *Communist Resistance in Nazi Germany* (London, 1985), p. 213.

42 Illustrated by contemporary reports on German public opinion in Heinz Boberach (ed.), *Meldungen aus dem Reich: 1938–1945* (Herrsching, 1985), pp. 400, 415, 365.

43 Erich Honecker, *From My Life* (New York, 1981), p. 102.

44 Leonhard, op. cit., pp. 96–7.

45 Egbert Krispyn, *Anti-Nazi Writers in Exile* (Athens, GA, 2010), p. 72.

46 Quoted in Klaus Völker, *Brecht: A Biography* (London, 1979), p. 265.

47 Brecht journal entry for 18 September 1939, quoted in John Willett, *Brecht in Context* (London, 1984), p. 193.

48 Bertolt Brecht, *The Resistible Rise of Arturo Ui* (London, 2013), pp. 7, 59.

49 Katharine Hodgson, 'The Soviet Union in the Svendborg Poems', in Ronald Spiers (ed.), *Brecht's Poetry of Political Exile* (Cambridge, 2000), p. 79.

50 Quoted in Horst Duhnke, *Die KPD von 1933 bis 1945* (Cologne, 1972), p. 343.

51 Quoted in Gollancz, op. cit., pp. 30–5.

52 Quoted in Duhnke, op. cit., p. 345.

53 *Rote Fahne*, 'Macht Front gegen die imperialistischen Bestrebungen!', June 1940, reproduced in Margot Pikarski & Günter Uebel, *Der Antifaschistische Widerstandskampf der KPD in Spiegel des Flugblattes 1933–1945* (Berlin, 1978).

54 Statistics quoted in Detlef Peukert, *Die KPD im Widerstand* (Wuppertal, 1980), p. 333 fn.

55 Boberach (ed.), op. cit., p. 1305.

56 Hugh Trevor-Roper, in his foreword to Terence Prittie, *Germans against Hitler* (London, 1964), p. 13.

57 *Der Spiegel*, 'Nachts kamen Stalin's Häscher', 42/1978.

58 Octavio Brandao, quoted in Leonhard, op. cit., p. 17.

59 Quoted in ibid., p. 16.

60 Ibid., p. 18.

61 Jesus Hernandez, quoted in ibid., p. 14.

62 Ruth von Mayenburg, *Blaues Blut und Rote Fahnen* (Munich, 1969), p. 268.

63 Quoted in Leonhard, op. cit., p. 23.

64 Katerina Clark, *Moscow, The Fourth Rome* (London, 2011), p. 341.

65 Quoted in Alfred Erich Senn, *Lithuania 1940, Revolution from Above* (New York, 2007) p. 66, fn 120.

66 Victor Kravchenko, *I Chose Freedom* (New York, 1946), p. 332.

67 Ibid., p. 333.

68 Leonhard, op. cit., p. 54.

69 Kravchenko, op. cit., p. 334.

70 Richard Taylor, *Film Propaganda: Soviet Russia and Nazi Germany* (London, 1998), p. 89.

71 Kyril Anderson, *Kremlevskij Kinoteatr, 1928–1953, Dokumenty* (Moscow, 2005), p. 539.

72 Quoted in Terry Charman, *Outbreak 1939: The World Goes to War* (London, 2009), p. 52.

73 Clark, op. cit., p. 341.

74 'Val'Kiriia', *Pravda*, 23 November 1940, p. 4.

75 Charles E. Bohlen, *Witness to History, 1929–1969* (New York, 1973), p. 89.

76 Nikita Khrushchev, *Khrushchev Remembers* (London, 1971), p. 112.

77 Quoted in Orlando Figes, *The Whisperers: Private Life in Stalin's Russia* (London, 2007), p. 374.

78 See Sarah Davies, *Popular Opinion in Stalin's Russia: Terror, Propaganda and Dissent, 1934–1941* (Cambridge, 1997), p. 97.

79 Ibid., p. 98.

80 Ibid., p. 99.

81 'The Russo-German Deal' in *The Times*, 23 August 1939, p. 13.

82 'Portuguese Anger over Soviet–Nazi Pact' in *The Times*, 28 August 1939, p. 9, and 'Hungary suspends Judgment' in *The Times*, 23 August 1939, p. 11.

83 Hugh Gibson (ed.), *The Ciano Diaries 1939–1943* (New York, 1946), p. 125.

84 Ibid., p. 131.

85 *Documents on German Foreign Policy, 1918–1945*, Series D, Vol. VII (Washington DC, 1954), No. 183, p. 191.

86 Quoted in Robert Skidelsky, *Oswald Mosley* (London, 1990), pp. 442–3.

87 Quoted in West, op. cit., p. 128.

88 Richard Griffiths, *Patriotism Perverted* (London, 1998), p. 237.

89 Elke Fröhlich (ed.), *Die Tagebücher von Joseph Goebbels*, Part 1, Vol. 7 (Munich, 1998), p. 73.

90 Alfred Rosenberg's Diary, 22 August 1939, United States Holocaust Memorial Museum, p. 267. www.ushmm.org.

91 The National Archives, Kew, London (hereafter 'TNA'), CAB 65/4/22 – 123-4, Foreign Office Memorandum, 29 November 1939.

92 Rosenberg's Diary, 26 August 1939, op. cit., p. 277.

93 Quoted in Hitler's Obersalzberg Speech in Anthony P. Adamthwaite, *The Making of the Second World War* (London, 1977), pp. 219–20.

94 Fritz Thyssen, *I Paid Hitler* (London, 1941), pp. 47, 56. Though the authenticity of this memoir is disputed, the letters quoted here are considered genuine.

95 *Völkischer Beobachter*, 25 August 1939, p. 1.

96 *Das Schwarze Korps*, 31 August 1939, p. 3.

97 *Völkischer Beobachter*, 1, 18 and 19 September 1939.

98 Rosenberg's Diary, entry date unclear, op. cit., p. 269.

99 *Völkischer Beobachter*, 26 August 1939, p. 8, and 3 September 1939, p. 9.

100 Daniil Granin, *Zubr* (Moscow, 1989), p. 125.

101 William Shirer, *This is Berlin: Reporting from Germany 1938–1940* (London, 1999), p. 56.

102 Karl Neumann's Diary, 24 August 1939, held at Deutsches Tagebucharchiv, Emmendingen, ref: 1346/1,3.

103 Ruth Andreas-Friedrich, *Berlin Underground, 1938–1945* (New York, 1947), p. 45.

104 Rainer Hamm, unpublished memoir, held at Deutsches Tagebucharchiv, Emmendingen, p. 25, ref: 1815,3.

105 Victor Klemperer, *I Shall Bear Witness, 1933–1941* (London, 1998) p. 293.

106 Hans Gisevius, *To the Bitter End* (New York, 1998), p. 364.

107 Jürgen Förster, 'The German Military's Image of Russia', in Ljubica Erickson & Mark Erickson (eds.), *Russia: War, Peace and Diplomacy* (London, 2005), p. 122.

108 Heinz Guderian, *Panzer Leader* (London, 1952), pp. 84–5.

109 Ulrich von Hassell, *The Ulrich von Hassell Diaries, 1938–1944* (Barnsley, 2011), pp. 43, 40.

110 Rosenberg's Diary, 5 October 1939, op. cit., p. 307.

111 TNA, War Cabinet memorandum, CAB/66/4/11, 7 December 1939.

112 Charman, op. cit., pp. 48–9.

113 Hugh Trevor-Roper (ed.), *Hitler's Table Talk, 1941–1944* (London, 2000), p. 481.

114 David Welch, *Propaganda and the German Cinema: 1933–1945* (London, 2006), p. 212.

115 Charman, op. cit., p. 57.

116 Erik Levi, *Music in the Third Reich* (London, 1994), pp. 201–2.

117 *Hamburger Tageblatt*, advertisement for the 'Siberian Cossack Choir', 29 May 1940, p. 7.

118 See *Deutsche Allgemeine Zeitung*, June 1941.

119 Morgan, op. cit., p. 117.

5 *A Rough, Uncertain Wooing*

1 Winston S. Churchill, *The Second World War* (London, 1989), p. 158.

2 Stephen Howarth, *August 1939* (London, 1989), p. 130.

3 The National Archives, Kew, London (hereafter 'TNA'), FO 371/23686/N 4146/243/38, 26 August 1939.

4 Henry 'Chips' Channon, quoted in Irene Taylor & Alan Taylor (eds.), *The Secret Annexe* (London, 2004), p. 436; Harold Nicolson quoted in Nigel Nicolson (ed.), *Harold Nicolson: Diaries and Letters 1930–1939* (London, 1966), p. 411; Sir Alexander Cadogan quoted in David Dilks (ed.), *The Diaries of Sir Alexander Cadogan 1938–1945* (London, 1971), p. 200.

5 Mass Observation Archive (hereafter 'MOA'), University of Sussex, August 1941 file, ref: SxMOA1/2/25/4/A/3.

6 Ibid., ref: SxMOA1/2/25/4/A/3/6.

7 Keith Jeffery, *MI6: The History of the Secret Intelligence Service, 1909–1949* (London, 2010), p. 312.

8 Hugh Dundas, quoted in Patrick Bishop, *Bomber Boys* (London, 2007), p. 103.

9 'The Russo-German Deal' in *The Times*, 23 August 1939, p. 13.

10 Andrew Roberts, *The Holy Fox* (London, 1991), p. 2.

11 Edward Raczyński, *In Allied London* (London, 1962), p. 20.

12 Anthony Carty & Richard A. Smith, *Sir Gerald Fitzmaurice and the World Crisis* (London, 2000), p. 286, quoting TNA, FO 371/23130/C12124.

13 Cadogan minute, from FO 371/23130/C11884, quoted in Carty & Smith, op. cit., p. 286, fn. 139.

14 Graham Stewart, *His Finest Hours: The War Speeches of Winston Churchill* (London, 2007), pp. 17, 21.

15 Robert Rhodes James (ed.), *The Diaries of Sir Henry Channon* (London, 1967), p. 215.

16 Mass Observation Diarist 5269–5, quoted in Juliet Gardiner, *Wartime Britain: 1939–1945* (London, 2004), p. 5.

17 Walter Schellenberg, *Invasion 1940: The Nazi Invasion Plans for Britain* (London, 2000), p. 217.

18 Low cartoons: 'Uncle Joe's Pawnshop' in *Evening Standard*, 2 October

1939; 'Someone is taking Someone for a Walk' in *Evening Standard*, 21 October 1939.

19 'Stalin shows his hand' in *The Times*, 18 September 1939.

20 TNA, War Cabinet, CAB 65/1/18, 17 September 1939, pp. 141–2.

21 Cadogan minute from 23 September 1939, quoted in Paul W. Doerr, '"Frigid but Unprovocative": British Policy towards the USSR from the Nazi–Soviet Pact to the Winter War, 1939' in *Journal of Contemporary History*, Vol. 36, No. 3, 2001, p. 428.

22 TNA, War Cabinet, CAB 65/1/34, 2 October 1939, pp. 271–2.

23 Ibid., p. 272.

24 TNA, Chiefs of Staff Committee Memorandum, CAB 66/2/24, 9 October 1939, pp. 196–206.

25 Quoted in Stewart, op. cit., pp. 20–1.

26 TNA, War Cabinet, CAB 65/1/57, 23 October 1939, p. 478.

27 TNA, War Cabinet, CAB 65/2/45, 11 December 1939, p. 383.

28 Roberts, op. cit., p. 190.

29 Halifax, quoted in Doerr, op. cit., p. 429.

30 TNA, Economic Warfare weekly report, CAB 68/4/39, 28 January 1940, p. 8.

31 TNA, War Cabinet, CAB 65/6/22, 29 March 1940, p. 187.

32 Quoted in Patrick Osborn, *Operation Pike: Britain versus the Soviet Union, 1939–1941* (London, 2000), p. 121. Patrick Osborn's excellent book is the only authority on this fascinating episode.

33 Quoted in TNA, War Cabinet, CAB 65/6/22, 29 March 1940, p. 188.

34 Quoted in Jukka Nevakivi, *The Appeal That Was Never Made* (London, 1976), p. 109.

35 Charles Richardson, 'French Plans for Allied Attacks on the Caucasus Oil Fields January–April 1940' in *French Historical Studies*, Vol. 8, No. 1, 1975, p. 156.

36 Osborn, op. cit., p. 141.

37 Ibid., p. 147. It is not impossible, but is nonetheless unlikely, that the aircraft that were seen were really Messerschmitt Bf-109s. Only five such aircraft had been delivered to the USSR, so the chances of one being sighted over Baku were slim.

38 Quoted in ibid., pp. 108–9.

39 Quoted in Harry Hanak, 'Sir Stafford Cripps as British Ambassador in Moscow, May 1940 to June 1941' in *English Historical Review*, Vol. 94, No. 370, January 1979, p. 55.

40 Quoted in Osborn, op. cit., p.148.

41 Richard Overy, *The Bombing War* (London, 2013), p. 267.

42 Hansard, 19 March 1940, quoted in Osborn, op. cit., p. 118.

43 Quoted in ibid., p. 247.

44 MOA, June 1939 Directive, ref: SxMOA1/1/6/8/36.

45 Paul Addison & Jeremy A. Crang (eds.), *Listening to Britain* (London, 2011), pp. 98, 130.

46 Ibid., p. 193.

47 Ibid., p. 222.

48 Ibid., pp. 289, 292.

49 Mary E. Glantz, *FDR and the Soviet Union* (Kansas, 2005), pp. 48, 51.

50 Robert Dallek, *Franklin D. Roosevelt and American Foreign Policy 1932–1945* (Oxford, 1995), p. 208.

51 Quoted in ibid., p. 209.

52 Quoted in Lynne Olson, *Those Angry Days: Roosevelt, Lindbergh, and America's Fight over World War Two, 1939–1941* (New York, 2013), p. 95.

53 Quoted in Dallek, op. cit., p. 212.

54 Glantz, op. cit., p. 53.

55 Stephen Ambrose, *Rise to Globalism: American Foreign Policy since 1938* (London, 1991), pp. 5, 7.

56 Quoted in Churchill, op. cit., p. 303.

57 Nigel West, *MI5: British Security Operations 1909–1945* (London, 1981), p. 126.

58 Text cited in Aaron Goldman, 'Defence Regulation 18B: Emergency Internment of Aliens and Political Dissenters in Great Britain during World War II' in *Journal of British Studies*, Vol. 12, No. 2, May 1973, p. 122.

59 Ibid., p. 129.

60 Gardiner, op. cit., p. 295.

61 Goldman, op. cit., p. 129.

62 Gardiner, op. cit., p. 300.

63 TNA, War Cabinet, CAB 65/11/25, 7 February 1940, p. 222.

64 TNA, FO 371/24844 5853, 23 June 1940, quoted in Hanak, op. cit., p. 59.

65 Churchill, op. cit., p. 280.

66 Hanak, op. cit., p. 57.

67 Quoted in Gabriel Gorodetsky, *Stafford Cripps' Mission to Moscow 1940–42* (Cambridge, 1984), p. 52.

68 Ibid., pp. 76, 78.

69 Stephen Dorril, *MI6: Inside the Covert World of Her Majesty's Intelligence Service* (London, 2002), p. 194.

70 TNA, FO 371/29464 1604, 22 October 1940, quoted in Hanak, op. cit., p. 66.

71 Hanak, op. cit., p. 67.

72 Ivan Maisky, *Memoirs of a Soviet Ambassador: The War 1939–1943* (London, 1967), p. 142.

73 Ibid., p. 143.

74 Laurence Collier, head of the Northern Department of the Foreign Office, quoted in Gorodetsky, op. cit., p. 129.

75 Llewellyn Woodward, *British Foreign Policy in the Second World War*, Vol. I (London, 1970), p. 607.

76 Gorodetsky, op. cit., p. 131.

77 Ibid., p. 147.

78 Ibid., p. 55.

79 Ibid., p. 76.

6 Oiling the Wheels of War   169 - 199

1   The *Prinz Eugen* would meet her end in 1946, when she was used as a test vessel for the US atomic test at Bikini Atoll, before being towed to Kwajalein Atoll, where she capsized.

2   Erich Raeder, *My Life* (New York, 1980), p. 199.

3   Quoted in Walter Laqueur, *Russia and Germany: A Century of Conflict* (London, 1965), p. 123.

4   Statistics from ibid., p. 132, and Paul N. Hehn, *A Low Dishonest Decade* (New York, 2002), p. 246.

5   Statistics quoted in Hehn, op. cit., pp. 245–6.

6   For details of the Kandelaki mission, see Lew Besymenski, 'Geheimmission in Stalins Auftrag?' in *Vierteljahrshefte für Zeitgeschichte*, Vol. 40, No. 3 (1992), pp. 339–57.

7   This is suggested by KGB defector Walter Krivitsky, *In Stalin's Secret Service* (New York, 2000), p. 196, and is reported in the more reliable study by Christopher Andrew & Oleg Gordievsky, *KGB: The Inside Story of its Foreign Operations from Lenin to Gorbachev* (London, 1990), p. 187.

8   Manfred Zeidler, 'German–Soviet Economic Relations during the Hitler–Stalin Pact', in Bernd Wegner (ed.), *From Peace to War: Germany, Soviet Russia and the World, 1939–1941* (Oxford, 1997), pp. 100–1.

9   Adam Tooze, *The Wages of Destruction* (London, 2006), p. 659.

10 Quoted in ibid., p. 288.

11 William Carr, *Arms, Autarky and Aggression* (London, 1972), p. 106.

12 *New York Times*, 'Reich is Accelerating Inflation of Currency', 27 September 1939, p. 1.

13 Tooze, op. cit., p. 296.

14 Max Domarus, *Hitler, Speeches and Proclamations, 1932–1945*, Vol. III (London, 1997), p. 1444.

15 Edward E. Ericson III, 'Karl Schnurre and the Evolution of Nazi–Soviet Relations, 1936–1941' in *German Studies Review*, Vol. 21, No. 2 (May 1998), p. 265.

16 Ibid., p. 268.

17 Richard Bessel, *Germany after the First World War* (Oxford, 1993), p. 41.

18 Zeidler in Wegner (ed.), op. cit., p. 98.

19 Ibid., p. 99.

20 Quoted in Jane Degras (ed.), *Soviet Documents on Foreign Policy*, Vol. III (Oxford, 1953), p. 367.

21 Edward E. Ericson III, *Feeding the German Eagle: Soviet Economic Aid to Nazi Germany, 1933–1941* (London, 1999), pp. 71, 79.

22 Quoted in Seweryn Bialer (ed.), *Stalin and his Generals: Soviet Military Memoirs of World War II* (London, 1970), p. 117.

23 Quoted in ibid., p. 117.

24 Quoted in ibid., p. 118.

25 Quoted in ibid., p. 118.

26 Valentin Berezhkov, *At Stalin's Side* (New York, 1994), pp. 81–2.

27 See William Green & Gordon Swanborough, 'Heinkel's High Speed Hoaxer: The Annals of the He-100' in *Air Enthusiast*, January–April 1989.

28 Tobias R. Philbin III, *The Lure of Neptune: German–Soviet Naval Collaboration and Ambitions 1919–1941* (Columbia, SC, 1994), pp. 68–70.

29 Ericson, *Feeding the German Eagle*, op. cit., p. 125.

30 *Documents on German Foreign Policy, 1918–1945* (hereafter '*DGFP*'), Series D, Vol. VIII (Washington DC, 1954), pp. 472–5.

31 Ibid., Ritter telegram to Schulenburg, 11 December 1939, Document 442, pp. 516–17.

32 Ibid., Ritter telegram to Berlin, 27 December 1939, addendum to Document 487, p. 575.

33 Ibid., Ribbentrop Memorandum, 11 December 1939, Document 438, p. 513.

34 Ericson, *Feeding the German Eagle*, op. cit., p. 92.

35 Ibid., p. 98.

36 William Shirer, *Berlin Diary 1934–1941*, illustrated edition (London, 1997), p. 131.

37 Ericson, *Feeding the German Eagle*, op. cit., p. 205.

38 *DGFP*, op. cit., Ribbentrop telegram to Schulenburg, 3 February 1940, Document, 594, p. 739.

39 Ibid., Text of the German–Soviet Economic Agreement, 11 February 1940, Document 607, pp. 763–9.

40 *Izvestia*, 16 February 1940, p. 1.

NOTES TO PAGES 155–175

41 Quoted in Zeidler in Wegner (ed.), op. cit., p. 96.

42 *National-Zeitung*, quoted in Bogdan Musial, *Stalins Beutezug* (Berlin, 2010), p. 27.

43 *DGFP*, op. cit., Schnurre Memorandum, 26 February 1940, Document 636, pp. 814–15.

44 Gustav Hilger & Alfred Meyer, *The Incompatible Allies: A Memoir-History of German–Soviet Relations, 1918–1941* (New York, 1953), p. 317.

45 *DGFP*, op. cit., Economic Agreement, 11 February 1940, Document 607, pp. 763–4.

46 D. A. Sobolev & D. B. Khazanov, 'Heinkel He-100 for the USSR' at www.airpages.ru/eng/ru/he100_2.shtml.

47 See *DGFP*, op. cit., Economic Agreement, Document 607, pp. 762–9, and Schnurre Memorandum, Document 636, pp. 814–17.

48 German offer of 152 million Reichsmarks is in Ericson, *Feeding the German Eagle*, op. cit., p. 100; and construction cost of *Lützow* is given as 83,590,000 Reichmarks in Erich Gröner, *German Warships 1815– 1945*, Vol. 1 (London, 1990), p. 65.

49 *DGFP*, op. cit., Economic Agreement, Document 607, p. 763.

50 Quote from Ericson, *Feeding the German Eagle*, op. cit., p. 115.

51 Statistics quoted in ibid., Table 1.6, p. 192.

52 Philbin, op. cit., p. 48.

53 Statistics quoted in Ericson, *Feeding the German Eagle*, op. cit., Table 1.5, p. 191.

54 Statistics quoted in Heinrich Schwendemann, 'German–Soviet economic relations at the time of the Hitler–Stalin Pact, 1939–1941' in *Cahiers du Monde russe*, XXXVI (1–2), January–June 1995, p. 176.

55 See statistics quoted in Ericson, op. cit., Table 4.1, p. 207. Average monthly percentage for July–December 1940 for German exports to the Soviet Union is 67.6 per cent of the total.

56 Nikolai Tolstoy, *Stalin's Secret War* (London, 1981), p. 188, quoted in Andrew & Gordievsky, op. cit., p. 202.

57 Statistics quoted in Ericson, *Feeding the German Eagle*, op. cit., Table 3.2, p. 202, and Musial, op. cit., pp. 28–9.

58 Ericson, *Feeding the German Eagle*, op. cit., p. 207.

59 Ibid., Table 4.1, p. 207, and Mark Harrison (ed.), *The Economics of World War II* (Cambridge, 1998), p. 10.

60 Statistics quoted in Ericson, *Feeding the German Eagle*, op. cit., Table 1.1, p. 187.

61 Zeidler in Wegner (ed.), op. cit., p. 110.

62 Statistics quoted in Ericson, *Feeding the German Eagle*, op. cit., Tables 1.3, 1.4, pp. 189–90.

63 The work of engineering designers Aleksandr Moskalyev and Arkhip Liul'ka respectively. On the latter, see Mark Harrison (ed.), *Guns and Rubles: The Defense Industry in the Stalinist State* (New Haven, 2008), pp. 216–17.

64 Mark Harrison, *Soviet Planning in Peace and War* (Cambridge, 1985), pp. 30–1.

65 Musial, op. cit., pp. 36–40.

66 Ibid., pp. 53, 54.

67 Statistics quoted in Ericson, *Feeding the German Eagle*, op. cit., Tables 3.1, 3.2, pp. 201–2, and Heinrich Hassmann, *Oil in the Soviet Union* (Princeton, 1953), Table 37, p. 148.

68 Ericson, *Feeding the German Eagle*, op. cit., pp. 124, 130, fn 7.

69 Dietrich Eichholtz, *War for Oil: The Nazi Quest for an Oil Empire* (Washington DC, 2012), p. 30.

70 Statistics quoted in Harrison, *Soviet Planning*, op. cit., Appendix 2, p. 253.

71 *DGFP*, op. cit., Document 481, p. 564.

72 Burton Klein, *Germany's Economic Preparedness for War* (Harvard, 1953), p. 58.

73 Statistics quoted in ibid., p. 45, and Ericson, *Feeding the German Eagle*, op. cit., Table 3.3, p. 203.

74 Bernd C. Wagner, *IG Auschwitz: Zwangsarbeit und Vernichtung von Häftlingen des Lagers Monowitz 1941–1945* (Munich, 2000), p. 39.

75 Ibid., pp. 281–2.

76 Primo Levi, *Survival in Auschwitz* (London, 1996), p. 72.

77 See Roger Moorhouse, *Berlin at War: Life and Death in Hitler's Germany* (London, 2010), pp. 74–99.

78 Ericson, *Feeding the German Eagle*, op. cit., Tables 3.5, 5.1, pp. 205, 210.

79 Ibid., p. 125.

80 Hilger & Meyer, op. cit., p. 317.

81 Andor Hencke, 'Die deutsch-sowjetischen Beziehungen zwischen 1932 und 1941', unpublished protocol held at the Institut für Zeitgeschichte, Munich, MA 1300/2, p. 32.

82 Yakovlev in Bialer (ed.), op. cit., p. 119.

83 Elke Fröhlich (ed.), *Die Tagebücher von Joseph Goebbels*, Part 1, Vol. 8 (Munich, 1998), p. 240.

84 Ericson, *Feeding the German Eagle*, op. cit., pp. 116, 120, fn 80.

85 Ibid., Tables 2.1, 2.2, p. 195.

86 Ibid., pp. 135–6.

87 Zeidler in Wegner (ed.), op. cit., p. 108.

88 Berezhkov, op. cit., pp. 90–1.

89 Nikita Khrushchev, *Khrushchev Remembers* (London, 1971), p. 114.

90 Ericson, *Feeding the German Eagle*, op. cit., pp. 125, 130, fn 24.

91 Ibid., p. 126.

92 Quoted in Gabriel Gorodetsky, *Grand Delusion: Stalin and the German Invasion of Russia* (New Haven & London, 1999), p. 24.

93 Zeidler in Wegner (ed.), op. cit., p. 103.

94 Gorodetsky, op. cit., p. 16.

95 See Bronis Kaslas, 'The Lithuanian Strip in Soviet–German Secret Diplomacy, 1939–1941' in *Journal of Baltic Studies*, Vol. 4, No. 3 (1973), pp. 211–25.

96 Geoffrey Roberts, *Stalin's Wars: From World War to Cold War, 1939–1953* (New Haven, 2006), p. 55.

97 This aspect is well covered in Gorodetsky, op. cit., pp. 23–47.

98 Transcript of the Hitler–Mannerheim discussion is in Ahti Jäntti & Marion Holtkamp (eds.), *Schicksalschwere Zeiten: Marschall Mannerheim und die deutsch-finnischen Beziehung 1939–1945* (Berlin, 1997), pp. 76–87. Translated from the German by the author.

99 *DGFP*, Series D, Vol. X (London, 1957), No. 13, pp. 12–13.

100 Quoted in Gorodetsky, op. cit., p. 56.

101 Philbin, op. cit., pp. 122–5.

102 *Izvestia*, 'Istoriya boevich korablei', 13 October 1940, p. 1.

103 *DGFP*, Series D, Vol. IX (Washington DC, 1956), pp. 291–7.

104 Ibid., pp. 353–4.

105 Quoted in Gorodetsky, op. cit., p. 58.

7 *Comrade 'Stonearse' in the Lair of the Fascist Beast*

1 Gustav Hilger & Alfred G. Meyer, *The Incompatible Allies* (New York, 1953), p. 322.

2 Ibid.

3 Valentin Berezhkov, *History in the Making: Memoirs of World War Two Diplomacy* (Moscow, 1983), p. 19.

4 Paul Schmidt, *Statist auf diplomatischer Bühne* (Wiesbaden, 1986), p. 514. This is disputed by eyewitnesses and consequently misreported by historians. Hitler's interpreter Paul Schmidt recalls that only the 'Presentation March' was played, and that the 'Internationale' was avoided, for fear that communist Berliners might be tempted to join in. Soviet interpreter Valentin Berezhkov, meanwhile, claims that the Soviet anthem *was* played. See Berezhkov, *History*, op. cit., p. 20. Newsreel footage available online shows the 'Presentation March'

clearly being played, so on that basis I consider Schmidt's account to be more reliable.

5   Elke Fröhlich (ed.), *Die Tagebücher von Joseph Goebbels*, Part 1, Vol. 8 (Munich, 1998), p. 416.

6   Schmidt, *Statist*, op. cit., p. 515. It is also referenced in the edited English edition of the memoir: Paul Schmidt, *Hitler's Interpreter* (New York, 1951), p. 209.

7   Karl-Heinz Janßen, 'Wir müssen Freunde bleiben' in *Die Zeit*, 14 June 1991.

8   The contemporary French newsreel of Molotov's arrival is 2'47", while the German version is only 2'13". See http://www.youtube.com/watch?feature=endscreen&v=2dPLEOC-uUo&NR=1 and http://www.youtube.com/watch?v=LzanQARfV2Q.

9   Felix Chuev & Albert Resis (eds.), *Molotov Remembers: Inside Kremlin Politics* (Chicago, 1993), pp. 16–17.

10 Berezhkov, *History*, op. cit., p. 21.

11 Ernst A. Busche, *Bellevue* (Leipzig, 2011), pp. 105–34.

12 Berezhkov, *History*, op. cit., p. 21.

13 Ibid., pp. 21–2.

14 Ribbentrop letter, quoted in Rudolf von Ribbentrop, *Mein Vater: Joachim von Ribbentrop, Erlebnisse und Erinnerungen* (Graz, 2013), p. 318.

15 Quoted in Albert Seaton, *Stalin as Warlord* (London, 1976), p. 94.

16 Not, as is sometimes maintained, in the Reich Chancellery, or the Bellevue Palace. See Schmidt, *Interpreter*, op. cit., p. 210.

17 Schmidt, *Statist*, op. cit., p. 516.

18 Ribbentrop–Molotov meeting, 12 November 1940, *Documents on German Foreign Policy, 1918–1945* (hereafter 'DGFP'), Series D, Vol. XI (London, 1961), pp. 533–7.

19 Ibid., p. 539.

20 Ibid., p. 541.

21 Schmidt, *Interpreter*, op. cit., p. 213.

22 Berezhkov, *History*, op. cit., p. 23.

23 Ibid.

24 Richard Overy, *The Dictators* (London, 2004), p. 20.

25 Quoted in Gabriel Gorodetsky, *Grand Delusion: Stalin and the German Invasion of Russia* (New Haven & London, 1999), p. 74.

26 *DGFP*, op. cit., p. 544.

27 Chuev & Resis (eds.), op. cit., p. 15.

28 Schmidt, *Statist*, op. cit., p. 519.

29 *DGFP*, op. cit., p. 548.

30 Schmidt, *Interpreter*, op. cit., p. 520.

31 Berezhkov, *History*, op. cit., p. 25, and Schmidt, *Statist*, op. cit., p. 520.

32 *DGFP*, op. cit., pp. 548–9.

33 Valentin Berezhkov, *At Stalin's Side* (New York, 1994), pp. 157–8.

34 Chuev & Resis (eds.), op. cit., p. 20.

35 Ibid., p. 16.

36 'Perepiska V. M. Molotova so I. V. Stalinym. Noiabr 1940g' in *Voenno-istoricheskii zhurnal*, No. 9 (1992), p. 18, quoted in Aleksandr M. Nekrich, *Pariahs, Partners, Predators: German–Soviet Relations, 1922–1941* (New York, 1997), p. 199.

37 Fröhlich (ed.), op. cit., p. 418.

38 *DGFP*, op. cit., pp. 550–3.

39 Ibid., p. 554.

40 Hans-Adolf Jacobsen (ed.), *The Halder War Diary 1939–1945* (London, 1988), p. 282.

41 *DGFP*, op. cit., p. 556.

42 Ibid., pp. 558–9.

43 Chuev & Resis (eds.), op. cit., p. 18.

44 *DGFP*, op. cit., pp. 559–60.

45 Ibid., p. 561.

46 Schmidt, *Statist*, op. cit., p. 523.

47 Chuev & Resis (eds.), op. cit., p. 16.

48 *DGFP*, op. cit., p. 562.

49 Berezhkov, *History*, op. cit., p. 42. A similar version of this exchange is related in the record of post-war interviews with Molotov: see Chuev & Resis (eds.), op. cit.

50 Schmidt, *Statist*, op. cit., p. 524.

51 *DGFP*, op. cit., pp. 564–5.

52 Ibid., p. 565.

53 Quoted in Ribbentrop, op. cit., p. 319.

54 *DGFP*, op. cit., pp. 566–9.

55 Winston Churchill, *Their Finest Hour* (London, 1949) p. 516.

56 Berlin Air Raid records, reproduced in Wieland Giebel & Sven Felix Kellerhof (eds.), *Als die Tage zu Nächten wurden* (Berlin, 2003), p. 217.

57 The official *DGFP* record of the discussion makes no mention of this last exchange, and neither does the memoir of the interpreter present, Gustav Hilger. First mention of it comes, via Stalin, from Churchill. See Churchill, op. cit., p.518. It is considered by some to be apocryphal.

58 Berezhkov, *History*, op. cit., p. 42.

59 Gorodetsky, op. cit., p. 76.

60 Quoted in Walter Warlimont, *Inside Hitler's Headquarters: 1939–45* (London, 1964), p. 113.

61 Ibid., p. 135.

62 Ibid.

63 Jacobsen (ed.), op. cit., p. 260.

64 Quoted in Gorodetsky, op. cit., p. 70.

65 Hugh Trevor-Roper (ed.), *Hitler's War Directives 1939–1945* (London, 1964), p. 86.

66 Jacobsen (ed.), op. cit., p. 286.

67 *DGFP*, op. cit., pp. 714–15.

68 Quoted in Ribbentrop, op. cit., p. 320.

69 Gorodetsky, op. cit., p. 85.

70 'Fresh Tension Reported' in the *New York Times*, 1 January 1941, p. 4.

71 Trevor-Roper (ed.), op. cit., p. 95.

8 *Riding the Nazi Tiger*

1 See William Brumfield, *Landmarks of Russian Architecture* (New York, 1997), p. 230.

2 *Pravda*, 22 December 1940, p. 5.

3 *Pravda*, 25 December 1940, p. 6, and 28 December 1940, p. 5.

4 The list of participants for the conference is available at http://militera. lib.ru/docs/da/sov-new-1940/90.html.

5 General M. I. Kazakov, quoted in Seweryn Bialer (ed.), *Stalin and his Generals: Soviet Military Memoirs of World War II* (London, 1970), p. 139.

6 Text of Meretskov's presentation is at http://militera.lib.ru/docs/da/ sov-new-1940/02.html and Russian State Military Archive (hereafter 'RSMA'), f. 4, Op. 18, 55, l. 3–45.

7 RSMA, f. 4, Op. 18, 56, l. 1–52.

8 Georgy Zhukov, *Reminiscences and Reflections*, Vol. 1 (Moscow, 1985), pp. 220–1.

9 RSMA, f. 4, Op. 18, 56, l. 85–92

10 Nikita Khrushchev, *Khrushchev Remembers* (London, 1971), pp. 145–6.

11 RSMA, f. 4, Op. 18, 59, l. 1–41.

12 Quoted in Geoffrey Roberts, *Stalin's Wars: From World War to Cold War, 1939–1953* (London, 2008), p. 71.

13 Text of Timoshenko's speech is at http://militera.lib.ru/docs/da/ sov-new-1940/88.html.

14 Gabriel Gorodetsky, *Grand Delusion: Stalin and the German Invasion of Russia* (New Haven & London, 1999), p. 124.

15 Quoted ibid., p. 125.

16 Ibid., pp. 125–6.

17   Simon Sebag Montefiore, *Stalin: The Court of the Red Tsar* (London, 2006), p. 302.

18   Ibid., p. 295.

19   Zhukov, op. cit., p. 224.

20   Ibid.

21   Quoted in Bialer (ed.), op. cit., p. 144.

22   Montefiore, op. cit., p. 296.

23   Geoffrey Roberts, *Stalin's General: The Life of Georgy Zhukov* (London, 2012), pp. 91–2, 97.

24   Quoted in Hugh Trevor-Roper (ed.), *Hitler's War Directives 1939–45* (London, 1964), p. 129 and http://avalon.law.yale.edu/imt/12–10–45. asp, p. 339.

25   Albert Seaton, *Stalin as Warlord* (London, 1976), p. 94.

26   Ibid., p. 95.

27   Valentin Berezhkov, *At Stalin's Side* (New York, 1994), p. 53.

28   Zhukov, op. cit., p. 234.

29   John Erickson, *The Soviet High Command: A Military-Political History, 1918– 1941* (London, 1962), p. 557.

30   Zhukov, op. cit., p. 234.

31   Roberts, *Zhukov*, op. cit., p. 92.

32   Neil Short, *The Stalin and Molotov Lines: Soviet Western Defences, 1928–41* (Oxford, 2008), p. 38.

33   David Glantz, *The Military Strategy of the Soviet Union: A History* (London, 1993), p. 75.

34   Gorodetsky, op. cit., p. 242.

35   Robert E. Tarleton, 'What really happened to the Stalin Line?' in *Journal of Slavic Military Studies*, Vol. 6, No. 1 (1993), p. 43.

36   Short, op. cit., p. 14.

37   Quoted in Gorodetsky, op. cit., p. 242.

38   Quoted in Edward E. Ericson III, *Feeding the German Eagle: Soviet Economic Aid to Nazi Germany, 1933–1941* (London, 1999), p. 147.

39   Ibid., p. 149.

40   Quoted in Manfred Zeidler, 'German–Soviet Economic Relations during the Hitler–Stalin Pact', in Bernd Wegner (ed.), *From Peace to War: Germany, Soviet Russia and the World, 1939–1941* (Oxford, 1997), pp. 108, 109.

41   Quoted in Ericson, op. cit., p. 160.

42   Heinrich Schwendemann, 'German–Soviet Economic Relations at the Time of the Hitler–Stalin Pact 1939–1941' in *Cahiers du Monde russe*, XXXVI (1–2), January–June 1995, p. 167.

43   Zeidler in Wegner (ed.), op. cit., p. 110.

44 Ericson, op. cit., p. 160.

45 J. B. Hoptner, *Yugoslavia in Crisis: 1934–1941* (New York, 1962), p. 240.

46 Gorodetsky, op. cit., p. 142.

47 Quoted in Trevor-Roper (ed.), op. cit., p. 107.

48 Frederick Taylor (trans. and ed.), *The Goebbels Diaries, 1939–1941* (London, 1982), p. 307.

49 Text of the Soviet–Japanese Neutrality Pact is available at http://avalon.law.yale.edu/wwii/s1.asp.

50 Quoted in Gorodetsky, op. cit., p. 199.

51 Quoted in Montefiore, op. cit., p. 308.

52 Taylor (trans. and ed.), op. cit., p. 315.

53 Text of the Anti-Comintern Pact is available at http://avalon.law.yale.edu/wwii/tri1.asp.

54 Ivo Banac (ed.), *The Diary of Georgi Dimitrov: 1933–1949* (New Haven & London, 2003), pp. 155–6.

55 Gorodetsky, op. cit., p. 200.

56 Zhores A. Medvedev & Roy A. Medvedev, *The Unknown Stalin* (London, 2006), p. 222.

57 David E. Murphy, *What Stalin Knew: The Enigma of Barbarossa* (New Haven, 2005), p. 170.

58 Speech is put together from various eyewitness accounts, such as Walter Warlimont, *Inside Hitler's Headquarters: 1939–45* (London, 1964), pp. 160–2 and Nicolaus von Below, *At Hitler's Side: The Memoirs of Hitler's Luftwaffe Adjutant, 1937–1945* (London, 2004), pp. 91–3. An interesting assessment of the various accounts is given in Jürgen Förster & Evan Mawdsley, 'Hitler and Stalin in Perspective: Secret Speeches on the Eve of Barbarossa' in *War in History*, Vol. 11, No. 1 (2004).

59 Quoted in Förster & Mawdsley, op. cit., p. 76.

60 Below, op. cit., p. 92.

61 Ibid.

62 Pavel Sudoplatov, *Special Tasks* (London, 1994), p. 117.

63 Medvedev & Medvedev, op. cit., p. 218.

64 M. J. Broekmeyer, *Stalin, the Russians, and Their War: 1941–1945* (Madison, WI, 2004), p. 21.

65 Vyacheslav Malyshev, quoted in Medvedev & Medvedev, op. cit., p. 219.

66 Quoted in Broekmeyer, op. cit., p. 21.

67 Quoted in Förster & Mawdsley, op. cit., pp. 101–2.

68 Quoted in Broekmeyer, op. cit., p. 22.

69 *Pravda*, 6 May 1941, p. 1.

70 The best analysis of the speech, and the various sources, is in Förster & Mawdsley, op. cit., pp. 61–103.

71 A theory popularised by Russian author Viktor Suvorov.

72 See, for instance, Gorodetsky, op. cit., p. 208.

73 Medvedev & Medvedev, op. cit., p. 221.

74 Taylor (trans. and ed.), op. cit., p. 364.

75 See Lothar Kettenacker, 'Mishandling a Spectacular Event: The Rudolf Hess Affair', in David Stafford (ed.), *Flight from Reality: Rudolf Hess and his Mission to Scotland, 1941* (London, 2002), pp. 19–37.

76 Quoted in David Dilks (ed.), *The Diaries of Sir Alexander Cadogan, 1938–1945* (London, 1971), p. 382.

77 Quoted in Robert Service, *Spies and Commissars: The Bolshevik Revolution and the West* (London, 2011), p. 184.

78 Nikita Khrushchev, *Khrushchev Remembers* (London, 1971), p. 116.

79 Memoir of Yury Chadayev, quoted in S. Berthon & J. Potts, *Warlords* (New York, 2006), p. 72.

80 On the Soviet reaction to the Hess story, see John Erickson, 'Rudolf Hess: A Post-Soviet Postscript', in Stafford (ed.), op. cit., pp. 38–60.

81 Quoted in Zhukov, op. cit., p. 268.

82 Roberts, *Zhukov* op. cit., p. 91.

83 Quoted in Seaton, op. cit., p. 95.

84 Gorodetsky, op. cit., p. 244.

85 Quoted in Roberts, *Zhukov* op. cit., p. 93.

86 Neil Short, *The Stalin and Molotov Lines: Soviet Western Defences, 1928–41* (Oxford, 2008), pp. 39, 41.

87 Zhukov, op. cit., pp. 263–4.

88 Ericson, op. cit., p. 170.

89 Schwendemann, op. cit., p. 168.

90 Kuznetzov in Bialer (ed.), op. cit., p. 191.

91 Ericson, op. cit., p. 172.

92 Quoted in ibid., p. 162.

93 Quoted in Robert Service, *Stalin* (London, 2008), p. 405.

94 Taylor (trans. and ed.), op. cit., p. 414.

95 Alfred Gottwaldt & Diana Schulle, *Die 'Judendeportationen' aus dem Deutschen Reich 1941– 1945* (Wiesbaden, 2005), p. 51.

96 Christopher Browning, *The Origins of the Final Solution: The Evolution of Nazi Jewish Policy, 1939–1942* (London, 2005), p. 90.

97 Saul Friedländer, *The Years of Extermination: Nazi Germany and the Jews, 1939– 1945* (London, 2007), p. 139.

98 Quoted in Herbert Rosenkranz, *Verfolgung und Selbstbehauptung: Die Juden in Österreich, 1938– 1945* (Vienna, 1978), p. 262.

99 Quoted in Friedländer, op. cit., p. 166.

100 Browning, op. cit., pp. 102–3.

101 Dumitru Nimigeanu, *Însemările unui țăran deportat din Bucovina* (Bucharest, 2006), p. 26.

102 Testimony given in K. Pelékis, *Genocide: Lithuania's Threefold Tragedy* (Germany, 1949), p. 47.

103 Nimigeanu, op. cit., pp. 31–2.

104 Guzevičius order, 28 November 1940, quoted in *Select Committee on Communist Aggression*, Vol. III (Washington DC, 1954), pp. 470–2.

105 Latvian State Archive. Fond Nr. 1987, Nr. 1 – Madona, Case Nr. 16272, Page 2. With thanks to Nauris Larmanis for supplying the documentation and translation.

106 Arvydas Anušauskas, *Terror and Crimes against Humanity: The First Soviet Occupation, 1940–1941* (Vilnius, 2006), p. 72.

107 The 'Serov Instructions', text quoted in Aleksandras Shtromas, *Totalitarianism and the Prospects for World Order* (Oxford, 2003), p. 292.

108 Quoted in Astrid Sics (ed.), *We Sang Through the Tears: Stories of Survival in Siberia* (Riga, 1999), p. 72.

109 Quoted in Kristi Kukk & Toivo Raun (eds.), *Soviet Deportations in Estonia: Impact and Legacy* (Tallinn, 2007), p. 165.

110 Quoted in Tadeusz Piotrowski (ed.), *The Polish Deportees of World War Two: Recollections of Removal to the Soviet Union and Dispersal Throughout the World* (London, 2004), p. 30.

111 Lidija Vilnis, in Sics (ed.), op. cit., p. 91.

112 Sandra Kalniete, *With Dance Shoes in Siberian Snows* (Riga, 2006), p. 62.

113 Nicolae Enciu, '12–13 iunie. Primele deportari staliniste' in 'Art-Emis' online magazine, http://www.art-emis.ro/istorie/1642–12–13-iunie-primele-deportari-staliniste.html.

114 Quoted in Kukk & Raun (eds.), op. cit., p. 204.

115 Herta Kaļiņina, quoted in Sics (ed.), op. cit., p. 73.

116 Quoted in Kukk & Raun (eds.), op. cit., p. 167.

117 Melãnija Vanaga, in Sics (ed.), op. cit., p. 60.

118 Statistics quoted in Romuald Misiunas & Rein Taagepera, *The Baltic States: Years of Dependence 1940–1980* (London, 1983), p. 42.

119 The Commission for study and appreciation of the totalitarian communist regime in Moldova, *Moldovenii sub teroarea bolşevică*, 2010, http://www.scribd.com/doc/51121384/Moldovenii-sub-teroarea-bol%C5%9Fevic%C4%83, p. 40.

120 This figure, as with many others from the deportations, is disputed and comes from Keith Sword *Deportation and Exile: Poles in the Soviet Union 1939–48* (Basingstoke, 1994), p. 26. A much lower figure of 22,353 is cited in Timothy Snyder, *Bloodlands: Europe between Hitler and Stalin* (London, 2010), p. 151.

121 Quoted in Erickson, *Soviet High Command*, op. cit., p. 574.

122 Quoted in Winston Churchill, *The Second World War* (London, 1989), p. 452.

123 Quoted in John Lukacs, *June 1941: Hitler and Stalin* (New Haven, 2006), pp. 78–9.

124 Felix Chuev & Albert Resis (eds.), *Molotov Remembers: Inside Kremlin Politics* (Chicago, 1993), p. 31.

125 Ruth Andreas-Friedrich, *Berlin Underground, 1938–1945* (New York, 1947), pp. 67–8.

126 Montefiore, op. cit., p. 313.

127 Quoted in Gorodetsky, op. cit., p. 299.

128 Fediuninskii in Bialer (ed.), op. cit., p. 241.

129 Mihai Sebastian, *Journal 1935–1944* (London, 2003), p. 369.

130 Details quoted in an interview with historian Arsan Martirosyan in *Komsomolskaya Pravda*, 20 June 2011, http://www.kp.ru/daily/25706/906806/.

131 Wolfgang Leonhard, 'Wer war Alfred Liskow, und was hatte er mit Dimitroff zu tun?' in *Frankfurter Allgemeine Zeitung*, No. 278, 29 November 2000.

132 Gorodetsky, op. cit., p. 309.

133 See ibid., pp. 311–13, and Montefiore, op. cit., pp. 323–4.

9 *No Honour among Thieves*

1 John Erickson, *The Road to Stalingrad* (London, 1993) pp. 115–16.

2 Valentin Berezhkov, quoted in Seweryn Bialer (ed.), *Stalin and his Generals: Soviet Military Memoirs of World War II* (London, 1970), pp. 217–18.

3 Max Domarus, *Hitler: Reden und Proklamationen 1932–1945*, Vol. III (Wiesbaden, 1973), pp. 1731–2, English text from the *New York Times*, 23 June 1941.

4 Frederick Taylor (trans. and ed.), *The Goebbels Diaries, 1939–1941* (London, 1982), pp. 424–5.

5 John Colville, *The Fringes of Power: Downing Street Diaries 1939–1955* (London, 1985), p. 481.

6 Anthony Eden, *The Eden Memoirs: The Reckoning* (London, 1965), p. 270.

7 Winston S. Churchill, *The Second World War* (abridged edition, London, 1959), p. 455.

8 Anatoly Liberman (trans. and ed.), *Mikhail Lermontov: Major Poetical Works* (Minneapolis, 1983), p. 101.

9 Alexander Nekrich, *1941 22 iiunia* (Moscow, 1995), p. 204.

10   Constantine Pleshakov, *Stalin's Folly* (London, 2005), p. 6.

11   Quoted in Bialer (ed.), op. cit., p. 197.

12   Rodric Braithwaite, *Moscow 1941* (London, 2006), p. 79.

13   Ivo Banac (ed.), *The Diary of Georgi Dimitrov, 1933–1949* (New Haven & London, 2003), p. 166.

14   Quoted in Catherine Merridale, *Ivan's War: The Red Army 1939–1945* (London, 2005), p. 77, and Geoffrey Roberts, *Molotov: Stalin's Cold Warrior* (Washington DC, 2012), p. 51. Text also at http://www.emersonkent.com/speeches/our_cause_is_just.htm.

15   Quoted in Braithwaite, op. cit., p. 75.

16   Quoted in David Glantz, *Barbarossa: Hitler's Invasion of Russia 1941* (Stroud, 2001), pp. 242–3.

17   Pleshakov, op. cit., p. 130.

18   Erickson, op. cit., p. 129.

19   Quoted in Merridale, op. cit., p. 76.

20   Christer Bergström, *Barbarossa – The Air Battle: July–December 1941* (London, 2007), p. 20.

21   Nicolaus von Below, *At Hitler's Side: The Memoirs of Hitler's Luftwaffe Adjutant, 1937–1945* (London, 2004), p. 107.

22   Simon Sebag Montefiore, *Stalin: The Court of the Red Tsar* (London, 2003), p. 326.

23   Glantz, op. cit., p. 36.

24   Steven J. Zaloga, *T-34/76 Medium Tank 1941–45* (Oxford, 1994), p. 12.

25   Account from the 1st Panzer Division, quoted in Paul Carell, *Hitler Moves East: 1941–1943* (Boston, 1964), p. 23.

26   Zaloga, op. cit., p. 12.

27   Stephen Zaloga & James Grandsen, *Soviet Tanks and Combat Vehicles of World War Two* (London, 1984), p. 127.

28   R. Tarleton, 'What Really Happened to the Stalin Line?' (Part II) in *Journal of Slavic Military Studies*, Vol. 6, No. 1, March 1993, p. 51.

29   J. E. Kaufmann & Robert M. Jurga, *Fortress Europe: European Fortifications of World War Two* (London, 1999), p. 362.

30   Heinz Guderian, *Panzer Leader* (London, 1952), pp. 146–7.

31   Christian Ganzer & Alena Paškovič, '"Heldentum, Tragik, Tapferkeit": Das Museum der Verteidigung der Brester Festung' in *Osteuropa*, 60. Jg., 12/2010, pp. 81–96.

32   Glantz, op. cit., p. 80.

33   See above p. 188. Total German oil stocks in the period 1939–41 amounted to around 8 million tons, of which the USSR had supplied approximately 1 million.

34   Edward E. Ericson III, *Feeding the German Eagle: Soviet Economic Aid to Nazi Germany, 1933–1941* (London, 1999), p. 179.

35   Alexander Yakovlev in Bialer (ed.), op. cit., p. 170.

36   Tobias Philbin, *The Lure of Neptune: German–Soviet Naval Collaboration and Ambitions, 1919–1941* (Columbia, SC, 1994), p. 128.

37   Quoted in Geoffrey Roberts, *Stalin's Wars: From World War to Cold War 1939–1953* (London, 2006), p. 85.

38   Romuald Misiunas & Rein Taagepera, *The Baltic States: Years of Dependence 1940–1990* (London, 1983), p. 48.

39   Boris Takk, quoted in Ene Kõresaar (ed.), *Soldiers of Memory: World War II and Its Aftermath in Estonian Post-Soviet Life Stories* (New York, 2011), p. 188.

40   Valdis Lumans, *Latvia in World War II* (New York, 2006), p. 155.

41   L'vov from Merridale, op. cit., p. 83, and Kovel from Alexander Werth, *Russia at War, 1941–1945* (London, 1964), p. 149

42   Merridale, op. cit., pp. 79–81.

43   Quoted in Braithwaite, op. cit., p. 77.

44   Hans von Luck, *Panzer Commander* (London, 1989), p. 70.

45   Braithwaite, op. cit., p. 85.

46   Quoted in Merridale, op. cit., p. 82.

47   William Spahr, *Stalin's Lieutenants: A Study of Command under Duress*, (Novato, CA, 1997), p. 265.

48   Colonel I. T. Starinov, quoted in Bialer (ed.), op. cit., p. 237.

49   Georgi Zhukov, *Reminiscences and Reflections*, Vol. 1 (Moscow, 1985), p. 309, and Montefiore, op. cit., p. 330.

50   Geoffrey Roberts, *Stalin's General: The Life of Georgy Zhukov* (London, 2012), pp. 106–7.

51   Mikoyan, quoted in Montefiore, op. cit., p. 330.

52   See, for example, Jonathan Lewis & Phillip Whitehead, *Stalin: A Time for Judgement* (New York, 1990), and Alan Bullock, *Hitler and Stalin: Parallel Lives* (London, 1991).

53   Zhores A. Medvedev & Roy A. Medvedev, *The Unknown Stalin* (London, 2006), p. 232.

54   See, for example, Montefiore, op. cit., p. 332.

55   English translation of Stalin's 3 July 1941 speech is at: http://www.ibiblio.org/pha/policy/1941/410703a.html.

56   Lieutenant General Ivan Boldin, Pavlov's deputy commander, quoted in Werth, op. cit., pp. 157–8.

57   Erickson, op. cit., p. 176.

58   Quoted in Robert Gellately, *Lenin, Stalin and Hitler: The Age of Social Catastrophe* (London, 2007), p. 478.

59 Michael Parrish, *The Lesser Terror: Soviet State Security, 1939–1953* (London, 1996), p. 77.

60 Ibid., p. 81.

61 Karel Berkhoff, *Harvest of Despair: Life and Death in Ukraine under Nazi Rule* (Cambridge, MA, 2004), p. 14.

62 Quoted in Bogdan Musial, *Konterrevolutionäre Elemente sind zu erschießen* (Berlin, 2000), p. 101.

63 Grzegorz Hryciuk, 'Victims 1939–1941: The Soviet Repressions in Eastern Poland', in Elazar Barkan, Elizabeth A. Cole & Kai Struve (eds.), *Shared History, Divided Memory: Jews and Others in Soviet-Occupied Poland, 1939–1941* (Leipzig, 2007), pp. 193–4.

64 Report of the Estonian Historical Commission, Phase I, *The Soviet Occupation of Estonia in 1940–1941*, p. 14., at http://www.mnemosyne.ee/hc.ee/pdf/conclusions_en_1940–1941.pdf.

65 *The Rainiai Tragedy: A Forgotten Soviet War Crime* (Vilnius, 2007), p. 12, at http://www.e-library.lt/resursai/Mokslai/LRS%20mokslininkai/V.Landsbergis/Rainiai/Rainiai_EN_Book.p df.

66 Romanian National Archive, f. 680, inv. 1, d. 4232, p. 3, f. 545–546, cited in Iulian Chifu, *Basarabia sub ocupatie sovietica si tentative contemporane de revenire sub tutela Moscovei* (Bucharest, 2004), p. 86.

67 Musial, op. cit., pp. 97, 138.

68 For details, see ibid., p. 102 and *passim*.

69 Quoted in ibid., p. 115.

70 Lumans, op. cit., p. 138.

71 *Rainiai Tragedy*, op. cit., p. 9.

72 Estonian Historical Commission Report, op. cit., p. 14.

73 Hryciuk, op. cit., p. 183. Higher figure of 20,000–30,000 is given by Musial, op. cit., p. 138.

74 Jan Gross, *Revolution from Abroad* (Princeton, 1988), p. 228.

75 Ernst Klee, Volker Reiss & Willi Dressen (eds.), *'Schöne Zeiten' Judenmord aus der Sicht der Täter und Gaffer* (Frankfurt am Main, 1988), pp. 35–6.

76 Ibid., p. 39.

77 Timothy Snyder, *Bloodlands* (London, 2010), p. 192.

78 Musial, op. cit., p. 172.

79 Ibid., pp. 177, 179.

80 Quoted in ibid., p. 188.

81 Wendy Lower, '"Anticipatory Obedience" and the Nazi Implementation of the Holocaust in the Ukraine: A Case Study of Central and Peripheral Forces in the Generalbezirk Zhytomyr, 1941–1944' in *Holocaust and Genocide Studies*, Vol. 16, No. 1 (2002).

82 Quoted in Richard Rhodes, *Masters of Death* (Oxford, 2002), p. 45.

83 Geoff Swain, *Between Stalin and Hitler: Class War and Race War on the Dvina* (London, 2004), p. 40.

84 Zvi Gitelman (ed.), *Bitter Legacy: Confronting the Holocaust in the* USSR (Bloomington, 1997), p. 266.

85 Klee et al., op. cit., p. 39.

86 Quoted in Andrew Ezergailis, *The Holocaust in Latvia 1941–1945* (Riga, 1996), p. 104.

87 Snyder, op. cit., p. 194.

88 Henry W. Flannery, *Assignment to Berlin* (London, 1942), p. 259.

89 Victor Klemperer, *I Shall Bear Witness* (London, 1998), p. 373.

90 Marie Vassiltchikov, *The Berlin Diaries of Marie 'Missie' Vassiltchikov: 1940–45* (London, 1985), p. 55.

91 Ruth Andreas-Friedrich, *Berlin Underground, 1938–1945* (New York, 1947), p. 68.

92 Quoted in 'Himmler letters: "I am travelling to Auschwitz. Kisses. Your Heini"' in *Daily Telegraph*, 26 January 2014, at http://www.telegraph.co.uk/news/worldnews/europe/germany/10597344/Himmler-letters-I-am-travelling-to-Auschwitz.-Kisses.-Your-Heini.html.

93 Author interview with Leopold Gernhardt, April 2008. See also Roger Moorhouse, 'The Nazi Final' in *BBC History Magazine*, June 2008.

94 Andreas-Friedrich, op. cit., p. 68.

95 Heinz Kühnrich, *Die KPD im Kampf gegen die faschistische Diktatur 1933–1945* (Berlin, 1987), p. 180.

96 Quoted in Braithwaite, op. cit., p. 75.

97 Molotov speech quoted in Werth, op. cit., p. 163; vox pop quoted in Braithwaite, op. cit., p. 80.

98 Werth, op. cit., pp. 177–8.

99 Ibid., p. 168.

100 Alex Danchev & Daniel Todman (eds.), *War Diaries 1939–1945: Field Marshal Lord Alanbrooke* (London, 2001), p. 166.

101 Nigel Nicolson (ed.), *Diaries and Letters of Harold Nicolson* (London, 1970), p. 173.

102 Churchill, op. cit., p. 462 ; Eden, op. cit., p. 270.

103 Nicolson, op. cit., p. 173; Danchev & Todman (eds.), op. cit., p. 166.

104 Gabriel Gorodetsky, *Stafford Cripps' Mission to Moscow, 1940–42* (Cambridge, 1984), p. 168.

105 Joseph P. Lash, *Roosevelt and Churchill, 1939–1941: The Partnership that Saved the West* (London, 1977), p. 343.

106 Quoted in Graham Stewart, *His Finest Hours: The War Speeches of Winston Churchill* (London, 2007), pp. 102–5.

107   Nicolson (ed.), op. cit., p. 173.

108   Colville, op. cit., p. 480.

109   Richard Toye, *The Roar of the Lion* (London, 2013), pp. 107–8.

110   Quoted in ibid., p. 108.

111   John Mahon, *Harry Pollitt: A Biography* (London, 1976), p. 269.

112   Quoted in Lynne Olson, *Those Angry Days: Roosevelt, Lindbergh, and America's Fight over World War Two, 1939–1941* (New York, 2013), p. 346.

113   Ivan Maisky, *Memoirs of a Soviet Ambassador: The War 1939–1943* (London, 1967), p. 172.

114   Glantz, op. cit., pp. 40, 45, 53.

115   Maisky, op. cit., p. 172.

116   Anna Cienciala, 'General Sikorski and the Conclusion of the Polish–Soviet Agreement of July 30, 1941: A Reassessment' in *Polish Review*, Vol. 41, No. 4 (1996), p. 413.

117   Halik Kochanski, *The Eagle Unbowed: Poland in World War Two* (London, 2012), p. 166.

118   David Dilks (ed.), *The Diaries of Sir Alexander Cadogan, 1938–1945* (London, 1971), p. 391.

119   Kochanski, op. cit., p. 167.

120   Cienciala, op. cit., p. 427.

121   Winston S. Churchill, *The Second World War: The Grand Alliance* (London, 1950), p. 349.

122   Maisky, op. cit., p. 174.

123   Eden, op. cit., p.273.

124   Gabriel Gorodetsky (ed.), *Stafford Cripps in Moscow, 1940–1942* (London, 2007), p. 132.

125   English language text of the agreement is at http://avalon.law.yale.edu/wwii/polsov.asp.

126   Colville, op. cit., p. 502.

Epilogue: Life After Death

1   Hugh Trevor-Roper (ed.), *Hitler's Table Talk, 1941–1944* (London, 2000), p. 24.

2   Text reported by the *New York Times*, 4 October 1941.

3   Hitler to Mussolini, 21 June 1941, quoted in R. J. Sontag and J. S. Beddie (eds.), *Nazi–Soviet Relations, 1939 –1941* (Washington, 1948), pp. 351, 353.

4   Quoted in Ann Tusa and John Tusa, *The Nuremberg Trial* (London, 1983),

p. 194.

5 Exchange quoted in James Owen, *Nuremberg: Evil on Trial* (London, 2006), pp. 250–1.

6 Tusa and Tusa, op. cit., pp. 297, 179–80.

7 Ibid., pp. 410–12.

8 The collection is available online, http://www.ibiblio.org/pha/nsr/nsr-preface.html.

9 Sovinformburo, *Falsifiers of History* (Moscow, 1948), pp. 6, 27 and 44.

10 Ibid., p. 41.

11 Ibid., p. 43.

12 John Erickson, 'How the Soviets Fought the War', in *Problems of Communism*, November 1963, p. 53.

13 Matthew P. Gallagher, *The Soviet History of World War II* (New York, 1963), p. 169.

14 Nikita Khrushchev, *Khrushchev Remembers* (London, 1971), p. 112.

15 Felix Chuev & Albert Resis (eds.), *Molotov Remembers: Inside Kremlin Politics* (Chicago, 1993), p. 23.

16 Ibid., p. 13.

17 Ann Imse, 'Baltic Residents Form Human Chain in Defiance of Soviet Rule', *Associated Press*, 23 August 1989.

18 David Remnick, 'Kremlin Condemns Baltic Nationalists; Soviets Warn Separatism Risks "Disaster"', *Washington Post*, 27 August 1989.

19 On this, see Keiji Sato, 'Die Molotow-Ribbentrop-Kommission 1989 und die Souveränitätsansprüche post-sowjetischer sezessionistischer Territorien', in Anna Kaminsky, Dietmar Müller & Stefan Troebst (eds.), *Der Hitler-Stalin-Pakt 1939 in den Erinnerungskulturen der Europäer* (Göttingen, 2011), pp. 199–215.

20 Text of the report in Gerhart Hass, *23. August 1939. Der Hitler-Stalin-Pakt* (Berlin, 1990), pp. 300–1.

21 Jerzy Borejsza, Klaus Ziemer and Magdalena Hułas, *Totalitarian and Authoritarian Regimes in Europe* (Oxford, 2006), p. 521.

22 'Chronology 1990: The Soviet Union and Eastern Europe', *Foreign Affairs*, 1990, p. 212.

23 See, for instance, Katja Wezel, 'Lettland und der 23. August 1939: Vom "weißen Fleck" der sowjetischen Geschichtsschreibung zum transnationalen Gedenktag?', in Kaminsky et al. (eds.), op. cit., pp. 309–25.

24 Siiri Oviir, quoted at http://www.europarl.europa.eu/sides/getDoc.do?type=CRE&reference=20090402&secondRef=ITEM-010&language=EN&ring=P6-RC-2009-0165#4-176 (accessed March 2014).

25 Written submission of Athanasios Palfilis, recorded at http://www.europarl.europa.eu/sides/getDoc.do?type=CRE&reference=20090402

&secondRef=ITEM-010&language=EN&ring=P6-RC-2009-0165#4-176 (accessed February 2014).

26 Jonathan Steele, 'History is too important to be left to politicians', *Guardian/CiF*, 19 August 2009.

27 Report from *Rossiyskaya Gazeta*, reproduced at http://www.telegraph. co.uk/sponsored/rbth/6106486/The-Molotov-Ribbentrop-Pact-between-Nazi-Germany-and-the-Soviet-Union-70-years-on.html.

28 Sergei Markov, quoted in Andrew Osborn, 'Medvedev Creates History Commission', *Wall Street Journal*, 21 May, 2009, at http://online.wsj. com/news/articles/SB124277297306236553?mg=reno64-wsj&url= http%3A%2F%2Fonline.wsj.com%2Farticle%2FSB124277297306236553.html.

Bibliography

PRIMARY SOURCES, UNPUBLISHED

Andor Hencke, *Die deutsch-sowjetischen Beziehungen zwischen 1932 und 1941*, unpublished protocol held at the Institut für Zeitgeschichte, Munich, MA 1300/2

Kriegstagebuch des Generalkommandos XIX AK über den Feldzug in Polen, September 1939

PRIMARY SOURCES, PUBLISHED

Ruth Andreas-Friedrich, *Berlin Underground, 1938–1945* (New York, 1947)

Ivo Banac (ed.), *The Diary of Georgi Dimitrov, 1933–1949* (New Haven & London, 2003)

Janusz Bardach, *Man is Wolf to Man* (London, 1998)

Hans Baur, *Hitler's Pilot* (London, 1958)

Nicolaus von Below, *At Hitler's Side* (London, 2004)

Valentin Berezhkov, *History in the Making: Memoirs of World War Two Diplomacy* (Moscow, 1983)

Valentin Berezhkov, *At Stalin's Side* (New York, 1994)

Heinz Boberach (ed.), *Meldungen aus dem Reich: 1938–1945* (Herrsching, 1984)

Charles Bohlen, *Witness to History, 1929–1969* (New York, 1973)

Margarete Buber-Neumann, *Under Two Dictators* (London, 2008)

Felix Chuev & Albert Resis (eds.), *Molotov Remembers: Inside Kremlin Politics* (Chicago, 1993)

Winston S. Churchill, *The Second World War* (London, 1989)

John Colville, *The Fringes of Power: Downing Street Diaries 1939–1955* (London, 1985)

Alex Danchev & Daniel Todman (eds.), *War Diaries 1939–1945: Field Marshal Lord Alanbrooke* (London, 2001)

Jane Degras (ed.), *The Communist International, 1919–1943 Documents* (New York, 1965)

Jane Degras (ed.), *Soviet Documents on Foreign Policy*, Vol. III (New York, 1978)

David Dilks (ed.), *The Diaries of Sir Alexander Cadogan 1938–1945* (London, 1971)

Documents on German Foreign Policy 1918–1945, Series D, Vols VII, VIII, IX, X, XI (London, 1961)

Anthony Eden, *The Eden Memoirs: The Reckoning* (London, 1965)

Elke Fröhlich (ed.), *Die Tagebücher von Joseph Goebbels* (Munich, 1998)

Hugh Gibson (ed.), *The Ciano Diaries: 1939–1943* (New York, 1946)

Hans-Bernd Gisevius, *To the Bitter End* (Boston, 1947)

Heinz Guderian, *Panzer Leader* (London, 1952)

Hans-Adolf Jacobsen (ed.), *The Halder War Diary 1939–1945* (London, 1988)

Ulrich von Hassell, *The Ulrich von Hassell Diaries, 1938–1944* (London, 2011)

Johnnie von Herwarth, *Against Two Evils* (London, 1981)

Gustav Hilger, *Wir und den Kreml* (Berlin, 1956)

Gustav Hilger & Alfred G. Meyer, *The Incompatible Allies* (New York, 1953)

Adolf Hitler, *Mein Kampf* (London, 1939)

Eric Hobsbawm, *Interesting Times* (London, 2002)

Heinrich Hoffmann, *Hitler was my Friend* (Barnsley, 2011)

Nikita Khrushchev, *Khrushchev Remembers* (London, 1971)

Peter Kleist, *Zwischen Hitler und Stalin, 1939–1945* (Bonn, 1950)

Victor Klemperer, *I Shall Bear Witness, 1933–1941* (London, 1998)

Semyon Krivoshein, *Mezhdubure* (Voronezh, 1964)

Ivan Maisky, *Memoirs of a Soviet Ambassador: The War 1939–1943* (London, 1967)

Nigel Nicolson (ed.), *Harold Nicolson: Diaries and Letters 1930–1939* (London, 1966)

Edward Raczyński, *In Allied London* (London, 1962)

Paul Schmidt, *Hitler's Interpreter* (New York, 1951)

Paul Schmidt, *Statist auf diplomatischer Bühne* (Wiesbaden, 1984)

Mihail Sebastian, *Journal 1935–1944* (Chicago, 2000)

Select Committee on Communist Aggression, Vol. III (Washington DC, 1954)

Dorothy Sheridan (ed.), *Among You Taking Notes… The Wartime Diary of Naomi Mitchison 1939–1945* (London, 1985)

William Shirer, *This is Berlin: Reporting from Germany 1938–1940* (London, 1999)

R. J. Sontag & J. S. Beddie, *Nazi–Soviet Relations 1939–1941* (Washington DC, 1948)

Albert Speer, *Inside the Third Reich* (London, 1970)

Walter Warlimont, *Inside Hitler's Headquarters* (London, 1964)

Georgy Zhukov, *Reminiscences and Reflections*, 2 vols. (Moscow, 1985)

SECONDARY SOURCES

Paul Addison & Jeremy A. Crang (eds.), *Listening to Britain* (London, 2011)

Christopher Andrew & Oleg Gordievsky, *KGB: The Inside Story of its Foreign Operations from Lenin to Gorbachev* (London, 1990)

Arvydas Anušauskas, *Terror and Crimes against Humanity: The First Soviet Occupation, 1940–1941* (Vilnius, 2006)

Elazar Barkan, Elizabeth A. Cole & Kai Struve (eds.), *Shared History – Divided Memory. Jews and Others in Soviet-Occupied Poland 1939–1941*, Leipziger Beiträge zur Jüdischen Geschichte und Kultur (Leipzig, 2007)

Sergo Beria, *Beria, My Father* (London, 2001)

Karel Berkhoff, *Harvest of Despair: Life and Death in Ukraine under Nazi Rule* (Cambridge, MA, 2004)

Lew Besymenski, 'Geheimmission in Stalins Auftrag?' in *Vierteljahrshefte für Zeitgeschichte*, Vol. 40, No. 3 (1992)

Seweryn Bialer (ed.), *Stalin and his Generals: Soviet Military Memoirs of World War II* (London, 1970)

Wolfgang Birkenfeld, 'Stalin als der Wirtschaftspartner Hitlers, 1939–1941' in *Vierteljahrshefte für Sozial und Wirtschaftsgeschichte*, Vol. 53 (1966)

Gerhard Bisovsky et al (eds.), *Der Hitler-Stalin-Pakt: Voraussetzungen, Hintergründe, Auswirkungen* (Vienna, 1990)

Jochen Böhler, *Zbrodnie Wehrmachtu w Polsce* (Kraków, 2009)

Jerzy Borejsza, Klaus Ziemer & Magdalena Hułas, *Totalitarian and Authoritarian Regimes in Europe* (Oxford, 2006)

Rodric Braithwaite, *Moscow 1941* (London, 2006)

Christopher Browning, *The Origins of the Final Solution: The Evolution of Nazi Jewish Policy, 1939–1942* (London, 2005)

Christopher Browning, *Remembering Survival* (London, 2010)

J. W. Brügel, 'Das Sowjetische Ultimatum an Rumänien im Juni 1940' in *Vierteljahrshefte für Zeitgeschichte*, Vol. 11, No. 4 (1963)

Achim Bühl (ed.), *Der Hitler-Stalin-Pakt: Die sowjetische Debatte* (Cologne, 1989)

Alan Bullock, *Hitler and Stalin: Parallel Lives* (London, 1991)

Angus Calder, *The Myth of the Blitz* (London, 1991)

Anna Cienciala, 'General Sikorski and the Conclusion of the Polish-Soviet Agreement of July 30, 1941: A Reassessment' in *Polish Review*, Vol. 41, No. 4 (1996)

Anna Cienciala, Natalia Lebedeva & Wojciech Materski (eds.), *Katyn: A Crime without Punishment* (New Haven, 2007)

Katerina Clark, *Moscow, The Fourth Rome* (London, 2011)

Robert Conquest, *Stalin: Breaker of Nations* (London, 1991)

Ion Constantin & Valeriu Florin Dobrinescu, *Basarabia în anii celui de al doilea război mondial: 1939–1947* (Iaşi, 1995)

Stéphane Courtois, *The Black Book of Communism: Crimes, Terror, Repression* (Cambridge, MA, 1999)

Robert Dallek, *Franklin D. Roosevelt and American Foreign Policy 1932–1945* (Oxford, 1995)

Norman Davies, *God's Playground: A History of Poland*, Vol. 2 (Oxford, 1981)

Norman Davies & Antony Polonski (eds.), *Jews in Eastern Poland and the USSR, 1939–46* (London, 1990)

Sarah Davies, *Popular Opinion in Stalin's Russia: Terror, Propaganda and Dissent, 1934–1941* (Cambridge, 1997)

Peter Davison (ed.), *Orwell and Politics* (London, 2001)

Paul W. Doerr, '"Frigid but Unprovocative": British Policy towards the USSR from the Nazi–Soviet Pact to the Winter War, 1939' in *Journal of Contemporary History*, Vol. 36, No. 3 (2001)

Max Domarus, *Hitler, Speeches and Proclamations, 1932–1945*, Vol. II (London, 1992)

Horst Duhnke, *Die KPD von 1933 bis 1945* (Cologne, 1972)

Dennis J. Dunn, *Caught Between Roosevelt & Stalin* (Kentucky, 1997)

James Eaden & David Renton, *The Communist Party of Great Britain since 1920* (Basingstoke, 2002)

Robert Edwards, *White Death: Russia's War on Finland 1939–40* (London, 2006)

Dietrich Eichholtz, *War for Oil: The Nazi Quest for an Oil Empire* (Washington DC, 2012)

Eloise Engel & Lauri Paananen, *The Winter War* (London, 1973)

John Erickson, *The Road to Stalingrad* (London, 1993)

John Erickson, *The Soviet High Command: A Military-Political History, 1918–1941* (London, 1962)

Ljubica Erickson & Mark Erickson (eds.), *Russia: War, Peace and Diplomacy* (London, 2005)

Edward E. Ericson III, *Feeding the German Eagle: Soviet Economic Aid to Nazi Germany, 1933–1941* (London, 1999)

Edward E. Ericson III, 'Karl Schnurre and the Evolution of Nazi–Soviet Relations, 1936–1941' in *German Studies Review*, Vol. 21, No. 2 (May 1998)

Andrew Ezergailis, *The Holocaust in Latvia 1941–1945* (Riga, 1996)

Orlando Figes, *The Whisperers: Private Life in Stalin's Russia* (London, 2007)

Fridrikh I. Firsov, Harvey Klehr & John Earl Haynes, *Secret Cables of the Comintern, 1933–1943* (New Haven & London, 2014)

Ingeborg Fleischhauer, *Der Pakt: Hitler, Stalin und die Initiative der deutschen Diplomatie 1938–39* (Frankfurt am Main, 1990)

Ingeborg Fleischhauer, 'Der Deutsch-Sowjetische Grenz- und Freundschaftsvertrag vom 28. September 1939' in *Vierteljahrshefte für Zeitgeschichte*, Vol. 39, No. 3 (1991)

Jürgen Förster et al., *Deutschland und das bolschewistische Rußland von Brest-Litowsk bis 1941* (Berlin, 1991)

Jürgen Förster & Evan Mawdsley, 'Hitler and Stalin in Perspective: Secret Speeches on the Eve of Barbarossa' in *War in History*, Vol. 11, No. 1 (2004)

Hans Frank, *Das Diensttagebuch des deutschen Generalgouverneurs in Polen 1939–1945* (Stuttgart, 1975)

Saul Friedländer, *The Years of Extermination: Nazi Germany and the Jews, 1939–1945* (London, 2007)

Christian Ganzer & Alena Paškovič, '"Heldentum, Tragik, Tapferkeit": Das Museum der Verteidigung der Brester Festung', in *Osteuropa*, 60. Jg., 12/2010

Juliet Gardiner, *Wartime Britain: 1939–1945* (London, 2004)

Jósef Garliński, *Poland in the Second World War* (London, 1985)

Robert Gellately, *Lenin, Stalin and Hitler: The Age of Social Catastrophe* (London, 2007)

Albert Gerutis, 'Der Hitler-Stalin Pakt und seine Auswirkung im Baltikum' in *Acta Baltica*, Vol. 19 (1981)

Robert Gerwarth, *Hitler's Hangman: The Life of Heydrich* (London, 2011)

Wieland Giebel & Sven Felix Kellerhof (eds.), *Als die Tage zu Nächten wurden* (Berlin, 2003)

Zvi Gitelman (ed.), *Bitter Legacy: Confronting the Holocaust in the USSR* (Bloomington, 1997)

Dinu Giurescu, *Romania in the Second World War* (New York, 2000)

David Glantz, *Barbarossa: Hitler's Invasion of Russia 1941* (Stroud, 2001)

Mary E. Glantz, *FDR and the Soviet Union* (Kansas, 2005)

Aaron Goldman, 'Defence Regulation 18B: Emergency Internment of Aliens and Political Dissenters in Great Britain during World War II', in *Journal of British Studies*, Vol. 12, No. 2, May 1973

Gabriel Gorodetsky, *Grand Delusion: Stalin and the German Invasion of Russia* (New Haven & London, 2001)

Gabriel Gorodetsky, *Stafford Cripps' Mission to Moscow 1940–42* (Cambridge, 1984)

Gabriel Gorodetsky, 'Stalin und Hitlers Angriff auf die Sowjetunion: Eine Auseinandersetzung mit der Legende von deutschen Präventativschlag' in *Vierteljahrshefte für Zeitgeschichte*, Vol. 37 (1989)

Olaf Groehler, *Selbstmörderische Allianz: Deutsch-russische Militärbeziehungen, 1920–1941* (Berlin, 1992)

Jan Gross, *Neighbors* (Princeton, 2001)

Jan Gross, *Revolution from Abroad* (Princeton, 1988)

Harry Hanak, 'Sir Stafford Cripps as British Ambassador in Moscow, May 1940 to June 1941' in *English Historical Review*, Vol. 94, No. 370, January 1979

Richard Hargreaves, *Blitzkrieg Unleashed: The German Invasion of Poland 1939* (Barnsley, 2008)

Mark Harrison (ed.), *The Economics of World War II* (Cambridge, 1998)

Jonathan Haslam, 'Soviet-German Relations and the Origins of the Second

World War: The Jury is Still Out' in *Journal of Modern History*, Vol. 69, No. 4 (1997)

Gerhart Hass, *23. August 1939. Der Hitler–Stalin-Pakt. Dokumentation* (Berlin, 1990)

Paul N. Hehn, *A Low Dishonest Decade* (New York, 2002)

Ulrich Herbert, *Hitler's Foreign Workers* (Cambridge, 1997)

John Hiden, Vahur Made & David J. Smith (eds.), *The Baltic Question during the Cold War* (London, 2008)

Toomas Hiio, Meelis Maripuu & Indrek Paavle (eds.), *Estonia 1940–45: Reports of the Estonian Commission for the Investigation of Crimes against Humanity* (Tallinn, 2006)

Stephen Howarth, *August 1939* (London, 1989)

Bair Irincheev, *War of the White Death* (Barnsley, 2011)

Keith Jeffery, *MI6: The History of the Secret Intelligence Service, 1909–1949* (London, 2010)

Roy Jenkins, *Churchill* (London, 2001)

Teresa Jeśmanowa (ed.), *Stalin's Ethnic Cleansing in Eastern Poland* (London, 2008)

Philip Jowett & Brent Snodgrass, *Finland at War 1939–1945* (Oxford, 2006)

Sandra Kalniete, *With Dance Shoes in Siberian Snows* (Riga, 2006)

Anna Kaminsky, Dietmar Müller & Stefan Troebst (eds.), *Der Hitler-Stalin-Pakt 1939 in den Erinnerungskulturen der Europäer* (Göttingen, 2011)

Bronis J. Kaslas, 'The Lithuanian Strip in Soviet-German Diplomacy, 1939–1941' in *Journal of Baltic Studies*, Vol. 4, No. 3 (1973)

Ian Kershaw, *Hitler 1936–1945* (London, 2000)

Francis King & George Matthews (eds.), *About Turn: The British Communist Party and the Second World War* (London, 1990)

David Kirby, *Finland in the Twentieth Century* (London, 1979)

Ernst Klee, Volker Reiss & Willi Dressen (eds.), *'Schöne Zeiten' Judenmord aus der Sicht der Täter und Gaffer* (Frankfurt am Main, 1988)

Halik Kochanski, *The Eagle Unbowed: Poland and the Poles in the Second World War* (London, 2012)

Ene Kõresaar (ed.), *Soldiers of Memory: World War II and Its Aftermath in Estonian Post-Soviet Life Stories* (New York, 2011)

Victor Kravchenko, *I Chose Freedom* (New York, 1946)

Kristi Kukk & Toivo Raun (eds.), *Soviet Deportations in Estonia: Impact and Legacy* (Tallinn, 2007)

Walter Laqueur, *Russia and Germany: A Century of Conflict* (London, 1965)

Wolfgang Leonhard, *Betrayal: The Hitler–Stalin Pact of 1939* (New York, 1989)

Wendy Lower, '"Anticipatory Obedience" and the Nazi Implementation of the Holocaust in the Ukraine: A Case Study of Central and Peripheral

Forces in the Generalbezirk Zhytomyr, 1941–1944' in *Holocaust and Genocide Studies*, Vol. 16, No. 1 (2002)

John Lukas, *Forgotten Holocaust: The Poles under German Occupation, 1939–1944* (Lexington, 1986)

John Lukacs, *June 1941: Hitler and Stalin* (New Haven, 2006)

Valdis Lumans, *Himmler's Auxiliaries: The Volksdeutsche Mittelstelle and the German National Minorities of Europe, 1933–1945* (London, 1993)

Valdis Lumans, *Latvia in World War II* (New York, 2006)

Frank McDonough, *Neville Chamberlain, Appeasement and the British Road to War* (Manchester, 2010)

John Mahon, *Harry Pollitt: A biography* (London, 1978)

Mark Mazower, *Hitler's Empire: Nazi Rule in Occupied Europe* (London, 2008)

Zhores A. Medvedev & Roy Medvedev, *The Unknown Stalin* (London, 2006)

Catherine Merridale, *Ivan's War: The Red Army 1939–1945* (London, 2005)

Allan Merson, *Communist Resistance in Nazi Germany* (London, 1985)

Romuald Misiunas & Rein Taagepera, *The Baltic States: Years of Dependence 1940–1980* (London, 1983)

Roger Moorhouse, *Berlin at War: Life and Death in Hitler's Germany* (London, 2010)

Kevin Morgan, *Harry Pollitt* (Manchester, 1993)

Edward Mortimer, *The Rise of the French Communist Party 1920–1947* (London, 1984)

David E. Murphy, *What Stalin Knew: The Enigma of Barbarossa* (New Haven, 2005)

Bogdan Musial, *'Konterrevolutionäre Elemente sind zu erschießen'* (Berlin, 2000)

Bogdan Musial, *Stalins Beutezug* (Berlin, 2010)

Aleksandr Nekrich, *Pariahs, Partners, Predators: German-Soviet Relations, 1922–1941* (New York, 1997)

Erwin Oberländer (ed.), *Hitler-Stalin-Pakt 1939* (Frankfurt am Main, 1989)

Lynne Olson, *Those Angry Days* (New York, 2013)

Patrick Osborn, *Operation Pike: Britain versus the Soviet Union, 1939–1941* (London, 2000)

Fraser Ottanelli, *The Communist Party of the United States* (New Brunswick, 1991)

Richard Overy, *The Bombing War* (London, 2013)

Richard Overy, *The Dictators* (London, 2004)

Artis Pabriks & Aldis Purs, *Latvia: The Challenges of Change* (London, 2013)

Joseph Pajaujis-Javis, *Soviet Genocide in Lithuania* (New York, 1980)

Allen Paul, *Katyn, Stalin's Massacre and the Triumph of Truth* (DeKalb, IL, 2010)

K. Pelékis, *Genocide: Lithuania's Threefold Tragedy* (Germany, 1949)

Detlef Peukert, *Die KPD im Widerstand* (Wuppertal, 1980)

Tobias R. Philbin III, *The Lure of Neptune: German-Soviet Naval Collaboration and Ambitions, 1919–1941* (Columbia, SC, 1994)

Tomasz Piesakowski, *The Fate of Poles in the USSR 1939–1989* (London, 1990)

Bianka Pietrow, *Stalinismus, Sicherheit, Offensive* (Melsungen, 1983)

Margot Pikarski & Günter Uebel, *Der Antifaschistische Widerstandskampf der KPD in Spiegel des Flugblattes 1933–1945* (Berlin, 1978)

Tadeusz Piotrowski (ed.), *The Polish Deportees of World War Two: Recollections of Removal to the Soviet Union and Dispersal Throughout the World* (London, 2004)

Constantine Pleshakov, *Stalin's Folly* (London, 2005)

Richard Raack, *Stalin's Drive to the West, 1938–1945* (Stanford, 1995)

Richard Raack, 'Stalin's Plans for World War II' in *Journal of Contemporary History*, Vol. 26 (1991)

Anthony Read & David Fisher, *The Deadly Embrace* (London, 1988)

Laurence Rees, *World War Two Behind Closed Doors: Stalin, the Nazis and the West* (London, 2008)

Albert Resis, 'The Fall of Litvinov: Harbinger of the German-Soviet Non-Aggression Pact' in *Europe-Asia Studies*, Vol. 52, No. 1 (2000)

Rudolf von Ribbentrop, *Mein Vater: Joachim von Ribbentrop, Erlebnisse und Erinnerungen* (Graz, 2013)

Charles Richardson, 'French Plans for Allied Attacks on the Caucasus Oil Fields January-April 1940' in *French Historical Studies*, Vol. 8, No. 1 (1975)

Andrew Roberts, *The Holy Fox* (London, 1991)

Geoffrey Roberts, *Molotov: Stalin's Cold Warrior* (Washington DC, 2012)

Geoffrey Roberts, *The Soviet Union and the Origins of the Second World War: Russo-German Relations and the Road to War, 1933–1941* (Basingstoke, 1995)

Geoffrey Roberts, *Stalin's General: The Life of Georgy Zhukov* (London, 2012)

Geoffrey Roberts, *Stalin's Wars: From World War to Cold War, 1939–1953* (New Haven, 2006)

Geoffrey Roberts, *The Unholy Alliance* (London, 1989)

Geoffrey Roberts, 'Infamous Encounter? The Merekalov–Weizsäcker Meeting of 17 April 1939' in *Historical Journal*, Vol. 35, No. 4 (1992)

Geoffrey Roberts, 'The Soviet Decision for a Pact with Nazi Germany' in *Soviet Studies*, Vol. 44, No. 1 (1992)

Herbert Rosenkranz, *Verfolgung und Selbstbehauptung: Die Juden in Österreich, 1938–1945* (Vienna, 1978)

Alexander B. Rossino, *Hitler Strikes Poland: Blitzkrieg, Ideology and Atrocity* (Kansas, 2003)

Phillip T. Rutherford, *Prelude to the Final Solution: The Nazi Program for Deporting Ethnic Poles 1939–1941* (Kansas, 2007)

Leonas Sabaliūnas, *Lithuania in Crisis: 1939–1940* (London, 1973)

Hans Schafranek, *Zwischen NKWD und Gestapo* (Frankfurt am Main, 1990)

Hartmut Schustereit, "Die Mineralöllieferungen der Sowjetunion an das Deutsche Reich" in *Vierteljahrshefte für Sozial und Wirtschaftsgeschichte*, Vol. 67 (1980)

Heinrich Schwendemann, 'German–Soviet economic relations at the time of the Hitler–Stalin Pact, 1939–1941' in *Cahiers du Monde russe*, XXXVI (1–2), January–June 1995

Ioan Scurtu & Constantin Hlihor, *Anul 1940: drama românilor dintre Prut si Nistru* (Bucharest, 1992)

Simon Sebag Montefiore, *Stalin: The Court of the Red Tsar* (London, 2003)

Alfred Erich Senn, *Lithuania 1940, Revolution from Above* (New York, 2007)

Robert Service, *Spies and Commissars: The Bolshevik Revolution and the West* (London, 2011)

Robert Service, *Stalin* (London, 2008)

Neil Short, *The Stalin and Molotov Lines: Soviet Western Defences, 1928–41* (Oxford, 2008)

Astrid Sics (ed.), *We Sang Through Tears: Stories of Survival in Siberia* (Riga, 1999)

Vieda Skultans, *The Testimony of Lives: Narrative and Memory in Post-Soviet Latvia* (London, 1998)

Sergej Slutsch, '17. September 1939: Der Eintritt der Sowjetunion in den Zweiten Weltkrieg' in *Vierteljahrshefte für Zeitgeschichte*, Vol. 48 (2000)

Sergej Slutsch, 'Stalins "Kriegsszenario 1939": Eine Rede, die es nie gab' in *Vierteljahrshefte für Zeitgeschichte*, Vol. 52, No. 4 (2004)

Timothy Snyder, *Bloodlands* (London, 2010)

Mark Spoerer, *Zwangsarbeit unter dem Hakenkreuz* (Stuttgart, 2001)

David Stafford (ed.), *Flight from Reality: Rudolf Hess and his Mission to Scotland, 1941* (London, 2002)

G. Bruce Strang, 'Once more unto the Breach: Britain's Guarantee to Poland, March 1939' in *Journal of Contemporary History*, Vol. 31, No. 4 (1996)

Pavel Sudoplatov, *Special Tasks* (London, 1994)

Keith Sword, *Deportation and Exile: Poles in the Soviet Union, 1939–48* (Basingstoke, 1994)

Keith Sword (ed.), *The Soviet Takeover of the Polish Eastern Provinces, 1939–41* (Basingstoke, 1991)

Robert E. Tarleton, 'What really happened to the Stalin Line?', in *Journal of Slavic Military Studies*, Vol. 6, No. 1 (1993)

Albert Tarulis, *Soviet Policy towards the Baltic States: 1918–1945* (Notre Dame, 1959)

Frederick Taylor (trans. & ed.), *The Goebbels Diaries: 1939–41* (London, 1982)

Richard Taylor, *Film Propaganda: Soviet Russia and Nazi Germany* (London, 1998)

Adam Tooze, *The Wages of Destruction* (London, 2006)

Richard Toye, *The Roar of the Lion* (London, 2013)

Hugh Trevor-Roper (ed.), *Hitler's War Directives 1939–1945* (London, 1964)

William R. Trotter, *A Frozen Hell: The Russo-Finnish Winter War of 1939–1940* (Chapel Hill, 2000)

Gerd Überschär, *Hitler und Finnland: 1939–1941* (Wiesbaden, 1978)

Adam B. Ulam, *Expansion and Coexistence: Soviet Foreign Policy 1917–73* (New York, 1974)

Peep Varju, 'The Destruction of the Estonian Political Elite during the Soviet Occupation' in *History Conference of the Estonian Memento Association*, Tallinn, 2007

Derek Watson, *Molotov: A Biography* (Basingstoke, 2005)

Donald Cameron Watt, *How War Came* (London, 1989)

Donald Cameron Watt, 'The Inititation of the Negotiations Leading to the Nazi–Soviet Pact: A Historical Problem', in C. Abramsky (ed.), *Essays in Honour of E. H. Carr* (London, 1974)

Bernd Wegner (ed.), *From Peace to War: Germany, Soviet Russia and the World, 1939–1941* (Oxford, 1997)

Gerhard L. Weinberg, 'The Nazi–Soviet Pacts: A Half-Century Later' in *Foreign Affairs*, Vol. 68, No. 4 (1989)

David Welch, *Propaganda and the German Cinema: 1933–1945* (London, 2006)

Alexander Werth, *Russia at War 1941–1945* (London, 1965)

Nigel West, *MI5: British Security Service Operations 1909–1945* (London, 1981)

Llewellyn Woodward, *British Foreign Policy in the Second World War*, Vol. 1 (London, 1970)

Janusz K. Zawodny, *Death in the Forest* (London, 1971)

Index

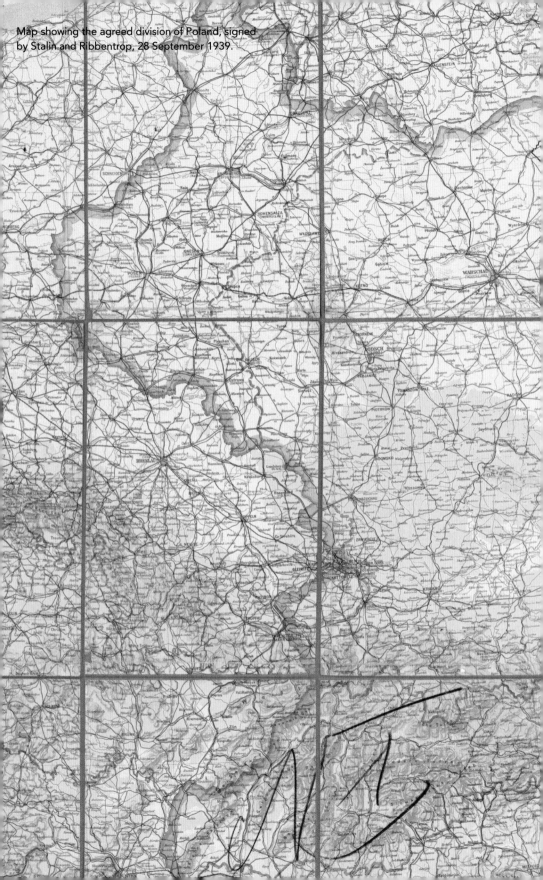

Map showing the agreed division of Poland, signed
by Stalin and Ribbentrop, 28 September 1939.